The Audience Studies Reader

Has political propaganda ever been effective? To what extent do African American families interpret their favourite television show differently from their white neighbours? Are romance novels and teenage magazines reactionary fantasies, or can they provide women with an important space of their own?

The Audience Studies Reader brings together key writings exploring questions of reception, interpretation and interactivity, reprinting forgotten pieces and combining key essays with new research. Beginning with a general introduction to the Reader, each extract is placed in its historical context with specially written Part introductions and annotated suggestions for further reading.

Organised thematically and chronologically, the seven Parts address:

- Paradigm shift – from 'effects' to 'uses and gratifications'
- Moral panic and censorship
- Reading as resistance and the active audience
- The spectator and the audience – shifts in screen theory
- The fan audience
- Female audiences – gender and reading
- Interpretive communities – nation and ethnicity
- Internet audiences, convergence and increased levels of interactivity.

The *Audience Studies Reader* provides a guide to historical approaches and suggests new ways of looking at the relationship between media texts and those who receive, consume and interpret them.

Essays by: Theodor Adorno, Ien Ang, Camille Bacon-Smith, Martin Barker, Bernard Berelson, Jacqueline Bobo, Eunice Cooper, Dawn H. Currie, Michel de Certeau, Helen Dinerman, Rebecca Dobash, Russell Dobash, Barbara Ehrenreich, John Fiske, Hazel Gaudet, Marie Gillespie, Sara Gwenllian-Jones, Miriam Hansen, Elizabeth Hess, Richard Hoggart, Gloria Jacobs, Henry Jenkins, Sut Jhally, Elihu Katz, Paul F. Lazarsfeld, Justin Lewis, Tamar Liebes, Angela McRobbie, Robert K. Merton, David Morley, David Muggleton, Laura Mulvey, Janice Radway, Philip Schlesinger, Esther Sonnet, Jackie Stacey, C. Kay Weaver, Fredric Wertham, Charles Winick, Gregory Woods.

Will Brooker is Assistant Professor in Communication at Richmond, the American International University in London. His books include *Batman Unmasked* and *Using the Force*.
Deborah Jermyn is Senior Lecturer in Film Studies at Southampton Institute. She is the co-editor of *The Cinema of Kathryn Bigelow: Hollywood Transgressor*.

The
Audience Studies
Reader

Edited by

Will Brooker and Deborah Jermyn

Routledge
Taylor & Francis Group

LONDON AND NEW YORK

First published 2003
by Routledge
11 New Fetter Lane, London EC4P 4EE

Simultaneously published in the USA and Canada
by Routledge
29 West 35th Street, New York, NY 10001

Routledge is an imprint of the Taylor & Francis Group

Typeset in Bell Gothic and Bembo by M Rules, London
Printed and bound in Great Britain by
TJ International Ltd, Padstow, Cornwall

British Library Cataloguing in Publication Data
A catalogue record for this book is available from the British Library

Library of Congress Cataloging in Publication Data
The audience studies reader / [edited by] Will Brooker and Deborah Jermyn.
    p.   cm.
Includes bibliographical references and index.
1. Motion picture audiences. 2. Motion picture audiences – Psychology.
3. Television viewers. 4. Television viewers – Psychology. 5. Reading.
I. Brooker, Will, 1970– II. Jermyn, Deborah, 1970–
PN1995.9.A8 A93 2002
302.23'43 – dc21   2002031688

ISBN 0–415–25434–5 (hbk)
ISBN 0–415–25435–3 (pbk)

Contents

Notes on contributors

Theodor Wiesengrund Adorno (1903–69) is best known for his involvement with the Frankfurt Institute for Social Research and his association with scholars such as Walter Benjamin, Herbert Marcuse, Max Horkheimer and Jürgen Habermas. Adorno's period with the Institute was primarily during the late 1930s and 1940s, at which point it had relocated in New York. He worked with Paul Lazarsfeld on the Princeton Radio Research Project and published his most celebrated work, *Dialectic of Enlightenment*, with Horkheimer in 1944. He became Director of the Institute in 1959 following Horkheimer's retirement, and died in Switzerland while working on his book *Aesthetic Theory*.

Ien Ang is currently Professor of Cultural Studies and Director of the Institute for Cultural Research at the University of Western Sydney. Her books in the field of media and audience studies include *Watching Dallas* (1985), *Desperately Seeking the Audience* (1991) and *Living Room Wars* (1996). Her most recent book is *On Not Speaking Chinese: Living Between Asia and the West* (2001).

Camille Bacon-Smith is a folklorist and the author of numerous fantasy and mystery novels in addition to her ethnographic studies of science fiction texts and their fan communities. Her work includes *Eye of the Daemon*, *Eyes of the Empress* and *Enterprising Women: Television Fandom and the Creation of Popular Myth*; her most recent non-fiction book is *Science Fiction Culture* (2000).

Martin Barker is Professor of Film and Television Studies at the University of Wales, Aberystwyth. He is the author of eleven books on various aspects of the media and culture, with particular attention to media censorship campaigns and the study of audiences of despised media. His most recent publications are (with Thomas Austin) *From Antz to Titanic: Reinventing Film Analysis* (2000) and (with Jane Arthurs and Ramaswami Harindranath) *The Crash Controversy: Censorship Campaigns and Film Reception* (2001). He is currently completing a study of a stage adaptation of *Crash*, exploring both cast and crew's understandings of its narrative, and the responses of local audiences.

Bernard Berelson became a key figure in the field of political communications following his work with Paul F. Lazarsfeld at Columbia University on *The People's Choice: How The Voter Makes Up His Mind in A Presidential Campaign* (1944). He is recognised as having popularised the term 'behavioural science' and co-authored *Human Behaviour: An Inventory of Scientific Findings* (with Gary Steiner) in 1964.

Jacqueline Bobo is Professor and Chair of the Women's Studies Program at the University of California, Santa Barbara. She holds a PhD in Film and is the author of *Black Women as Cultural Readers* (1995), *Black Women Film and Video Artists* (1998) and *Black Feminist Cultural Criticism* (2001).

Will Brooker is Assistant Professor in Communication at Richmond, the American International University in London. He has published widely on audience and interpretation, with a particular focus on fandom and cultural power. His work includes *Batman Unmasked* (Continuum, 2000) and *Using the Force: Creativity, Community and Star Wars Fans* (Continuum, 2002).

Eunice Cooper was a staff member at the Department of Scientific Research of the American Jewish Committee with the Institute of Social Research in the late 1940s, before moving to the Research Center for Human Relations at New York University.

Dawn H. Currie is Associate Professor of Sociology at the University of British Columbia. She is co-editor of *Anatomy of Gender: Women's Struggles for the Body* (1992) and *Exploring the Social World: Social Research in Action* (1999).

Michel de Certeau (1925–86) was born in Chambery, France. Having taken degrees in Classics and Philosophy, he joined the Jesuit order in 1950 and spent the next two decades undertaking research into religious history and contributing to French Catholic journals. Following the social uprising of 1968, de Certeau published an assessment of the year's events, *Starting to Speak: Towards a New Culture*, and shifted his research interests from religion towards more varied social and intellectual issues. His subsequent work includes *Culture in the Plural* (1974) and *The Practice of Everyday Life* (1980).

Helen Dinerman was a staff member at the Department of Scientific Research of the American Jewish Committee with the Institute of Social Research in the late 1940s, before moving on to International Public Opinion Research Inc. In 1981 the World Association of Public Opinion Research established the annual Helen Dinerman Award in recognition of her scientific achievements over three decades of public opinion research.

Rebecca Emerson Dobash is Professor of Social Research in the Department of Applied Social Science at the University of Manchester. Her main area of research is violence and the policies and interventions relating to it. With Russell Dobash she has co-authored numerous books, government reports and articles on these themes including *Rethinking Violence Against Women* (1999) and *Changing Violent Men* (2000).

Russell Dobash is Professor of Criminology and Social Policy in the Department of Applied Social Science at the University of Manchester. His research spans a number of areas – prisons, child sexual abuse – but he is best known for his research on violence which includes numerous co-authored projects with Rebecca Emerson Dobash. He regularly serves as an adviser to women's groups and criminal justice agencies in the UK and elsewhere.

Barbara Ehrenreich is a social and political essayist who has written for *The Nation*, *The Progressive* and *Harper's*. Her books include *Fear of Falling: The Inner Life of the Middle Class* (1989), *The Worst Years of Our Lives: Irreverent Notes from a Decade of Greed* (1990) and most recently *Nickel and Dimed: On (Not) Getting By in America* (2001).

John Fiske was, until his retirement in 2001, Professor of Communication Arts at the University of Wisconsin-Madison, USA; he has previously taught in Australia and Great Britain. He is best known for his work on popular culture and resistant interpretation, including *Television Culture* (1988), *Reading the Popular* (1989) and *Understanding Popular Culture* (1989), while his collaborative work includes *Reading Television* with John Hartley (1979) and *Myths of Oz* with Bob Hodge and Graeme Turner (1988).

Hazel Gaudet was a researcher at the Bureau of Applied Social Research co-authoring *The People's Choice* (1944) with Paul F. Lazarsfeld and Bernard Berelson. Her other pioneering studies in the field includes co-authorship of *The Invasion from Mars* (1940) which examined audience responses to Orson Welles and The Mercury Theatre's notorious 1938 radio broadcast of H.G. Wells' *War of the Worlds*.

Marie Gillespie is Senior Lecturer in Sociology at the Open University. Her recent research and writing on the cultural politics of transnational communities include a collaborative project on the coverage and reception of satellite TV narratives on September 11 and after in multilingual households.

Sara Gwenllian-Jones is Lecturer in Television and Digital Media at Cardiff University. She is co-author of *Intensities: The Journal of Cult Media* and is currently writing a book on cult television. She enjoys riding her mountain bike through forests during thunderstorms.

Miriam Hansen is Ferdinand Schevill Distinguished Service Professor in the Humanities at the University of Chicago, where she teaches in the Department of English and the Committee on Cinema and Media Studies. She is the author of *Babel and Babylon: Spectatorship in American Silent Films* (1991) and numerous articles on American and German film history, film theory, and debates on mass culture and the public sphere. She is completing a study of 'The Other Frankfurt School: Kracauer, Benjamin, and Adorno on Cinema, Mass Culture, and Modernity.'

Elizabeth Hess began her career as a journalist in the 1970s, and has written for *Ms*, *The Washington Post* and *The Village Voice*. She has lectured and written widely on feminism, art and censorship, and more recently began reporting on animal issues. She is co-author with Barbara Ehrenreich and Gloria Jacobs of *Re-Making Love: The*

Feminization of Sex (1986) and author of *Lost and Found: Dogs, Cats and Everyday Heroes at a Country Animal Shelter* (1998).

Richard Hoggart's distinguished career has involved him in many roles. As a teacher of literature and founder of the Centre for Contemporary Cultural Studies at Birmingham University, he was largely responsible, with Stuart Hall, for legitimising the study of popular culture and what we now know as media studies. He was a member of the Pilkington Committee on the Future of Broadcasting in the early 1960s, and served for five years as an Assistant Director-General of UNESCO. He was Warden of Goldsmiths' College, London, from 1976 to 1984, and chaired the Arts Council from 1978 to 1982. His many books include the seminal *The Uses of Literacy*, a three-volume autobiography and, most recently, *First and Last Things*, and *Between Two Worlds*.

Gloria Jacobs has edited *New York Woman* and the pioneering feminist magazine *Ms*. She is co-author, with Elizabeth Hess and Barbara Ehrenreich, of *Re-Making Love: The Feminization of Sex* (1986).

Henry Jenkins, director of the Comparative Media Studies Program at MIT, has spent his career studying media and the way people incorporate it into their lives. He has published articles on a diverse range of topics relating to popular culture, and testified in 1999 before the US Senate during the hearings on media violence that followed the Littleton, Colorado, shootings. He has published six books and more than fifty essays on popular culture. His books include *From Barbie to Mortal Kombat: Gender and Computer Games* (1998), *Science Fiction Audiences: Watching Doctor Who and Star Trek* (1995) and *Textual Poachers: Television Fans and Participatory Culture* (1992).

Deborah Jermyn is Senior Lecturer in Film Studies at the Southampton Institute, UK. She has published widely on women and popular culture and is co-editor of *The Cinema of Kathryn Bigelow: Hollywood Transgressor* (Wallflower Press, 2002).

Sut Jhally is Professor of Communication at the University of Massachusetts at Amherst and founder and executive director of The Media Education Foundation in Northampton. His books include *The Codes of Advertising: Fetishism and the Political Economy of Meaning in the Consumer Society* (1987) and *Cultural Politics in Contemporary America* with Ian H. Angus (1989). He has produced over twenty videos, including *Dreamworlds* I and II, and *Advertising and the End of the World*.

Elihu Katz is Trustee Professor of Communication at the Annenberg School, University of Pennsylvania. His long-standing interest in the interaction of mass and interpersonal communication began with *Personal Influence* (1955), the book he co-authored at Columbia with Paul F. Lazarsfeld. Further expressions of this interest are *Medical Innovation* (1960) with James S. Coleman and Herbert Menzel and *The Export of Meaning: Cross-Cultural Readings of Dallas* (1990) with Tamar Liebes. Katz served as founding director of Israel Television, and long-time consultant on social research to the BBC.

Paul F. Lazarsfeld was Professor of Sociology for thirty years and Director of Columbia's Bureau of Applied Social Research. He was a pioneering figure in the field, helping the Bureau become the 'birthplace' of mass communication research and contributing to numerous studies of the impact of radio and television on the American public.

Justin Lewis is Professor of Communication and Cultural Industries at Cardiff University. He has written several books about media and culture. His most recent books: *Constructing Public Opinion: How Elites Do What they Like and Why We Seem to Go Along With It* is an analysis of the media and public opinion.

Tamar Liebes is Chair of the Department of Communication and Journalism at the Hebrew University of Jerusalem. She has written on issues of cultural imperialism arising from the reception of American popular TV series in *The Export of Meaning: Cross-Cultural Readings of Dallas* with Elihu Katz (1990) and TV news as locus of political socialisation in *Reporting the Arab/Israel Conflict: How Hegemony Works* (1997). Liebes' recent work includes a book on the Americanisation of Israeli media and politics entitled *American Dreams, Hebrew Subtitles: Globalization from the Receiving End*.

Angela McRobbie is Professor in the Department of Media and Communications at Goldsmiths' College, University of London. She is author of *British Fashion Design: Rag Trade or Image Industry?* (1998) and *In The Culture Society: Art, Fashion and Popular Music* (1999).

Robert K. Merton is recognised as one of the most significant American sociologists of the post-war era. Most of his career was spent at Columbia University. In 1994 he was presented with the National Medal of Science in recognition of his work on the sociology of science, the first sociologist ever to be awarded this medal.

David Morley is Professor of Communications in the Department of Media and Communications, Goldsmiths' College, University of London. He is the author of a number of books about media audiences, including *Family Television* with Stuart Hall (1988), *Spaces of Identity* with Kevin Robins (1995), *The Nationwide Audience Studies* with Charlotte Brunsdon (1999) and most recently *Home Territories* (2000).

David Muggleton is Senior Lecturer in Sociology in the School of Sport, Exercise and Health at University College, Chichester, UK. His main research interests are youth culture and the sociology of sport.

Laura Mulvey is Professor of Film and Media Studies in the School of Art, Film and Visual Media at Birkbeck, University of London. She has co-directed a number of experimental films including *Disgraced Monuments* (1996) and her books include *Fetishism and Curiosity* (1996).

Janice Radway is Frances Fox Professor of Literature at Duke University, North Carolina. She has served as editor of the *American Quarterly* and is author of *A Feeling for Books: The Book-of-the-Month Club, Literary Taste, and Middle Class Desire*.

Philip Schlesinger is Professor of Film and Media Studies at the University of Stirling, where he is Director of Stirling Media Research Institute. He is also Visiting Professor of Media and Communication at the University of Oslo and an editor of *Media, Culture and Society* journal. He is the author of *Putting 'Reality' Together* (1987, 2nd edn) and *Media, State and Nation* (1992) and has co-authored *Televising 'Terrorism'* (1983), *Women Viewing Violence* (1992), *Reporting Crime* (1994), *Men Viewing Violence* (1998) and *Open Scotland?* (2001). He is presently working on questions of collective identity.

Esther Sonnet is Reader and Principal Lecturer in Media and Cultural Studies at Southampton Institute. She has published widely on film, feminism, gender and popular culture and is currently completing the book *Masquerades of Desire: Women's Fiction in an Age of Postfeminism* from which the article in this volume is drawn.

Jackie Stacey is Professor in Women's Studies and Cultural Studies in the Department of Sociology at Lancaster University and co-editor of the film and television studies journal *Screen*. She has written on numerous subjects within feminist cultural criticism and has further research interests in the body and changing health cultures. Her books include *Teratologies: A Cultural Study of Cancer* (1997).

C. Kay Weaver is a Senior Lecturer in the Department of Management Communication, University of Waikato, New Zealand. She is a co-author of *Women Viewing Violence* (1992) and *Violence and the Media* (in press). Her work has also appeared in a number of journals and edited book collections. She is an associate editor of *Feminist Media Studies*.

Fredric Wertham (1895–1981) was born in Munich, Germany. As a postgraduate, correspondence with Sigmund Freud led him to take up psychiatry as his life's work. Wertham is notorious for his campaign against horror and crime comic books in the 1950s. Following a series of articles that identified what he saw as corruptive elements in contemporary comic books, Wertham published *Seduction of the Innocent* in 1954 and played a key role in the Senate Subcommittee hearings of the following year, indirectly contributing to the self-censorship and partial collapse of the comic book industry. Though often vilified by comic fans as a reactionary 'witchfinder general', Wertham's association with liberal causes, his campaigning against racism and his testimonials against censorship are often overlooked by critics.

Charles Winick is a noted researcher, Professor of Sociology at the GSUC, as well as the faculty of the City College of CUNY. He is the author of over 100 articles on diversive aspects of drug use and abuse. Professor Winick has, since 1984, been Director of the Training Program in Behavioral Science Research in Drug Abuse, sponsored by NIDA in cooperation with the New York State Division of Substance Abuse Services. He previously served as Director of Research at the American Social Health Association; Program Director at the National Information Center on Drugs, and Consultant to the United Nations Division of Narcotic Drugs; the World Health Organization Project on Coded Information on Drugs, and the President's Commission on Marijuana and Drug Abuse.

Gregory Woods is Professor of Gay and Lesbian Studies at the Nottingham Trent University. His was the first such appointment in the United Kingdom. His books of cultural history include *Articulate Flesh: Male Homo-eroticism and Modern Poetry* (1987) and *A History of Gay Literature: The Male Tradition* (1998). Three volumes of his poetry have been published by Carcanet Press.

Acknowledgements

The editors wish to thank the following:

Christopher Cudmore at Routledge for his advice and encouragement throughout the development of this book. Robert Peck at the University of Westminster, who taught us both on the MA in Film and Television and introduced us to many of the articles included below.

Will Brooker thanks Fiona Graham for her reserves of practical and psychological support during the editing process. Deborah Jermyn offers special thanks for all their support to Kath Barrow, Steph Beecher, Tom Corr, Su Holmes, Pat Pitt-Jones and Portia Tertullien.

Permission given by the following copyright holders and authors for the extracts and articles in this collection is gratefully acknowledged.

Extract from T. W. Adorno, *The Culture Industry*, London: Routledge (1991). Reprinted with permission of the publisher. Extract from Ien Ang, *Living Room Wars: Rethinking Audiences for a Postmodern World*, London: Routledge (1996). Reprinted with permission of the publisher. Extract from Camille Bacon-Smith, 'Suffering and Solace: The Genre of Pain', in *Enterprising Women*, Philadelphia: University of Pennsylvania Press (1992). Reprinted with permission of the publisher. © Camille Bacon-Smith. Martin Barker, 'The Newson Report', in Martin Barker and Julian Petley (eds), *Ill Effects*, London: Routledge (1997). Reprinted with permission of the publisher and author. © Martin Barker. Extract from Jacqueline Bobo, '*The Color Purple*: Black Women as Cultural Readers', in E. Deirdre Pribham (ed.) *Female Spectators*, London: Verso (1992). Reprinted with permission of the publisher. © 1992 Verso. Eunice Cooper and Helen Dinerman, 'Analysis of the Film *Don't Be A Sucker*: A Study in Communication', *Public Opinion Quarterly*, vol. 15, no. 2 (Summer 1951). Reprinted with permission of the University of Chicago Press. © 1951 University of Chicago Press. Extract from Dawn H. Currie, *Girl Talk: Adolescent Magazines and Their Readers*, Toronto: University of Toronto Press (1999). Reprinted with permission of the publisher © 1999 University of Toronto Press. Extract from Michel de Certeau, *The Practice of Everyday Life*, Minneapolis: University of Minneapolis Press (1998). Reprinted with permission of the publisher. Extract from Barbara Ehrenreich, Elizabeth Hess and Gloria Jacobs, 'Beatlemania: Girls Just Want To Have Fun', in Lisa A. Lewis (ed.) *The Adoring Audience*, London: Routledge (1992). Reprinted with permission of the publisher. Extract from John Fiske, *Understanding Popular Culture*, London: Routledge (1989). Reprinted with permission of the publisher. Extract from Marie Gillespie, *Television, Ethnicity and Cultural Change*, London: Routledge (1995). Reprinted with permission of the publisher. Sara Gwenllian-Jones, 'Histories, Fictions and *Xena: Warrior Princess*', *Television and New Media*, vol. 1, no. 4 (November 2000). Reprinted with permission of Sage Publications, Inc. © 2000 Sage Publications, Inc. Extract from Miriam Hansen, *Babel and Babylon: Spectatorship in American Silent Film*, Cambridge, MA: Harvard University Press (1991). Reprinted by permission of the publisher. © The President and Fellows of Harvard College. Extract from Richard Hoggart, *The Uses of Literacy*, London: Chatto and Windus (1957). Reprinted with permission of The Random House Group. Extract from Henry Jenkins, 'Out of the Closet and Into the Universe: Queers and *Star Trek*', in John Tulloch and Henry Jenkins (eds) *Science Fiction Audiences: Watching Doctor Who and Star Trek*, London: Routledge (1995). Reprinted with permission of the publisher. Extract from Sut Jhally and Justin Lewis, *Enlightened Racism: The Cosby Show, Audiences and the Myth of the American Dream*, Oxford: Westview Press (1992). Reprinted by permission of Westview Press, a division of Perseus Books L.L.C. ©1992 by Westview Press, a division of Perseus Books L.L.C. Paul. F. Lazarsfeld, Bernard Berelson and Hazel Gaudet, *The People's Choice: How the Voter Makes Up His Mind in a Presidential Campaign*, New York: Columbia University Press (1944). Reprinted with permission of the publisher. © 1944 Columbia University Press. Extract from Tamar Liebes and Elihu Katz, *The Export of Meaning: Cross-Cultural Readings of Dallas*, Oxford: Oxford University Press (1990). Reprinted with permission of the publisher. Extract from Angela McRobbie, '*Jackie* Magazine: Romantic Individualism and the Teenage Girl', *Feminism and Youth Culture*, Basingstoke: Macmillan (2000) (2nd edition). Reprinted with permission of the author © 2000 Angela McRobbie. Robert K. Merton, *Mass Persuasion: The Social Psychology of a War Bond Drive*, New York: Harper and Brothers (1946). Reprinted with permission of The Free Press, a division of Simon and Schuster, Inc. © 1946, renewed 1974 by Robert K. Merton. Extract from David Morley, *The Nationwide Audience*, London: BFI (1980). Reprinted with permission of the publisher. Extract from David Muggleton, *Inside Subculture: The Postmodern Meaning of Style*, London: Berg (2000). Reprinted with permission of the publisher. Laura Mulvey (1975) 'Visual Pleasure and Narrative Cinema', *Screen*, vol. 16, no. 3 (Autumn) pp. 6–18. Reprinted with permission of Oxford University Press and the author. Extract from Janice Radway, *Reading the Romance: Women, Patriarchy and Popular Literature*, Chapel Hill and London: University of North Carolina Press (1984). Reprinted with permission of the publisher © 1984, 1991 University of North Carolina Press. Extract from Philip Schlesinger, Rebecca Dobash, Russell Dobash and C. Kay Weaver, *Women Viewing Violence*, London: BFI (1992). Reprinted with permission of the authors © 1992 Philip Schlesinger *et al*. Extract from Jackie Stacey, *Stargazing: Hollywood Cinema and Female Spectatorship*, London: Routledge (1994). Reprinted with permission of the publisher. Extract from Fredric Wertham, *Seduction of the*

Innocent, London: Museum Press (1955). Permission applied for. Extract from Charles Winick, 'Tendency Systems and the Effects of a Movie Dealing With A Social Problem', *Journal of General Psychology* (April 1963) pp. 290–305. Reprinted with permission of Helen Dwight Reid Education Foundation. Published by Heldref Publications, 1318 Eighteenth St., NW, Washington, DC, 20036–1802. © 1963. Extract from Gregory Woods, 'We're Here, We're Queer and We're Not Going Catalogue Shopping', in P. Burston and C. Richardson (eds) *A Queer Romance: Lesbians, Gay Men and Popular Culture*, London:. Reprinted with permission of the publisher and author. © Gregory Woods.

INTRODUCTION

'It's out there ... somewhere': locating the audience for *The Audience Studies Reader*.

IT IS CUSTOMARY IN books of this nature to provide an Introduction that offers the reader a map of the book's terrain, gesturing toward key debates, interventions and sites of conflict in the field, sketching a brief history of the area and pointing out landmarks to look out for along the way. This kind of guiding information is invaluable, a crucial part of a Reader like this one: and you will find it here, though not gathered in one place. Instead of rushing the reader through a vast range of articles and arguments at the start of the book – instead of reeling off decades of history before the journey even begins – we have chosen to offer context and explanation at key points on that journey, through brief essays at the start of each Part.

This book collects essays that cross disciplinary fields in pursuit of the audience, and they are divided into seven clearly signposted Parts, organised both chronologically and thematically. Each Part is preceded by an Editors' Introduction that explains the rationale behind that Part's theme, provides concise and informative summaries to prepare the reader for the extracts that follow and suggests further reading.

The first three Parts give a historical context to early studies of the media audience, offering examples of key theoretical paradigms as research shifted from a preoccupation with 'effects' to an increasing recognition of the 'active audience'. We include a number of historically significant texts from the 1940s and 1950s that have rarely been made available in their original form since they were first published; although they might now in some ways have been intellectually 'superseded', they offer fascinating insights into the discipline's evolution.

In Parts Four and Five we examine the different connotations and conceptualisations of the terms 'spectators' and 'fans' in relation to the broader notion of the audience. Part Six provides an overview of the ways in which female audiences and feminist criticism have been pivotal in the history of audience research, while Part Seven brings together a diverse selection of essays that foreground the influence of nation, ethnicity or class on audience interpretation. Finally, in our Conclusion, we suggest possible questions for the future of audience studies and ask whether the concepts of 'overflow' and 'convergence' may raise new issues for the discipline.

The articles reprinted in this volume, then, give a sense of audience studies in all its variations, offering breadth – the conceptual and historical development of audience studies across disciplines including media studies, film studies and sociology – and depth, through a collection of representative work within contemporary cultural studies. The Reader collates major essays from some of the most respected writers in these disciplines while also including a number of recent and less familiar articles, suggesting new avenues within audience studies and providing a fresh context in which to situate the more established and canonical research.

We want to pause for a moment here and turn our attention from existing studies of audience to a real audience member: you, the reader. The fact that you have felt intrigued enough to pick up this book and browse through this Introduction – whether at home, in a bookshop or a library – means that you are in some sense, however tentatively and temporarily, part of our audience. The fact that you are reading this means we, the editors, have succeeded in finding you.

Who are you though? An undergraduate looking for help with an essay? An interested media-industry professional? An academic wondering whether to add this collection to a reading list? Each of you will find different strengths and weaknesses in what follows. Some of your needs will be met, others inevitably will be frustrated. In this Introduction we do not want to follow the customary trail through a history of the field, which in any case would only be duplicated, and done in more depth, in our section introductions and extracts. Rather, we want to reflect briefly on our own process of developing and editing this book; the ways in which, throughout that process, we had to continually construct and revise our concept of you, its audience, and by extension, what this might tell us about the nature of audiences *per se*.

In fact, there are and already have been a number of 'audiences' for this book, some of which encountered it long before publication. In some respects, we were our own first audience, from the moment we began to discuss this project some five years prior to the current time of writing. Teaching and researching different approaches to the subject, we began to realise there might be a need for a book that brought the essays and themes explored here together in one place. We imagined that an *Audience Studies Reader* would be useful to us, making our work easier by clarifying key themes, strands and interventions in audience studies and drawing out the connections between them. In this sense, it was a book meant broadly for us, and for other academics 'like us'.

But the other audience we imagined was, of course, our students in film and communication studies. This book would make their lives easier too, by collecting all these readings in a single volume and providing helpful introductions, enabling them to find useful readings at once instead of having to chase up multiple sources. They, and students in related disciplines, would surely welcome a book that did the chasing for them and made the readings more accessible, both in practical terms and in terms of the context and explanation we as editors would provide. Already we were constructing *The Audience Studies Reader* with their needs in mind, mentally selecting the essays that such a book would need to include and fitting them within sketched-out structures on scrap paper.

When it came to writing a book proposal for our publishers, however, we had to consider not just the student audience, but a new audience made up of our peers and the publishers themselves. If these 'audiences' – Routledge and its representatives; a jury of international scholars – didn't approve, then the project would simply fall by the wayside. In agreeing the final structure of this book, then, our search for its audience necessitated a process of negotiation. Clearly, for the publisher, commercial viability had to be a key consideration. Our editor at Routledge agreed that there was a market for the book; but was our vision of it shared elsewhere? Our initial proposal was sent to a number of anonymous readers – audience studies academics from around the world – for their comments.

Each of the academic readers who considered our proposal wanted related but distinct things of an *Audience Studies Reader*; and their needs had to be met, balanced and compromised as the book progressed from an initial idea to actual publication. We thought our ideas were valid; now we had to choose which of our original selections to defend and which to abandon, wavering between our investment in the initial proposal and our desire to see the book published, even in a modified form. While we had a good idea of what our students' needs were and what we wanted, these notions had to be traded off against the demands of publishers and reviewers; a movement that illustrates the operation of what Janice Radway has called 'the institutional matrix' (Radway, 1984), the shifting power dynamic that exists between readers, writers and publishers. Our reviewers' responses, though overwhelmingly positive and useful, also proved both helpful and contradictory, both encouraging and frustrating; it would prove impossible to fulfil all the various requests of even this small and select audience group.

To illustrate this let us take a specific example: our reprinting of Laura Mulvey's seminal 1975 essay on film and spectatorship, 'Visual Pleasure and Narrative Cinema'. We argued that though it was already widely reproduced elsewhere, such was its impact on the way theories of spectatorship developed, and indeed its ubiquity as required reading on a whole range of courses, that it still warranted inclusion in this collection. 'Reader A' agreed, and in fact was unhappy that the follow-up (see Mulvey, 1981) wasn't included; 'Why isn't Laura Mulvey's response to her own seminal essay included here?' 'Reader C' offered a different perspective; 'I also wonder if Mulvey's piece needs to be included. It is reprinted in many other places and its undeniable influence . . . could be summarised.' Mulvey's own position brought another perspective to bear when we contacted her to seek her permission to reprint the essay. In agreeing to its use she also commented 'To tell the truth, I am continually amazed that people still want to anthologise VP and NC' as if, despite the significance of its polemical status at the time of publication, it was now so familiar that it no longer had currency in the contemporary landscape of audience studies. (Personal correspondence with author, 23 August 2001). Which of these observations is correct? Should Mulvey's essay be here at all? How were we to meet every reader's suggestions, while respecting Mulvey's wishes and preserving our own sense of the book's structure and intended purpose?

The answer, of course, is that we couldn't. Each of the readers welcomed different extracts and decried the absence of others according to their own specialist fields, research interests, teaching needs and geographical location; almost all of them asked for more extracts from their own national context. As editors we could only compromise, defend our choices and aim to address the widest audience possible while maintaining the principles and aims of the book's rationale. There is no such thing as a complete or ideal Reader, one that would mean all things to all people – any more than there is such thing as an ideal reader, whose every need would be satisfied by our collection.

Just as each audience member brings their own history and socio-cultural specificities to bear on each media text, transforming it into something distinct and unique to them, so each reader could argue the case for and against anything we have chosen to either include or omit here. The audience is 'out there', somewhere, and in reaching the end of this Introduction you have become part of our readership. But, as our editing of this collection has underlined, the 'audience' is equally and simultaneously identifiable and elusive, imaginable and unpredictable, and enduringly fascinating for all those reasons.

Will Brooker and Deborah Jermyn
March 2002

PART ONE

Paradigm shift
From 'effects' to 'uses and gratifications'

Introduction

IF ONE HAD TO pinpoint the first transitional moment in the twentieth century in terms of the rise of audience studies, it would perhaps be World War I. Its significance lies in the fact that it was from this historical moment onwards that 'propaganda' arguably emerged as a primary and indispensable weapon in any war effort while more generally, the popularisation of the term brought with it the enduring notion of 'the public' as a vulnerable and persuadable lot 'at risk' from propaganda. With these shifts came a fascination with understanding how the public might be moved to respond or act in certain ways. In the inter-war period a 'myth' had grown up, arguably with some foundation, that Germany hadn't lost World War I solely due to military ineptitude. Rather, they had also lost a 'paper war'. Another decisive battle had been won by the dropping of British propaganda leaflets behind enemy lines, the contents of which were so devastating to German morale that they played a momentous role in Germany's defeat. According to this version of history at least, on this occasion the pen was at least as mighty as the sword.

It is in the context of the propaganda of World War I and the paranoia and suspicion that followed it in the inter-war period that one can better understand the first extracts in this Part. In Europe and the USA there was a surge of interest in trying to understand how propaganda worked, and a fear that an elite circle of skilled manipulators could use it to control the minds and behaviour of the masses. The rise of European dictatorships in this period lent further credence to this interest since they suggested that certain charismatic personalities, making full use of the growing modern media, were able to bend the masses to their will. It was in the 1920s and 1930s then that the mass-society or mass-culture thesis arose.

According to this thesis, modern society was characterised by the breakdown of traditional social responsibilities and ties, leading to a mass of alienated individuals who could be led and controlled. This approach to society was also endorsed by the Frankfurt School's theory of the 'Culture Industry' (led by T. W. Adorno and later

Max Horkheimer whose work can be read in Part Two of this collection). They argued that culture was imposed from 'above' on to a passive and malleable audience, thus further popularising a rather pessimistic and paternalistic view of the mass audience. In this context, early audience research sought to discern the 'effects' that the media had on its audiences, based on an assumption that a quantifiable audience response would be identifiable and predictable given a certain media stimulus. This phase of audience research, then, has become known as the 'effects' or 'hypodermic needle' model, a simple stimulus–response approach which imagines the media as a kind of narcotic and the relationship between media/audience as one where the audience can, it presumes, be straightforwardly 'injected' with a message.

As Chapter 1 in this Part from Lazarsfeld *et al.*'s *The People's Choice: How The Voter Makes Up His Mind in a Presidential Campaign* demonstrates, the shortcomings of the effects model began to emerge even as audience research began to tentatively examine how this relationship between audience and media operated. First published in 1944, Lazarsfeld's work examines the findings of a study undertaken by social scientists in Erie County, Ohio, USA, from May–November 1940 'to observe the progress and effect of the presidential campaign in that community' (Lazarsfeld *et al.*, 1968: xxii). In the run-up to voting, a core group of 600 respondents were questioned every month for seven months about how they intended to vote. Two main groups emerged – those who did not change their political opinion and those who did. These 'changers and shifters' were the group the study was most concerned with since they meant that researchers could chart the processes of opinion formation and change as they developed and, crucially, the factors that influenced them. Their 'personal characteristics, their contacts with other people and their exposure to radio and newspapers were carefully examined' and compared to those people who were 'constants' (ibid.). While this was a study concerned with home affairs, then, it was nevertheless part of a larger drive to understand how the media communicated its 'messages' effectively, a will fuelled not just by the desire for America to improve their own propaganda but to 'protect' their citizens from that of other nations.

The study's findings brought some surprises and in the Preface to the 1968 third edition Lazarsfeld reflected that in fact they had found that 'the role of mass-media turned out to be rather small'. Instead they had been surprised to note the significance of 'what seemed to be a great deal of person-to-person interaction'. At the time they were prevented from exploring this more thoroughly by the remit of the research, which meant that their 'primary efforts were directed towards establishing the role of the more formal media' (ibid.: vi.). Nevertheless, they had been able to identify the existence of a group of articulate individuals whom they termed 'opinion leaders'. It was these individuals and the mutual interaction of group members more generally, that played a decisive role in influencing the 'changers and shifters' above and beyond the mass media.[1] Quite radically, then, this suggested that campaign media propaganda had very limited effects on the audience in terms of 'converting' voters.

As we see in the extract here, Lazarsfeld *et al.* found that the relationship between audience and media was rather less direct than the stimulus–response model imagined by the effects approach. Instead they suggested it was more accurate to speak of a 'two-step flow of information'. Rather than the mass media 'injecting' their messages direct to the population, information was frequently filtered through to the 'less active' members of the audience via opinion leaders. These opinion leaders did not operate in the terms imagined by the mass-society thesis, however. This was not a simple 'top-down' model of influence. Rather, as Lazarsfeld noted in the Preface to the second edition, 'we found that that opinion leadership does not operate only vertically from top to bottom, but also horizontally: there are opinion leaders in every walk of life' (ibid.: xxxv). This, then, was an early reflection on how a range of local, social and familial loyalties, allegiances and pressures might be brought to bear on changes in opinion and behaviour. It was an account that undermined the concept of mass society as made up of isolated individuals, through its description instead of the influence of interlinked and overlapping social networks. Furthermore, it questioned the concept of the media being able to bring direct and quantifiable influence to bear on the individual; with its repeated descriptions of face-to-face contact superseding the media's dissemination of election campaign information, how pervasive for most people was the media's power in any direct sense after all? Already, then, we see how the effects model, with its neglect of the diverse and even conflicting 'cross-pressures' wrought on every individual by various social and cultural affiliations such as class, ethnicity and religion, would prove to be untenably simplistic. That said, we should remember that the effects tradition is still very much with us, emerging with predictable regularity every time the latest shooting or suicide is linked to the perpetrator having been a fan of a violent film or controversial rock star (a theme explored further in Part Two on the 'vulnerable audience').

Chapter 2, Robert K. Merton's (1946) study, *Mass Persuasion: The Social Psychology of a War Bond Drive*, bears a number of similarities to Lazarsfeld's and in fact it was Lazarsfeld, as Director of the Bureau of Applied Social Research of Columbia University, who originally suggested it be undertaken. Both were analyses of instances of group behaviour examined by social scientists, in the context of a prevailing concern with the powers and operation of propaganda, in order to better understand how people could be moved to respond in a given way – in this instance to buy war bonds. On War Bond Day, 21 September 1943, the popular US radio star Kate Smith broadcast intermittent appeals for 18 hours on Columbia Broadcasting System in an effort to persuade the public to buy war bonds. Merton's Preface sums up the impetus behind the research succinctly: 'A radio star succeeded in selling some $39,000,000 of war bonds in one day's broadcasts. Our study asks and seeks to answer one central question: how did this come about?' (Merton, 1971: xi). In order to answer this question, the researchers carried out 100 detailed interviews with people who had heard the Smith bond broadcasts, seventy-five of whom had telephoned their bond pledges to WABC radio in New York and twenty-five 'unpersuaded' listeners who had not bought bonds despite hearing the broadcasts.

This 'real-life' context differentiated the study from other social psychology studies or experiments in media effects of the time that were laboratory-based (a method, again, which is still with us). The lab setting of much effects research is one of the key criticisms that has been brought to bear on it. With its over-reliance on students as respondents, its decontextualisation of the processes of interaction with media texts and the danger of influence wrought by having the researcher present observing the subject, lab-based research has unsurprisingly been accused of conducting its work in artificial and therefore unrepresentative environments. For Merton, then, the grounding of his research in a 'real-life situation' was one of its 'genuine merits' (Merton, 1971: 4–5). The study considers individual motives for buying or not buying war bonds, accounts of which are seen here in the extract that follows, where Merton looks at what factors made people 'susceptible' to the drive in contrast to the 'predisposed' who had already decided to buy bonds in advance of the appeal. More broadly Merton's analysis also entailed a detailed analysis of the figure of Kate Smith; the impact of the longevity of the broadcast and its use of repetition; the content of the appeals and a 'thematic analysis' which suggested it was dominated by the leitmotif of 'sacrifice'; and the 'predispositions' and 'resistance' strategies of listeners.

Given that it appeared *after* Lazarsfeld's study and its conclusions, it is revealing that Merton's work seems *more* overtly marked by fears of a manipulative mass media and a vulnerable public who through 'exposing themselves to the content of print, movies and radio . . . may become susceptible to their influence' (ibid.: 1). Of course by the time of the War Bond Day in 1943 America's involvement in World War II was well underway and this can perhaps be seen as a further factor in the rather dark vision of modern society which is sometimes evident in the study. This is a world then where propaganda has taken on 'enlarged amplitude and heightened intensity' since,

> When values are in flux, when competing parties and factions and interests offer their distinctive ideological goods in the market place of opinion, when a unity of moral outlook has been suddenly shattered or has slowly decomposed into shapeless disagreements, the propagandist has his heyday.
>
> (ibid.: xi)

This pessimistic account of the operation of mass persuasion extends beyond the immediate political context, however, to wider cultural fears of manipulation by advertisers. Advertisers, of course, did indeed have a concerted interest in the findings of these research projects and the researchers' anxieties about contemporary advertising strategies come to the fore on more than one occasion. Merton suggests that the popular perception of Kate Smith's personal sincerity and integrity was a particularly persuasive factor for the respondents who in every aspect of their everyday lives.

> feel themselves the object of manipulation. They see themselves as the target for ingenious methods of control through advertising which cajoles, promises, terrorises; through propagandas that, utilizing available techniques, guide the unwitting audience into opinions which may or may not coincide with the best interests of themselves or their affiliates.
>
> (ibid.: 142)

Note, then, how in line with the Frankfurt School's position, we appear to return again here to the belief in the mass media – or more specifically here, advertisers – exerting a direct and pernicious influence on the 'unwitting' public. This is just one form of cynical interface Merton imagines the public have to contend with every day in a 'highly competitive, segmented, urban society' (ibid.: 143), a society where for many, Merton argues, the apparently accessible, genuine, non-materialistic Kate Smith was a breath of fresh air.[2] The study seems prompted, then, not just by a desire to understand how this act of mass persuasion was possible, but by a position that ultimately perceives human persuasibility as a 'general problem' from which we must seek to 'learn effective defenses' in an age characterised by a 'prevalently manipulative society' (ibid.: 2–10). Nevertheless by identifying and examining the relationship between certain 'stimuli' and 'clusters of motives', the study combines a 'scientific' approach to the respondents' behaviour with a growing awareness of how opinion and action are determined not by monolithic media but by interaction with them in broad cultural and individual contexts.

Interestingly, what Merton's account here also starts to point towards is the 'uses and gratifications' approach to audiences, where different audiences use the same media to meet different needs according to their own wants. He describes how certain listeners (typically mothers with sons fighting in the war) responded to the appeal to buy war bonds as a way of alleviating their sense of helplessness while others used it as a way of self-satisfyingly demonstrating their commitment to Kate Smith. Listener responses, then, were marked by *selectivity*. As the term suggests, the uses and gratifications approach to audiences credits them with being 'active' and/or discriminating in their engagement with the media in a way not envisaged by the effects model. This paradigm shift in audience studies led to acknowledgement that audiences may read or use the media in different, surprising, even 'aberrant' ways,[3] rather than responding in ways that might be predicted through controlled 'stimuli'.

Audience studies now acknowledged the potential for a 'boomerang effect' in the communication of propaganda, where the 'intended' meaning of a media text can be turned around by members of its audience who read it in a way which positively reverses the intended meaning. We first encountered this turn of phrase in this Part in the extract from Lazarsfeld's *The People's Choice* who described how 'the formal media *produced several boomerangs* upon people who resented what they read or heard and moved in the opposite direction from that intended' (Lazarsfeld, 1968: 154; italics mine). This form of audience engagement with and use of the media is discussed in more detail here in Chapter 3 by Cooper and Dinerman's (1951) study, 'Analysis of the Film *Don't Be A Sucker*: A Study in Communication'. An anti-prejudice, anti-fascist film, *Don't Be A Sucker*, which made comparisons between Germany and America, was distributed by the USA government to fighting forces during World War II and shortly afterwards in the USA as an educational film. Rather than instigating shifts in attitude or awareness regarding the dangers and proclivity of discrimination in the USA, Cooper and Dinerman found that for various reasons 'several of the messages "boomeranged" and produced unexpected and undesired attitude changes'.

For example, the German 'sucker' who goes on to become a Nazi and die in battle was played by attractive, recognisable star Kurt Krueger and was generally received more sympathetically than his American counterpart, the 'hero' Mike. Though Mike eventually resists the lure of fascist agitators, he was perceived as drab and gullible, thereby precluding audience identification with him and thus negating the motivational impact he was intended to have on audiences. This article shows not only how one text can carry a multiplicity of uses and meanings, but how futile it can be to try and second-guess them.

In Chapter 4, Charles Winick's 'Tendency Systems and the Effects of a Movie Dealing with a Social Problem', we see how the move towards the uses and gratifications model is brought to bear on his analysis of the reception of another film, *The Man With the Golden Arm* (Otto Preminger, 1955). Starring Frank Sinatra as a heroin junkie struggling to kick his habit, the film was intended as a moral, anti-drug drama. Winick circulated questionnaires about the film and attitudes towards drug addicts, both pre- and post-'exposure' to the film, to over a thousand teenagers at school in New York and examined their responses in relation to a number of hypotheses predicated on their race, class and gender and how 'adjusted' the respondent was.

A key objective was to discover whether viewing the film changed attitudes to drug addiction. In the event Winick found that other extra-textual factors such as the era's Congressional drug investigations and even the price paid for the cinema ticket also had a bearing on responses.

Perhaps the most illuminating results though came from interviews with fifty narcotics addicts who had seen the film. Winick's description of their responses might also be understood as an example of a 'boomerang effect'. Rather than acknowledging the film's anti-drug 'message' they instead saw it as a kind of endorsement of their lifestyle, or as one respondent put it, 'Now it's hip to be a junk' (Winick, 1963: 300). Furthermore, in their reading of the film, the casting of 'hip' star Frank Sinatra in the lead role transferred a certain cachet onto drug addiction and vindicated their fantasies. Different audiences 'used' the film to different ends, then, in that 'It would appear that the movie was almost a different movie for relatively less adjusted, relatively adjusted and addicted members of the audience. Each group perceived the film in a manner consonant with its own tendency system' (ibid.: 302). While, as noted above, the effects tradition maintains an enduring appeal, Winick's comments here nevertheless demonstrate just how far audience studies had come to revise the early simple stimulus–response model by this time.

Notes

1   These themes were returned to and explored later in *Personal Influence*, Katz and Lazarsfeld (1955).

2   This was all the more intriguing as Merton notes, given the confluence between Smith as a radio star and radio as a commercial venture; despite appearing on six sponsored radio programmes every week, Smith was able to maintain a persona as 'the epitome of sincerity and the exponent of truth' (Merton, 1971: 83). This persona was fully utilised by the carefully constructed and negotiated war bond media event she participated in. Merton's account then is of interest not just to the history of communications research but also to star studies.

3   This is a contention that would be explored later in more detail by Stuart Hall: see Part Three of this Reader.

Further reading

Abercrombie, N. and Longhurst, B. (1998) 'Changing Audiences; Changing Paradigms of Research', *Audiences: A Sociological Theory of Performance and Imagination*, London and Thousand Oaks, CA: Sage Publications, pp. 3–37.

Elliot, P. (1974) 'Uses and Gratifications Research: A Critique and a Sociological Alternative', in J. G. Blumler and E. Katz (eds) *The Uses of Mass Communication*, London and Beverly Hills: Sage, pp. 249–68.

Gauntlett, D. (1998) 'Ten Things Wrong with the "Effects" Model', in R. Dickinson, R. Harindranath and O. Linné (eds) *Approaches to Audiences: A Reader*, London: Arnold.

Katz E. and Lazarsfeld, Paul F. (1955) *Personal Influence*, Glencoe, IL: The Free Press.

Lazarsfeld, P. F., Berelson, B. and Gaudet, H. (1944. 3rd edition 1968), *The People's Choice:*

How the Voter Makes Up His Mind in a Presidential Campaign. New York: Columbia University Press.

Merton, R. K. (1946, reprinted 1971) *Mass Persuasion: The Social Psychology of a War Bond Drive*. Westport, CT: Greenwood Press Publishers.

Murphy, G., Murphy, L. B. and Newcomb T. M. (1937) *Experimental Social Psychology*. New York: Harper and Brothers.

Chapter 1

Paul F. Lazarsfeld, Bernard Berelson and Hazel Gaudet

THE PEOPLE'S CHOICE

How the voter makes up his mind in a presidential campaign

THE POLITICAL HOMOGENEITY OF social groups is promoted by personal relationships among the same kinds of people. But for a detailed and systematic study of the influence of such relationships – the political role of personal influence – a systematic inventory would be needed of the various personal contacts and political discussions that people had over a sample number of days. That would provide an index of personal exposure similar to the indices of exposure to the formal media developed in previous chapters. Such complete data are not available in the present study,[1] but enough information has been collected to indicate the importance of personal relationships so far as their direct political influence is concerned. Our findings and impressions will be summarized without much formal statistical data. The significance of this area of political behavior was highlighted by the study but further investigation is necessary to establish it more firmly.

In comparison with the formal media of communication, personal relationships are potentially more influential for two reasons: their coverage is greater and they have certain psychological advantages over the formal media.

Personal contacts reach the undecided

Whenever the respondents were asked to report on their recent exposure to campaign communications of all kinds, political discussions were mentioned more frequently than exposure to radio or print. On any average day, at least 10% more people participated in discussions about the election – either actively or passively – than listened to a major speech or read about campaign items in a newspaper. And this coverage 'bonus' came from just those people who had not yet made a final decision as to how they would vote. Political conversations, then, were more likely to reach those people who were still open to influence.

For example, people who made up their minds later in the campaign were more likely to mention personal influences in explaining how they formed their final vote decision. Similarly, we found that the less interested people relied more on conversations and less on the formal media as sources of information. Three-fourths of the respondents who at one time had not expected to vote but were then finally 'dragged in' mentioned personal influence. After the election, the voters were given a check list of 'sources from which they got most of the information or impressions that caused them to form their judgment on how to vote.' Those who had made some change during the campaign mentioned friends or members of their family relatively more frequently than did the respondents who kept a constant vote intention all through the campaign.

The two-step flow of communications

A special role in the network of personal relationships is played by the 'opinion leaders.' . . . we noted that they engaged in political discussion much more than the rest of the respondents. But they reported that the formal media were more effective as sources of influence than personal relationships. This suggests that ideas often flow *from* radio and print *to* the opinion leaders and *from* them to the less active sections of the population.

Occasionally, the more articulate people even pass on an article or point out the importance of a radio speech. Repeatedly, changers referred to reading or listening done under some personal influence. Take the case of a retired school teacher who decided for the Republicans: 'The country is ripe for a change . . . Willkie is a religious man. *A friend read and highly recommended* Dr. Poling's article in the October issue of the *Christian Herald* called "The Religion of Wendell Willkie".'

So much for the 'coverage of personal contacts.' The person-to-person influence reaches the ones who are more susceptible to change, and serves as a bridge over which formal media of communications extend their influence. But in addition, personal relationships have certain psychological advantages which make them especially effective in the exercise of the 'molecular pressures' finally leading to the political homogeneity of social groups. We turn now to a discussion of five such characteristics.

Non-purposiveness of personal contacts

The weight of personal contacts upon opinion lies, paradoxically, in their greater casualness and non-purposiveness in political matters. If we read or tune in a speech, we usually do so purposefully, and in doing so we have a definite mental set which tinges our receptiveness. Such purposive behavior is part of the broad area of our political experiences, to which we bring our convictions with a desire to test them and strengthen them by what is said. This mental set is armor against influence. The extent to which people, and particularly those with strong partisan views, listen to speakers and read articles with which they agree in advance is evidence on this point.

On the other hand, people we meet for reasons other than political discussion are more likely to catch us unprepared, so to speak, if they make politics the topic. One can avoid newspaper stories and radio speeches simply by making a slight effort, but as the campaign mounts and discussion intensifies, it is hard to avoid some talk of politics. Personal influence is more pervasive and less self-selective than the formal media. In short, politics gets through, especially to the indifferent, much more easily through personal contacts than in any other way, simply because it comes up unexpectedly as a sideline or marginal topic in a casual conversation. For example, there was the restaurant waitress who decided that Willkie would make a poor president after first thinking he would be good. Said she: 'I had done a little newspaper reading against Willkie, but the real reason I changed my mind was from *hearsay*. So many people don't like Willkie. Many customers in the restaurant said Willkie would be no good.' Notice that she was in a position to overhear bits of conversation that were not intended for her. There are many such instances. Talk that is 'forbidden fruit' is particularly effective because one need not be suspicious as to the persuasive intentions of the speakers; as a result one's defenses are down. Furthermore, one may feel that he is getting the viewpoint of 'people generally,' that he is learning how 'different people' think about the election.

Such passive participation in conversation is paralleled in the case of the formal media by accidental exposure, e.g., when a political speech is heard because it follows a favorite program. In both conversation and the formal media, such chance communication is particularly effective. And the testimony to such influence is much more frequent in the case of personal contacts. The respondents mentioned it time and again: 'I've heard fellows talk at the plant . . . I hear men talk at the shop . . . My husband heard that talked about at work . . .'

Flexibility when countering resistance

But suppose we do meet people who want to influence us and suppose they arouse our resistance. Then personal contact still has one great advantage compared with other media: the face-to-face contact can counter and dislodge such resistance, for it is much more flexible. The clever campaign worker, professional or amateur, can make use of a large number of cues to achieve his end. He can choose the occasion at which to speak to the other fellow. He can adapt his story to what he presumes to be the other's interests and his ability to understand. If he notices the other is bored, he can change the subject. If he sees that he has aroused resistance, he can retreat, giving the other the satisfaction of a victory, and come back to his point later. If in the course of the discussion he discovers some pet convictions, he can try to tie up his argument with them. He can spot the moments when the other is yielding, and so time his best punches.

Neither radio nor the printed page can do anything of the kind. They must aim their propaganda shots at the whole target instead of just at the center, which represents any particular individual. In propaganda as much as in other things, one man's meat is another man's poison. This may lead to boomerang effects, when arguments aimed at 'average' audiences with 'average' reactions fail with Mr. X. The formal media produced several boomerangs upon people who resented what they read or heard and moved in the opposite direction from that intended. But among 58 respondents who mentioned personal contacts as concretely influential, there was only one boomerang. The flexibility of the face-to-face situation undoubtedly accounted for their absence.

Rewards for compliance

When someone yields to a personal influence in making a vote decision, the reward is immediate and personal. This is not the case in yielding to an argument via print or radio. If a pamphlet argues that voting for the opposite party would be un-American or will jeopardize the future, its warning may sound too remote or improbable. But if a neighbor says the same things, he can 'punish' one immediately for being unimpressed or unyielding: he can look angry or sad, he can leave the room and make his fellow feel isolated. The pamphlet can only intimate or describe future deprivations; the living person can create them at once.

Of course all this makes personal contacts a powerful influence only for some people who do not like to be out of line. There are certainly some people who gain pleasure from being non-conformists, but under normal circumstances they are probably very much in the minority. Whenever propaganda by another person is experienced as an expression of the prevailing group tendencies, it has greater chances of being successful than the formal media because of social rewards. For example, here is a woman who was for Roosevelt until the middle of the campaign: 'I have always been a Democrat and I think Roosevelt has been all right. But my family are all for Willkie. They think he would make the best president and they have been putting the pressure on me.' She finally voted for Willkie. This aspect of personal contacts was especially important for women.

The rewards of compliance to other people are learned in early childhood. The easiest way for most children to avoid discomfort is to do what others tell them to do. Someone who holds no strong opinions on politics and hence makes up his mind late in the campaign may very well be susceptible to personal influences because he has learned as a child to take them as useful guides in unknown territory. The young man who was going to vote for Roosevelt because 'my grandfather will skin me if I don't' is a case in point.

Trust in an intimate source

More people put reliance upon their personal contacts to help them pick out the arguments which are relevant for their own good in political affairs than they do in the more remote and impersonal newspaper and radio. The doubtful voter may feel that the evaluations he reads or hears in a broadcast are plausible, for the expert writer can probably spell out the consequences of voting more clearly than the average citizen. But the voter still wonders whether these are the issues which are really going to affect *his own* future welfare. Perhaps these sources see the problem from a viewpoint entirely different from his own. But he can trust the judgment and evaluation of the respected people among his associates. Most of them are people with the same status and interests as himself. Their attitudes are more relevant for him than the judgments of an unknown editorial writer. In a formal communication the content can be at its best; but in a face to face contact the transference is most readily achieved. For example, here is the case of a young laborer who professed little or no interest in the campaign and who did not even expect to vote until late October: 'I've been discussing the election with *the fellows at the shop* and I believe I'll vote, but I haven't decided yet who for.' His constant exposure to the views of his fellow-workers not only brought him to the ballot booth but also brought out his final Democratic vote in line with his colleagues.

A middle-aged woman who showed great interest in the campaign was undecided until late October and then voted for Willkie: '*I was talking politics just this morning with a friend, a businessman.* He says business will improve if Willkie is elected and that Willkie promises to keep us out of the war. FDR is getting too much power. He shouldn't have a third term.' Her friend had apparently run out for her what amounted to a small catalogue of Republican arguments and he was impressive enough to clinch her vote, which had been in the balance throughout the campaign. Her trust in his judgment settled her mind.

Trust in another person's point of view may be due to his prestige as well as to the plausibility of what he has to say or its relevancy to one's interests. It is obvious that in all influences prestige plays a considerable role. The degree of conformity is greater the higher the prestige of the person in our group who seeks to influence us. The plausibility of the consequences he presents will seem greater if he is important. (Of course, the formal media are also important in this respect.) The heightening of trust through the prestige of certain personal contacts was clear in the case of the driver of a bread truck who changed to Willkie because the prominent president of a business firm had done him the honor of persuading him in that direction. Then, too, there is the case of a middle-aged housewife with little education who was for Willkie from May through September, became undecided in October, and finally voted for Roosevelt. She left Willkie because of the statements of people whom she considered authorities: 'I talked with *a college student* from Case, in Cleveland, and students are for Roosevelt because he has helped recreation. I talked, too, with a *man from Chicago who is very interested in politics*, and he doesn't seem to think that Willkie is a big enough man to handle international affairs.'

Persuasion without conviction

Finally, personal contacts can get a voter to the polls without affecting at all his comprehension of the issues of the election – something the formal media can rarely do. The newspaper or magazine or radio must first be effective in changing attitudes related to the action. There were several clear cases of votes cast not on the issues or even the personalities of the candidates. In fact, they were not really cast for the candidates at all. They were cast, so to speak, for the voters' friends.

'*I was taken to the polls* by a worker who insisted that I go.'

'*The lady where I work wanted me to vote.* She took me to the polls and *they all voted Republican so I did too.*'

In short, personal influence, with all its overtones of personal affection and loyalty, can bring to the polls votes that would otherwise not be cast or would be cast for the opposing party just as readily if some other friend had insisted. They differ from the formal media by persuading uninterested people to vote in a certain way without giving them a substantive reason for their vote. Fully 25% of those who mentioned a personal contact in connection with change of mind failed to give a real issue of the campaign as a reason for the change, but only 5% of those who mentioned the formal media omitted such a reason. When personal influence is paramount in this way, the voter is voting mainly for the personal friend, not the candidate.

Practical implications

In a way the outcome of the election in Erie County is the best evidence for the success of face-to-face contacts. It so happened that for some time the Republican machine in that area worked much more vigorously than its Democratic opponent. When asked whether they knew people who had good ideas about politics, our respondents mentioned considerably more Republican than Democratic local politicians. A few people who did not expect to vote but finally went to the polls mentioned Republican canvassers as the main influence, but we could not trace a similar success for the Democratic machine.

However, one should not identify the personal contacts discussed in this chapter with the efforts of the *professional* political machines. These personal contacts are what one might call *amateur machines* which spring up during elections – individuals who become quite enthusiastic or special groups that try to activate people within their reach. One might almost say that the most successful form of propaganda – especially last-minute propaganda – is to 'surround' the people whose vote decision is still dubious so that the only path left to them is the way to the polling booth. We do not know how the budget of the political parties is distributed among different channels of propaganda but we suspect that the largest part of any propaganda budget is spent on pamphlets, radio time, etc. But our findings suggest the task of finding the best ratio between money spent on formal media and money spent on organizing the face-to-face influences, the local 'molecular pressures' which vitalize the formal media by more personal interpretation and the full richness of personal relationships into the promotion of the causes which are decided upon the course of an election.

In the last analysis, more than anything else people can move other people. From an ethical point of view this is a hopeful aspect in the serious social problem of propaganda. The side which has the more enthusiastic supporters and which can mobilize grass-root support in an expert way has great chances of success.

Note

1   In two respects it is more difficult to get an index of personal exposure as compared with one of radio listening and newspaper reading. One involves a memory factor. Radio speeches are rather distinct events and people are not likely to listen to too many of them. Therefore if they are asked to remember those they have been exposed to, they are bound not to make too many mistakes. With newspapers it is still simpler because we can place the entire paper before them and their recognition is fairly reliable, as we have seen in various studies using this method. But people meet people the whole day long, and it is not nearly so likely that they can remember everything that passed between them in discussion. At least it would first be necessary to do some experimentation with personal contact diaries as suggested in the text.

To this we have to add the element of self-consciousness. If people know that they have to keep a record of what they talked about with other people, they might very well be affected in their selection of topic. Radio diaries have been tested and it seems that keeping such diaries makes people record their radio diet substantially. But this might be due to the fact that radio listening is a much more standardized pursuit; talking with people is much more flexible and might therefore be more affected by a request for systematic recording.

It is hoped that experimentation in this direction will be furthered.

Chapter 2

ROBERT K. MERTON

MASS PERSUASION
The social psychology of a war bond drive

Guilt and decision: the susceptible bond buyer

BEFORE EXPOSURE TO THE Smith broadcasts, the 28 informants in the 'susceptible' group felt that they had discharged their bond obligations. Eleven had previously met their self-set quota of bonds during the drive and the others felt 'we are doing all we can with payroll deductions.' Since their prior purchases satisfied their established standards, they had reached a temporary equilibrium in which their ego level could be preserved intact. 'I had bought bonds in the community the week before, and felt that was all I needed to buy." 'I wasn't going to buy a bond, because we've already bought *our bonds*.' 'I usually buy bonds through the bank. I thought I'd let it slip for a couple of months; *I was ahead of my pledge*.' 'We always buy our bonds the first day of the drive. *We had already bought our share when I heard her*.' Smith led these listeners to reassess the adequacy of their previous contributions. She disturbed the previously stabilized ego level by inviting a series of reappraisals of the implicit standards in terms of which a sense of adequacy had been attained. How did this come about?

As we have seen, a larger proportion of the susceptible buyers responded to all the persuasive elements of the broadcast: more were greatly devoted to Smith, more were impressed by the extent of her effort, and more were acutely interested in the content of her appeals. Furthermore, only four of the 28 had funds readily available for the purchase, in contrast to the predisposed who had, of course, specifically set aside their money for this purpose. And since they had a higher level of resistance, they listened to more appeals before deciding to pledge a bond (1 of every 4 heard Smith 20 times or more before coming to a decision).

It is significant that, in contrast to the predisposed group who characteristically explained their decision as a matter of convenience, the susceptible group phrased their 'motivation' in terms of a renewed sense of guilt. Various aspects of the Smith broadcasts served to redefine the appropriate amount of bonds to be purchased and, in the light of these modified norms, an acute sense of unworthiness and self-accusation intervened. Without implying that a single factor in the total situation initiated this process of self-revaluation, we can conveniently classify the susceptible listeners in three categories, according to the aspects of the broadcasts to which they chiefly responded.[1] Some repeatedly stressed the magnitude of Smith's effort and described in circumstantial detail how this led them to re-examine their own contributions to the war effort. Others phrased the basis for their behavior chiefly in terms of their affective relationship to Smith. And still others were primarily influenced by the accounts of sacrifice by soldiers which led to an upward revision of norms for their own conduct.

As the day wore on, listeners in the first category were increasingly affected by Smith's 'self-sacrifice.' In the context of her seemingly extreme and selfless effort, their own earlier contributions fell short. They were no longer convinced that they had done enough: 'By evening, she was still going so strong. I admired her endurance. *I felt if she had made such an effort, why shouldn't I make another bit of an effort?*'

The Phrasing of Motivation among Susceptible Bond Buyers

	No. of Cases
Smith's 'sacrifice' (the marathon)	16
Affective relationship (devotion to Smith)	5
Content of Smith appeals (others' sacrifices)	6
Unclassified	1
	—
Total	28

The recurring theme throughout these sixteen interviews is expressed in the following excerpts:

> I'd already bought one for the drive. Then I began to feel I should have done a little more than I had . . . *She was doing her bit to help the boys carry on.* I would have felt uneasy . . . I don't know . . . if I hadn't bought.

> *If she could stay on the radio all day like that, the least I could do was to buy another bond.* I wouldn't feel right listening all day and then going into a bank and not buying from her. *Maybe if she were only on for an hour or two, like the others, it wouldn't matter.*

Following the bond purchase, these listeners experienced a release of tension, as though they had again satisfied legitimate demands which had been laid upon them. They had regained their self-regard.

> After I bought, I could sleep – before that I couldn't close my eyes. It was almost one o'clock by the time I bought the bond. I thought, '*poor darling, she certainly earned that thirty million she sold.*' At one o'clock, I said, '*Now that I've done my little job, I thank God for giving me the wisdom to see clearly,*' and I turned off the radio.

For these persons, then, it was not what Smith said that day that prompted the purchase, but what she did. Accounts of the sacrifices of fighting men did not move them to self-reappraisal. They had previously bought sufficient bonds to alleviate any guilt feelings evoked by these more familiar themes. For them, the reappraisal came about through a more direct, forceful, and new impact – provided, in this instance, by Smith's personal example.

Among the five buyers who bought bonds primarily as a testimonial to their long-standing devotion to Smith, there was little activation of guilt. This is evidenced by their tendency to lose sight of the fact that they were buying *bonds*, rather than answering a request by Smith. Their beloved Kate was making an appeal, and they gave to *her*. Had she been asking for clothing for the worthy poor, books for the bedridden, or toys for deprived children, their response would probably have been the same: '*She asked for something*, and I gave it to her.' 'I bought as soon as I knew she wanted it . . . *If I like Kate Smith so much, I have to prove it.*' 'I said to myself, No, Kate, I won't let you down on this.' These pledges, then, did not stem from a reorientation toward war bonds or a revision of personal norms of bond purchases. In a sense, they did not so much represent war bond pledges as pledges of personal attachment to Smith.[2]

For the remaining six persons among the susceptible buyers, the process of persuasion was phrased in considerably different terms. They revised their bond obligations upward in response to the content of Smith's appeals. Closer examination of these six cases indicates that they were especially vulnerable to one of these appeals and for a particular reason.

We have noted that a central theme in the Smith broadcasts could be summarized in these terms: Buy a bond and bring your boy back home. And it was to this theme that these persons chiefly responded. A series of interlocking data indicate that the context of this selective response was provided by their deep personal involvement in the war. To begin with, four of the listeners in this category were mothers of sons in the armed forces; the fifth had a brother in the service, and the sixth was himself a veteran of the first World War. In contrast, only 9 of the 22 others in the susceptible category had close relatives (son, brother, husband or father) in some branch of the service.

Further data account for this selective response. These five persons were peculiarly beset by fears and anxiety concerning a son or brother who, in all five instances, was serving overseas. They were, therefore, peculiarly sensitive to Smith's vivid portrayals of the needs and sacrifices of men at the front. It was as though they visualized their own sons as the central figures in the dramatic episodes described by Smith. Phrases which were little more than clichés for others took on deep emotional significance for those who interpreted them in the light of their own longings and anxieties. Thus, almost echoing a Smith phrase, one informant in this category defined her bond purchase as a means of 'bringing my brother home sooner.'

Responded to Accounts of Soldier Sacrifice	*Close Relatives in Armed Forces*		
	Yes	*No*	*Total*
Yes	5	1	6
No	9	13	22
Total	14	14	28

Within this context of emotional stress, Smith's appeals were taken by mothers as presenting a means of coping with the apprehensions that crowded in upon them. They felt themselves at the mercy of incalculable circumstances. There was the ever-present imminence of fateful word from the War Department – We regret to inform you . . . Faced with these obsessive fears, it was psychologically difficult for them to arrive at the dispassionate judgment that nothing could be done to enhance the safety of their sons. All this generated a powerful need for 'doing something' about an unendurable situation and, under the goad of this desperate anxiety, the bond purchase took on an almost magical character.[3] For, tormented by terrible forebodings, these mothers acted as though the *particular* bond they bought would directly safeguard their own sons in battle, as though *their* bonds would set in motion circumstances which would bring their boys safe through the war. *Something* was being done, and the sense of helplessness and lack of control over an unbearable, ego-charged danger gave way to a feeling of having introduced some measure of control.[4] Smith's vivid accounts of the horrors to which fighting men are exposed thus had a double-edged character: they virtually terrorized these mothers into an added bond purchase and by doing so, provided a behavior formula for temporary escape from intolerable fears and anxieties.

Translating Smith's appeals into acutely personal terms, the anxious mother of a bombardier stationed in England felt that her bond was to serve as direct aid to her son.

> I remember she says, 'If you buy a bond, you buy a ticket for your son to come home.' [At this point, the interviewer was shown a photograph of her son.] She was just like speaking to me. Her voice . . . she helps mothers, our sons, I cried all the time. [She asks the interviewer: You think maybe our boys come home soon?] The way she speaks to mothers, it would break anyone's heart. I think: I am going to buy a bond. *I'll buy a bond for my boy. I wouldn't NOT have the money to help my son. I wouldn't be able to rest.*

A Brooklyn housewife, whose only son was overseas, similarly supplied a personal context for Smith's accounts of sacrifice, as the following excerpt indicates:

> The way she was talking, I had all I could do to get to the phone quickly. She was telling the story of a young fellow – I remember his name, Merrill – that didn't have any legs or arms and was happy and wanted no sympathy and that we should buy bonds in his name *and save some other boy from such a thing. It touched very deeply. Not only what she said. But my son's in the service for three years* . . . It got me so. I ran from the phone right over to his picture and started to cry. And I said: '*Sonny, if this will save one hair on your head*, I thank God, and I thank God that I live in the United States.'

In those instances where mothers had no knowledge of their sons' whereabouts or of the risks to which they were exposed, anxieties were all the more intensified. The absence of any secure basis for judgment gave free rein to all manner of apprehensions which they sought to escape by actively doing something for their boys:

> I tell you, I was pretty well upset. I sent my daughter to call her up. *I hadn't heard from my boy for some time and I was worried.* [Informant gives way to

tears.] It's funny how some people don't give. It's only a loan. If I had more money, I'd given it all. [Informant finds it increasingly difficult to speak.] I feel foolish, but I can't help myself. I'm so upset about my son on the Flying Fortress. *Every time she spoke, it meant more and more. I was so upset. It made me wish I could have given her all – everything I had to give up for the boy.* I was trying to get some money together to get curtains, but I put up with the old ones.

I was listening to Kate's stories and started to think of my son. He trained in the Seventh Regiment. It was just that she was asking for money and my boy is in the war. *I don't even know where he is now. His A.P.O. number has been changed.*

But all this does not explain why only 5 of the 14 listeners with close relatives in the armed forces responded in this fashion. What of the 'deviate' cases, those 9 who did *not* respond selectively to this phase of Smith's appeals. An analysis of the interviews provides the clue. The unresponsive persons had little basis for acute fears of anxiety concerning the safety of sons or brothers in the service. In five cases, their kin were stationed in this country and, therefore, their situation did not evoke immediate anxiety. And in another instance, where a son was overseas, he was far removed from any active war theater. Nor could a chief gunner's mate, the husband of another informant, be a source of anxiety, since at the time he was home on leave and listening with his wife to the Smith bond drive. Thus, the emotional context for selective listening was significantly different for the two categories of informants, although both had close relatives in the Army or Navy.

In review, then, the evidence suggests that susceptible listeners responded selectively in terms of distinctive sets of determinants. By taking 'close relatives in the service' as a crude index of direct emotional involvement with the war, we found a tendency for those who were emotionally involved to respond particularly to the 'sacrifice' theme of Smith's broadcasts. But this led to the problem of interpreting the absence of such selective response among some relatives of servicemen. A further refinement of our index in terms of those relationships which did or did not generate anxiety enabled us to account for such seeming 'exceptions.' It was against the background of acute anxiety concerning the safety of affectively significant persons in the armed services that some informants were particularly affected by the sacrificial theme.

This pattern suggests the apparent paradox that those who had already contributed most heavily to the national war effort – by giving a son or brother to the service and by previous bond purchases – were perhaps the most likely to continue giving more. Their initial emotional involvement provided the motivational basis for further cumulative contributions, whereas those who had a less immediate, a psychologically less compelling stake in the war were not as likely to have the same urgent drive for all-out sacrifice. Each successive emotional commitment induced further commitment, if only because it made for successive gratifications.[5] We do not know, of course, the frequency of *this pattern of cumulative and self-reinforcing response*[6] in the general population, but its occurrence among our informants suggests the possibility that the main weight of contributions to the war effort may be borne, for understandable psychological reasons, by particular sectors of the nation.[7]

Detachment and decision

As we have seen, eleven informants who bought a bond from Smith exhibited a comparatively unemotional, detached orientation toward war bonds. Eight of these – the 'indifferent' – had planned to buy additional bonds during the drive and three – the 'undisposed' – had no such intention. These are the persons who prevailingly regard war bonds as a 'practical investment,' rather than a patriotic symbol or an essential instrumentality in the war effort.

> *I think the investment part, the saving part, is important.* If the country fails, our money won't be any good anyway. If we win, we get it back.

> *It's just for a rainy day. I think that's a pretty logical reason.* Ten years from today, we don't know what straits we'll be in and then the money may come in handy. I don't want to cash in any of them. You know what I'd really like to do? If I could, I'd like to buy enough to take care of my son's education.

The paucity of cases in the two groups of 'detached' buyers does not permit us to establish comparative patterns of persuasion, but these few instances do provide a basis for interpretations which have some measure of plausibility. We can readily understand, for example, why the eight indifferent listeners who were poised for a bond purchase listened to an average of only eight broadcasts, fewer than that of any other predisposition group. In contrast to the predisposed group, they had little affective or emotional concern with war bonds, and in contrast to those who had no prior intent to buy a bond, they required little cumulative persuasion. Their decision was quickly made, and there was little further motivation for continued listening.

In accord with their prevalently utilitarian attitude toward bonds, their decision to purchase their bond from Smith rather than from others stemmed largely from promised gratifications which had little or no relation to bonds as a focus of sentiment. Thus the prospect of a personal, even though ephemeral, contact with a celebrity played a conspicuous role in their decision. Five of the eight persons in this category telephoned their pledge in the hope of speaking personally to Smith, whereas only 12 of the 55 other bond buyers were actuated by this consideration. The decision to buy was less a matter of purchasing a sentiment-laden bond than an occasion for direct personal contact with a prestigeful public figure. This motive was typically expressed by an informant who, to say the least, was otherwise atypical – she is an attendant to a 'half-woman, half-serpent freak' in a mid-Manhattan 'museum':

Predisposition Category	Expectation of Smith Personally Answering Telephone Pledge		
	+	−	Total
Indifferent	5	3	8
All other buyers	12	55	67
Total	17	58	75

Reptilina and I sat talking about it for a few minutes first. [At this point, the articulate Reptilina herself interrupted to explain: '*We thought about calling because we would be able to talk to Kate herself.*'] Then I said, well, I'll call up. I did, and found out that Kate was not talking to people. She really couldn't, now that I think of it, because so many people called up. But I couldn't back out then. I would have felt like a fool. Besides, I was going to buy one anyway.

Another basis for the decision, extraneous to any emotional meaning ascribed to bonds, is found in their affective ties to Smith. In seven cases, they were devoted fans who readily sought this new opportunity of expressing their sentiment. 'Being an admirer of hers, I just called.' The present experience occurred within the context of previous sentimental attachments to Smith, ties imbued with considerable affect. Thus, when one such listener heard the bond broadcasts, she was flooded with nostalgic images of what Smith had meant to her in the past:

About eleven or twelve years ago, I was very ill. I was sitting all alone. It was wintertime. The ground was all white with snow, the trees and everything. And nothing could be more realistic than Kate singing, 'When the Moon Comes Over the Mountain' . . . Thoughts came quickly back to me of that night when I was down in spirit and health, too. It's something I don't think anything can express. I was anxious to see her do well . . . *I think there's a natural desire where anyone you've contacted* . . . [and, then, as the actual character of the 'persona' tie is half-recognized] . . . *maybe, not personally. She had set her goal and I wanted to help her meet it.*

And, finally, since all these persons had planned to purchase their bonds at a post office or bank, they were not at all subjected to a conflict of personal loyalties.

This configuration of factors – detached attitude, immediate intent to purchase, comparatively slight attention devoted to the broadcasts, and primary concern with relationship to Smith – reduced the likelihood of any focus on the content of Smith's appeals. There is little evidence of any marked response to the themes of her broadcast among the 'indifferent' bond buyers. And, in consequence, there were no signs that these listeners experienced a reorientation toward their secular conception of war bonds. In large measure, Smith simply provided another, seemingly convenient occasion for the planned bond purchase and, in these instances at least, left unmodified the previous detached attitudes toward war bonds.

Among the 'undisposed' listeners, i.e., those who had a detached orientation toward war bonds and had no prior intent to buy a bond, the major element in persuasion was clearly their close affective tie to Smith. This becomes evident from a comparison between the three undisposed persons who finally pledged a bond to Smith and the six who were not persuaded to do so. We have seen that comparatively few persons in our sample expressed an unfavorable attitude towards Smith (only 18 per cent of our informants). But all six of the undisposed nonbuyers fall in this category, whereas all three who purchased a bond had positive feelings towards her.

Notes

1 At the risk of undue repetition, it should be emphasized that we do not thereby subscribe to the view that action results from isolated impulses or motives. We are here analyzing our informants' own phrasing of the aspects which led to a reconsideration of their previous decision not to buy additional bonds during the drive.

2 A similar pattern has been found in the field of political behavior. '. . . personal influence, with all its overtones of personal affection and loyalty, can bring to the polls votes that would otherwise not be cast or would be cast for the opposing party just as readily if some other friend had insisted . . . Fully 25% of those who mentioned a personal contact in connection with change of mind failed to give a real issue of the campaign as a reason for the change, but only 5% of those who mentioned the formal media omitted such a reason. When personal influence is paramount in this way, the voter is voting mainly for the personal friend, not the candidate.' P.F. Lazarsfeld, B. Berelson and H. Gaudet, *The People's Choice* (New York: Duell, Sloan & Pearce, 1944), p. 157.

3 Compare Malinowski's account of 'the type of situation in which we find magic.' 'Man, engaged in a series of practical activities, *comes to a gap*; the hunter is disappointed in his quarry, the sailor misses propitious winds, the canoe-builder has to deal with some material of which he is never certain that it will stand the strain, or the healthy person suddenly feels his strength failing. What does man do naturally under such conditions, setting aside all magic, belief and ritual? Forsaken by his knowledge, baffled by his past experience and by his technical skill, *he realises his impotence. Yet his desire grips him only the more strongly; his anxiety, his fears and hopes, induce a tension in his organism which drives him to some sort of activity.* Whether he be savage or civilised, whether in possession of magic or entirely ignorant of its existence, *passive inaction*, the only thing dictated by reason, *is the last thing in which he can acquiesce.* His nervous system and his whole organism drive him to some *substitute activity*. B. Malinowski, 'Magic, Science and Religion,' in *Science, Religion and Reality* (ed. by Joseph Needham) (New York: The Macmillan Company, 1925, p. 73). (Italics inserted).

4 'The function of magic is to ritualise man's optimism, to enhance his faith in the victory of hope over fear.' *Ibid.*, p. 83.

5 The previously quoted mother of a crew member of a Flying Fortress provides a case in point: 'I've given my blood to the Red Cross five times and I plan to go again soon . . .'

6 A similar pattern has been exhibited in other contexts. It is found in the 'self-selection of audiences,' so that, for example, opinion-shaping radio programs have audiences comprised in the main of persons in full agreement with the views being broadcast. Mass meetings centered about a *cause célèbre* ordinarily attract those who had the 'appropriate' attitudes at the outset and thus produce reinforcement rather than diffusion of attitudes. The effects tend to be cumulative rather than dispersive. Cf. P. F. Lazarsfeld 'The Effects of Radio on Public Opinion,' *Print, Radio and Film in a Democracy* (Douglas Waples, ed.) (University of Chicago Press, 1942), pp. 68–69.

7 This may be mitigated by a countertendency on the part of guilt-ridden persons to 'compensate' for their seemingly inadequate contributions to a common cause. The veteran who responded to the 'sacrifice theme' illustrates this pattern. 'I never gave buying a bond a thought before I heard her. The stories she told of the suffering of the boys on the other side comes right back to you. The last one she was telling got me. It reminded me of something that happened twenty-five years ago on the other side. And it made me want to buy. *At least I can buy a bond. I can't do anything else.*'

Chapter 3

Eunice Cooper and Helen Dinerman

ANALYSIS OF THE FILM *DON'T BE A SUCKER*
A study in communication

THIS REPORT, AND THE film which is the focus of study, are no longer timely. They belong to the 1940s. It is hoped, however, that the study approach described here may still be of interest to research workers in the field of mass communication on problems of intergroup relations.

How effective are films for the changing of attitudes in a desired direction? What kinds of themes are likely to be effective?

This article reports on the reactions of adult and high school groups to the film *Don't Be a Sucker*, which seeks to point out the futility of intergroup prejudice. The authors found that the film was most successful in routing specific messages to specific groups, but that several of the messages 'boomeranged' and produced unexpected and undesired attitude changes. The authors conclude that an appeal to enlightened self-interest proved to be the film's most successful means of communicating its message.

Miss Cooper is now at the Research Center for Human Relations, New York University. Mrs Dinerman is with International Public Opinion Research, Inc.

During World War II the Army Signal Corps produced a twenty-minute film intended to raise the morale of our fighting forces. After the war a shortened version of the film was widely shown both commercially and under educational auspices. The research reported here is an attempt to determine how effective the film was in influencing attitudes and to see what factors contributed to, or detracted from, its effectiveness.[1]

The principal appeal of the film is to the self-interest of the spectators. To the somewhat prejudiced or wavering individual the film-makers say, 'Prejudice is a device used by agitators to manipulate you for their own gain; you get nothing out of it; on the contrary, if you allow yourself to be duped into discrimination you are the one who loses out in the end.' For members of minority groups the film carries this message, 'If each of you protects the rights of others you will find in this unity the strength to eliminate discrimination.'

The story line is as follows:

The beginning of the film defines and describes typical 'suckers.' A young man drinking at a bar picks up a blonde, leaves with her, and is robbed in the alley-way by the blonde's accomplice. A train passenger is inveigled into a card game from which he emerges with a badly depleted bankroll. These are some of the suckers of the world.

The film then focuses upon a bright-looking young man, Mike, who is admiring the countryside from a train window. Mike is proud to be an American and happy about the limitless opportunities thus afforded him. But, we are told, there are those who want to cheat Mike of his birthright.

Upon alighting from the train, Mike stops to listen to a street speaker who is urging 'real Americans,' 'American Americans,' to take over jobs held by Negroes and by 'rich aliens with foreign accents.' Mike nods his agreement as the agitator attacks one minority group after another. But when the speaker attacks Masons, Mike is shocked into disagreement for he is himself a Mason.

An onlooker, noting Mike's initial agreement and his later dismay at being implicitly attacked, draws him aside and discusses the rabble-rouser with him. The newcomer introduces himself as a refugee professor who saw the same things happen in Berlin. He warns Mike that such talk is always motivated by the speaker's desire for gain and that people like Mike never profit from discrimination.

The refugee professor proceeds to draw the parallel between the present scene and Germany under Nazism. He describes a Nazi street speaker very much like the soap-box orator to whom Mike has been listening. One by one the Nazi succeeds in isolating each minority group so that all are vulnerable. But, the narrator points out, the one who was really being swindled was Hans, a pure German according to Nazi standards. To him the Nazis promised everything and he believed them. In destroying the liberty of others he lost his own freedom and life.

The refugee professor describes the persecution, the pillage and the wanton destruction which followed the Nazi rise to power. A German teacher is shown lecturing on the myth of 'master races.' He ironically refers to pictures of Hitler, Goebbels, and Goering as evidence that the mythical Aryans are not blue-eyed, tall and slender. As the teacher concludes his lecture uniformed Nazis stride in and attack him.

The narrator says that everybody in Germany suffered because the people did not stick together. By permitting attacks on the first minority, everyone lost out. When Germany was defeated even the 'true Aryans' whom Nazism promised jobs and security, ended their lives in nameless graves.

Mike is convinced by the professor's story. He tears up and tosses away the 'hate' pamphlet he had accepted from the American agitator.

In evaluating the overall effectiveness of the film, the main concerns were:

a.   the degree to which each of the film's several messages was accepted; and
b.   how the responses to each of these separate elements contributed to, or detracted from, the film's achievement of its more general purposes.

Within the present article, however, no attempt is made to report upon all these specific and interlocking details. Our purpose here is to present only data which bear on concepts more generally useful to students of propaganda.

Research methodology

There were two phases in the research: a first phase, devoted to determining the *nature* of the film's impact upon the audience; and the second phase, devoted to getting the *specific results of that impact in quantitative terms*. The film was shown to various audiences to determine the nature of its emotional impact. This qualitative phase of the study included four steps:

a. Presentation of the film to four groups of adults with the aid of Program-Analyzer apparatus. Group interviews were conducted immediately following each showing.
b. Intensive interviews with twenty-four individual students at a Manhattan girls' school one week after the film had been shown as part of a school Brotherhood Week program.
c. Group interviews with classes at the same school one week after the showing.
d. Administering a written questionnaire to 326 third and fourth-year students of the same high school one week after the showing.

The second phase of the study involved the following experimental procedure: Approximately one thousand second-year high school students were divided into a control and an experimental group. In the course of a regular assembly program, the experimental group was shown *Don't Be a Sucker* together with a film about vaccination. The control group, at a similar assembly, was shown the vaccination film and a South American travelogue. Teachers were instructed to hold no discussion with the students concerning the films or their purpose.

Four weeks later students in both groups were asked to complete a written questionnaire. The questionnaire contained one hundred items bearing upon attitudes toward such diverse subjects as political parties, the relations between labor and business, social conformity and social defiance, and school issues. The bulk of the items were such that responses to them could not reasonably be expected to have been influenced by the film. About one in every five items, however, dealt with intergroup relations in America or with discrimination in Nazi Germany, and the responses to these items were therefore susceptible to influence by the film. No direct reference to the film itself was made at any time.

After the questionnaires were completed, the two groups were compared with regard to various background characteristics, and cases were deleted as necessary to render the groups completely comparable. The control group contained 491 students and the experimental group 368. The two groups contained equal proportions of students identical with respect to certain social, personal and familial characteristics.

The equating of groups was apparently successful. On no item unrelated to the film was there any significant difference between the responses of the experimental group and the responses of the control group. Accordingly, differences between the responses of the experimental and the control groups to film-related items could be attributed to exposure to the film.

Because of the methods adopted, the applicability of the findings is limited. In the first place, although the qualitative data were derived from both adults and adolescents, the quantitative data were derived wholly from youngsters of high school age. The major conclusions of our research, based as they are largely on the quantitative data, cannot therefore be regarded as necessarily valid for adults, but only for the high school age group to which the statistics apply.

Secondly, from the description of methods, the quantitative materials bear only on *change* of opinion. No data are available on the film's reenforcement effects, that is, its tendency to intensify existent attitudes. Statements derived from the quantitative data are based on the assumption that the attitudes of the control and experimental groups were similar before exposure to the test film, and that any group differences in responses to the questionnaire items constitute a measure of change attributable to exposure to the film.

Selective perception

Communication research has abundantly demonstrated that the success or failure of the communication process depends as much on members of the audience and their predisposition as it depends on the content of the stimulus and the manner of its presentation.[2] Each member of an audience, consciously or not, modifies the stimulus he perceives according to his own predispositions. To determine the direction in which these subjective factors in perception work is a central question in much audience research and research on the impact of propaganda.

'Don't Be a Sucker' is designed to influence the attitudes of an audience which varies widely in age, interests, ethnic and religious backgrounds, and in its existent attitudes about prejudice. By no means unaware of these variations in audience predispositions, the producers of *Don't Be a Sucker* addressed specific appeals to different groups. But the diversity of the special appeals in a film cannot be expected to anticipate the usually far greater diversity of the audience. The producer must decide to which groups in the audience he will address himself. The producers of *Don't Be a Sucker* decided to appeal specifically to each major religious group in the audience; to show the Catholic, the Jew, and the Protestant that members of his own group suffered under the Nazi regime. Study of the film's impact thus involved the essential question of whether selective perception did indeed function in the manner anticipated by the producers; that is whether specific messages successfully reached their intended target groups.

'Don't Be a Sucker' is remarkable in the degree to which selective perception did operate with precision. From all the evidence, several of the messages scored precise hits on their intended target groups. The film is particularly emphatic in asserting that everyone suffers under Nazism. Nazi persecution is shown to have been directed against Catholics as well as Jews. Even the dominant group in Hitler's Germany is shown to have suffered under fascism. The appeal of these messages is clearly based on self-interest: American Catholics are assumed to be especially interested in the fate of German Catholics, and the persecution of German Protestants is supposed to hit American Protestants with special force.

These two groups perceived and reacted to the appropriate messages. Sixty-one per cent of American Catholics in the control group agreed that under Nazism, German Catholics were persecuted as much as Jews, while 72 per cent of the Catholic experimental group agreed with this statement.[3] The film apparently promoted this view among members of the group for which it was intended.[4] The American Protestants were led by the film to reject the idea that Hitler helped the German majority. Fifty-two per cent of the American Protestants who had not seen the film believed that

Hitler had helped the German majority but only 26 per cent of the group who had seen the film maintained this view.[5] These two messages were thus selectively perceived by the groups for which they were intended. Non-Catholics in the audience were not impressed by the message intended for Catholics, and non-Protestants ignored the message concerning the German Protestant majority. (There were no significant differences between the control group and the experimental group.)

Another example of selective response in *Don't Be a Sucker* is provided by the reactions to the American agitator scene. Part of the argument of the agitator is that jobs which rightfully belong to native Americans are being taken by Negroes and by 'alien foreigners with accents.' Presumably, one of the tasks of the film is to bring about more democratic attitudes on this score. Although the intended lesson, that there should be no employment discrimination, is never explicitly stated in the film, the hate slogan of the agitator is made explicit, and it was hoped that the lesson would be inferred by the audience:

Data from the quantitative phase reveal that only one subgroup of the audience did make the desired inference. The questionnaire contained the test item:

> In times of depression, it is only right that jobs should be given first to people born in America.

The more 'intelligent'[6] members of the audience who were themselves of native stock *and* somewhat prejudiced against Jews and Negroes seemed to learn the lesson of the film.[7] Only 27 per cent of all such persons in the experimental group agreed with the statement, as compared to 49 per cent of all such persons in the control group. While the less prejudiced students of non-native stock were also apparently influenced in the appropriate direction, differences in response to the test item between control and experimental groups were not large enough to be statistically significant.

Although the specific devices responsible for the degree to which selective perception operated cannot be isolated on the basis of available data, it is believed that the selective routing of messages was facilitated by the German agitator scene. As this scene opens a closely packed crowd is listening to the agitator; but as the agitator attacks various minorities by name, the listening crowd moves away from the representatives of those minorities. Thus when Jews are attacked, the crowd edges away from the Jewish student; when the Catholics are attacked, the Catholic boy is suddenly left standing alone. To the degree that each member of the movie audience identifies himself with the film representative of his own minority group, he feels also the isolation into which his film counterpart has been thrust. By emotionally dividing the movie audience into the same groups as are portrayed on the screen, this symbolic representation of the divide-and-conquer technique probably accomplishes what is rarely accomplished through mass media: each target group is made sufficiently self-conscious to perceive its appropriate message selectively.

'Boomerang' effects

Selective perception of propaganda sometimes counteracts the intent of the communicator and produces a 'boomerang.'[8] 'Boomerang' effects may operate in various ways. We shall here discuss and illustrate four:

a.   a message intended for a specific group may be intercepted by another, i.e., 'mis-perception.'
b.   the message may be contradicted by another element within the film.
c.   the message may be contradicted by the personal experience or previous knowledge of the audience.
d.   the message may resemble another, more familiar, extra-film concept of contrary implications.

The Message Intercepted

'Don't Be a Sucker' contains messages specifically intended for the dominant groups in this society and others for the minorities. Dominant groups are warned to be alert to the dangers of fascism and are shown that prejudice toward minorities may serve as an opening wedge for fascism. To minorities, the film points out that they are many and that if they stand united against prejudice toward any one group, they will be strong enough in union to defeat any attack. If the dominant group receives this message meant for the minorities, the effect may be exactly opposite to that intended by the film producers. If they are led to believe that the minorities are themselves strong enough to resist encroachments upon their rights so that they require no assistance from dominant group members in the struggle to maintain these rights, then this dominant group may become complacent rather than apprehensive about threats to any minority in their midst.

Such a mis-routing of messages did occur in some cases in *Don't Be a Sucker*. Comments made by some young Protestant adults during intensive interviews indicated that these respondents interpreted the message intended for the minorities as evidence that divide-and-conquer techniques were *ipso facto* doomed to failure in the United States:

> I don't think that would happen so much here, for the simple reason that we have no tremendous majority of people of one race. In Germany, it's predominantly German, and therefore if you can get a majority together, then you might be able to do something; but in this country you have all races, all creeds, and all religions; and therefore I don't think it would be quite so easy.

> Oh, we've got a race problem, but we've got a hundred of them over here; and they are all so balled up – I mean, none of them are any great threats; one person has certain prejudices and another has certain others, so that none is going to control or take over.

Thus, some American Protestants, upon seeing the film, came to regard prejudice as composed of a multiplicity of individual prejudices which, because they were often in competition with one another, constituted no great danger and no real step toward fascism.

The Message Contradicted by Another Element in the Film

The film-makers apparently failed in their attempt to impress upon the audience that there is a real possibility of fascism developing in the United States. Precisely the same proportion (29 per cent) of both control and experimental groups subscribed to the statement: 'What happened in Germany under the Nazis could never happen in America.' There is good reason to believe that this represents not merely a lack of impact, but rather a net result of several aspects of the film operating in a way to nullify the intended message.

The film relies almost exclusively upon one device, the parallel speeches by American and German soapbox orators, to communicate the idea that the beginnings of fascist activity, as manifested in Germany in the early thirties, are already (1940s) evident here. The film's success or failure in communicating the idea that 'it can happen here' is thus almost wholly dependent on the spectator's response to this one device. Our research reveals that for one or more of three reasons, the effectiveness of this device was nullified.

First, analysis of the film's content reveals that while the German agitator is but one of many aspects of Nazism depicted in the film, the American agitator is the sole symptom of fascist activity in America shown in the film. Secondly, numerous persons in the audience are impressed not so much with the similarities of the American and German agitator scenes, as with their dissimilarities. These persons are particularly impressed with the fact that the German agitator commands the attention and respect of his audience, whereas the American agitator is received with indifference and skepticism. Finally, the only person in the film who seems to take the American agitator seriously is the hero, Mike, who is later quite easily converted to approved views. Many members of the audience apparently regarded the ease of this reconversion as evidence that, even if Americans are momentarily blinded into following fascists, their native good sense soon brings them back to the path of democracy.

The Message Contradicted by Personal Experience

Interview material suggested that the device of the American agitator often 'boomeranged' because the audience apparently regarded soapbox speakers in general, as 'lamebrains,' not to be taken seriously:

> . . . you see these people down in Wall Street doing the same thing that the man was doing in that picture, and I just stand there and watch them to laugh at them. I mean, I get a big kick out of them.

> I've listened to several in New York City. But for the most part it's just a lot of talk and nonsense that doesn't mean much, and you do that just as a form of diversion.

The film's presentation of the sneering reception accorded the American agitator thus contributes to the boomerang concept that American agitators are innocuous. A number of the respondents who laughed at the American soapbox orators also believed, perhaps as a result of World War II propaganda, that Germans and

Americans are markedly dissimilar. Accordingly, they seized upon the different reactions to the two film agitators as evidence of American good sense, which would preclude the success of local fascist agitation:

> In the scene showing the Nazi speaker, you have the four boys standing out and the rest of the group moving away from them – coming under the spell of the speaker and falling under his sway. Whereas in the American scene the people walked away. They do have the sense, you might say. They walk away.

> Only one man clapped. The people listening were average Americans. They behaved like they would. They saw through it all.

Believing that Americans in general would not be taken in by such talk, these respondents regarded Americans who do applaud the agitator as uneducated, low-class, or in some other way inferior to themselves:

> People that did not have an education (were listening to the soapbox speaker). In the front row there were two workers who were eating away. Educated people wouldn't stand there and eat. At the back row two people looked at each other and moved away. That proves that educated people wouldn't listen.

By thus disidentifying themselves from Americans who might accept an agitator's view, these respondents came to believe that not only is the agitator innocuous, but the few persons he convinces are likewise of no importance or influence on the social scene.

To determine whether the boomerang thus suggested by the qualitative data actually increased the complacency of the audience, the following statement was tested: 'In America, hardly anyone would listen to a man trying to spread race hate.'

It is obvious that a definite boomerang effect toward increased complacency, did occur among the less prejudiced students. Twenty-nine per cent of the students who saw the film felt that there would be no audience for an American hate monger, as compared with only 19 per cent of the students who had not seen the film. There is some indication that among *more prejudiced* students the film may have had the opposite, more desirable, effect, but the difference between control and experimental groups among the more prejudiced is not statistically significant.

That this particular boomerang should have occurred only among the *less prejudiced* students is quite startling, and is not wholly explicable on the basis of available data. Ordinarily, the less prejudiced student would be expected to have a better understanding of the messages of anti-discrimination propaganda. It is possible, however, that such students so dislike fascist propaganda that when they were confronted with a scene in which a fascist agitator was in fact unsuccessful, their own wishes influenced them to believe that no such agitator could be successful.

The statistical data bear out the fact that the boomerang suggested in the first phase of the study did occur but was less serious than might have been anticipated. Occurring only among the less prejudiced, such a boomerang is not likely to be as harmful as it might be if it similarly affected the more prejudiced.

The Message Resembles a More Familiar Concept of Contrary Implication

It will be recalled that the film-makers tried to impress upon minority groups that in unity they will find strength. This message was also received by the majority, or dominant group, in the audience, among whom it re-enforced complacency. But even when it reached the minority group member for whom it was intended, this message seemed to arrive in somewhat garbled form. The distortion was perhaps due to the resemblance between this message and a more familiar idea of contrary implications.

The United States as a 'melting pot' is an old concept familiar to most Americans. Some persons find implicit in this idea the notion that there is in fact no real majority group and consequently no minority group is in danger of persecution. *Don't Be a Sucker* likewise asserts that America contains many minorities, but suggests that each minority *is* in danger of attack, a danger which can be averted only if all minorities stand together.

In an effort to determine the extent to which this 'melting pot' idea might cause the message of the film to boomerang, the following statement was tested: 'There are so many minorities in this country, that no single one would ever be persecuted.' The responses reveal that a boomerang effect did occur among the less intelligent members of minority groups; 44 per cent of such respondents who had seen the film agreed with the statement, as compared to only 26 per cent who had not seen the film. However, no significant difference appears among the more intelligent members of minority groups. The less intelligent members of minority groups interpreted the statements about the heterogeneity of the United States population as evidence that no minority in this country need fear persecution. Thus the film led them to be more complacent.

Notes

1 This study was conducted in 1947 and 1948 by the Department of Scientific Research of the American Jewish Committee with the Institute of Social Research. At that time the authors were staff members of the Department. They gratefully acknowledge the help they received from various members of the Department, and especially the help of Dean Mannheimer. Thanks are also due to Mr. Louis Novins of Paramount.

2 See, for example, Paul Lazarsfeld, Bernard Berelson, and Hazel Gaudet, *The People's Choice*. New York: Duell, Sloan and Pearce, 1944; Robert K. Merton, *Mass Persuasion*. New York: Harper's, 1947; 'The Effects of Presenting "One Side," Versus "Both Sides," On Changing Opinions On a Controversial Subject,' *Readings in Social Psychology*, edited by Newcomb and Hartley; Muzafer Sherif and Hadley Cantril, *The Psychology of Ego Involvements*. New York: Wiley and Sons, 1947. See especially chapters 3, 4.

3 The item was: 'The Catholics were persecuted as much as the Jews under the Nazis.'

4 American Catholics were apparently particularly interested in the fate of German Catholics even before seeing the film. Note that in the control group, i.e., among respondents not exposed to the film, 61 per cent of the American Catholics and only 42 per cent of others were aware of the extent of Nazi persecution of Catholics.

5 The item was: 'Hitler got Germany out of the depression, and before Germany went to war, he had improved conditions for the pure Germans.'

6 *Index of Intelligence*: Intelligence level was decided on the basis of course of study. Students

enrolled in the academic course were rated as more intelligent and those in the commercial course, as less intelligent. Support for such a procedure is to be found in the statistics taken from the Monograph of the National Survey of Secondary Education by G. N. Kefauver, called 'Horizontal Organization of Secondary Education,' 1932.

7 Degree of prejudice was determined from answers on eight questionnaire items concerning attitudes towards Negroes and Jews. An index of degree of prejudice was derived from the number of answers indicating prejudice, each item being given equal weight. Those who gave prejudiced responses to six or more of the eight items were classified as 'very highly prejudiced'; those who gave prejudiced responses to five were called 'highly prejudiced'; to four or three, 'of average prejudice'; to two, 'mildly prejudiced'; to none or one item, 'not prejudiced.'

8 A communication item is said to 'boomerang' when it produces a result directly opposite to that which its producers intend. See Robert K. Merton, and Patricia L. Kendall, 'The Boomerang Response,' *Channels*, Vol. xxi, No. 7 (June 1944).

Chapter 4

Charles Winick

TENDENCY SYSTEMS AND THE EFFECTS OF A MOVIE DEALING WITH A SOCIAL PROBLEM

R ECENT YEARS HAVE SEEN a fairly steady increase in the number of 'message' films which are concerned with a social problem. A movie of this kind was the subject of this study: *The Man With The Golden Arm*, starring Frank Sinatra and Kim Novak and released late in 1955. The film received enormous publicity because it was released even though it was refused a Motion Picture Production Code seal of approval. Its musical background became a best-selling phonograph record. A stylized stark arm was the basis for an extensive advertising campaign. The film was an adaptation of a novel by Nelson Algren, which represented addiction as a way of death rather than of life. Algren has disavowed the film as not being an adequate rendering of his novel.

Frank Sinatra plays Frankie Machine, a poker dealer who has shed both addiction and gambling and learned to be a jazz drummer. A poker dealer frames Machine into jail, after which he is an easy mark for a drug peddler. Machine returns to gambling and drugs. He is harassed by his wife and becomes friendly with a neighborhood singer, played by Kim Novak, who helps him 'kick' his addiction. His wife kills herself and the film ends with Machine presumably joining the singer in a new life. The film presents the addict's urgent need to take drugs and his suffering and victimization by peddlers. It avoids any representation of the pleasure or of the mechanics of taking heroin, although implicit in a number of scenes is the relief from jitters provided by narcotics. Narcotics addiction is presented as a very undesirable affliction, although the film presents no specific recommendations on how to handle addiction as a social problem.

The teenage group in New York was selected for study because of the great incidence of addiction in the city and because this is the age group most susceptible to drug addiction (6). It is also the most active movie-going group: only in the 15–19 age group has there been an increase (31 per cent) in the number of persons who now go to movies more often than they did several years ago (13).

Hypotheses

Six hypotheses were examined: (a) A process of self-selection would lead to a higher frequency of relatively less adjusted persons seeing the film than relatively adjusted persons. (b) Exposure to the film would lead to more permissive attitudes towards narcotics. (c) Recency of exposure would be associated with greater attitude change. (d) Relatively less adjusted viewers of the film would show greater attitude change than relatively adjusted viewers. (e) Lower-class, male, and Negro viewers would show greater attitude change after seeing the film than middle-class, female, and white viewers, respectively. (f) Drug addicts would perceive the film as a confirmation of their own image of addiction.

Procedure

Thirty statements dealing with attitudes toward addiction and drugs were developed on the basis of a pilot inquiry. These statements were designed to indicate restrictive versus permissive attitudes toward addiction rather than as a comprehensive scale. A six-point scale was used on each question: all-most-many-some-few-no, in order to provide an opportunity for the expression of attitudes ranging from complete favorableness to complete unfavorableness. These 30 statements were added to 150 statements taken from the Peterson–Thurstone scale of attitudes towards social problems, including scales on attitudes toward liquor, war, crime, capital punishment, Negroes, Chinese, punishment of criminals, and Germans (14). The total questionnaire of 180 items was administered in the fall of 1955, several months before the film's release, to young people of 16 and 17 who were attending secondary schools in the Metropolitan New York area. The respondents had previously taken the Bernreuter Personality Inventory. Drug addiction among young people in New York City is especially concentrated in certain parts of the city which provided approximately one-fifth of the total sample, so that the great majority of the 1,203 subjects were not environmentally sensitized to narcotic matters. The subjects' average age was 17.3; there were 652 boys and 551 girls.

Eight months later, by which time the film had completed its run at neighborhood movie theatres, the same questionnaire was administered to the same subjects, and 1,002 subjects could be reached in order to be retested. Sixty-one per cent of those retested were categorized as middle class and 39 per cent lower class. The classification into lower and middle class was in terms of three criteria: family income above or below $3,500, the neighborhood in which the respondents lived, and the rating of the occupation of their fathers on an adaptation of the Barr scale of occupational status (17).

Of the total retested, 54 per cent were male and 46 per cent were female; 71 per cent were white and 29 per cent were Negro. A total of 442 subjects said they had, and 560 said they had not seen the film. Approximately 43 per cent of the subjects retested had thus seen the film, or over three times as many people as saw *Sister Kenny*.

Each subject was classified as either relatively less adjusted or relatively adjusted, based on his scores on the Bernreuter (2). In order to be classified as a relatively less adjusted, a subject had to have a score in the upper quartile of the national norms for high school students on each of three scales of the test. These scales are neurotic tendency (B1–N), introversion–extroversion (B3–1), and self confidence (F1–C). The subjects whose scores were less than the upper quartile on one or more of these scales were classified as relatively adjusted. The classification in terms of adjustment is not completely satisfactory because it implies overt behavior, and the actual behavior of these young people may or may not directly mirror their test scores. However, one authoritative review of several hundred studies with the Bernreuter concluded that a low score on the neurotic tendency scale indicated a wholesome adjustment and a high score indicated poor adjustment to the environment (20).

Of the 442 subjects who saw the film, 145, or 32.8 per cent, were classed as relatively less adjusted and 297 as relatively adjusted. Of the 560 subjects who had not seen the film, 142, or 25.13 per cent, were considered relatively less adjusted and 418 relatively adjusted. The difference between the two groups, significant at the two per cent level ($p = 2.14$), tended to confirm the hypothesis of a greater self-selection of relatively less adjusted subjects who saw the film. It is possible that degree of adjustment masks either lower- or middle-class membership (1), and that it is this class membership with its movie-going patterns which accounts for the greater attendance at the film of the less adjusted respondents, since members of the middle class go to movies more frequently than members of the lower class (8). Table 4.1 gives the relationship between the social class of the subject and their personality, in terms of their exposure to the film. Chi square was .28, with one degree of freedom, with p between .50 and 70. The degree of adjustment of the viewers was thus independent of their social class.

Table 4.1 Degree of adjustment of viewers by class

Class	Number of relatively adjusted viewers	Number of relatively less adjusted viewers	N
Middle	184	86	270
Lower	113	59	172
	297	145	· 442

In order to measure changes attributable to exposure to the film, a number of before-and-after comparisons were made.

1. Test–retest scores of the entire group, both viewers and non-viewers, of the Peterson–Thurstone social attitudes scale were compared to establish whether the passage of time had any effect in changing these attitudes. Shift on the scales was measured for each person by whether he changed his answer on readministration, from one step to another. The net difference between the percentage of respondents changing their answers in one direction and the percentage changing their answers in the other direction was the measure of effect. A shift from any one step on the scale to any other step was counted as one shift.

2. The Peterson–Thurstone scores of those subjects who had seen the film were compared with those who had not, to determine if the self-selection process of seeing the film involved subjects whose attitudes on social issues were more

liberal as well as more subject to change and to determine the direction of any such change.

3. A comparison was made of the test–retest scores on the items dealing with addiction of those subjects who had not seen the film, to establish the extent to which their attitudes towards addiction had remained stable during the months between the two test situations. The same criterion of shift was used on the addiction scale as on the social attitude scale.
4. A comparison was made of the changes in the scores on the addiction scale of the subjects who had seen the film against the base line of the shift shown by the subjects who had not seen the film.
5. A comparison was made of the changes on the addiction scale of the subjects who saw the film soon after the initial test and those who saw it soon before the retest, to study the effect of recency of exposure.
6. The changes in the scores on the addiction scale of the relatively less adjusted and relatively adjusted subjects who had and who had not seen the film were compared.
7. Intensive interviewing was conducted of a sample of relatively less adjusted and relatively adjusted subjects who had seen the film, in order to obtain data on perception of the film's characters and plot.
8. Intensive interviewing was conducted of a sample of drug addicts who had seen the film, in order to determine how the subjects of a social problem reacted to the representation of the problem.

Findings on Test–Retest

1. Generalized social attitudes

Comparing the before and after scores of all the subjects on the questions from the Peterson–Thurstone scales did not reveal any significant shift in social attitudes as a whole. These attitudes were thus not substantially changed either by the passage of eight months or by specific events which occurred during this period.

2. Exposed versus unexposed subjects

The pre-film scores on the Peterson–Thurstone scales of those who subsequently saw the film were compared with the pre-film scores of those who had not. No significant differences between the two groups were found. The group which saw the film thus did not appear to be either more liberal or intrinsically readier for a change in social attitudes. The statements dealing with attitudes toward liquor which were adapted from the Peterson–Thurstone scales and which might possibly be related to attitudes toward drug addiction also did not differentiate the viewer from the nonviewer group. No significant shifts in social attitudes differentiated the viewer from the nonviewer group.

3. Stability of attitudes toward drug addiction

The before and after scores of the 30 addiction statements of the subjects who had not seen the film were compared. Measuring such changes provided a base line against which to measure changes in those exposed to the film. Nonviewers of the film did not show any significant differences, but exhibited a tendency to a shift on three statements. These items were: *drug peddlers are wicked men; drug addicts are poor people; people who want to buy drugs in a large city can do so.* In each case the direction of the shift was from the 'no' to the 'all' end of the scale. The direction of these shifts was consonant with contemporary and heavily publicized state and Congressional investigations of addiction.

4. Exposure to the film

With the base line established by the scores of the nonexposed group, it was assumed that the changes in the addiction attitudes of those who saw the film were attributable to the film. It is possible that there was some 'contamination' of nonviewers by viewers, through discussion. Table 4.2 lists the eight statements which exhibited a statistically significant shift in the subjects who saw the film. Twenty-two items did not show a significant shift.

The shift on all the questions but one was uniformly from the 'no' to the 'all' end of the scale, and thus in the direction of a more permissive attitude toward the narcotic addict. The question which showed a shift from the 'all' to the 'no' end is the statement on violence, which is a popular stereotype about addicts. It is probably a reflection of the extensive film footage devoted to the self-directed violence of the hero's withdrawal ordeal. Each of the other shifts can also be linked with specific content of the film. Many of the 22 questions on which there was no shift embodied relatively restrictive attitudes toward the drug user.

Table 4.2 Statements on addiction scale which showed significant pre-post exposure shift

Statement number	Percentage of subjects shifting	Critical ratio
1. Addicts are essentially decent people.	23	4.6★
2. Drug addicts are linked with violent behavior.	22	4.4★
3. Drug addicts can reform and become worthwhile citizens.	19	3.8★
4. People who take narcotic drugs may derive benefit from them.	19	3.8★
5. People who want to buy drugs in a large city can do so.	17	3.4★
6. Drug addicts may become the tools of criminals.	16	3.2★
7. Drug addicts may be quite intelligent	14	2.8★
8. Talented people may take narcotic drugs in order to help get over difficult times.	13	2.6★

★$p<.01$.

The changes in test–retest scores were computed without regard to where along the continuum from all-to-no, the shifts took place. There is a difference between a group shifting from a point near the 'all' end to a point even nearer, and another group shifting the same direction and distance from a point near the 'no' end. Ideally, shifts on such scales would be stated as a ratio of the possibilities of shifting, in an 'effectiveness index.' Such an index was not computed because its sampling distribution has not been satisfactorily worked out (9).

5. Recency of exposure

Some respondents saw the film soon after the first test experience, others shortly before the second, and still others sometime between the two test experiences. In order to evaluate the effect of recency of exposure, a comparison was made between the differences in the test–retest scores of the two extreme groups: the respondents who saw the film in the six weeks after the week in which they were first tested, and the respondents who saw the film in the six weeks before the week in which they were retested. Table 4.3 gives the results of this comparison in terms of the mean shift of each group, in per cent.

Table 4.3 Differences in test–retest scores of respondents who saw film soon after original test and respondents who saw it before retest

Statement	Group who saw film early (N = 73)	Group who saw film later (N = 114)	Critical ratio
1	32	21	1.64
2	17	33	2.56★★
3	20	31	1.73
4	20	24	0.66
5	11	27	2.9★
6	17	31	2.2★★
7	16	14	0.37
8	14	13	0.19

★$p<.01$.
★★$p<.05$.

On most of the statements, the differences between the scores of the early and late viewing groups are not significant. On the statement (No. 5) dealing with the ease of buying drugs in a large city, seeing the film soon before the retest had a significant effect on the respondent's responses. The statements on addicts becoming the tools of criminals (No. 6) and being linked with violence (No. 2) showed smaller shifts. In each case, the respondents who saw the film most recently showed greater change. Most of the statements did not show any significant change, so that the passage of a period of several months did not materially affect the ability of the film to modify attitudes. It is possible that the group which saw the film soon after the first test, and which had to pay premium prices to do so at first-run theatres, may have been especially responsive to the film's contents.

6. Relatively less adjusted and relatively adjusted subjects

It had been hypothesized that relatively less adjusted subjects who had seen the film would display greater shifts than would its relatively adjusted viewers because of their greater empathy with the protagonists and subject matter of the movie. Previous studies have suggested that there is a low but consistent positive correlation between sensitivity to art and high scores on the neurotic tendency and introversion scales on the Bernreuter (16, 21). There were three statements on which there were significant differences between the mean shifts of the relatively less adjusted and the relatively adjusted subjects who had seen the film, as shown in Table 4.4.

The shifts on the statements which exhibited a significant difference between the two groups were in the direction of a greater permissiveness toward drug users, since they involve increased perception of the addict as intelligent, talented, and likely to reform. A comparison of the before and after scores on the addiction scale of the members of each group who did not see the film did not yield any significant differences between the two groups, so that the viewers' change on the three statements may be attributable to their having seen the film. A comparison of the scores of the lower class relatively less adjusted viewers of the film with the middle class relatively less adjusted viewers yielded no significant differences; neither did a comparison of middle class relatively adjusted viewers with lower class relatively adjusted viewers.

Table 4.4 Statements on which there was a significant difference in the shift of two groups of viewers, in per cent

Statement	Shift of relatively less adjusted (N = 145)	Shift of relatively adjusted (N = 297)	Critical ratio
3	26	15	2.4**
7	19	10	2.4**
8	22	10	3.1*

*p<.01.
**p<.05.

7. Class, sex, and race differences

It had been hypothesized that lower class, male, and Negro subjects would be more likely than middle class, female, and white subjects, respectively, to shift on the addiction scale because of the greater incidence of addiction among the former three groups. A comparison of the shifts on the addiction scale of lower class with middle class, male with female, and Negro with white subjects, did not reveal any significant difference in attitudes between the groups compared.

Interviews on the film

In order to obtain more information on effects than could be provided by pre-post testing, interviews dealing with the film were conducted with approximately one-

Table 4.5 Major responses to questions on film

Question	Relatively less adjusted subjects' major responses	Per cent giving response	Relatively adjusted subjects' major responses	Per cent giving response
What is film about?	Man with troubles	31	Addict trying to break habit	63
	Addict with wife and girl friend	27	Musician-addict	19
Best scene	When Frankie went to pusher's apartment	32	Frankie breaking habit	54
	When wife is exposed	29	Kim and Frank arguing	16
Liked most about film	Kim helping Frankie	31	Acting	44
	Romance	16	Story	28
What kind of person is hero?	Man who is in trouble	41	Sick man	37
	Addict trying to be drummer	32	Man from bad environment	26
How did hero become drug user?	Pusher got to him	33	Weak character	41
	Wife nagged	28	Needed it	30
Describe hero	Takes responsibility	34	Weak person	37
	Interesting	21	Sick	26
What do you think of heroine?	Tries to help	37	Beautiful	31
	Beautiful	26	Dumb blonde	27
Scene recalled best	Frankie getting a shot	43	Frankie kicking habit	64
	Frankie kicking habit	34	In pusher's apartment	29

third (102 relatively less adjusted and 45 relatively adjusted) subjects who had seen the film. The interviews were conducted either in the respondents' homes or in a recreational center. Every third person who had seen the film was interviewed, with substitutions made in the small number of cases in which the respondent was unavailable. The interviews were conducted several weeks after the respondents had filled out the second round of attitude scale questionnaires.

The respondents had little difficulty in answering the eight questions, and there were practically no 'don't know' responses. The interviewees' responses were coded independently into categories by the author and another analyst, and the very few differences in coding were resolved by discussion. The two most important categories of response to each question for the two groups are shown in Table 4.5, in terms of the proportion of each group giving the response.

The responses of the two groups to the eight questions showed clear differences which were much more substantial than the differences elicited by the addiction scale scores. By and large, the relatively less adjusted viewers emphasized the positive and admirable qualities of the hero and heroine, and perceived the 'magic helper' theme in which the hero's passivity and circumstances beyond his control lead him into addiction, while the all-giving mother-imago (Kim Novak) helped him to solve his problems, including those with his wife, who was generally described by these subjects as evil and unpleasant. The relatively adjusted viewers generally saw the hero as a weak person beset by a variety of serious problems for which there was no easy solution. The relatively adjusted subjects were more likely to recall scenes of the hero abandoning addiction, while the relatively less adjusted subjects tended to recall scenes in which addiction is fostered.

In addition to their responses to these questions, the respondents were asked if they had thought about the film since seeing it. Sixty-one per cent of the relatively less adjusted and 34 per cent of the relatively adjusted subjects said that they had thought about the movie since seeing it. Practically all the subjects interviewed, regardless of degree of adjustment, when asked which character they admired most, used the real names of the stars rather than their film names. The use of the stars' names suggests the extremely high degree of identification of many viewers with actors and actresses over and above the obvious difficulties of recalling the characters in a film as compared with the ease of recalling its stars.

On the basis of the answers to these questions it is possible to regard this film as almost a kind of projective test. The viewer's personality was related to how he perceived its theme. One reason for the relative identification of some of the relatively less adjusted viewers with Frank Sinatra may be that he has become a kind of folk hero, who is a romantic symbol of total sexual expression and adventurous living. The audience tends to respond to its image of Frank Sinatra rather than to a character called Frankie Machine; a number of respondents volunteered that Frankie Machine sounded like an 'unreal' name! Identification with Kim Novak was probably facilitated by a great deal of publicity about her in some widely disseminated magazine articles.

The kind of analysis of the interviews detailed above on the dimension of personality was also made in terms of class, sex, and race. The differences on the dimensions of class and sex were less clearcut than were those for personality. The middle-class interview subjects ($N = 91$) tended to identify more with the hero than did lower-class respondents ($N = 59$). This may be because the squalor of the film's background was so stylized and unreal that it could have offended some lower-class viewers. Contrariwise, the arty representation of a lower-class milieu and the curious dated atmosphere and rococo background music may have been peculiarly attractive to middle-class viewers. Other studies have reported that middle-class youths are more receptive than lower-class youths to commercial films (22).

Male interviewees ($N = 77$) were more likely to identify with the film's hero than were females ($N = 73$). This may be related to the greater attractiveness of addiction to men than to women (22). It may also be related to Frank Sinatra's having more impact than Kim Novak. The interviews yielded no differences between Negroes ($N = 33$) and whites ($N = 117$) in response to the eight questions, possibly because the film has no Negroes.

Interviews with narcotic addicts

In order to discover how addicts perceived the film, 50 (42 male and eight female) narcotic addicts who had seen the film were interviewed in New York City. Access to the addicts was facilitated by Narcotics Anonymous. They were asked three questions: What did you think of the film? What did you like about it? What didn't you like about it?

The most eagerly voiced reaction of the addicts interviewed was that they enjoyed the film very much. Many saw it several times and enjoyed discussing it. Some addicts pointed out that '. . . taking drugs is now almost legitimate, like mental health or homosexuality. We're a real social problem at last . . .' As one addict expressed it: 'Now it's hip to be a junk.' The interest of addicts in this film was not unexpected: when an earlier drug film – *To The Ends of the Earth* – was premiered in New York City, it was almost mobbed by drug addicts eager to see it.

A number of addicts were particularly pleased that Frank Sinatra played the role of the drug user because they regarded him as a 'hip' person who has been successful in many of the ways in which addicts have fantasies of being successful. Many addicts' fantasy lives center around how they could be celebrities with their own 'weed farms.' The association of famous movie stars with drugs was seen by some addicts as a vindication of their fantasies, since the addict subculture thrives on stories of prominent persons who are secret drug users but who are not exposed because of their fame or 'connections,' as some addicts wryly observed.

The addicts were not distressed by the withdrawal scenes. There was little that addicts disliked about the film, although they delighted in their expertise in detecting errors. They noted: '. . . Frankie would walk around after getting a shot at Louie's, not lie down – a real junkie wouldn't ever change the cotton like Louie did – no connection ever talks like Louis – the junkie kicking in the jail wasn't realistic – no connection would ever raise the price like that, from $2 to $5 – that drumming scene was all fake . . .' Presumed accuracy was also noted: 'When that guy kicked candy by eating $27.68 worth in one night, that is so right; that is the only way to kick . . .,' thus reflecting many addicts' fantasy that the way to stop taking something is to take all you want of it.

Addicts enjoyed the movie, based on what they said in the interviews, not only because their traditional passivity was reinforced by having so important a symbol of society as a movie studio interested in them. They also enjoyed the film because they found it easy to empathize with a totally unreal yet immediate and magical resolution of the hero's very difficult reality situation, with his wife very conveniently killing herself. The addicts thus saw the film as a confirmation of their own view of addiction and as a reinforcement of their fantasies, with addiction almost glorified.

Discussion

One hypothesis of this study was largely disproved, one was partially confirmed, and the other four were confirmed. The hypothesis that lower class, male, and Negro viewers would be more likely to show changes in attitudes towards addiction after seeing *The Man With The Golden Arm* than middle class, female, and white viewers, respectively, was not confirmed by test–retest data. There was a greater tendency for middle-class and female viewers than for lower-class and male viewers, to identify with the film's hero, in the personal interviews. The hypothesis of recency of exposure affecting attitude change was only partially confirmed.

It was established that more of the relatively less adjusted subjects saw the film than relatively adjusted subjects. Exposure to the film was related to more permissive attitudes toward narcotics, with the relatively less adjusted viewers showing more change than the relatively adjusted viewers. Drug addicts who saw the film were pleased with it and saw it as a justification of addiction. Personal interviews dealing with the film proved to be a very useful tool for eliciting differences in perception of the film between subgroups in its audience.

The persons who saw the film did not significantly change their attitudes on most – 22 – of the statements on the addiction scale. Most of these items dealt with relatively restrictive attitudes about addiction as a social problem. The eight statements which showed significant shifts could be related to the content of the film, although the shifts appeared related more to individual scenes than to underlying themes. The statements showing change generally dealt with permissive attitudes toward addicts and the change was in the direction of greater permissiveness. Similar selectivity in perceiving emotional meaningful film content has been reported in other studies (23).

Almost every question which showed a shift could be related to some action of Frank Sinatra in the film. The shift could thus be partially attributed to the extent to which Sinatra had salience for the audience. This study found greater shifts in attitudes than previous research conducted in a naturalistic self selection context. One reason for this difference may be that most previous studies deal with educational or relatively low budget 'problem' films, which did not have stars and did not have the 'glamor' of a story involving jazz, illicit love, and crime.

The relatively less adjusted subjects who showed a greater shift than the relatively adjusted subjects on three items may have been readier to believe well of the addict than the latter group, may have identified more easily with the film's characters, or may have been more resistant to the manifest content of the film. In the interviews their greater empathy with the hero emerged very clearly. The differences between the two groups' perception of the film's action and characters suggests that this kind of questioning may sometimes be more useful than the traditional before-and-after exposure attitude scale method. The differences also point up the importance of obtaining as much background data on the subjects as possible, in addition to the usual socio-economic classificatory data. The interviews with addicts clearly demonstrated their ability to interpret the film in a manner consonant with their own attitudes. It would appear that the movie was almost a different movie for relatively less adjusted, relatively adjusted, and addicted members of the audience. Each group perceived the film in a manner consonant with its own tendency system.

How enduring might be the effect of seeing this film on its audiences? One effect of a single 'problem' film on the subjects of the 'problem' is summed up in a remark attributed to humorist Robert Benchley about the film *The Lost Weekend*: 'It's the kind of film that makes you stop drinking – for twenty minutes.'

One difference between this imputed effect of *The Lost Weekend* and the effect of *The Man With The Golden Arm* is that *not one* of the addicts interviewed mentioned stopping drug use after seeing the film, even though the film is concerned with the evils of addiction. Like the adolescent who has his fantasies and impressions confirmed by significant others through the process of 'consensual validation' (19), the addicts saw their fantasies about themselves confirmed by the film and were reinforced in their addiction.

We can only speculate about the effects of the film on its teen-age nonaddict viewers. The film would be only one of a very complex series of interrelated triggers which might have some relation to a person's attitudes toward drugs. Seeing a 'problem' film may initiate a learning process, but not change basic attitudes (15). The importance of differential association and socialization within a delinquent subculture as factors in addiction cannot be over-emphasized. However, it is possible to speculate that media stimuli may alert a sensitized young person to new possibilities for behavior and excitement which might not involve basic attitude changes. Although there is not likely to be any direct and specific way in which a viewer of a film on prejudice – the usual staple of media attitude change studies – can immediately implement any libertarian attitudes he acquires from the film, he can implement a more permissive attitude toward drug use by experimenting with drugs. Some viewers may have connected the producer's publicized flouting of the Code ban with Frankie's flouting of the law; both producer and Frankie thrived. It is certainly possible that seeing the film may have helped some teenagers toward a more permissive attitude toward drug use.

The film's success – it was seen by approximately 25 million Americans – seems to have had considerable impact on mass media in making addiction a more acceptable subject. The Motion Picture Code was liberalized in 1956 so that addiction could be a subject of code-approved films. Beginning with *Hatfull of Rain* and *Monkey on My Back* in 1957, each successive year has seen films, novels, and plays dealing with drug addiction. Whatever the artistic merits of these films, they have been successful in getting large audiences.

A curious aspect of the large audiences which these films have been getting is that the only major change in how communities express their social attitudes toward addiction since 1956 has been a constant *increase* in the penalties provided for narcotics users by legislation on both the Federal and state levels. Thus, the Federal Narcotic Control Act of 1956, and state legislative action since 1956, have consistently provided more and more severe jail terms for addicts, even though the spate of media output on addiction has generally provided a view of the addict which could be interpreted by audiences as being at least as sympathetic as that presented in *The Man With The Golden Arm*. There has been an actual *decrease* in hospital and other treatment facilities for addicts. This suggests as one possibility for speculation on the net effect of such films that the continued existence of the narcotics problem may serve some function of social control and that the public may actually not want to be 'solved.' Another speculative possibility is that the problem has little salience in terms of social action, or that the mass media are expressing advanced or deviant views which are not shared by legislative groups and the public. Yet another possibility is that some kind of cognitive dissonance or attitudinal homeostasis permits the general public to develop more sympathetic attitudes toward the addict simultaneously with its awareness of increasing penal provisions and diminishing treatment facilities. What society does about a social problem thus may not be related to what the creators of and audiences for media dealing with the problem may regard as appropriate socially ameliorative action.

References

Auld, F., Jr. Influence of social class on personality test responses. *Psychol. Bull.*, 1952, 49, 318–332.

Bernreuter, R. G. *Manual for the Personality Inventory*. Stanford: Stanford Univ. Press, 1935.

Blumer, H. *Movies and Conduct*. New York: Macmillan, 1933.

Blumer, H., Hauser, P. *Movies, Delinquency, and Crime*. New York: Macmillan, 1933.

Charters, W. W. *Motion Pictures and Youth*. New York: Macmillan, 1933.

Chein, I., and Rosenfeld, E. Juvenile narcotics use. *Law & Contemp. Problems*, 1957, 22, 52–68.

Cressey, P. G. The motion picture experience as modified by social background and personality. *Amer. Soc. Rev.*, 1938, 3, 516–525.

Handel, L. *Hollywood Looks At Its Audience*. Urbana: Univ. Illinois Press, 1950, 106–108.

Hovland, C. I., Lumsdaine, A., and Sheffield, F. D. *Experiments on Mass Communication*. Princeton Univ. Press, 1949, 284–289.

—. Reconciling conflicting results derived from experimental and survey studies of attitude change. *Amer. Psychol.*, 1959, 14, 3–17.

Hulett, J. E., Jr. Estimating the net effect of a commercial motion picture upon the trend of local public opinion. *Amer. Soc. Rev.*, 1949, 14, 263–275.

Klapper, J. T. *The Effects of Mass Media*. Glencoe: Free Press, 1960.

Opinion Research Corporation. *The Public Appraises Movies*. Princeton: The Corporation, 1957, 12–13.

Peterson, R. C. and Thurstone, L. L. *Motion Pictures and the Social Attitudes of Children*. New York: Macmillan, 1933, 107–128.

Raths, L. E. and Trager, F. N. Public opinion and Crossfire. *J. Educ. Soc.*, 1948, 21, 345–368.

Sisson, E. D. and Sisson, B. Introversion and the aesthetic attitude. *J. Gen. Psychol.*, 1940, 22, 203–208.

Springer, N. N. The influence of general social status on the emotional stability of children. *J. Genet. Psychol.*, 1938, 53, 321–328.

Stouffer, S. A. A sociologist looks at communications research. In Douglas Waples (Ed.), *Print, Radio, and Film in a Democracy*. Chicago: Univ. Chicago Press, 1942, 133–146.

Sullivan, H. S. *The Interpersonal Theory of Psychiatry*. New York: Norton, 1953, 28–29.

Super, D. The Bernreuter personality inventory: A review of research. *Psychol. Bull.*, 1942, 39, 94–120

Wheatley, L. A. and Sumner, F. C. Measurement of neurotic tendency in Negro students of music. *J. of Psychol.*, 1946, 22, 247–252.

Wiese, M. J., and Cole, S. G. A study of children's attitudes and the influences of a commercial motion picture. *J. of Psychol.*, 1946, 21, 151–171.

Wilner, D. Attitudes as a determinant of perception in the mass media of communication: Reactions to the motion picture *Home of the Brave*. Ph.D. Dissertation, University of California at Los Angeles, 1950.

PART TWO

Moral panic and censorship
The vulnerable audience

Introduction

THE EXTRACTS IN THIS Part have in common the concept of the mass audience as easily influenced and open to persuasion, usually from 'new' media forms. All of them, tellingly, employ an image of the child audience – sometimes as a specific group that is particularly in need of protection, sometimes as a metaphor for the docile, unresisting nature of the audience as a whole. Although these pieces span forty years, from Fredric Wertham's contribution to the American Senate Subcommittee on comic books in 1954 (Chapter 6) to Martin Barker's attack on the British Government's Criminal Justice Bill of 1994 (Chapter 8), their concerns and core ideas are very similar. All of the writers here, with the exception of Martin Barker who argues powerfully against the enforced 'protection' of the audience, share a suspicion of the latest popular culture and a sense of responsibility, sometimes combined with disdain, for those who consume it.

Richard Hoggart (Chapter 7) and Fredric Wertham, despite their different cultural contexts – Hoggart's work, largely based on literary criticism, is now regarded as an early example of British cultural studies, whereas Wertham emerges from American social psychology – have much in common in terms of their attitudes towards 1950s' pulp fiction and its readers. Significantly, Wertham's attacks on comic books are a critique of his own national culture, and can be seen as part of a contemporary drive to contain internal threats to American values; Hoggart, on the other hand, celebrates a notion of 'traditional' British values – 'older, neighbourhood rhythms' (p. 68) – which he contrasts to the shallow and degraded culture permeating from America.

However, the texts they discuss are extremely similar: *Crime Inc* and *Crime Does Not Pay* for Wertham, *Crime Unlimited* and *Crime Doesn't Pay* for Hoggart. Their methods are based on a common technique of quoting particularly shocking material out of context – both dispense with footnotes or sources, in Hoggart's case because he invents his examples – in order to bring the nature of this degraded entertainment home to a readership who might never have come into contact with pulp magazines.

It is easy to find fault with Hoggart's device of quoting 'typical' passages from his own imagination, and with Wertham's method of presenting his own notes from discussion with 'delinquent' children as proof of comic books' harmful effects. Hoggart makes sweeping generalisations about the magazines' audience – 'many of them are, on the whole, bored' (p. 67) – while Wertham fails to see that his tame 'delinquents' may be parroting back exactly what he wants to hear, having found a way of passing their own responsibility onto the cynical comic book publishers.

However, both writers exhibit an apparently genuine worry about the effects of pulp literature on an emotionally immature and vulnerable audience, and some of their concerns are harder to laugh off. Hoggart's examples of 'sexy' periodicals may seem coy to us decades later, for instance, but his arguments against exploitative advertisements for 'body-building' and their influence on teenage insecurities have echoes in more recent debates about young girls' susceptibility to idealised female images in teenage magazines.

In Chapter 5, T. W. Adorno, writing here in 1975, re-examines his own conception of the 'culture industry' which was originally based on his experience of Germany – as a Jewish-Italian academic – in the 1930s, and of the USA – as a Marxist and exile – in the 1940s. Adorno clearly sees no reason to update his first impressions of a passive audience in thrall to a soulless, degrading mass culture; moreover, unlike Hoggart and Wertham, Adorno considers these consumers as lost souls, long past protecting. The culture industry is a *fait accompli*, astonishingly successful in its project of creating false needs and satisfying them with its own products. Consumers have been duped into their role as cogs in the industry's machinery, keeping it running by subscribing to its ideals and to the illusion of individual control. 'The customer is not king . . . not its subject, but its object' (p. 55).

Adorno's work is notoriously lacking in either an ethnographic engagement with any kind of 'real' audience or a detailed textual analysis of the commodities he derides. He does, however, single out the American cinema industry as an example of mass culture's ability to offer pseudo-individuality – the illusion of difference and novelty, often embodied in the latest movie star – in an essentially standardised, conveyor-belt genre product from a dehumanised production line. 'What parades as progress in the culture industry, as the incessantly new . . . remains the disguise for an eternal sameness' (p. 56).

Modern culture, then, is empty, only temporarily satisfying and ultimately degrading to its consumers. The culture industry, Adorno states, despises its audiences; Adorno certainly seems to despise its audiences, for their pathetic weakness and inability to resist; and ultimately, the audiences of Adorno's account despise themselves, as they glimpse the prison they are building around themselves but blind themselves to it, preferring deception and transitory fulfilment to the more challenging alternatives. The culture industry has largely succeeded in its aim to regress adult consumers into 'eleven year-olds' (p. 59). To throw off their fetters and struggle towards genuine enlightenment, this audience would have to 'come of age' as adults.

Martin Barker provides a voice from the other side of the debate. Barker argues fiercely against the assumption that media texts have identifiable and negative effects, and by extension against the very concept of a vulnerable audience. Picking apart the arguments of the 1994 Newson Report, which itself fed a contemporary moral panic around 'video nasties', Barker suggests that the focus on children as an audience group in particular need of protection is a canny emotional ploy to win support for increased censorship.

We have seen that Wertham presented children as helpless targets for the comic companies' dangerous messages, and that Hoggart warned of the effects similar magazines would have on 'young men on National Service', 'juke-box boys' and 'adolescents of below the average intelligence' (p. 70). Adorno, in turn, suggested that the mass audience as a whole had been regressed into exposed, passive children. Barker warns that we must resist such rhetoric, making the counter-argument that such an image of children constructs them as 'incompetent' and as such could have harmful effects on their own self-perception.

In contrast to the other writers here, Barker employs tenacious analysis of the texts themselves. Rather than assuming the worst of the video *Child's Play III* and accepting the received opinion of its role in the murder of James Bulger, Barker takes us through the film's narrative and concludes that, while 'not a very good film' (p. 078), its message is the opposite to that assumed by Elizabeth Newson. This refusal to accept a text's 'meanings' without examining it at first hand is a useful lesson. Barker's previous work has already applied the same technique of re-reading to some of the horror and crime comics discussed by Wertham, with similar results; a close analysis of the magazines glossed by Hoggart and the Western movies referred to offhandedly by Adorno might well overturn many of their assumptions and perhaps allay some of their fears.

Further reading

Arnold, M. (1869, reprinted 1970) *Culture and Anarchy*. Harmondsworth: Penguin.

Barker, M. (1984) *A Haunt of Fears*, London: Pluto.

Brooker, W. (2000) *Batman Unmasked*, London: Continuum.

Gilbert, J. (1986) *A Cycle of Outrage*, New York: Oxford University Press.

Leavis, F. R. (1933) *Culture and Environment*, London: Chatto and Windus.

Nyberg, A. K. (1998) *Seal of Approval: The History of the Comics Code*, Jackson: University Press of Mississippi.

Chapter 5

T. W. Adorno

CULTURE INDUSTRY RECONSIDERED

THE TERM CULTURE INDUSTRY was perhaps used for the first time in the book *Dialectic of Enlightenment*, which Horkheimer and I published in Amsterdam in 1947. In our drafts we spoke of 'mass culture'. We replaced that expression with 'culture industry' in order to exclude from the outset the interpretation agreeable to its advocates: that it is a matter of something like a culture that arises spontaneously from the masses themselves, the contemporary form of popular art. From the latter the culture industry must be distinguished in the extreme. The culture industry fuses the old and familiar into a new quality. In all its branches, products which are tailored for consumption by masses, and which to a great extent determine the nature of that consumption, are manufactured more or less according to plan. The individual branches are similar in structure or at least fit into each other, ordering themselves into a system almost without a gap. This is made possible by contemporary technical capabilities as well as by economic and administrative concentration. The culture industry intentionally integrates its consumers from above. To the detriment of both it forces together the spheres of high and low art, separated for thousands of years. The seriousness of high art is destroyed in speculation about its efficacy; the seriousness of the lower perishes with the civilizational constraints imposed on the rebellious resistance inherent within it as long as social control was not yet total. Thus, although the culture industry undeniably speculates on the conscious and unconscious state of the millions towards which it is directed, the masses are not primary, but secondary, they are an object of calculation; an appendage of the machinery. The customer is not king, as the culture industry would have us believe, not its subject but its object. The very word mass-media, specially honed for the culture industry, already shifts the accent onto harmless terrain. Neither is it a question of primary concern for the masses, nor of the techniques of communication as such, but of the spirit which sufflates them, their master's voice. The culture industry misuses its concern for the masses in order to duplicate, reinforce and strengthen their mentality, which it presumes is given and unchangeable. How this mentality might be changed is excluded throughout. The masses are not the measure but the ideology of the culture industry, even though the culture industry itself could scarcely exist without adapting to the masses.

The cultural commodities of the industry are governed, as Brecht and Suhrkamp expressed it thirty years ago, by the principle of their realization as value, and not by their own specific content and harmonious formation. The entire practice of the culture industry transfers the profit motive naked onto cultural forms. Ever since these cultural forms first began to earn a living for their creators as commodities in the market-place they had already possessed something of this quality. But then they sought after profit only indirectly, over and above their autonomous essence. New on the part of the culture industry is the direct and undisguised primacy of a precisely and thoroughly calculated efficacy in its most typical products. The autonomy of works of art, which of course rarely ever predominated in an entirely pure form, and was always permeated by a constellation of effects, is tendentially eliminated by the culture industry, with or without the conscious will of those in control. The latter include both those who carry out directives as well as those who hold the power. In economic terms they are or were in search of new opportunities for the realization of capital in the most economically developed countries. The old opportunities became increasingly more precarious as a result of the same concentration process which alone makes the culture industry possible as an omnipresent phenomenon. Culture, in the true sense, did not simply accommodate itself to human beings; but it always simultaneously raised a protest against the petrified relations under which they lived, thereby honouring them. In so far as culture becomes wholly assimilated to and integrated in those petrified relations, human beings are once more debased. Cultural entities typical of the culture industry are no longer *also* commodities, they are commodities through and through. This quantitative shift is so great that it calls forth entirely new phenomena. Ultimately, the culture industry no longer even needs to directly pursue everywhere the profit interests from which it originated. These interests have become objectified in its ideology and have even made themselves independent of the compulsion to sell the cultural commodities which must be swallowed anyway. The culture industry turns into public relations, the manufacturing of 'goodwill' *per se*, without regard for particular firms or saleable objects. Brought to bear is a general uncritical consensus, advertisements produced for the world, so that each product of the culture industry becomes its own advertisement.

Nevertheless, those characteristics which originally stamped the transformation of literature into a commodity are maintained in this process. More than anything in the world, the culture industry has its ontology, a scaffolding of rigidly conservative basic categories which can be gleaned, for example, from the commercial English novels of the late seventeenth and early eighteenth centuries. What parades as progress in the culture industry, as the incessantly new which it offers up, remains the disguise for an eternal sameness; everywhere the changes mask a skeleton which has changed just as little as the profit motive itself since the time it first gained its predominance over culture.

Thus, the expression 'industry' is not to be taken too literally. It refers to the standardization of the thing itself — such as that of the Western, familiar to every movie-goer — and to the rationalization of distribution techniques, but not strictly to the production process. Although in film, the central sector of the culture industry, the production process resembles technical modes of operation in the extensive division of labour, the employment of machines and the separation of the labourers from the means of production – expressed in the perennial conflict between artists active in the culture industry and those who control it – individual forms of production are nevertheless maintained. Each product affects an individual air; individuality itself serves to reinforce ideology, in so far as the illusion is conjured up that the completely reified and mediated is a sanctuary from immediacy and life. Now, as ever, the culture industry exists in the 'service' of third persons, maintaining its affinity to the declining circulation process of capital, to the commerce from which it came into being. Its ideology above all makes use of the star system, borrowed from individualistic art and its commercial exploitation. The more dehumanized its methods of operation and content, the more diligently and successfully the culture industry propagates supposedly great personalities and operates with heart-throbs. It is industrial more in a sociological sense, in the incorporation of industrial forms of organization even when nothing is manufactured – as in the rationalization of office work – rather than in the sense of anything really and actually produced by technological rationality. Accordingly, the misinvestments of the culture industry are considerable, throwing those branches rendered obsolete by new techniques into crises, which seldom lead to changes for the better.

The concept of technique in the culture industry is only in name identical with technique in works of art. In the latter, technique is concerned with the internal organization of the object itself, with its inner logic. In contrast, the technique of the culture industry is, from the beginning, one of distribution and mechanical reproduction, and therefore always remains external to its object. The culture industry finds ideological support precisely in so far as it carefully shields itself from the full potential of the techniques, contained in its products. It lives parasitically from the extra-artistic technique of the material production of goods, without regard for the obligation to the internal artistic whole implied by its functionality (*Sachlichkeit*), but also without concern for the laws of form demanded by aesthetic autonomy. The result for the physiognomy of the culture industry is essentially a mixture of streamlining, photographic hardness and precision on the one hand, and individualistic residues, sentimentality and an already rationally disposed and adapted romanticism on the other. Adopting Benjamin's designation of the traditional work of art by the concept of aura, the presence of that which is not present, the culture industry is defined by the fact that it does not strictly counterpose another principle to that of aura, but rather by the fact that it conserves the decaying aura as a foggy mist. By this means the culture industry betrays its own ideological abuses.

It has recently become customary among cultural officials as well as sociologists to warn against underestimating the culture industry while pointing to its great importance for the development of the consciousness of its consumers. It is to be taken seriously, without cultured snobbism. In actuality the culture industry is important as a moment of the spirit which dominates today. Whoever ignores its influence out of scepticism for what it stuffs into people would be naive. Yet there is a deceptive glitter about the admonition to take it seriously. Because of its social role, disturbing questions about its quality, about truth or untruth, and about the aesthetic niveau of the culture industry's emissions are repressed, or at least excluded from the so-called sociology of communications. The critic is accused of taking refuge in arrogant esoterica. It would be advisable first to indicate the double meaning of importance that slowly worms its way in unnoticed. Even if it touches the lives of innumerable people, the function of something is no guarantee of its particular quality. The blending of aesthetics with its residual communicative aspects leads art, as a social phenomenon, not to its rightful position in opposition to alleged artistic snobbism, but rather in a variety of ways to the defence of its baneful social consequences. The importance of the culture industry in the spiritual constitution of the masses is no dispensation for reflection on its objective legitimation, its essential being, least of all by a science which thinks itself pragmatic. On the contrary: such reflection becomes necessary precisely for this reason. To take the culture industry as seriously as its unquestioned role demands, means to take it seriously critically, and not to cower in the face of its monopolistic character.

Among those intellectuals anxious to reconcile themselves with the phenomenon and eager to find a common formula to express both their reservations against it and their respect for its power, a tone of ironic toleration prevails unless they have already created a new mythos of the twentieth century from the imposed regression. After all, those intellectuals maintain, everyone knows what pocket novels, films off the rack, family television shows rolled out into serials and hit parades, advice to the lovelorn and horoscope columns are all about. All of this, however, is harmless and, according to them, even democratic since it responds to a demand, albeit a stimulated one. It also bestows all kinds of blessings, they point out, for example, through the dissemination of information, advice and stress reducing patterns of behaviour. Of course, as every sociological study measuring something as elementary as how politically informed the public is has proven, the information is meagre or indifferent. Moreover, the advice to be gained from manifestations of the culture industry is vacuous, banal or worse, and the behaviour patterns are shamelessly conformist.

The two-faced irony in the relationship of servile intellectuals to the culture industry is not restricted to them alone. It may also be supposed that the consciousness of the consumers themselves is split between the prescribed fun which is supplied to them by the culture industry and a not particularly well-hidden doubt about its blessings. The phrase, the world wants to be deceived, has become truer than had ever been intended. People are not only, as the saying goes, falling for the swindle; if it guarantees them even the most fleeting gratification they desire a deception which is nonetheless transparent to them. They force their eyes shut and voice approval, in a kind of self-loathing, for what is meted out to them, knowing fully the purpose for which it is manufactured. Without admitting it they sense that their lives would be completely intolerable as soon as they no longer clung to satisfactions which are none at all.

The most ambitious defence of the culture industry today celebrates its spirit, which might be safely called ideology, as an ordering factor. In a supposedly chaotic world it provides human beings with something like standards for orientation, and that alone seems worthy of approval. However, what its defenders imagine is preserved by the culture industry is in fact all the more thoroughly destroyed by it. The colour film demolishes the genial old tavern to a greater extent than bombs ever could: the film exterminates its imago. No homeland can survive being processed by the films which celebrate it, and which thereby turn the unique character on which it thrives into an interchangeable sameness.

That which legitimately could be called culture attempted, as an expression of suffering and contradiction, to maintain a grasp on the idea of the good life. Culture cannot represent either that which merely exists or the conventional and no longer binding categories of order which the culture industry drapes over the idea of the good life as if existing reality were the good life, and as if those categories were its true measure. If the response of the culture industry's representatives is that it does not deliver art at all, this is itself the ideology with which they evade responsibility for that from which the business lives. No misdeed is ever righted by explaining it as such.

The appeal to order alone, without concrete specificity, is futile; the appeal to the dissemination of norms, without these ever proving themselves in reality or before consciousness, is equally futile. The idea of an objectively binding order, huckstered to people because it is so lacking for them, has no claims if it does not prove itself internally and in confrontation with human beings. But this is precisely what no product of the culture industry would engage in. The concepts of order which it hammers into human beings are always those of the status quo. They remain unquestioned, unanalysed and undialectically presupposed, even if they no longer have any substance for those who accept them. In contrast to the Kantian, the categorical imperative of the culture industry no longer has anything in common with freedom. It proclaims: you shall conform, without instruction as to what; conform to that which exists anyway, and to that which everyone thinks anyway as a reflex of its power and omnipresence. The power of the culture industry's ideology is such that conformity has replaced consciousness. The order that springs from it is never confronted with what it claims to be or with the real interests of human beings. Order, however, is not good in itself. It would be so only as a good order. The fact that the culture industry is oblivious to this and extols order *in abstracto*, bears witness to the impotence and untruth of the messages it conveys. While it claims to lead the perplexed, it deludes them with false conflicts which they are to exchange for their own. It solves conflicts for them only in appearance, in a way that they can hardly be solved in their real lives. In the products of the culture industry human beings get into trouble only so that they can be rescued unharmed, usually by representatives of a benevolent collective; and then in empty harmony, they are reconciled with the general, whose demands they had experienced at the outset as irreconcilable with their interests. For this purpose the culture industry has developed formulas which even reach into such non-conceptual areas as light musical entertainment. Here too one gets into a 'jam', into rhythmic problems, which can be instantly disentangled by the triumph of the basic beat.

Even its defenders, however, would hardly contradict Plato openly who maintained that what is objectively and intrinsically untrue cannot also be subjectively good and true for human beings. The concoctions of the culture industry are neither guides for a blissful life, nor a new art of moral responsibility, but rather exhortations to toe the line, behind which stand the most powerful interests. The consensus which it propagates strengthens blind, opaque authority. If the culture industry is measured not by its own substance and logic, but by its efficacy, by its position in reality and its explicit pretensions; if the focus of serious concern is with the efficacy to which it always appeals, the potential of its effect becomes twice as weighty. This potential, however, lies in the promotion and exploitation of the ego-weakness to which the powerless members of contemporary society, with its concentration of power, are condemned. Their consciousness is further developed retrogressively. It is no coincidence that cynical American film producers are heard to say that their pictures must take into consideration the level of eleven-year-olds. In doing so they would very much like to make adults into eleven-year-olds.

It is true that thorough research has not, for the time being, produced an airtight case proving the regressive effects of particular products of the culture industry. No doubt an imaginatively designed experiment could achieve this more successfully than the powerful financial interests concerned would find comfortable. In any case, it can be assumed without hesitation that steady drops hollow the stone, especially since the system of the culture industry that surrounds the masses tolerates hardly any deviation and incessantly drills the same formulas on behaviour. Only their deep unconscious mistrust, the last residue of the difference between art and empirical reality in the spiritual make-up of the masses explains why they have not, to a person, long since perceived and accepted the world as it is constructed for them by the culture industry. Even if its messages were as harmless as they are made out to be – on countless occasions they are obviously not harmless, like the movies which chime in with currently popular hate campaigns against intellectuals by portraying them with the usual stereotypes – the attitudes which the culture industry calls forth are anything but harmless. If an astrologer urges his readers to drive carefully on a particular day, that certainly hurts no one; they will, however, be harmed indeed by the stupefication which lies in the claim that advice which is valid every day and which is therefore idiotic, needs the approval of the stars.

Human dependence and servitude, the vanishing point of the culture industry, could scarcely be more faithfully described than by the American interviewee who was of the opinion that the dilemmas of the contemporary epoch would end if people would simply follow the lead of prominent personalities. In so far as the culture industry arouses a feeling of well-being that the world is precisely in that order suggested by the culture industry, the substitute gratification which it prepares for human beings cheats them out of the same happiness which it deceitfully projects. The total effect of the culture industry is one of anti-enlightenment, in which, as Horkheimer and I have noted, enlightenment, that is the progressive technical domination of nature, becomes mass deception and is turned into a means of fettering consciousness. It impedes the development of autonomous, independent individuals who judge and decide consciously for themselves. These, however, would be the precondition for a democratic society which needs adults who have come of age in order to sustain itself and develop. If the masses have been unjustly reviled from above as masses, the culture industry is not among the least responsible for making them into masses and then despising them, while obstructing the emancipation for which human beings are as ripe as the productive forces of the epoch permit.

Chapter 6

Fredric Wertham

SEDUCTION OF THE INNOCENT

A T THE BEGINNING OF World War II, I started a special form of group therapy for delinquent and predelinquent children in the Mental Hygiene Clinic for the Queens General Hospital. This was intended primarily for treatment, but it turned out unexpectedly to be one of the most revealing channels of information about the influence of comic books. When this group started I had no intention of taking up that problem, but the subject turned up spontaneously again and again.

The usual age range of members of this group was from thirteen to sixteen. The majority were boys, but there were always some girls. As therapy, the club was more successful than any other method of child guidance, especially of delinquents. This was attested by probation officers and juvenile law enforcement authorities. Some 90 per cent of all those who attended the sessions for prolonged periods (that is, at least one year) are no longer problems to their families, the authorities or themselves. Only children who had got into some kind of trouble were eligible, and the minimum trouble was playing hookey. In many cases much more serious offenses were involved. Most of the children came from one-family-house, middle-class sections of the population.

The name Hookey Club started in this way. I was confronted with several children one day who were truants. While interviewing them as a group, they began questioning one another. This went so well that I asked them to return in a group. Little by little, whenever children with truancy problems came, my assistants would feed them into the group-therapy class. Once, before one of the weekly meetings, I said to a social worker, 'I see the Hookey Club is coming in today.' She laughed and repeated the remark, and the name stuck. The Hookey Club developed into a regular institution. The sessions were strictly secret, with only myself and usually a stenographer present. All details remained confidential. At each session the case of one boy or girl or some general topic on someone's mind was discussed. One child functioned as chairman to maintain order. Every boy or girl at the session could question the child whose case was taken up. And everyone could express his opinion about the case. Among the children were always some experts in various forms of delinquency who questioned the child who was up for discussion. Whatever a child might have learned from comic books for the commission of a delinquent act, the group never accepted that as an excuse. Nor did any child ever spontaneously bring it up as an excuse.

Children are more isolated than we think, and have few in whom they can confide without fear of misunderstanding or recrimination. Adults rarely realize how serious children are about their conflicts. They want to be straightened out. They shrink from a judge; but in the Hookey Club, where they were even more severely questioned by their peers, they could speak out fully and openly about anything whatsoever. When children question one another, one can readily see how the troubles of children reflect the troubles and conflicts of society. My experiences with the Hookey Club have confirmed me in my opinion that valuable personality assets slumber in delinquent children. By regarding these children as inferior or emotionally sick or psychopathic, we miss the constellation of social and individual forces that leads to delinquency and deprives these children of really scientific help. To characterize them merely by negative qualities is both unjust and scientifically inaccurate.

Forms of delinquency that adults know little about and children frequently encounter, like juvenile extortion rackets, were discussed. 'Why did you steal the five dollars?' the thirteen-year-old chairman of one session asked. 'I'll explain it to you,' answered the fourteen-year-old whose case was being probed. 'The older kids in school were getting up a mob and if I did not pay them some money they'd get after me and beat me up.' To an adult this may sound like an untrue excuse, but there were always some juvenile experts in the Hookey Club who recognized a social reality when they saw it.

Often boys who practiced the extortion racket themselves were questioned by the group:

Q.: Where did it happen?
A.: In the school yard.
Q.: How did you know he had money?
A.: I asked him how much money has he got, he said a dollar.
Q.: How old was the boy?
A.: About thirteen.
Q.: How did you know he couldn't beat you up?
A.: I took money from him before, two weeks before that. I got a wallet and fifteen cents before that.
Q.: Did you do anything worse than the other things?
A.: Yes. I stabbed a boy.
Q.: When was that?
A.: That was last year. The boy was about twelve years old. I stabbed him with a knife, a pocket knife. I stabbed him in the back. They put me in the shelter for two weeks.

In such cases I often found that the whole comic-book ideology and methodology were apparent in both those who answered and those who questioned. The boys evaluated this influence in a matter-of-fact way. A boy replied to questions about a burglary he committed:

'I read comic books where they broke into a place. I got the idea to break into the house. I wanted the money. I couldn't go through the front door because I didn't have the key. I didn't think of the comic book.'

Questioner: 'You don't have to think of it, it is in the back of your mind, in your subconscious mind.'

A boy who had been arrested because he kicked another boy was questioned:

Q.: What did you do?

A.: We were pitching pennies in school. This kid was cheating. One guy grabbed me and pushed me against a water faucet. He bent down to get the pennies. I took my foot and kicked him in the head. He had two or three stitches in the head.

Q.: It wouldn't have been so bad if you had punched him in the head, but kicking is not right. When you see a comic book, the point is with most fellows, they see that a certain fellow in there does that, they want to be like him and think they are tough and can do the same. In the comic book they might get away with it, in this case you don't.

ANOTHER BOY: The guy who thinks he is a tough guy, he isn't really tough.

The effect of comic-book reading was scrutinized by the club members, because there were always some who had reading difficulties. The members were more critical than some of the pseudo-educators who proclaim that comic books are good for reading. At a session where classics comic books were mentioned, a fourteen-year-old boy said in reply to questions:

'I don't read the comic books. I just look at the pictures. I can read, but I just don't take the time out. Sometimes, when it is a good story, I read it. You would be surprised how much you can learn just by looking at the pictures. If you have a good mind, you can figure things out for yourself. I like the horror science-fiction ones. I just look at the pictures.'

In the Hookey Club the group was both judge and jury. I functioned merely as advisor. The children could recommend that a boy be allowed to leave school and given his working papers, or that he should stay in school. They could suggest that a boy should not be taken off parole or that he should be. When I had to make a report about a child, the Hookey Club members discussed whether the child should be referred to the Children's Court or should receive supervision by the Juvenile Aid Bureau or should just be left under Hookey Club jurisdiction. Sometimes they suggested that no report be made until they had seen the child in question longer.

Going over the protocols of the Hookey Club it is hard to see how adults can be so naive about the role comic books play in the lives of children. The accounts of the sessions bristled with revealing bits about comic books, a topic that came up again and again in very different connections: a boy bought his switchblade knife through an advertisement from a comic book; a girl bought some phony medicine from a comic book to reduce her weight, which she was self-conscious about; different methods of stealing, burglarizing and hurting people were learned from comic books; comic books were cited to justify cunning, distrust and race ridicule; and so on. The excuses of the industry's experts that comic books show methods to hurt, wound and kill people in order to teach children self-defense did not go with the experts of the Hookey Club. They knew better. Nor did they believe that comic books taught not to commit delinquencies. They knew that what they demonstrate is that one should not make mistakes in committing them. A girl of fourteen who had been stealing had a comic book with her at one session:

THIRTEEN–YEAR–OLD CHAIRMAN: Which comic books do you read mostly?

A.: Girls read mostly *Crimes by Women*.

Q.: Which crimes do women commit?

A.: Murder. They marry a man for his life insurance and then kill him, then marry another man, and then just go on like that until they finally get caught. Or they will be a dancer and meet the wrong kind of a guy and get involved in a bank robbery.

Q.: What's the fun for you in reading that?

A.: It shows you other people's stupid mistakes.

Here are some samples from Hookey Club proceedings:

A FIFTEEN–YEAR–OLD DELINQUENT GIRL: In some of the crime comic books kids pick up ideas. They give them ideas of robbery and sex . . .

Q.: Sex?

A.: Yes, plenty of sex. They show you unexposed [sic] women, men beating up girls and breaking their arms. The fellows see them and they want to try it. They try to wrestle with them and get ideas. I know of fellows who do imitate comic books. When I was young I used to read comic books and I watched the fellows and how they imitated what they did in the books. They tried it with the girls around my way. They tied them up. The boys were around ten or twelve, the girls were the same age. They used to always read the comic books. I asked them what made them do that. They said they saw it in the comic books. They read *Crime, Murder Inc., Crime Does Not Pay*, most of those crime books.

A boy who burglarized stores explained, 'I read the comic books to learn how you can get money. I read about thirty a week. I read *Crime Does Not Pay, Crime and Punishment, Penalty, Wanted*. That is all I can think of. There was this one case. It was in back of a factory with pretty rich receipts, money. It showed how you get in through the back door. I didn't copy that. I thought the side door was the best way. I just switched to the skylight. I carried it out practically the same way as the comic book did it, only I had to open two drawers to do it. I didn't do every crime book, some of them were difficult. Some of them I just imitated. I had to think the rest out myself. I know other boys who learned how to do such jobs from comic books.'

From the discussion of the case of a fourteen-year-old girl who had been caught shoplifting.

TWELVE–YEAR–OLD BOY: I saw a comic book where they do shoplifting. This girl was shoplifting and she was caught. They took her down to the Police Department. It was a love story. When she got married she still shop-lifted and she broke down and told her husband. I didn't like it. It was the only thing I had to read. It might give a girl ideas to shoplift.

FIFTEEN–YEAR–OLD BOY: They get the idea, if she gets away with it, why can't I get away with it. I saw a book where a man has a hanger in his coat with hooks on. It was a crime comic book . . . The kids see that these men get away with it. They say, let's try it. They learn the method of putting it in a jacket. They teach you how to do it in the comic book. They didn't notice it until somebody jumped on this man and the things fell out. Otherwise they would not have caught him.

From a discussion on fighting in school:

THIRTEEN-YEAR-OLD BOY: I learned from crime comic books when you want to hit a man don't get face to face – hit him in the back.

FIFTEEN-YEAR-OLD (contradicting): In comic books they hit them in the eye!

From an all-round discussion on fairy tales:

> *Superman* is a fairy story.
> No, it is not a fairy story. It is a comic book. The comic books, they are mostly murder or something funny, but the fairy tales, they are just stories.
> The comics like *Superman* are not true, they don't happen, but they might happen or could happen. The fairy tales, they just can't happen.
> In the fairy tales they don't get killed.

At one Hookey Club session I had another psychiatrist present as a guest. The question of comic books and my criticism of them came up:

FOURTEEN-YEAR-OLD (*addressing Dr. W.*): I think it is stupid. You are the only psychiatrist who is really interested. Maybe there are five others . . . out of five thousand – how can you get any headway? You spend close to maybe a thousand dollars and it is stupid. You can't stand a chance against these comic-book publishers.

FIFTEEN-YEAR-OLD: That is right, because they got the police to put in a good word for the comic books. Like before, they used to have policemen and policewomen say it is a good influence for the children. They had a police lady and a police chief in every edition of *Crime Does Not Pay*. That is one of the reasons why you have no chance.

THE FOURTEEN-YEAR-OLD: I noticed in *Crime Does Not Pay* they give two dollars a letter for what's on your mind. People write beautiful letters saying this comic book is good for children – anything to earn two dollars.

ANOTHER FIFTEEN-YEAR-OLD: Gals don't approve of guys going to poolrooms in Brooklyn. They pay for protection. They take a switchblade and if a guy don't pay them a dollar, they will rip up the table . . . I have been in with them . . . You could learn that from a comic book, too. . . . I read some of that in *Crime Does Not Pay*.

SIXTEEN-YEAR-OLD: The guys, the big racketeers and stuff, they pay the guys maybe to put something in crime comic books that is good. The other boys think it is a good idea. So they start doing it and get into the Youth House, and when they get back they work for the racketeers. They make a lot of money and everything and stuff. They want the young boys to read the crime comic books to get ideas. The boys are about seventeen when the racketeers use them for dope and stuff, to peddle it, and to run the numbers . . . I think crime comic books are there to make the kids into bad boys, so that they can make some money. I figure maybe these gangsters they say: a couple of years from now, when these guys grow up, I'll give them a number racket and I can be the big guy then. Sometimes they need gunmen to eliminate the other big guys. The comic books show about that, too, about racing and stuff.

GUEST PSYCHIATRIST: What was that you said about Youth House?

THE SIXTEEN-YEAR-OLD: The racketeers want to send you to Youth House, and Warwick, too, so that you get really bad . . . They want you to go there so that people will be scared of you . . . If you have a record, everybody will be scared of you. You know how people are in the neighborhood, people say so-and-so was in Youth House and in Warwick . . . If you walk in with a gun, they are scared of you.

THE FOURTEEN-YEAR-OLD (*addressing the psychiatric guest*): This is no insult to you. If you got a thousand dollars check for these funny books, would you talk against them? They give some people side money, so they write, 'Approved by Dr. So-and-So: Good Reading Matter for Children.'

My psychiatric guest felt that the Hookey Club was a little rough.

Chapter 7

Richard Hoggart

THE USES OF LITERACY

The newer mass art: sex in shiny packets

A. The juke-box boys

THIS REGULAR, INCREASING, AND almost entirely unvaried diet of sensation without commitment is surely likely to help render its consumers less capable of responding openly and responsibly to life, is likely to induce an underlying sense of purposelessness in existence outside the limited range of a few immediate appetites. Souls which may have had little opportunity to open will be kept hard-gripped, turned in upon themselves, looking out 'with odd dark eyes like windows' upon a world which is largely a phantasmagoria of passing shows and vicarious stimulations. That this is not today the position of many working-class people is due mainly to the capacity of the human spirit to resist; to resist from a sense, even though it is not usually defined, that there are other things which matter and which are to be obeyed.

But it may be useful to look now at some of those points in English life at which the cultural process described in the last two chapters is having its strongest effect. We should see there the condition which might already have been reached were it not for the resistances I have repeatedly stressed. One such illustration is to be found in the reading of young men on National Service. For two years many of them are, on the whole, bored; they are marking time until they go back to their jobs; they are adolescent and have money to spare. They are cut off from the unconsciously felt but important steadying effect of home, of the web of family relationships; perhaps also from the sense, at their place of work, of being part of an organization which has a tradition in its own kind of skill. They are as a result open to the effects of the reading, both fragmentary and sensational, so freely provided for them. The only bound books read by a great many, my own experience strongly suggests, are likely to be those written by the most popular crime novelists. Otherwise, they read comics, gangster novelettes, science and crime magazines, the newer-style magazines or magazine/newspapers, and the picture-dailies. Luckily, National Service lasts only two years; after that, they go home and back to work, still readers of these publications, but soon also men with commitments, with more demands on their time and money, probably with a good chance of picking up older, neighbourhood rhythms, with a good chance of escaping from the worst effects of what can be a glassily hermaphrodite existence ('life like a permanent wank [masturbation] inside you,' as a soldier once described it to me), and one not connected to any meaningful sense of personal aim. I know there are exceptions and that much is being done to improve matters; but, given the background described in the preceding chapters, this is for many the predominant atmosphere during the period of National Service.

Perhaps even more symptomatic of the general trend is the reading of juke-box boys, of those who spend their evening listening in harshly lighted milk-bars to the 'nickelodeons'. There are, of course, others who read the books and magazines now to be discussed − some married men and women, perhaps in particular those who are finding married life a somewhat jaded affair, 'dirty old men', some schoolchildren − but one may reasonably take those who, night after night, visit these bars as typical or characteristic readers of these most developed new-style popular journals.

Like the cafés I described in an earlier chapter, the milk-bars indicate at once, in the nastiness of their modernistic knick-knacks, their glaring showiness, an aesthetic breakdown so complete that, in comparison with them, the layout of the living-rooms in some of the poor homes from which the customers come seems to speak of a tradition as balanced and civilized as an eighteen-century town house. I am not thinking of those milk-bars which are really quick-service cafés where one may have a meal more quickly than in a café with table-service. I have in mind rather the kind of milk-bar − there is one in almost every northern town with more than, say, fifteen thousand inhabitants − which has become the regular evening rendezvous of some of the young men. Girls go to some, but most of the customers are boys aged between fifteen and twenty, with drape-suits, picture ties, and an American slouch. Most of them cannot afford a succession of milk-shakes, and make cups of tea serve for an hour or two whilst − and this is their main reason for coming − they put copper after copper into the mechanical record-player. About a dozen records are available at any time; a numbered button is pressed for the one wanted, which is selected from a key to titles. The records seem to be changed about once a fortnight by the hiring firm; almost all are American; almost all are 'vocals' and the styles of singing much advanced beyond what is normally heard on the Light Programme of the B.B.C. Some of the tunes are catchy; all have been doctored for presentation so that they have the kind of beat which is currently popular; much use is made of the 'hollow-cosmos' effect which echo-chamber recording gives. They are delivered with great precision and competence, and the 'nickelodeon' is allowed to blare out so that the noise would be sufficient to fill a good-sized ballroom, rather than a converted shop in the main street. The young men waggle one shoulder or stare, as desperately as Humphrey Bogart, across the tubular chairs.

Compared even with the pub around the corner, this is all a peculiarly thin and pallid form of dissipation, a sort of spiritual dry-rot amid the odour of boiled milk. Many of the customers − their clothes, their hair-styles, their facial expressions all indicate − are living to a large extent in a myth-world compounded of a few simple elements which they take to be those of American life.

They form a depressing group and one by no means typical of working-class people; perhaps most of them are rather less intelligent than the average, and are therefore even more exposed than others to the debilitating mass-trends of the day. They have no aim, no ambitions, no protection, no belief. They are the modern equivalents of Samuel Butler's mid-nineteenth-century ploughboys, and in as unhappy a position as theirs:

> The row of stolid, dull, vacant plough-boys, ungainly in build, uncomely in face, lifeless, apathetic, a race a good deal more like the pre-Revolution French peasants as described by Carlyle than is pleasant to reflect upon – a race now supplanted . . .

For some of them even the rough sex-life of many of their contemporaries is not yet possible; it requires more management of their own personalities and more meeting with other personalities than they can compass.

From their education at school they have taken little which connects with the realities of life as they experience it after fifteen. Most of them have jobs which require no personal out-going, which are not intrinsically interesting, which encourage no sense of personal value, of being a maker. The job is to be done day by day, and after that the rest is amusement, is pleasure; there is time to spare and some money in the pocket. They are ground between the millstones of technocracy and democracy; society gives them an almost limitless freedom of the sensations, but makes few demands on them – the use of their hands and of a fraction of their brains for forty hours a week. For the rest they are open to the entertainers and their efficient mass-equipment. The youth clubs, the young people's institutes, the sports clubs, cannot attract them as they attract many in their generation; and the commercial people ensure, by the inevitable process of development in commercial entertainment, that their peculiar grip is retained and strengthened. The responsibilities of marriage may gradually change them. Meanwhile, they have no responsibilities, and little sense of responsibilities, to themselves or to others. They are in one dreadful sense the new workers; if, by extrapolation simply from a reading of newer working-class entertainment literature, one were to attempt to imagine the ideal readers for that literature, these would be the people. It is true, as I have said, that they are not typical. But these are the figures some important contemporary forces are tending to create, the directionless and tamed helots of a machine-minding class. If they seem to consist so far chiefly of those poorer intelligence or from homes subject to special strains, that is probably due to the strength of a moral fibre which most cultural providers for working-class people are helping to de-nature. The hedonistic but passive barbarian who rides in a fifty-horse-power bus for threepence, to see a five-million-dollar film for one-and-eightpence, is not simply a social oddity; he is a portent.

B. The 'spicy' magazines

What are such men likely to read, apart from picture-dailies, the more sensational Sunday papers, and newspaper/magazines? The public library has no appeal, nor even perhaps those stationers' fourpenny libraries whose main function is to hold a large stock of the kinds of fiction – 'Crime' or 'Tec' or 'Mystery', 'Westerns', and

'Romance' or 'Love', as the shelves are usually headed – of which the public libraries never have enough copies. One needs to look rather at those 'magazine shops' of which there is always one in every large working-class shopping-area. Their window-space is littered and over-hung with paper-backs in varying stages of disintegration, since they operate a system of exchanges – an expensive one, usually, since paper-backs originally costing two shillings change hands at sixpence a time. Here, too, there is a rough division of material into three themes – Crime, Science Fiction, and Sex novelettes.

I noted from one window on one day the following characteristics of the main groups; the magazines were not displayed in their sections, of course, but in the usual profuse order:

A. *Crime*. The prevailing note here, since most are from America and have been published since the American outcry against magazines which seemed to glorify crime, is that 'Crime Doesn't Pay'. They are likely to have sub-titles such as, 'Published in the cause of the Reduction of Crime'. Whatever the formal professions, the interest and excitement remain all with the gangster, or the detectives are tem-peramentally gangsters who chance to be on the side of the law. Titles run on these lines:

Super Detective	F.B.I. Crime Cases
H.Q. Police Stories	Thrilling Police Cases
True Detective	Secret Detective Stories
Crime Unlimited	Top-Flight Detective Tales
Smashing Police Stories	Candid Camera Detective
Hot-Spot Police Tales	

The format is almost always the same; flat paper, crude print, vivid glossy cover: obviously there is much 'ghosting' and interchange of material.

B. *Science*. Here the titles ring the changes on 'Science', 'Space Science', and 'Spaceways', with adjectival support from 'Startling', 'Weird', 'Future', 'Astounding', 'Fantastic', 'Super', 'Thrilling', and 'Authentic'.

Again, the same flat paper with glossy covers. This is the sort of science fiction which preceded, and presumably goes on unaffected by, the elevation of some writing on similar themes into a subject for serious discussion in the literary weeklies. The manner and situations are alike extremely limited. In most stories there is a nubile girl, dressed in what a costume-designer for a second-class touring revue might be expected to consider a 'futuristic' outfit. This usually means a very short and pleated white skirt, and an abbreviated top incorporating some sort of modernistic motif. This is 'sex stuff' with zip-fasteners instead of the old-fashioned blouses and skirts; vicarious fornication (with no details) on a spaceship moving between Mars and Venus.

Of the third group, the sex-novelettes, I shall say more, separately. These three groups cover almost the whole non-periodical stock of my specimen shop and the others of its kind. The old 'Westerns' and 'Boxing', which would have been major groups twenty years ago, exist only on the fringes today.

These magazines appear to have a particular appeal, I have suggested, for adoles-cents of below the average intelligence and for others who, for one reason or other, have not developed or do not feel themselves adequate. The advertisements are pre-dominantly compensatory. This may be a convenient place at which to digress briefly about compensatory advertising of the more elementary kind, which constantly appears both in the type of magazine now being discussed and in a much wider range of periodicals.

At their simplest such advertisements appeal to a sense of physical inferiority, they urge the reader to learn how to stop smoking and so acquire a clearer eye and brain, a steadier and firmer hand grip; 'Be Tall', they urge, 'Build Your Physique', 'Why Be Scraggy?', 'Glowing Vitality for *You*', '*They* took my course . . .' says an extremely muscular advertiser, 'and look at the difference in *Them*! *You* send for details and I'll give *You* a husky body.'

From there it is a short step to the nerve-advertisements, and the inferiority-complex advertisements:

> Do you suffer from nervousness, inferiority-feeling, lack of confidence, stammering, failure of necessary poise, hesitation and humility? – all these indicate a fundamental maladjustment arising from a SUBCONSCIOUS FAILURE OF NERVE-ORIENTATION.
>
> Learn to generate POSITIVE instead of NEGATIVE Drives! Create for yourself a DOMINANT and ASSERTIVE personality!

or to some things which seem even more powerful:

> IT SEEMS INCREDIBLE
> How far have YOU tapped your own immense forces of potential development?
> DO YOU WISH TO? [A modernistic drawing is likely to appear here of a male figure with rays of vital force streaming from him.]
> Then free them and control them – from the day you master this amazing system.
> USE to the full your own ASTONISHING HIDDEN DYNAMIC! This volume can REDIRECT YOUR LIFE.

Often the same organization makes both the basic appeals (are you simply nerve-ridden?) and those more positive, where the sense of inadequacy is not so strongly stressed, but still it is assumed that you would like to win more friends and influence more people. You may discover how to do so by paying, say, £2 for a book on 'The secret of successful personality-selling'. New ones, making even bigger and better claims and with yet more dynamic titles and similarly large prices, come out at frequent intervals.

> Is Life giving YOU the rewards you want and deserve? Do you want to go on living fruitlessly and purposelessly . . . nagged by timidity and fear?
> If not, here is the solution you seek.
> From it you will win money, power, fame, and the esteem of all your acquaintance [a strange echo of the close of Freud's twenty-third Introductory Lecture, on the artist as a self-rewarding phantast – 'He has won – through this phantasy – what before he could win only in phantasy: honour, power and the love of women.' Stranger still, how such a would-be resounding final chord sounds a thin egocentric echo to Bacon on 'the

farthest end of knowledge': 'for the glory of the Creator, and the relief of man's estate'].

To return to the magazines themselves: there are a number of 'spicy', 'off-the-shoulder' periodicals, or sex-and-bittiness weeklies and monthlies, whose bark is in an illuminating way much worse than their bite. They can be bought from almost any newsagent, not only from the 'magazine shops', and some of them have considerable sales. I have not been able to find figures of their distributions by class, but know them to be popular among working-class and lower middle-class young men.

They are, first, repositories of jokes, many of them illustrated and with the emphasis on very obvious, limited, and only moderately exceptionable sexual innuendoes. Each of them usually has a crossword, a page on sport, fortune-telling-by-the-stars, and short-short stories. The stories might be expected, from the layout and drawings, to be sexy, but prove to be as domestically whimsical as those in a modern women's home magazine. The narrator is a young man who is either not long married or, to judge from the mildness of his whistles after the girls, won't be long before he settles down with a decent lass.

Nowadays there is sometimes a film-serial, with *décolleté* photographic illustrations. For the rest, there are a great many drawings of various sizes, with jokes underneath. Most of these magazines aim to be very smart and modern, although in general their layout is hardly slicker than that of some family magazines. They establish their claim to modernity and sophistication largely by using artists in the newer style. Their pages have not, therefore, the quieter domestic lines of the older magazine artists, but rather those of the Englishmen who have learned from the Americans, notably from Varga. There have to be photographic pin-ups, and in the absence of a considerable use of colour photography and some of the more expensive devices which help their rivals, most of these magazines seem to try to ensure that their photographs shall be as daring as possible and that the models really shall appear to be coming right out of the page at the reader.

They are all consciously sexy-naughty, aware that they are being daring, having a bit of a fling, at least in their illustrations. But obviously one can feel like that only by assuming the existence of values which one is flouting. There is little that is ingrown or overheated about these magazines; they belong to the same world as the older women's magazines, after all. The strongest objection is not to their sexiness but, as so often with the newer kinds of magazine, to their triviality: they get the thrill of naughtiness so easily and on such slight and spurious evidence.

There exists a number of more narrowly working-class magazines, which, partly because of their local and specific character, differ strikingly from the group I have just described. None of them seem to have long lives, but new magazines in the same tradition appear almost as soon as police action has led to the closing of their predecessors. Usually, they appear monthly and sell for sixpence. I shall describe the character of some which circulate mainly in the north, but there are local magazines of a similar type in the south. The more successful northern magazines may be bought, to my knowledge, from Manchester to Hull and from Middlesbrough to Nottingham. At least one reached a sale of more than one hundred thousand copies of each issue, which suggests a readership of not less than one-third of a million. This particular magazine was certainly read predominantly by members of the urban working-classes in the north-east.

The composition of each issue of a magazine of this type is very simple. There is usually a small sports item, something on films, an odd short-story (meant to look sexy, but really pure froth), and a few advertisements (for lucky charms and the like). The rest of the space is generally devoted to jokes, printed plain in double columns, and to drawings, either illustrating the jokes or in their own right, because they are suggestive. There are not many photographs of models, perhaps – this is a guess – because they would be too expensive. Instead, these magazines tend to use for their more important illustrations, for those which take the place of the photographic pin-ups in the more elaborate magazines, drawings which seem to have been executed originally in heavily-shaded pencilling and then photographed. The final effect is roughly similar to that of the usual photographic pin-ups. Photographed drawings have this further advantage, I imagine: that the artist, who usually works in the Varga idiom, can let himself go on what he regards as suitable parts of the girls' bodies so as to produce a picture even more boldly suggestive than the normal photographic pin-up. One such magazine used to make a particular feature of accentuating the nipples as they protruded underneath a dress. Similarly, the breasts can be very boldly shaped and divided.

In general, these magazines belong to the world of the dirtier picture-postcards; they have a similar vulgarity and a similarly circumscribed view of the possible situations for humour – backsides, 'jerries', knickers, 'belly buttons', breasts (and now 'falsies', the most popular new feature in all the sex-joke magazines). They may be a little cruder than the postcards. When I say this, I am not thinking of such features as the outstanding nipples and the implausibly swelling thighs. The crudest elements in all these magazines is usually the drawing of the girls' faces, especially in the larger studies; they are of a quality I have not seen in the postcards. They have a large-mouthed and brassy vulgarity of expression. I do not think I am speaking here of something which a more generous spirit would recognize as 'rough but earthy gusto, the Chaucerian touch'. This is a pseudo-sophisticated and knowing urban coarseness which it would be a romantic folly to mistake for anything else. These magazines hold their readers, I should guess, by the peculiar suggestiveness of their photographed drawings, and by a certain recognizable quality in the faces and properties shown in them. I open one issue at a double-page drawing of a girl in shorts, with a hugely plunging neckline to her blouse, club-riding on a sports bicycle as so many girls from the northern town do at week-ends. She has unmistakably the face of the one in most large groups of working-class girls who blatantly 'knows what it's for'. In this very restricted sense, a limited realism of expression, these magazines belong to the working-classes in a way that the nationally distributed 'spicy' magazines – and the popular modern magazine/newspapers for that matter – do not.

Chapter 8

Martin Barker

THE NEWSON REPORT
A case study in 'common sense'

IN JUNE 1994, THE *Christian Democrat* celebrated a famous victory. It had forced the Home Secretary, Michael Howard, to amend his Criminal Justice Bill to make the British Board of Film Classification much more stringent about what was allowed on to video. Howard hadn't adopted their amendment – one which had been drafted at a meeting of the Movement for Christian Democracy in March – outright. But its main thrust, without question, was accepted.

How had they done this? By a combination of arguing and lobbying. They had talked of the need to protect children. They had spoken of gratuitously violent films and videos, and how bad they are for the young. And they had played on memories of recent cases where young people, even children, had so obviously gone bad. And they got their argument into every newspaper in the land, and on to many radio and television programmes. The effect, as their Parliamentary sponsor David Alton himself put it, was that they had 'changed the terms of reference' in which 'films of this kind' would henceforth be discussed.

That was no small achievement. And it owed much to one thing: a report by Professor Elizabeth Newson published in April 1994, just two weeks before the 'Alton Amendment' reached the floor of the House of Commons – a report which, as this essay aims to demonstrate, was wildly misleading (Newson, 1994). But the most important thing to note is not just its appalling quality of evidence and argument, but that, *because of the nature of what it was arguing, those weaknesses went wholly unnoticed*. What we have, in the Newson Report, is a classic case of 'common sense writ large'. By this I mean that its claims have the same status as medieval witchcraft accusations. When a 'witch' was denounced, a whole array of evidences and proofs could be adduced; but these could only ever convince because those hearing them were already completely persuaded that these were the only likely explanations. You can only believe someone to be a witch if you believe there are 'witch-events'. The facts adduced only look like evidence and arguments if you are already within that frame of reference. So the Newson Report.

In this chapter, I aim to demonstrate just how bad the Newson Report was. But my broader aim is to push to the centre of our attention the question: why don't we spot this more easily? And I focus on the Newson Report because it is so symptomatic. There, condensed within a few pages, are all the marks of a contemporary witch-craze. Few will now remember the details of what Newson wrote. And yet look how the same framework of ideas was so easily reactivated in more recent attacks: on magazines for young girls (for 'encouraging young girls to experiment sexually'); on *The X-Files* (for 'encouraging young people to play with the supernatural'); on any photography of naked children (for 'pandering to child pornographers'); on 'porn on the Internet' (for giving access to a 'vast array of corrupting materials'); and so on and on. Newson's report allows us to see in miniature all these processes.

How does 'common sense' operate?

The aftermath of the murder of James Bulger in Liverpool gave a huge fillip to the prosecution case against TV, film and video. At the trial, the judge speculated on what might have prompted the killing. He wondered if there wasn't a connection with violent videos. He didn't mention any particular films, but the press had been primed, and one film, *Child's Play III*, became their target. However, it soon became clear that, despite police efforts, there was not a scrap of evidence that the boys had watched the film. Did this failure produce retractions of the claim? Did any of the newspapers, or Alton, or the other campaigners, admit they had been wrong? Not one. So urgent is the wish to find such a link, it seems, that when an exemplar like this falls apart the response is simply to carry on.

In fact, several things happened. Some retreat to the position 'Well, they certainly had/could have had access to films of this sort; after all, we all know children will find ways . . .', or: 'Of course, there was an evil climate that surrounds children from films like this, whether they actually see them or not.' (This apparently weaker position is in fact rhetorically stronger. For what would count as a test of it?) Others escape by arguing 'Well, maybe not that time – but here's another . . .', and cite another new case, in its turn difficult to check.

These strategies were all at play in the Granada TV programme, *TV Violence – Will It Change Your Life?* on 1 May 1994, intended as television's riposte to the threatening resonances of the Bulger case. Granada had arranged for one of the Merseyside police investigators to be present, to 'give the facts'. And he did so, briefly acknowledging that they had found no link. But he continued: no, they hadn't seen that film, but they *had* grown up in a 'violent video culture'. And, to see the harm that could do, look at the case of Suzanne Capper in Manchester, a young woman brutally murdered in a drugs case. Inevitably a warm round of applause greeted this rebuttal. The trouble is, the claimed link in the Capper case was just as bogus, but no one was there to show it. The story most people remember is the story as the press told it – as the Liverpool policeman retold it, having heard it from the press.

Most of us have no chance to check claims in cases like this. We are therefore dependent on how the facts are presented to us by the media. In fact, if we want an example of media effects, this is probably the clearest we can get! And it is very tempting to welcome and accept quick-fix explanations that seem to 'make sense'.

They speak in a vocabulary that we recognise. So, even when refuted, such cases don't go away. They linger like ghosts, always half-alive to 'explain' the next 'inexplicable'. Long after the link in the Bulger and Capper cases had been thoroughly disapproved, journalists and others were happily repeating them as if they were established truths.

This isn't something new, though it currently has a new vigour. In the 1950s, for example, when there was a scare about the possible effects of horror comics on the young, a story hit the press which seemed to prove the point perfectly. A young Borstal absconder, Alan Poole, was killed in a police shoot-out. The press story was that when the police broke into his hideout they found him surrounded by hundreds of crime and horror comics.

Or did they? Some months later the Home Secretary had to make a statement to Parliament:

> Take the case of Alan Poole the Borstal absconder who shot a policeman and was himself then killed resisting arrest. In that case it was reported in the press that he had a library of 50 of these comics. Indeed a social worker said that he had a collection of over 300 . . . [I]n spite of all the publicity, we found that this particular lad had one 'Western' comic in his possession, and that not a very alarming one.
>
> (cited in Barker, 1984a, p. 30)

Yet, despite this official refutation, the case of Alan Poole was cited as proof for a long time after. It suggests that these claims are not part of a rational debate.

But we need to take this further: these arguments have a very particular nature and structure. There are many horrible events 'out there', but only certain very specific kinds of explanation are mobilised to account for them. In the Bulger case, it seemed to 'make sense' to explain their behaviour by saying they had been 'corrupted' by watching videos – and never mind that they hadn't actually watched them at all. They could have, might have; it could all make sense if they had.

Then, what about this?

> FATHER STABBED BABY TO DEATH 'AS SACRIFICE TO WARD OFF EVIL': A father who thought he was Joseph, his wife was Mary and they and their children were on the way to the Garden of Eden killed his 17-month-old daughter as a sacrifice, an Old Bailey court was told yesterday . . . Before the attack in June, he had . . . watched the film *King of Kings*, about the life of Christ.
>
> (*Guardian*, 21 December 1994)

Not one newspaper which recounted this sad story thought it worth suggesting that *King of Kings* is a potential cause of murder. Why not? Actually there is probably *more* evidence to sustain such a link, because of the tendency for certain very disturbed violent offenders to adopt a 'killer-missionary' role; they explain their violence as a command from God. The reason why such a link wouldn't be proposed is because it doesn't seem 'obvious' – and that is the problem we must explore.

Newson's assumptions

David Alton may have used the good offices of the Movement for Christian Democracy to prepare and promote his case, but he also apparently had science on his side, in the form of Elizabeth Newson's Report, co-signed by twenty-four other child professionals. I want to put that 'science' to the test. One of the problems has been the disparity between its size and scope, and its impact. Here is a short report, making no claim to present new evidence. It mainly tells of a supposed change of heart by twenty-five people. Its tone is certainly thoughtful and concerned. It makes no obvious wild claims. Follow, then, its narrative, to see where steps are taken that might give us cause to question.

Newson begins with the Bulger case. She is careful not to assert that the two boys really did see *Child's Play III* or other equivalent films. Rather, the boys are depicted as exemplars of a new cruelty in children. Something exceptional must explain this new viciousness. And here Newson acts as spokesperson for a group who have been growing increasingly worried: the child professionals. It is their view that there are now new kinds of film, and that these films have disturbing 'messages'. To confirm this, we are referred to two films as examples, and to a large body of research evidence which (we are assured) now concludes that these messages are doing harm. The conclusion is inevitable: professionals must forgo their traditional liberalism. The problems are just too overwhelming.

We need to get behind this narrative. For it is built on a series of claims, all of which have to be true for her argument to hold up. There are eight such claims:

1   the murder of James Bulger was so special as to require special explanation;
2   such an explanation has to be some singular change. The most singular recent change is the easy availability of sadistic images within films;
3   these films offer a distinctive message which can be traced and correlated with the attitudes and/or behaviour of James's killers. *Child's Play III* might well be an example of such a film;
4   there is also now a new kind of film, in which 'the viewer is made to identify with the *perpetrator* of the act, not the victim';
5   these four propositions are linked to a general claim: 'The principle that what is experienced vicariously will have *some* effect on *some* people is an established one, and is the reason why industry finds it worth while to spend millions of pounds on advertising';
6   this new kind of film is the start of a worsening curve, as film-makers, video games writers and the like exploit the growing potential of their technologies. Therefore their effects are almost certain to get worse;
7   a great deal of research has already been done, with consistent conclusions: 'media violence' is linked via 'heavy viewing' to 'aggressive behaviour';
8   there is now a vast world literature on this topic, which consistently supports this link.

Eight claims, then, so common to debates on these issues they could be endlessly reproduced. Unfortunately not one of them can be justified. Not one of these claims can be supported by either evidence or logic, as I aim to demonstrate. Yet each one looked disturbingly obvious and persuasive. So persuasive in fact that only a fool or a villain would ignore that obviousness. I will tackle them through four key themes around which they are organised: How do we tell what the 'message' of a film is? How can we understand 'media influence'? Is there, as claimed, an overwhelming body of evidence for 'harm'? And just what is 'media violence'?

How can we tell what the 'message' of a film is?

There have been claims about 'new, bad media images' for a very long time. An example:

> Granted, my dear sir, that your young Jack, or my twelve year old Robert, have minds too pure either to seek after or to crave after literature of the sort in question, but not infrequently it is found without seeking. It is a contagious disease, just as cholera and typhus and the plague are contagious, and, as everybody is aware, it needs not personal contact with a body stricken to convey either of these frightful maladies to the hale and hearty. A tainted scrap of rag has been known to spread plague and death through an entire village, just as a stray leaf of *Panther Bill* or *Tyburn Tree* may sow the seeds of immorality amongst as many boys as a town may produce.
>
> (see Barker, 1989, p. 102)

Thus a nineteenth-century campaigner against 'penny dreadfuls'.
   Or again:

> Before these children's greedy eyes with heartless indiscrimination horrors unimaginable are . . . presented night after night . . . Terrific massacres, horrible catastrophes, motor-car smashes, public hangings, lynchings . . . All who care for the moral well-being and education of the child will set their faces like flint against this new form of excitement.

Thus *The Times*, eighty years ago (see Pearson, in Barker, 1984b, p. 88).
   Or again:

> I find that many parents and teachers are blissfully ignorant of the contents of comics and they would be wise when the opportunity occurs to examine them in detail. They will not be impressed by the printing, colouring, drawing or literary contents, and they will soon see that the comics can be broadly divided into two classes, harmful and harmless.

Thus one of the 1950s campaigners (Barker, 1984a, p. 81).
   If we look carefully at these three quotations we can discern the core of critics' claims. There are 'bad materials' out there, and we only have to look to know that they are bad. One contact can be enough (if in the nineteenth century the favourite metaphor for this was disease, today it is drug addiction), so the dangers when we are 'bombarded' with 'floods' of these things are incalculable. So how do we tell 'bad' materials from 'good'? Let us take Newson's examples head-on.
   Child's Play III is not a very good film. But the point is: what *kind* of film is it, and

what could reasonably be claimed about it? Not many people will have seen it, and therefore it is interesting to ask readers to fill out a mental image of what it must be like. After all, the film was widely claimed to be the possible trigger for the murder of James Bulger. What sort of a film is it in your imagination?

The most remarkable thing about this film is that a great majority of the film is devoted to a desperate attempt to save a small child from being killed. It is a horror film, no question. In part it is scary, sometimes a bit bloody. But judge for yourselves whether it fits your mental image. Here is a synopsis:

The story is the third in a series in which teenager Andy Barclay is forced to do battle with a 'Good Guy' doll which has been possessed by the mind of a former murderer. The title sequence shows a doll forming out of plastic contaminated with the blood of the murderer: evil is returning. The opening scene shows the chairman of the doll-making company resolving to resume production of the doll. He is a cynical man – 'Let's face it,' he sneers at one of his executives, 'what are children, after all, but consumer trainees?' For that he will get his comeuppance. That night, he takes home the first doll off the production line, and it comes alive and kills him gleefully. 'Don't fuck with the Chuck,' it rudely pronounces.

The remainder of the film takes place around a military academy for the young, where Andy Barclay has been sent to help him 'grow up'. From the start, he is viewed as a troublemaker, and is victimised, especially by a sadistic Sergeant who cuts all their hair, and by the young Lieutenant Shelton. On his first parade, he is saved from the worst of the bullying by the intervention of da Silva, a tough-cookie girl who doesn't mind standing up to Shelton. Barclay and da Silva are attracted to each other. Soon Andy sees on television an advertisement for the newly released Good Guy dolls, and knows trouble is brewing. A parcel delivered to him is opened by Tyler, a tiny wide-eyed black boy who only loves to play. In it is Chucky.

We see Chucky attempting to take over Tyler's body. Interrupted, it reverts to its 'lifeless' form, and is thrown out as rubbish. Chucky uses a ruse to escape from the garbage truck, killing the driver in the process. On the parade ground, Andy guesses what has happened.

There follows a series of episodes as Andy discovers that Chucky is targeting little Tyler; he again and again tries to capture Chucky to destroy him, only to find himself misunderstood and humiliated by Shelton, who sees him just as a wimp. Chucky's level of mayhem rises. Finally, the Colonel dies of a heart attack when confronted with a talking doll.

The next day is a War Game, and it will go ahead in honour of the dead Colonel. Tyler is separated from Andy and da Silva. Andy absconds to try to save him. Chucky meantime has substituted live bullets in one team's guns, and lures Shelton to his death. In the final showdown at a nearby fairground, da Silva is wounded and has to leave Andy Barclay to stop Chucky alone. As Chucky once more begins the chant to transfer his soul into Tyler, an injured Andy manages to throw him off the top of a 'ghost mountain'. Chucky falls into the blades of a wind machine, and is destroyed. The film ends with Andy saying goodbye to da Silva as she is taken away by ambulance – and he is once more taken into care . . .

Even this short synopsis demonstrates that *Child's Play III* is the *exact opposite* of everything that was said about it; this is in fact one of a thousand films which show a sort of rite of passage of adolescence: a misunderstood, essentially gentle boy gains courage and a girlfriend through the need to confront evil. Misunderstood and mal-treated by the adults around him, he does the right thing, no matter what the cost to himself. This is a very *moral* tale.

Of course that is not all there is to say about this film. Any horror film has to *show* evil to make sense of the hero's struggle. And Chucky is a curious form of evil: the idea of an animated doll, a cuddlesome thing that might turn on you, is 'risky'. But, then, a horror film can only work because it deals in notions which are potentially frightening. Interestingly, the film also displays a most cynical view of big business, and its attitude to children – and it would not be the first time that a political strain in a film has led to attacks on it in the name of 'protecting children'.

If Newson and so many others can be so wrong about *Child's Play III*, let us check the other film she obliquely references as especially dangerous because of that issue of 'identification':

> A parallel in a recently released film is where we witness in lit silhouette the multiple rape of a woman by a queue of men, and hear her agonised screams, all in the context of an intent to punish her.

What film is this? It proved very hard to track down. Even Professor Newson herself, when I asked her, was not sure of its title – an odd situation for someone quoting it in a published report. Finally, I identified the film as Peter Greenaway's *The Baby of Macon*. Once again, what kind of film was this, and can it carry the reading that Newson makes of it?

The Baby of Macon is, like all Greenaway films, a highly stylised art-house product. Every scene is filmed at slow speed, lit and set like classical oil-paintings. The film deals with social power, symbolised in the conflicts between the Church and a young woman whose baby brother has miraculous powers. Who will control his powers? But there is also a play-within-the-film; we see that the story of the Church, the woman and the baby is being acted to an audience; and below stage we see the actors also living out various conflicts. The scene to which Newson refers comes right at the end of the film. Her account of it is seriously misleading. We do not see the woman being raped in lit silhouette in the way she suggests. An enclosed four-poster bed is just about visible. It is hidden from us by the Church representatives who, having won control over the Baby, calmly ignore the woman's screams while discussing their new power over women. Even this meaning is complicated by the fact that at this point the gap between the story and the actors is breaking down. The 'rape' is meant to be sim-ulated but the male actors have decided to take revenge for being up-staged by the young actress. They will *really* rape her, but no one will notice, because they will assume her screams are simulated. In no sense at all will this narrative, and this scene within it, support a claim of 'getting the viewers to identify with the attackers'. The whole film is about male domination, and the forms through which it is enforced. It is precisely these ambiguities, and the deliberate breakdown of the narrative, which makes this scene so meaningful, and so powerful.

The reason for spending so much time on this is because it throws into relief the question: *how can we know what the 'message' of a film is?* There is now a body of research into film and all other kinds of media, into how they work to produce mean-ings, and how audiences receive and make sense of those meanings. This is a developing field, and a great deal is still being explored and debated. But two things are clear: neither Elizabeth Newson or any of her co-signatories has any expertise in this field. And the possible 'effects' they imputed to these films, and their audiences, contradict everything practitioners in the field do know – but which nobody wanted to hear.

All this inevitably provokes the question: how do people like Newson get away with making unsubstantiated and insupportable claims about films, on the basis of unblemished ignorance of all such matters? Imagine the situation where a bunch of amateurs published claims about the way 'chemicals' affect the body, claiming that sulphur affects our 'humours', and that if we ingest it in particular ways it is guaranteed to make us hum . . . imagine the scorn that would fall on them. The scorn which is regularly visited on those who do have expertise in these matters looks remarkably like that visited on those who questioned the claims of the witch-finders.

What can we say more generally about the kinds of media material that get labelled in this way? In fact there is a growing body of research which suggests that the labelling of media materials as 'bad influences' is not the innocent process it proffers itself as being. Histories of censorship, for instance, show how repeatedly the censors act in self-serving ways to limit or bar materials which might embarrass them. Yet, in attacking them, they always do so by calling them 'harmful'. Examples are legion. In the nineteenth century, critics of the 'penny dreadfuls' reserved their worst hatred for the 1866 publication *Wild Boys of London*. Yet, when examined (something made difficult by the fact that the police were persuaded to break into the printers, and smash the printing plates), it turns out not to be the catalogue of gang warfare and delinquency that the title might seem to suggest. In fact, the story connects closely with a deep-running sore of the time: the problem of orphans and the urban poor.[1] Annette Kuhn has shown how censorship of early films was predicted on the concerns of Empire, and in particular on the imposition of a definition of proper female sexuality (Kuhn, 1988). Between the two world wars, film censorship was used to prevent embarrassment in foreign affairs (Mathews, 1994).

My own work on the 1950s horror comics campaign showed how particular comics were targeted which dealt with strongly political issues, including anti-McCarthyite stories (Barker, 1984a). In the 1970s, the film *Scum* was barred from television for a long time; in fact it is a powerful critique of the brutality of the Borstal system, and the way it can make its inmates more desperate and violent. And it raised embarrassing questions at a time when the Conservative Party was pressing the introduction of 'short, sharp shock' schemes for young offenders. Again it was banned on grounds of being 'violent'. In fact it seems that the word 'violence' frequently acts as a code-word for objections made to materials on quite other, often political, grounds. We need to bear this in mind when we come to the final part of this chapter. For it raises acutely the question: Is it meaningful to research into such a question at all?

How can we understand 'media influence'?

In Elizabeth Newson's report, there is one classic sentence which has been heard so often, if in different words, it has become like a mantra. 'The principle that what is experienced vicariously will have *some* effect on *some* people is an established one, and is the reason why industry finds it worth while to spend millions of pounds on advertising.' What does this amount to? One very typical problem faced by those who reject the rhetorics of the anti-media campaigners is the challenge: then, are you saying that television has no influence at all? If that was the case, then advertisers wouldn't be willing to spend all that money, would they? Isn't that sufficient proof that TV must have *some* effect? Given that, what is the problem with admitting that TV violence might cause people to go out and commit real-life violence?

This is, I suspect, the most commonly repeated move by anti-violence campaigners. It was certainly there in 1984 at the height of the campaign against video nasties. The evangelical Christian Action, Research and Education (the equivalent then of David Alton's Movement for Christian Democracy) urged:

> Organisations spend around £1.6bn in advertising each year. They must believe that by seeing an advertisement on TV, on a poster etc, the consumer will be persuaded to purchase a product, make a donation or change their behaviour. The Government itself has used advertising to portray messages about safe sex, drinking and driving, and firework safety in an attempt to change the behaviour of the public. All the political parties make broadcasts before elections to persuade voters to cast their vote in a particular direction. There must be instances when each of us can recall seeing a product that had been recently advertised and deciding just to 'try it out'. It would be trite to stretch the argument and say that after seeing one episode of violence, an individual is going to commit a crime. But the point is illustrated: what we see *does* affect our behaviour.
>
> (CARE, 1994, p. 29)

This argument is evidently felt to be a clincher. Yet even a cursory examination shows it to be palpable nonsense. The simple error the campaigners make is to assume that, if TV, or film, or whatever, has *some* influence, it must have the kinds of influence they want to ascribe to it. It would be a very stupid person who denied that television had any influence at all – but only if 'influences' includes all the following and many more (add your own examples to our list):

1   interesting us in things we didn't previously know about;
2   making us stay up too late;
3   giving us a sense of our place in the world, through its ability to take us to events as they are happening;
4   making us smile, laugh, be sad, cry, feel nostalgic, patriotic, disturbed, uneasy, want to join in, bored, disenchanted with our own lives;
5   making us think about things, shaking our assumptions, making us complacent, talking to us in languages we feel comfortable or uncomfortable with;
6   and so on.

All these are effects, no question. They are a very small part of any list of possible effects. So, why so firmly dismiss the analogy with advertising, and challenge the idea that television violence might cause violence? There are a number of strands to this argument which must be disentangled in turn.

Consider the following (real) cases:

1   A man takes a gun and shoots his entire family after watching the news. Arrested
     and tried, he explains his actions on the basis that the world news was so bad
     there seemed no point anyone going on living.
2   A paedophile is convicted of molesting a young boy. In his house, the police
     reported, he has a collection of newspaper cuttings about court cases involving
     paedophiles.
3   An elderly woman commits suicide after watching *Schindler's List*. In a note, she
     expresses an overwhelming sense of guilt at being a survivor of the Nazi camps.

What is the difference between cases like these and putative cases of television causing violence? In the first case, any explanation would have to refer to the man's mental
state (he must have been already depressed, perhaps there were already signs of disturbance or family breakdown, etc.). So it could not be put down simply to the
'effects of the news'; the man's reaction was non-normal, unpredictable, and therefore
could not provide us with grounds for judging the suitability or rightness of the news.
It was he who was aberrant, not the news.

The second case poses an interesting problem. We are well used to hearing of
claims that sexual attackers possessed pornographic materials – with the implication
that this provides a causal factor. But we know that the press material this man collected will have been condemnatory of paedophilia. Yet somehow the man 'used'
them. What judgement could be based on this – that we should ban even the word
'paedophilia', lest it stimulate the desires?

In the third case, a woman is 'induced' to suicide by a film. Not by the violence of
the film (of which there is some, and very disturbing it is, too), but by a sense of deep
shame when she relates the film to her own and other Jewish people's lives. Yet curiously my suspicion is that, however sad her death, the judgement would be that this
only proves the *worth* and *quality* of the film.

This is not what the anti-media campaigners mean. In each of these cases, they will
argue that while TV or press or films were factors they can't be blamed as causes. But
when they make claims about TV or films causing violence they change the way the
explanation works.

There is something very strange about the way they argue this, as I have argued
before (see Barker, 1984b). Their claim is that the materials they judge to be 'harmful' can only influence us by trying to make us be the same as them. So horrible
things will make us horrible – not horrified. Terrifying things will make us terrifying – not terrified. To see something aggressive makes us feel aggressive – not
aggressed against. And the nastier it is, the nastier it is likely to make us. This idea is
so odd, it is hard to know where to begin, in challenging it. Let me start, then, by
saying that if it were true, then their own whole analogy with advertising breaks
down, and collapses even more completely if we add in that notion of 'vicarious
viewing'. This is why.

Mass advertising began in the 1880s, with the arrival of brand names. Research to
make that advertising more effective developed in the 1920s. Since then, the overwhelming tendency of advertisers has been towards more and more targeted
advertising, precisely because they know that advertising that depends on 'vicarious
contact' – that is, on our happening to see an advertisement which isn't really aimed
at us, which we haven't selected for any reason – is singularly ineffective.

Advertisers have also learnt another principle, and that concerns the difficulties of negative advertising. From the 1950s at least, advertisers have understood that products associated with negative images are unlikely to be acceptable. The most notorious example of this is the cigarette campaign with the slogan 'You're never alone with a Strand'. The assumption that you might be alone but for the cigarette did no good for its sales, and it bombed. The kinds of film which the campaigners attack are, on this principle, the *least likely to be influential*, since they depend on the construction of feelings of negativity: fear, anxiety, shock, horror, and so on.

Advertisers work from the premise that vicarious contact with their materials is the least likely to be effective, and that it if has any 'effect' at all it is likely to be the opposite of what they are seeking. The only advertising materials which use negative images are *educational* materials, which are *intended to make us think critically* – anti-drink/driving campaigns, for instance. So everything we know about the way advertisements work conflicts with the notion that filmic violence is likely to promote audience copying.

Is there a consistent and overwhelming body of evidence in favour of the proposition that 'media violence causes violence'?

It is now common to hear that 'more than 70% of published studies support this conclusion'. A current publisher's catalogue asserts without qualification that

> the consensus among the psychologists, media theorists, sociologists and educators presented is that there is a direct, causal link between the excessive viewing of violence, or the playing of video games, to becoming stimulated to acting violently or to becoming desensitised to violence.

It is certainly true that endless experiments have been conducted. Since the 1930s, in particular in America, vast sums of money have been obtained to test this relationship. But curiously, and with hardly an exception, researchers in this field have hardly ever set up what are called 'critical experiments'.

In any branch of science, not all experiments are of equal worth – and not just because some are better designed or conducted than others. An experiment is useful to the extent that it can add to our knowledge, not just by confirming what we think we know, but by clarifying aspects which are not yet clear. As knowledge accumulates, it becomes necessary to develop theories and models that can make sense of what we think we know. Without theories, information is dry and uninformative. But theories always and of necessity go wider and involve more than the evidence on which they claim to be based. Theories involve generalisations, they assert patterns and causal links, they even perhaps allow predictions. So, a critical test is one which focuses on some particular feature of a theory or model, and asks: are we sure that it really works like that? Designing experiments that really do this is especially hard – because very often theories point towards hidden, non-obvious processes.

Take, then, a simple example. Many claims about media influence talk about viewers 'identifying' with a film character. This is a *theoretical* claim. It amounts to arguing that a viewer may become persuaded by a film *because* (causal linkage) they have identified with a character. There is nothing wrong with claims of this kind. Any theory has to make them. And the theory of media/violence connections frequently depends on it, because it offers an explanation as to how and why people are linked to elements in a film.[2] But note: 'identification' is not something you can *see* happening. An observer can't look at someone, and say: 'Look, s/he is identifying!' Still less can an observer look at four people, and see one as more prone to identification than the others.

So what can researchers do in this situation? They have to develop *models* of what might be going on in 'identification', and then design *tests* to see if things happen according to the predictions of the model. For example, they will have to have measures for who is an 'identifier' (making as sure as possible that there is something there to be measured, of course). Suppose they do this, how will they know if they have done it well? The trouble is, since no one can *see* an identifier – it is not an observable act – there are only limited ways to be sure they have really located the process. Researchers can use *consistency* – using several tests that ought, if they are right, to come up with the same results. They can use *repeatability* – doing the same test several times, while varying supposedly irrelevant conditions. They can test for *critical links* – that is, taking two measures, and seeing if the predicted link is as expected between them. What good science does, then, is to carry out experiments that can help guard against 'experimental artefacts', that is, results that only mean something because of the way the experiment was set up.

In the field of media effects work researchers are extraordinarily careless about such basic requirements of theory as these. In another work, for example, I re-examined the basic research which has been seen as providing the justification for the concept of 'identification'. It had two problems. First, the research was virtually non-existent – concepts such as 'identification' have been so much taken for granted that it has not been felt necessary to test them directly at all. Instead, research has been carried out that *assumes* its presence. Second, the research was grossly self-contradictory – but no one had bothered to check. On only two occasions had research been conducted to see whether the claimed process of 'identification' could be discovered at all – and on both occasions the answer was negative (see Barker, 1989, Chapter 6).[3]

This carelessness about critical tests then links with the other unexplored problem, which we might call the 'problem of accumulated results'. Essentially, it has been assumed that if two studies of media-effects both come up positive, then they can be added together – eventually to generate that '70% of all studies'. Guy Cumberbatch addresses this issue (Cumberbatch and Howitt, 1989). What he shows is that published studies contradict each other on a whole range of dimensions: on which groups are most 'vulnerable'; on the kinds of stimulus that might trigger responses; on whether films make us prone to copy directly, or just generally raise aggressive levels; and on the contexts most conducive to effects. To take just two of his examples: he shows that William Belson's much-cited work in fact conflicts with many others:

> Belson . . . finds no evidence, that high exposure to television reduces boys' respect for authority, or that it desensitises them, makes them less considerate for others, produces sleep disturbances or (in an earlier study . . .) is associated with stealing. Belson's findings contradict many previous studies.
>
> (p. 48)

Cumberbatch also draws attention to the awkward fact that research has shown that 'aggression can be raised by *humorous* films as much as by aggressive ones' (p. 38). In other words, the studies simply don't support each other. Indeed, to the extent that some of them might be right, then others have to be counted as wrong. It is once again only a grim determination not to ask difficult questions that allows claims like this to go unchallenged.

This tendency can be illustrated in another way. Earlier, I used three quotations drawn from a wide historical period. It is commonplace to researchers that such objections to 'dangerous media' go back a very long way. In the nineteenth century, when such objections first reached full flood, the charges were brought against 'penny dreadfuls' (in Britain) and dime novels (in America). By the turn of the century, music hall (Britain) and vaudeville (America) were the objects of dismay. Then cinema. Then radio. Then comic books. Then television, video, video games, computers, and most recently the Internet. The litany of threats is remarkable for the way each new medium was cited as marking a virtual collapse of civilization.

But not only did no one think to check or research these claims, or wonder at their extravagance when they could pass so regularly into history; but in fact the claims are mutually contradictory. When 'penny dreadfuls' were attacked, a major part of their danger was the fact that they were found 'on the streets' – they were the street literature of their time. That being so, you might have thought that the security of cinema would make it less dangerous. Not so – here, it was the 'moral dangers of darkness' which appalled critics. But, then, television, which is mostly viewed with the light on, must be less dangerous. Not so – now a new danger emerged, the 'invasion of the home' (though of course that would imply the relative safety of cinema, wouldn't it?).

But cinema and film did, so it was said, have the shared risk that they scroll past you uncontrollably. But, then, in that case, video should have been seen as an improvement because viewers can stop and start it. Ah, not so – now the dangers were that viewers would obsessively rerun their 'favourite bad bits'. But, in that case, film and TV must have been safer than we first thought. Not so, because . . . and so the game goes on. These claims cannot all be true. If one medium is damned, the others must be excused. But the most important point is that all these are made as *ad hoc* assertions, with no attempt to prove or disprove them. Simply, no one has bothered to ask, because it is all so obvious – the witches are out there, aren't they?

What exactly is 'media violence'?

Everything I have been arguing comes together at this point. The expression 'media violence' has to be one of the most commonly repeated, and one of the most ill-informed, of all time. It is supposed to encompass everything from cartoons (ten-ton blocks dropped on Tom's head by Jerry, Wily Coyote plummeting down yet another mile-deep canyon); children's action adventure films (the dinosaurs of *Jurassic Park* alongside playground scuffles in *Grange Hill* and last-reel shootouts in westerns); news footage from Rwanda and Bosnia; documentary footage showing the police attacking Rodney King in Los Angeles; horror films from Hammer to cult gore movies; the range from Clint Eastwood as the voiceless hard man of *Dirty Harry* to Arnie as the violent humorist of almost any of his films, etc, etc.

And therein lies the point: no single ground has ever been given for us to suppose that such a list has any single property in common other than that certain critics don't

like them. It is a useless conflation of wholly different things. Yet somehow that conflation endlessly continues. And whenever the phrase 'media violence' is used it
conjures up one image above all else: an image of motiveless mayhem, to which words
such as 'gratuitous' easily attach themselves. A trip to America intervened in the draft-
ing of this chapter. While I was there, President Clinton put his signature to a Bill
requiring TV manufacturers to fit 'V-Chips' on TVs; and with immaculate timing a
'new report' on TV violence simultaneously came out. Among its findings was the
assertion that over 73 per cent of violence in programmes went unpunished. That
sounds worrying. It is the kind of datum that seems to require a concerned response –
until we note, as an acid commentary in an American magazine did, that this figure
related to punishment of the perpetrator *in that scene*. It went on:

> But to do the opposite, a violent program would have to create a scene in
> which, let's say, a man is shot, a cop sees it happen, and the criminal is
> arrested on the spot. US television chooses to do things the old fashioned
> way. There's something called a *plot*.
>
> (*Electronic Media*, 1996)

This is not a point of detail. The moment 'plot' is allowed in, the whole category
'media violence' dissolves into meaninglessness. And that is precisely what needs to be
asserted. *There simply is no category 'media violence' which can be researched; that is why over
seventy years of research into this supposed topic have produced nothing worthy of note.* 'Media
violence' is the witchcraft of our society. This is such an important point, yet its significance seems constantly to get lost. Imagine that medical researchers were to
propose a classification of drugs according to whether they taste nice or nasty. Not
only that, but they add that they are going to research – and be funded for more than
seventy years for the purpose – into the claim that nasty-tasting drugs do you harm,
whereas nice-tasting drugs do you good. What would we say? Quite apart from
folksy responses, the scientific response would have to be that there is no reason to
suppose that 'nasty-tasting drugs' can be a research object at all. Not everyone finds
the same drugs unpleasant. Taste may be a wholly incidental aspect of a chemical's
behaviour. Finding them unpleasant may equally be a function of being told that you
have to 'take your medicine'. And so on. In other words, *it wouldn't be worth doing the
research at all, because there is nothing there worth researching.*

Hard though it may be to accept that an entire research tradition is based on thin
air, this is my case. I challenge the research tradition to show a single reason why we
should treat cartoons, news, horror, documentaries, police series, westerns, violent
pornography and action adventure as having anything in common. Let it be noted: for
any one of these that is withdrawn from the list, that '70 per cent of all studies' must
be instantly reduced, because some of the studies have (usually without telling us) used
just such a mix of genres as their research-objects. And every single 'count' of 'acts of
violence' will have to be redone, to eliminate those no longer included.

Pending a reply to my challenge, I end this chapter by proposing a different
research agenda.

1   Many opinion polls show wide public concern for limiting 'violence' on televi-
     sion and film. Yet the same people, when asked, have much greater trouble
     naming the films and programmes which they think have too much. My proposal

is that we need to research *how different segments of the public develop their category 'media violence', and what they mean by it.*

2   In a study of children's responses to violence, a Dutch researcher found that children simply do not think of cartoons as violent at all – though they agree generally with adults' concerns and estimates about violence (see Morrison, 1993, for details; see also Buckingham, 1996). While media researchers tend to *count* 'incidents of violence', it seems that the children follow the *story-lines*, and are always aware of the *kind* of film or programme they are watching. My proposal is that we need to study *how children develop a 'sense of story', and how does this relate to their liking for the kinds of material that the critics worry about?*

3   The languages employed to describe how much people use the media are loaded: from 'heavy viewing' to 'excessive'. These judgemental terms distort research. There has recently been a body of research on 'fans', including fans of supposedly problematic materials such as horror (see Kermode, 19977; also Penley, 1992; Bacon-Smith, 1992; Sconce, 1996; and Sanjek, 1990). My proposal is that we need to study *how viewers who choose to commit themselves to a medium, genre or series differ in their understandings of them from those whose relationship with them is more casual.*

4   We need to deepen our investigation of the moral campaigners, and their relationship to the research community, in a number of ways. The first is the problem of language. One of the disturbing aspects of the anti-media campaigners' way of arguing is their tendency to hyperbole and emotional talk. This infects the researchers who start to talk of people being 'bombarded' with images of violence, of an 'incessant menu' of 'particularly damaging' and 'gratuitous' materials. Even when no damaging consequences are being implied, this kind of language is still used. So reports of the girl who had a fascination (no doubt long since ended) with *Silence of the Lambs* always talked of her as 'addicted' to the film – whereas a man who went to see *The Flintstones* forty times was called a 'fan'. Quite different images of the people and their reasons for seeing the film are conjured up by the two expressions. *We need to research the invasion of 'effects research' by these languages.*

5   Then there is the talisman against which to test everything: the protection of children. This is the cornerstone of common sense thinking on this topic. Replying to a letter from me, Elizabeth Newson said this:

> I have throughout been careful to stick to my last, which is the protection of children, despite the fact that many correspondents have made the point that adults too might be vulnerable to such images, however presented or wrapped up . . . I hope that any arguments you wish to present will acknowledge that my case is about children, not adults.

Why does Professor Newson think this makes the argument stronger? Because 'children' in our culture are seen as specially in need of care and protection. Now that really is a hard one to get past – but we have to try. We have to get past it because the argument is making quite illegitimate use of our feelings for our individual children to make a case for something quite different, called 'childhood'. *We need to research the way the lives of actual children have been affected by the predominant image of themselves as incompetent.*

6   What can we positively say about the media preference of those who become involved in delinquency and crime? As yet, not much. But the little we do know contradicts all the claims of the campaigners. The ignored study by the Policy Studies Institute (Hagell and Newburn 1994) may have been limited, but it provided at least a genuine starting point. It was ignored because its findings didn't 'fit'. For they found that the only slightly significant differences between delinquent and non-delinquent boys were in the former's liking for *The Bill* and for the *Sun*! Actually, it wouldn't be difficult to offer an explanation of these preferences: *The Bill* as a police procedural, helping them to prepare for what would happen if they get caught; and the *Sun* for its melodramatic view of the world. The trouble is that this *kind* of explanation is not at all what the campaigners want to hear. It treats the delinquents as normal people, using the media in exactly the same complicated ways as everyone else. *We need further research not only into what media preferences delinquents have, but also into how they understand and use them.*

7   Finally, there are the anti-media campaigns themselves. From much that is shown in this book, it should be clear that these campaigns are not the innocent things they manage to appear. At best, they are blind and ignorant forms of protectiveness, at worst disguised political campaigns. *We need urgently to research and gather together a historical picture of such campaigns.*

I am not meaning to imply that none of this research has been done – it has, in fragments. But there is now an urgent need to counter-attack; and our part as critical researchers and academics is to pull together what is known, and to press this agenda that will cut away the ground from under them. They hide their nonsense in a fog of their making, but also of our unquestioning.

Notes

1   *Wild Boys of London* was published in complete form in 1866, and began republication in 1873, until the police action prevented its completion. At the time of suppression, two parallel stories were running. One concerned a group of boys who had stowed away to the West Indies, where they were captured by pirates. But this was no simple adventure, for the pirates were all escaped slaves roaming the Caribbean looking for slaving ships, in order to free the slaves and kill their captains. The boys debate the morality of such killings, and conclude that they are indeed justified. The second story-line involved the arrival in London of a group of foreigners to pursue their political cause: Fenians. There can be little doubt that the act of suppression was a political act. But what is just as important is that it was passed off as an act of morality, for the 'protection of children'.

2   It is of course not the only one. Another commonly claimed candidate is 'desensitisation'. Lack of space prevents me dealing with all such claims equally, but it must be noted that the two are not compatible with each other. If media influence worked via 'identification', then we would have to concern ourselves with different kinds of film, and different kinds of audience, than if it worked via 'desensitisation'. They are not simply alternatives we can shift between, or add together.

3   This fact may be uncomfortable to many working within the media studies field itself, where also that assumption has largely gone unquestioned.

References

Bacon-Smith, Camille (1992) *Enterprising Women: Television Fandom and the Creation of Popular Myth*, Philadelphia, PA: University of Pennsylvania Press.

Barker, Martin (1984a) *A Haunt of Fears: The Strange History of the British Horror Comics Campaign*, London: Pluto Press.

Barker, Martin (1984b) *The Video Nasties: Freedom and Censorship in the Arts*, London: Pluto Press.

Barker, Martin (1989) *Comics: Ideology, Power and the Critics*, Manchester: Manchester University Press.

Buckingham, David (1996) *Moving Image: Children's Emotional Responses to Television*, Manchester: Manchester University Press.

CARE (Christian Action, Research and Education) (1994) *Evidence to the Home Affairs Committee*, London: HMSO, pp. 27–33.

Cumberbatch, Guy and Howitt, Dennis (1989) *A Measure of Uncertainty: the Effects of the Media*, London: John Libbey.

Electronic Media (1996) 'Getting moving on violence', 12 February, p. 12.

Hagell, A. and Newburn, T. (1994) *Young Offenders and the Media: Viewing Habits and Preferences*, London: Policy Studies Institute

Kermode, M. (1997) 'I was a teenage horror fan: or: how I learned to stop worrying and love Linda Blair', in M. Barker and J. Petley (eds) *Ill Effects*, London: Routledge, Chapter 4.

Kuhn, Annette (1988) *Cinema, Censorship and Sexuality, 1909–1925*, London: Routledge.

Mathews, Tom Dewe (1994) *Censored: The Story of Film Censorship in Britain*, London: Chatto & Windus.

Morrison, David (1993) 'The idea of violence', in A. Millwood-Hargrave (ed.), *Violence in Factual Television*, London: John Libbey, pp. 124–8.

Newson, Elizabeth (1994) *Video Violence and the Protection of Children*, Report of the Home Affairs Committee, London: HMSO, 29 June, pp. 45–9.

Penley, Constance (1992) 'Feminism, psychoanalysis, and the study of popular culture', in L. Grossberg *et al* (eds), *Cultural Studies*, London: Routledge, pp. 479–500.

Sanjek, David (1990) 'Fans notes: the horror film magazine', *Literature/Film Quarterly*, 18: 3, pp. 150–60.

Sconce, Jeffrey (1996) 'Trashing the academy: taste, excess and the emerging politics of cinematic style', *Screen*, 36: 4, pp. 371–93.

PART THREE

Reading as resistance

The active audience

Introduction

T HE EXTRACTS HERE TAKE a very different view to most of those in the preceding Part. Rather than analysing primary texts and assuming a predictable, often negative 'effect' on the intended audience, these writers propose a two-way relationship between audiences and texts whereby readers can resist, engage with and create their own meanings from the culture they receive from 'above'.

John Fiske in Chapter 11 makes an explicit contrast between his own approach and that typified by Adorno – the notion of 'a mass culture imposed upon a powerless and passive people by a culture industry whose interests were in direct opposition to theirs' (p. 115). In place of this 'quiescent, passive mass' of consumers, Fiske, like Michel de Certeau, constructs audiences as fighters in a semiotic guerrilla war, snatching interpretations and creating a space for themselves.

In turn, where Hoggart bemoaned the passing of an authentic 'folk' culture made by the people, de Certeau in Chapter 10 advises against such nostalgia. 'The operational models of popular culture cannot be confined to the past, the countryside or primitive peoples. They exist in the heart of the stronghold of the contemporary economy' (p. 105). The practice that produced Hoggart's favourite pub songs has shifted towards 'making do' with the consumer texts audiences are given; the culture may no longer be home-made, but the meanings are.

David Morley's *The Nationwide Audience* in Chapter 9 emerged from the ethnographic research tradition at the Birmingham Centre for Contemporary Cultural Studies. Morley's work here is based on a theoretical framework proposed by Stuart Hall, who had served as Chair of the 'Birmingham School' while Morley was a postgraduate student. Hall's theory of texts as possessing 'encoded' meanings, which are then 'decoded' by the audience, is offered as a progression from the 'uses and gratifications' model (see Part One), which Morley sees as too imprecise. He argues, after Hall, that texts remain 'structured in dominance' by the preferred reading – that is, the meaning which the producers encoded and which they want the audience to receive.

In this case, British viewers of the TV news magazine *Nationwide* either accept the preferred reading, propose their own 'oppositional' reading or negotiate between the two, accepting some of the programme's encoded values and resisting others. In principle a text may be read in any number of different ways, but in practice the audience's group affiliations and social preconceptions – factors such as age, ethnicity, social class, political convictions – will limit and shape the potential interpretations. Morley's concept of audience response, then, is far broader than Adorno, Hoggart or Wertham's bleak picture of a docile crowd lapping up media messages – one of his groups here rejects and mocks much of the programme's content – but it remains deliberately cautious.

John Fiske, by contrast, has occasionally been accused of over-optimism in his celebration of audiences' powers of 'resistance'. Drawing on de Certeau's notions of 'making do' within the frameworks of power, Fiske begins this extract by discussing the small-scale rebellion inherent in ripping a pair of bought jeans and transforming them into the wearer's own, individual creation, then extends the image into a broader, metaphorical notion of 'ripping' as cultural appropriation. His example of Judy Garland as a mainstream icon who was 'torn' and reworked for the gay community is particularly relevant with regard to Gregory Woods' piece below.

Of course, the ripping of jeans or the queering of a Judy Garland poster is, on the face of it, a 'tiny gesture', a micropolitical rebellion rather than a challenge to the structures of power. As Fiske admits, the jeans industry quickly incorporates such acts of resistance by producing its own pre-ripped jeans and drawing localised creativity back into the system; but consumers in turn find new ways of constructing their own, genuinely popular culture from the texts they are given. This is the 'guerrilla warfare' described by de Certeau: the ways in which audiences use their own wiles and cunning within an imposed framework. A North African in a low-income Parisian housing development finds 'ways of using the constraining order of the place', and indeed of the French language (p. 108). An office worker practises '*la perruque*' by working on her own website during work hours. A gay fan of a science fiction TV show 'poaches' stories of homoerotic love between the two main characters from the heterosexual narrative (see Henry Jenkins, Chapter 17, Part Five). All these practices are 'tactics' for working with the dominant culture.

In his use of the word 'bricolage', de Certeau recalls the work of Richard Dyer, who applied the term specifically to gay interpretations of mainstream, heterosexual cinema. Gregory Woods, in Chapter 12, takes up this method of piecing together 'queer' meanings from straight culture, writing stories in the gaps and filling in textual spaces. Like Fiske, he chooses to study the everyday examples of fashion imagery, and again we see how the meaning of blue jeans can be anchored in a 'preferred' meaning or be 'ripped' by an active reader, to be read against the grain. Woods wryly draws out the stolidly heterosexual, even homophobic message encoded in clothes catalogues, revealing that even the images we would pass over as 'common sense' examples are loaded with the dominant ideology. A shirtless man in jeans is fixed as aggressively masculine by the caption stressing their 'hard, brash' connotation; a mug featuring the Chippendales male strippers is labelled 'Ladies this is for you!' in a clumsy attempt to deter gay readings. Shirts for men are available in every colour but pink, while potentially homoerotic images of men in dressing gowns are made 'safe' with the addition of an admiring, and otherwise irrelevant, female spectator

We should note, though, that this careful policing of the text to enforce its dominant, heterosexual meaning does not prevent readers like Woods from producing their own, gleefully playful readings of the 'delicious' models in 'little white briefs'; despite the even heavier taboos around young gay sexuality, Woods is able to read a queer relationship into a picture of two boys in Spider-Man and Fido Dido pyjamas. However, the question remains with all these examples: is it enough to celebrate small-scale resistance and minor acts of rebellion within an imposed structure? The gay consumer still finds himself unrepresented in the Littlewoods catalogue, the North African still lives in low-income French housing, the teenage rebel still buys Levis and the trade unionist still watches *Nationwide* for want of a better news magazine. These practices of negotiating and even opposing are laudable, but they remain limited in their cultural power.

Further reading

Dyer, R. (1977) *Gays and Film*, London: BFI.
Fiske, J. (1987) *Television Culture*, London: Routledge.
Fiske, J. (1989) *Reading the Popular*, London: Routledge.
Hebdige, D. (1979) *Subculture: The Meaning of Style*, London: Methuen.
McRobbie, A. (2000) *Feminism and Youth Culture*, London: Routledge.
Tulloch, J. (2000) *Watching the TV Audience*, London: Arnold.
Willis, P. (1977) *Learning to Labour*, Farnborough: Saxon House.

Chapter 9

David Morley

THE *NATIONWIDE* AUDIENCE

Phase 2: *Nationwide* 'Budget Special' 29/3/77

P HASE 2 OF THE PROJECT, using a *Nationwide* programme on the March 1977 Budget, was designed to focus more clearly on the decoding of political and economic issues, as opposed to the coverage of 'individuals' and 'social oddities' represented in the programme used in Phase 1. In particular this sample of groups was chosen so as to highlight the effects of involvement in the discourse and practice of trade unionism on decoding patterns. The groups chosen were managers, university and F.E. students, full-time TU officials and one group of shop stewards.

The programme was introduced by Frank Bough, as follows:

> And at 6.20 what this 'some now, some later' Budget will mean to you. Halma Hudson and I will be looking at how three typical families across the country will be affected. We'll be asking . . . union leader Hugh Scanlon and industrialist Ian Fraser about what the Budget will mean for the economy.

Three main sections from the programme were selected for showing to the various groups:

1) A set of vox pop interviews with afternoon shoppers in Birmingham city centre on the question of the tax system and whether:
   a) taxes are too high, and
   b) the tax system is too complicated.

These interviews are then followed by an extensive interview with Mr Eric Worthington, who is introduced as 'a taxation expert'. Mr Worthington moves from technical discussion of taxation to expound a philosophy of individualism and free enterprise and the need for tax cuts to increase 'incentives', combined with the need for cuts in public expenditure. It is notable here that the interviewer hardly interrupts the speaker at all; the interview functions as a long monologue in which the speaker is prompted rather than questioned.

2)   The main section of the programme, in which *Nationwide* enquires into:

> how this Budget will affect three typical families . . . and generally speaking most people in Britain fall into one of the three broad categories represented by our families here . . . the fortunate 10% of managers and professionals who earn over £7,000 p.a., the less fortunate bottom fifth of the population who are the low paid, earning less than £2,250 p.a., and the vast majority somewhere in the middle, earning around £3,500 p.a.

The three families are then dealt with one at a time. Each 'case study' begins with a film report that includes a profile of the family and their economic situation, and an interview which concludes with the husbands being asked what they would like to see the Chancellor do in his Budget. Following the film report, the account then passes back to the studio where Bough and Hudson work out by how much each family is 'better off' as a result of the Budget. Each family (the husband and the wife) is then asked for its comments.

The families chosen are those of an agricultural labourer, Ken Ball, a skilled toolroom fitter, Ken Dallason, and a personnel manager, John Tufnall. The general theme of the programme is that the Budget has simply 'failed to do much for anyone, though the plight of the personnel manager (as representative of the category of middle management) is dealt with most sympathetically.

3)   The third section is again introduced by Bough:

> Well now, with one billion pounds' worth of Mr Healey's tax cuts depending upon a further round of pay agreement, we are all now, whether we are members of trade unions or not, actually in the hands of the trade unions.

There follows a discussion between Hugh Scanlon (Associated Union of Engineering Workers) and Ian Fraser (Rolls Royce), chaired by Frank Bough, which concentrates on the question of the power of the unions to dictate pay policy to the government. Here Scanlon is put on the spot by direct questions from both Ian Fraser and Frank Bough in combination, whereas Fraser is asked 'open' questions which allow him the space to define how he sees 'the responsibility of business'.

[. . .]

Group 21

A group of white, mainly male bank managers, with an upper middle class background, on a two-week in-service training course at a private college run by the Midland Bank; aged 29–52; predominantly Conservative.

The predominant focus of concern for this group is the mode of address or presentation of the programme. This is so out of key with the relatively academic/serious forms of discourse, in TV and the press, to which they are attuned that their experience is one of radical disjuncture at this level. This is a level of discourse with which they make no connections:

> Well, speaking for myself, if I'd wanted to find out about the Budget I'd probably rely on the next day's newspaper . . . something like the *Telegraph* . . . or the *Money Programme* . . .

(From a quite different perspective, they repeat the comments of the predominantly black F.E. groups; cf. group 12: 'If I'd been watching at home I'd have switched off, honestly . . .')

Further, when asked:

> Q: How did that come across as a message about the Budget?

They replied:

> It wasn't sufficient, to be quite frank . . .
> . . . it didn't do anything for me . . .
> . . . I find that kind of plot embarrassing . . .
> . . . I just squirm in embarrassment for them.
> . . . I'd far rather have a discussion between three or four opposing views . . .
> . . . I mean it's much more rewarding . . . more ideas . . . they are articulate . . .

It is *ideas*, not 'people', which are important to them:

> Q: What about the actuality sequences – going into people's homes?

> I don't think you need it – if we're talking about ideas.

Rather than the immediacy of 'seeing for yourself' someone's experiences, which many of the working class groups (e.g. 1–6) take as at least a partial definition of what 'good TV' is, for this group it has to be about considered judgement and facts.

> In that programme, what have we heard? We've heard opinions from various people which don't necessarily relate to facts . . . some of the information . . . or background . . . all you've picked up are people's reactions . . . not considered . . .

> I mean . . . the point was made [by Ian Fraser of Rolls Royce] 'I'm not prepared to comment on the Budget till I've seen it in full tomorrow . . .'

As far as this group are concerned, *Nationwide* are:

> exploiting raw emotion . . . they encourage it . . .

> sensationalising items . . .

It's entertainment . . . raw entertainment value . . .

It's basically dishonest . . . I don't think it's representative . . .

As entertainment that's . . . maybe . . . acceptable . . . you can lead people by the nose . . . now if you're talking about communicating to the public and you're actually leading them, I think that's dishonest . . .

In startling contrast, for example, with group 17's insistence that items should be short, fast and to the immediate point, a perspective from which *Nationwide* was seen to fall short, this group feel that *Nationwide*:

. . . try and pack far too much into one particular programme . . . questions are asked, and before somebody had really got time to satisfactorily explain . . . it's into another question . . . and you lose the actual tack . . .

I can't bear it . . . I think it's awful . . . one thing . . . then chop, chop, you're onto the next thing.

This concern with the coherence and development of an argument leads them to single out the interview with the tax expert, Mr Worthington, as praiseworthy. They feel that the item was a little unbalanced:

Particularly that accountant from Birmingham . . . was . . . very much taking a view very strongly, that normally would only be expressed with someone else on the other side of the table . . .

But their predominant feeling is that at least the item contained a fully developed and coherent argument:

There he was allowed to develop it . . .

The programme certainly fails to provide this group with a point of identification, presumably because of the disjunction at the level of the programme's mode of address:

I couldn't identify with any of them.

I didn't identify myself with the middle management . . .

For them the whole tone of the programme makes it quite unacceptable to them, and they hypothesise, perhaps for others:

There's a great danger, I'm sure Frank Bough isn't doing it deliberately, of being patronising or condescending . . . and this I found irritating – that 'there's going to be £1.20 on your kind of income' . . . to me, Frank Bough on £20,000 a year . . . it's enough for a . . .

They hypothesise that the target audience is:

The car worker . . . the middle people . . . and below.

and wonder aloud that the programme might have been:

talking down . . . even to the lowest paid worker.

They place an emphasis on what this meant to the British worker . . . to a range of workers . . . I think it needed the same thing in a much more intelligent way – appealing to the more intelligent aspects of the people involved . . .

I wonder if they've underestimated their audience.

But this is a perspective which is not unchallenged; their view of the 'middle people . . . and below' also leads them to wonder:

Would many of the population be capable of absorbing the information . . . even the simple part of the question . . . especially in a programme of that sort . . .

Because, they argue:

they do not understand – the man in the street does not understand the issues: they understand '£10 a week' . . .

The ideological problematic embedded in the programme provokes little comment. It is largely invisible to them because it is so closely equivalent to their own view. The lack of comment is I suggest evidence of the non-controversial/shared nature of the problematic. Indeed, they go so far as to deny the presence of *any* ideological framework; it's so 'obvious' as to be invisible:

Q: What was the implicit framework?

I don't think they had one . . .

. . . there wasn't a theme . . . like an outline of the Budget . . .

The only point made by the presentation of the Budget, as far as they can see, is:

It left you with a view . . . the lasting impression was that [Healey] didn't do very much for anyone . . .

But they are very critical of this 'superficial' view precisely because it has not explored what they see as the crucial socio-political background:

There is another side to the coin, he didn't do a lot, but there was full reason at the time why he couldn't do a lot, and that was virtually ignored . . .

Group 22

An all male group of white, full-time, trade union officials (Transport and General Workers Union, Union of Shop, Distributive and Allied Workers, Union of Construction, Allied Trades and Technicians, Bakers, Food and Allied Workers Union, National Union of Agricultural and Allied Workers), aged 29–64, with a working-class background, on a TUC training course; exclusively Labour.

The group find the problematic of the programme quite unacceptable and accompany the viewing of the videotape with their own spontaneous commentary:

Programme	Commentary
Link after vox pop interviews: 'Well, there we are, most people seem agreed the tax system is too severe . . .'	'That's a bloody sweeping statement, isn't it? . . . from four bloody edited interviews!'
Interview with Mr Worthington:	'Is this chap a tax expert? Seems like a berk . . .' 'Poor old middle management!' 'Aaaagh!'
'. . . ambitious people . . .'	'Avaricious people, did he say?' 'What about the workers!!' 'Let's watch *Crossroads*.'
'. . . and of course the lower paid workers will benefit . . . from . . . er . . . the . . . er . . .'	'Extra crumbs falling from the table!'
Three Families Section-Manager: 'He doesn't own a car . . .' 'A modest bungalow . . .'	'Ha, Ha! That's a good one!' 'Family mansion! His lav's bigger than my lounge!'
'. . . we can't have avocados any more . . .'	'Did you hear that!' 'Those aren't Marks & Spencer's shoes he's wearing.'
Mr Tufnall digging in his garden 'However much you get – someone else is waiting to take it away . . .'	'Good! Redistribution of wealth and fat . . .'
'What, of course is a tragedy is in respect of his child still at college . . .'	'They didn't mention that for the other peasants.'
'One has to run a car . . .'	'Does one! He doesn't "run a car".'
'His child at college . . .'	'I worked nights to do that.'
'actually in the hands of the trades unions . . .'	'Yurgh!'

This group began by commenting that the programme was:

Obviously contrived, wasn't it, the whole thing . . . all contrived from start to finish to put the image over . . . I'm of the opinion the ones we've got to watch for the image creation are the local programmes.

This they see as an unacceptably right-wing perspective, also seen as characteristic of:

most ordinary TV programmes; serials . . . you get, em, *General Hospital*. It's so right-wing it's unbelievable – it's pushing the senior management at the people all the time. 'You must respect the consultants and doctors', and 'they're the people who make the decisions . . . and they know what they're doing' . . .

They say of the vox pop sequence in the programme that it is far too narrow and class-specific a sample of opinion to provide the 'ground' which *Nationwide* represents it as providing for their 'summation' of 'what most people think'.

Then the way the actual interviews were . . . very carefully selected in the centre of Birmingham, mid-afternoon . . . with the shoppers and business-men – there wasn't one dustman around . . . there wasn't any agricultural workers with their welly-boots on . . . it was purely middle class shoppers out buying their avocado pears or something; then at the end he says 'everybody agrees' – he's met four people. I don't know how many people live in Birmingham, but there's more than four . . . he only shows what he wants to show.

Mr Worthington, the tax expert, is dismissed as a 'berk':

Of course everybody believes that this chap is the expert, the TV tells us so, and the things he was saying, he might as well be reading a brief from Tory Central Office, which I think he probably was anyway . . . and they didn't just ask him to lay out the facts, they actually asked him his opinion, and to me an independent expert is supposed to tell you the facts, not necessarily give you their opinion on general policy . . .

The group feel that Mr Worthington is allowed 'free rein' in the programme, very dif-ferent from their experience of being interviewed by the media:

The development of the scene was allowed to go on and on, wasn't it? Glamour boy [i.e. the interviewer] just sat back and let him get on with it . . .

We've found that local sort of media – y'know we've got good relations – and yet we're cut all the time, as compared with the management's views.

The group do, at one point, comment on the form of the programme's presentation, or mode of address:

My major complaint against most of the *Nationwide* programmes, apart from the political ones, is the way in which they trivialise every topic they seem to take up – and just when the topic begins to blossom out, they suddenly say, 'well that's it . . .'

But crucially, as distinct for instance from Group 21, for whom the mode of address of the programme is the dominant issue, for this group it is the political perspective or problematic of the programme which is the dominant focus of their concerns. The perspective is one which they vehemently reject:

> The perspective was that of the poor hard-pressed managerial section . . . they had the farm worker there . . . that was, sort of, 'well, you've got £1.90 now – are you happy with that – now go away' and then 'Now, you, poor sod, you're on £13,000 p.a. . . . and a free car . . . Christ, they've only given you £1.10 – I bet you're speechless!' . . .

> . . . the sympathy was, you're poor, and you're badly paid and we all know that, because probably it's all your own bloody fault anyway – the whole programme started from the premise that whatever the Budget did it would not benefit the country unless middle management was given a hefty increase – that was the main premise of the programme, they started with that . . . they throw the farm worker in simply for balance at the other end of the scale.

The visibility of this distinct 'premise' for this group is in striking contrast, again, with group 21, for whom this premise is so common-sensical as to be invisible and for whom the programme had no particular theme or premise of this kind.

This group feel that *Nationwide*, because of its politics, is not a programme for them. It is:

> Not for TU officials. For the middle class.

> Undoubtedly what they regard as being the backbone of the country, the middle class . . . they allowed the agricultural worker to come in so as the middle class can look down on him and say 'poor sod, but I can't afford to give him anything because I've had to do without me second car, etc!'

As far as they are concerned the whole union/employer discussion is totally biased against Scanlon:

> He [interviewer] was pushing him into a corner . . . that was the first comment, immediately getting him into a corner, then the opponent [i.e. Fraser] who was supposed to have been equal . . . more or less came in behind Bough to support Bough's attack on Scanlon.

> Yes, except you've got to realise Scanlon slipped most of those punches expertly – a past master . . .

> but pointed, direct questions . . .

There is, however, another thread to this group's comments which emerges particularly around the question of tax and incentives. In line with the group's dominant political perspective, there is some defence of progressive taxation:

> What about the social wage? It's only distribution . . . the taxation takes it from you and gives it to me . . . I mean, if you're not taking income tax from those who can afford to pay, you can't give anything to those who aren't paying . . .

> So long as I get benefit for the tax I pay, I'm happy enough.

But at this point a more 'negotiated' perspective appears which shares much in common with the Labour 'Realpolitik' of some of group 20's comments; they say that to criticise *Nationwide*'s perspective on tax and incentives is misguided:

> It's not necessarily a criticism of the programme . . . a lot of highly paid skilled operatives fall into exactly the same trap . . . they probably listen to the programme themselves . . .

As they somewhat uneasily put it, extending in a sense, some of Scanlon's own comments on the need to 'look after' the 'powerful . . . skilled elements':

> One of the main objects of the full-time official is to maintain differentials . . .

> I'm not saying differentials are good . . . but as a trade unionist you've got to be able to maintain it . . .

Indeed they extend this to a partial defence of *Nationwide*'s perspective; at least to an implicit agreement about what, in matters of tax, is 'reasonable':

> . . . I think we should try to get the income tax in this country to a respectable level to allow everyone to work and get something out of it . . . because there's no doubt about it, the higher up the ladder you go, the harder you're hit for income tax.

They remark in justification of this perspective that the problem is that 'incentives' have been destroyed, because:

> They've increased the income tax in this country to such a degree that it don't matter how hard you work . . .

Indeed, they also take up one of the other themes of the dominant media discourse about trade unionism:

> There's a lot of . . . unions in this country that could produce a lot more . . . British Leyland's one for a start-off.

This is not to say that they wholeheartedly endorse this negotiated/'realist' perspective. They cannot, for it is in contradiction with much of the rest of their overall political outlook. It is rather to point to the extent to which this is a discourse of 'negotiated' code, crossed by contradictions with different perspectives in dominance in relation to different areas, or levels, of discussion.

Chapter 10

Michel de Certeau

THE PRACTICE OF EVERYDAY LIFE

THE OPERATIONAL MODELS OF popular culture cannot be confined to the past, the countryside, or primitive peoples. They exist in the heart of the strongholds of the contemporary economy. Take, for example, what in France is called *la perruque*, 'the wig.' *La perruque* is the worker's own work disguised as work for his employer. It differs from pilfering in that nothing of material value is stolen. It differs from absenteeism in that the worker is officially on the job. *La perruque* may be as simple a matter as a secretary's writing a love letter on 'company time' or as complex as a cabinetmaker's 'borrowing' a lathe to make a piece of furniture for his living room. Under different names in different countries this phenomenon is becoming more and more general, even if managers penalize it or 'turn a blind eye' on it in order not to know about it.[1] Accused of stealing or turning material to his own ends and using the machines for his own profit, the worker who indulges in *la perruque* actually diverts time (not goods, since he uses only scraps) from the factory for the work that is free, creative, and precisely not directed toward profit. In the very place where the machine he must serve reigns supreme, he cunningly takes pleasure in finding a way to create gratuitous products whose sole purpose is to signify his own capabilities through his *work* and to confirm his solidarity with other workers or his family through *spending* his time in this way. With the complicity of other workers (who thus defeat the competition the factory tries to instill among them), he succeeds in 'putting one over' on the established order on its home ground. Far from being a regression toward a mode of production organized around artisans or individuals, *la perruque* reintroduces 'popular' techniques of other times and other places into the industrial space (that is, into the Present order).

Many other examples would show the constant presence of these practices in the most ordered spheres of modern life. With variations, practices analogous to *la perruque* are proliferating in governmental and commercial offices as well as in factories. No doubt they are just as widespread as formerly (though they ought still to be studied), just as widely suspected, repressed, or ignored. Not only workshops and offices, but also museums and learned journals penalize such practices or ignore them. The authority of ethnological or folklore studies permits some of the material or linguistic objects of these practices to be collected, labelled according to place of origin and theme, put in display cases, offered for inspection and interpretation, and thus that authority conceals, as rural 'treasures' serving to edify or satisfy the curiosity of city folk, the legitimization of an order supposed by its conservators to be immemorial and 'natural.' Or else they use the tools and products taken from a language of social operations to set off a display of technical gadgets and thus arrange them, inert, on the margins of a system that itself remains intact.

The actual order of things is precisely what 'popular' tactics turn to their own end, without any illusion that it will change any time soon. Though elsewhere it is exploited by a dominant power or simply denied by an ideological discourse, here order is *tricked* by an art. Into the institution to be served are thus insinuated styles of social exchange, technical invention, and moral resistance, that is, an economy of the '*gift*' (generosities for which one expects a return), an esthetics of '*tricks*' (artists' operations) and an ethics of *tenacity* (countless ways of refusing to accord the established order the status of a law, a meaning, or a fatality). 'Popular' culture is precisely that; it is not a corpus considered as foreign, fragmented in order to be displayed, studied and 'quoted' by a system which does to objects what it does to living beings.

The progressive partitioning of times and places, the disjunctive logic of specialization through and for work, no longer has an adequate counterpart in the conjunctive rituals of mass communications. This *fact* cannot become our *law*. It can be gotten around through departments that, 'competing' with the gifts of our benefactors, offer them products at the expense of the institution that divides and pays the workers. This practice of economic *diversion* is in reality the return of a sociopolitical ethics into an economic system. It is no doubt related to the *potlatch* described by Mauss, an interplay of voluntary allowances that counts on reciprocity and organizes a social network articulated by the 'obligation to give.'[2] In our societies, the market economy is no longer determined by such an 'emulation': taking the abstract individual as a basic unit, it regulates all exchanges among these units according to the code of generalized equivalence constituted by money. This individualistic axiom is, of course, now surfacing as the question that disturbs the free market system as a whole. The a priori assumption of an historical Western option is becoming its point of implosion. However that may be, the *potlatch* seems to persist within it as the mark of another type of economy. It survives in our economy, though on its margins or in its interstices. It is even developing, although held to be illegitimate, within modern market economy. Because of this, the politics of the 'gift' *also* becomes a diversionary tactic. In the same way, the loss that was voluntary in a gift economy is transformed into a transgression in a profit economy: it appears as an excess (a waste), a challenge (a rejection of profit), or a crime (an attack on property).

This path, relative to our economy, derives from another; it compensates for the first even though it is illegal and (from this point of view) marginal. The same pathway allows investigations to take up a position that is no longer defined only by an acquired power and an observational knowledge, with the addition of a pinch of nostalgia. Melancholy is not enough. Certainly, with respect to the sort of writing that separates domains in the name of the division of labor and reveals class affiliations, it would be 'fabulous' if, as in the stories of miracles, the groups that formerly gave us our masters and that are currently lodged in our corpus were to rise up and themselves mark their comings and goings in the texts that honor and bury them at the same time. This hope has disappeared, along with the beliefs which have long since vanished from our cities. There are no longer any ghosts who can remind the living of reciprocity. But in the order organized by the power of knowledge (ours), as in the order of the countryside or the factories, a diversionary practice remains possible.

Let us try to make a *perruque* in the economic system whose rules and hierarchies are repeated, as always, in scientific institutions. In the area of scientific research (which defines the current order of knowledge), working with its machines and making use of its scraps, we can divert the time owed to the institution; we can make textual objects that signify an art and solidarities; we can play the game of free exchange, even if it is penalized by bosses and colleagues when they are not willing to 'turn a blind eye' on it; we can create networks of connivances and sleights of hand; we can exchange gifts; and in these ways we can subvert the law that, in the scientific factory, puts work at the service of the machine and, by a similar logic, progressively destroys the requirement of creation and the 'obligation to give.' I know of investigators experienced in this art of diversion, which is a return of the ethical, of pleasure and of invention within the scientific institution. Realizing no profit (profit is produced by work done for the factory), and often at a loss, they take something from the order of knowledge in order to inscribe 'artistic achievements' on it and to carve on it the graffiti of their debts of honor. To deal with everyday tactics in this way would be to practice an 'ordinary' art, to find oneself in the common situation, and to make a kind of *perruque* of writing itself.

[. . .]

In spite of measures taken to repress or conceal it, *la perruque* (or its equivalent) is infiltrating itself everywhere and becoming more and more common. It is only one case among all the practices which introduce *artistic* tricks and competitions of *accomplices* into a system that reproduces and partitions through work or leisure. Sly as a fox and twice as quick: there are countless ways of 'making do.'

From this point of view, the dividing line no longer falls between work and leisure. These two areas of activity flow together. They repeat and reinforce each other. Cultural techniques that camouflage economic reproduction with fictions of surprise ('the event'), of truth ('information') or communication ('promotion') spread through the workplace. Reciprocally, cultural production offers an area of expansion for rational operations that permit work to be managed by dividing it (analysis), tabulating it (synthesis) and aggregating it (generalization). A distinction is required other than the one that distributes behaviors according to their *place* (of work or leisure) and qualifies them thus by the fact that they are located on one or another square of the social checkerboard – in the office, in the workshop, or at the movies. There are differences of another type. They refer to the *modalities* of action, to the *formalities* of practice. They traverse the frontiers dividing time, place, and type of action into one part assigned for work and another for leisure. For example, *la perruque* grafts itself onto the system of the industrial assembly line (its counterpoint, in the same place), as a variant of the activity which, outside the factory (in another place), takes the form of *bricolage*.

Although they remain dependent upon the possibilities offered by circumstances, these transverse *tactics* do not obey the law of the place, for they are not defined or identified by it. In this respect, they are not any more localizable than the technocratic (and scriptural) *strategies* that seek to create places in conformity with abstract models.

But what distinguishes them at the same time concerns the *types of operations* and the role of spaces: strategies are able to produce, tabulate, and impose these spaces, when those operations take place, whereas tactics can only use, manipulate, and divert these spaces.

We must therefore specify the operational schemas. Just as in literature one differentiates 'styles' or ways of writing, one can distinguish 'ways of operating' – ways of walking, reading, producing, speaking, etc. These styles of action intervene in a field which regulates them at a first level (for example, at the level of the factory system), but they introduce into it a way of turning it to their advantage that obeys other rules and constitutes something like a second level interwoven into the first (for instance, *la perruque*). These 'ways of operating' are similar to 'instructions for use,' and they create a certain play in the machine through a stratification of different and interfering kinds of functioning. Thus a North African living in Paris or Roubaix (France) insinuates *into* the system imposed on him by the construction of a low-income housing development or of the French language the ways of 'dwelling' (in a house or a language) peculiar to his native Kabylia. He superimposes them and, by that combination, creates for himself a space in which he can find *ways of using* the constraining order of the place or of the language. Without leaving the place where he has no choice but to live and which lays down its law for him, he establishes within it a degree of *plurality* and creativity. By an art of being in between, he draws unexpected results from his situation.

These modes of use – or rather re-use – multiply with the extension of acculturation phenomena, that is, with the displacement that substitute manners or 'methods' of transiting toward an identification of a person by the place in which he lives or works. That does not prevent them from corresponding to a very ancient art of 'making do.' I give them the name of uses, even though the word most often designates stereotyped procedures accepted and reproduced by a group, its 'ways and customs.' The problem lies in the ambiguity of the word, since it is precisely a matter of recognizing in these 'uses' 'actions' (in the military sense of the word) that have their own formality and inventiveness and that discreetly organize the multiform labor of consumption.

Use, or consumption

In the wake of the many remarkable works that have analyzed 'cultural products,' the system of their production,[3] the geography of their distribution and the situation of consumers in that geography,[4] it seems possible to consider these products no longer merely as data on the basis of which statistical tabulations of their circulation can be drawn up or the economic functioning of their diffusion understood, but also as parts of the repertory with which users carry out operations of their own. Henceforth, these facts are no longer the data of our calculations, but rather the lexicon of users' practices. Thus, once the images broadcast by television and the time spent in front of the TV set have been analyzed, it remains to be asked what the consumer *makes* of these images and during these hours. The thousands of people who buy a health magazine, the customers in a supermarket, the practitioners of urban space, the consumers of newspaper stories and legends – what do they make of what they 'absorb,' receive, and pay for? What do they do with it?

The enigma of the consumer-sphinx. His products are scattered in the graphs of televised, urbanistic, and commercial production. They are all the less visible because the networks framing them are becoming more and more tightly woven, flexible, and totalitarian. They are thus protean in form, blending in with their surroundings, and liable to disappear into the colonizing organizations whose products leave no room where the consumers can mark their activity. The child still scrawls and daubs on his schoolbooks; even if he is punished for this crime, he has made a space for himself and signs his existence as an author on it. The television viewer cannot write anything on the screen of his set. He has been dislodged from the product; he plays no role in its apparition. He loses his author's rights and becomes, or so it seems, a pure receiver, the mirror of a multiform and narcissistic actor. Pushed to the limit, he would be the image of appliances that no longer need him in order to produce themselves, the reproduction of a 'celibate machine.'[5]

In reality, a rationalized, expansionist, centralized, spectacular and clamorous production is confronted by an entirely different kind of production, called 'consumption' and characterized by its ruses, its fragmentation (the result of the circumstances), its poaching, its clandestine nature, its tireless but quiet activity, in short by its quasi-invisibility, since it shows itself not in its own products (where would it place them?) but in an art of using those imposed on it.

The cautious yet fundamental inversions brought about by consumption in other societies have long been studied. Thus the spectacular victory of Spanish colonization over the indigenous Indian cultures was diverted from its intended aims by the use made of it: even when they were subjected, indeed even when they accepted their subjection, the Indians often used the laws, practices, and representations that were imposed on them by force or by fascination to ends other than those of their conquerors; they made something else out of them; they subverted them from within – not by rejecting them or by transforming them (though that occurred as well), but by many different ways of using them in the service of rules, customs or convictions foreign to the colonization which they could not escape.[6] They metaphorized the dominant order: they made it function in another register. They remained other within the system which they assimilated and which assimilated them externally. They diverted it without leaving it. Procedures of consumption maintained their difference in the very space that the occupier was organizing.

Is this an extreme example? No, even if the resistance of the Indians was founded on a memory tattooed by oppression, a past inscribed on their body.[7] To a lesser degree, the same process can be found in the use made in 'popular' milieus of the cultures diffused by the 'elites' that produce language. The imposed knowledge and symbolisms become objects manipulated by practitioners who have not produced them. The language produced by a certain social category has the power to extend its conquests into vast areas surrounding it, 'deserts' where nothing equally articulated seems to exist, but in doing so it is caught in the trap of its assimilation by a jungle of procedures rendered invisible to the conqueror by the very victories he seems to have won. However spectacular it may be, his privilege is likely to be only apparent if it merely serves as a framework for the stubborn, guileful, everyday practices that make use of it. What is called 'popularization' or 'degradation' of a culture is from this point of view a partial and caricatural aspect of the revenge that utilizing tactics take on the power that dominates production. In any case, the consumer cannot be identified or qualified by the newspapers or commercial products he assimilates: between the person (who uses them) and these products (indexes of the 'order' which is imposed on him), there is a gap of varying proportions opened by the use that he makes of them.

Use must thus be analyzed in itself. There is no lack of models, especially so far as language is concerned; language is indeed the privileged terrain on which to discern the formal rules proper to such practices. Gilbert Ryle, borrowing Saussure's distinction between '*langue*' (a system) and '*parole*' (an act), compared the former to a fund of *capital* and the latter to the *operations* it makes possible: on the one hand, a stock of materials, on the other, transactions and uses.[8] In the case of consumption, one could almost say that production furnishes the capital and that users, like renters, acquire the right to operate on and with this fund without owning it. But the comparison is valid only for the relation between the knowledge of a language and 'speech acts.' From this alone can be derived a series of questions and categories which have permitted us, especially since Bar–Hillel's work, to open up within the study of language (*semiosis* or *semiotics*) a particular area (called *pragmatics*) devoted to use, notably to *indexical expression*, that is, 'words and sentences of which the reference cannot be determined without knowledge of the context of use.'[9]

We shall return later to these inquiries which have illuminated a whole region of everyday practices (the use of language); at this point, it suffices to note that they are based on a problematics of enunciation.[10] By situating the act in relation to its circumstances, 'contexts of use' draw attention to the traits that specify the act of speaking (or practice of language) and are its effects. Enunciation furnishes a model of these characteristics, but they can also be discovered in the relation that other practices (walking, residing, etc.) entertain with non-linguistic systems. Enunciation presupposes: (1) a *realization* of the linguistic system through a speech act that actualizes some of its potential (language is real only in the act of speaking); (2) an *appropriation* of language by the speaker who uses it; (3) the postulation of an interlocutor (real or fictive) and thus the constitution of a relational *contract* or allocation (one speaks to someone); (4) the establishment of a *present* through the act of the 'I' who speaks, and conjointly, since 'the present is properly the source of time,' the organization of a temporality (the present creates a before and an after) and the existence of a 'now' which is the presence to the world.[11]

These elements (realizing, appropriating, being inscribed in relations, being situated in time) make of enunciation, and secondarily of use, a nexus of circumstances, a nexus adherent to the 'context' from which it can be distinguished only by abstraction. Indissociable from the present *instant*, from particular circumstances and from a *faire* (a peculiar way of doing things, of producing language and of modifying the dynamics of a relation), the speech act is at the same time a use *of* language and an operation performed *on* it. We can attempt to apply this model to many non-linguistic operations by taking as our hypothesis that all these uses concern consumption.

We must, however, clarify the nature of these operations from another angle, not on the basis of the relation they entertain with a system or an order, but insofar as *power relationships* define the networks in which they are inscribed and delimit the circumstances from which they can profit. In order to do so, we must pass from a linguistic frame of reference to a polemological one. We are concerned with battles or games between the strong and the weak, and with the 'actions' which remain possible for the latter.

Notes

1 See in particular A. Huet *et al.*, *La Marchandise culturelle* (Paris: CNRS, 1977), which is not satisfied merely with analysing products (photos, records, prints), but also studies a system of commercial repetition and ideological reproduction.

2 See, for example, *Pratiques culturelles des Français* (Paris: Secrétariat d'Etat à la Culture – SER, 1974), 2 vol. Alvin Toffler, *The Culture Consumers* (Baltimore: Penguin, 1965), remains fundamental and pioneering, although it is not statistically based and is limited to mass culture.

3 On the premonitory theme of the 'celibate machine' in the art (M. Duchamp, *et al.*) or the literature (from Jules Verne to Raymond Roussel) of the early twentieth century, see J. Clair *et al.*, *Les Machines célibataires* (Venice: Alfieri, 1975).

4 See, for example, on the subject of the Aymaras of Peru and Bolivia, J.-E. Monast, *On les croyait Chrétiens: les Aymaras* (Paris: Cerf, 1969).

5 See M. de Certeau, 'La Longue marche indienne,' in *Le Réveil indien en Amérique latine*, ed. Yves Materne and DIAL (Paris: Cerf, 1976), 119–135.

6 G. Ryle, 'Use, Usage and Meaning,' in *The Theory of Meaning*, ed. G. H. R. Parkinson (Oxford: Oxford University Press, 1968), 109–116. A large part of the volume is devoted to use.

7 Richard Montague, 'Pragmatics,' in *La Philosophie contemporaine*, ed. Raymond Klibansky (Firenze: La Nuova Italia, 1968), I, 102–122. Y. Bar-Hillel thus adopts a term of C. S. Peirce, of which the equivalents are, in B. Russell, 'ego-centric particulars'; in H. Reichenbach, 'token-reflexive expressions'; in N. Goodman, 'indicator words'; in W. V. Quine, 'non-eternal sentences'; etc. A whole tradition is inscribed in this perspective. Wittgenstein belongs to it as well, the Wittgenstein whose slogan was 'Don't ask for the meaning; ask for the use' in reference to normal use, regulated by the institution that is language.

8 See 'The Proverbial Enunciation,' p. 18.

9 See Emile Benveniste, *Problèmes de linguistique générale* (Paris: Gallimard, 1974), II, 79–88.

10 Fernand Deligny, *Les Vagabonds efficaces* (Paris: Maspero, 1970), uses this word to describe the trajectories of young autistic people with whom he lives, writings that move through forests, wanderings that can no longer make a path through the space of language.

11 See 'Indeterminate,' p. 199.

Chapter 11

John Fiske

UNDERSTANDING POPULAR CULTURE

The commercial and the popular

THE RELATIONSHIP BETWEEN POPULAR culture and the forces of commerce and profit is highly problematic, and it is one of the themes that runs throughout this book. We can begin to examine some of the issues by looking in more detail at the example of torn jeans.

At the simplest level, this is an example of a user not simply consuming a commodity but reworking it, treating it not as a completed object to be accepted passively, but as a cultural resource to be used. A number of important theoretical issues underlie the differences between a user of a cultural resource and a consumer of a commodity (which are not different activities, but different ways of theorizing, and therefore of understanding, the same activity).

Late capitalism, with its market economy, is characterized by commodities — it is awash with them, it would be impossible to escape them, even if one wanted to. There are a number of ways of understanding commodities and their role in our society: in the economic sphere they ensure the generation and circulation of wealth, and they can vary from the basic necessities of life to inessential luxuries, and, by extension, can include non-material objects such as television programs, a woman's appearance, or a star's name. They also serve two types of function, the material and the cultural. The material function of jeans is to meet the needs of warmth, decency, comfort, and so on. The cultural function is concerned with meanings and values: All commodities can be used by the consumer to construct meanings of self, of social identity and social relations. Describing a pair of jeans, or a TV program, as a commodity emphasizes its role in the circulation of wealth and tends to play down its separate, but related, role in the circulation of meaning . . .

This difference of emphasis (on money or meanings) carries with it a corresponding difference in conceptualizing the balance of power within the exchange. The commodity–consumer approach puts the power with the producers of the commodity. It is they who make a profit out of its manufacture and sale, and the consumer who is exploited insofar as the price he or she pays is inflated beyond the material costs to include as much profit as the producer is able to make. This exploitation, in the case of jeans, often takes on a second dimension, in that the consumer may well be a member of the industrial proletariat whose labor is exploited to contribute to the same profit (the principle remains even if the commodity produced by the worker is not the actual jeans bought in his or her role as consumer).

When this approach tackles the question of meaning, it does so through a theory of ideology that again situates power with the owners of the means of production. Here, the theory would explain that jeans are so deeply imbued with the ideology of white capitalism that no one wearing them can avoid participation in it and therefore extending it. By wearing jeans we adopt the position of subjects within that ideology, become complicit with it, and therefore give it material expression; we 'live' capitalism through its commodities, and, by living it, we validate and invigorate it.

The producers and distributors of jeans do not *intend* to promote capitalist ideology with their product: they are not deliberate propagandists. Rather, the economic system, which determines mass production and mass consumption, reproduces itself ideologically in its commodities. Every commodity reproduces the ideology of the system that produced it: a commodity is ideology made material. This ideology works to produce in the subordinate a false consciousness of their position in society, false for two reasons: first because it blinds them to the conflict of interest between the bourgeoisie and proletariat (they may well be aware of the difference, but will understand this difference as contributing to a final social consensus, a liberal pluralism in which social differences are seen finally as harmonious, not as conflictual), and second because it blinds them to their common interests with their fellow workers – it prevents the development of a sense of class solidarity or class consciousness. Ideology works in the sphere of culture as economics does in its own sphere, to naturalize the capitalist system so that it appears to be the only one possible.

So how much of a resistance to this is wearing torn jeans? In the economic sphere there is a trace of resistance in that for jeans to become naturally ragged they need to be worn long past the time when they would normally be considered worn out and thus need replacing with another pair. Reducing one's purchase of commodities can be a tiny gesture against a high-consumption society, but its more important work is performed in the cultural sphere rather than the economic. One possible set of meanings here is of a display of poverty – which is a contradictory sign, for those who *are* poor do not make poverty into a fashion statement. Such a signified rejection of affluence does not necessarily forge a cultural allegiance with the economically poor, for this 'poverty' is a matter of choice, although it may, in some cases, signify a sympathy toward the situation of the poor. Its main power is in the negative, a resuscitation of jeans' ability in the 1960s to act as a marker of alternative, and at times oppositional, social values. But more significant than any other possible meaning of ragged jeans is the fact that the raggedness is the production and choice of the user, it is an excorporation of the commodity into a subordinate subculture and a transfer of at least some of the power inherent in the commodification process. It is a refusal of commodification and an assertion of one's right to make one's own culture out of the resources provided by the commodity system.

Such 'tearing' or disfigurement of a commodity in order to assert one's right and ability to remake it into one's own culture need not be literal. The gay community made a heroine out of Judy Garland by 'tearing' or disfiguring her image of the all-

American, all-gingham girl-next-door, and reworked her as a sign of the masquerade necessary to fit this image, a masquerade equivalent to that which, in the days before sexual liberation, permeated the whole of the social experience of gays (see Dyer 1986).

Excorporation is the process by which the subordinate make their own culture out of the resources and commodities provided by the dominant system, and this is central to popular culture, for in an industrial society the only resources from which the subordinate can make their own subcultures are those provided by the system that subordinates them. There is no 'authentic' folk culture to provide an alternative, and so popular culture is necessarily the art of making do with what is available. This means that the study of popular culture requires the study not only of the cultural commodities out of which it is made, but also of the ways that people use them. The latter are far more creative and varied than the former.

The vitality of the subordinate groups that, in various shifting social allegiances, constitute the people is to be found in the ways of using, not in what is used. This results in the producers having to resort to the processes of incorporation or containment. Manufacturers quickly exploited the popularity of ragged (or old and faded) jeans by producing factory-made tears, or by 'washing' or fading jeans in the factory before sale. This process of adopting the signs of resistance incorporates them into the dominant system and thus attempts to rob them of any oppositional meanings.

This approach claims that incorporation robs subordinate groups of any oppositional language they may produce: it deprives them of the means to speak their opposition and thus, ultimately, of their opposition itself. It can also be understood as a form of containment – a permitted and controlled gesture of dissent that acts as a safety valve and thus strengthens the dominant social order by demonstrating its ability to cope with dissenters or protesters by allowing them enough freedom to keep them relatively content, but not enough to threaten the stability of the system against which they are protesting.

So Macy's advertises 'Expressions – Faded attraction . . . the worn out jean from Calvin Klein Sport.' 'Worn out in all the right places,' the copy continues, 'brand new jeans slip on with the look and feel of old favorites. And when Calvin's cool white crew neck is added (a soon-to-be new favorite) you're set for a totally relaxed mood.' Any possible oppositional meanings are incorporated and tamed into the unthreatening 'old favorites.' The producers exert their control over the signs of wear by ensuring that they occur only in the 'right places,' and then use this incorporated and thus defused language of opposition to sell more commodities (the white crew neck) to the people they have stolen it from. In such ways, the theory of incorporation tells us, signs of opposition are turned to the advantage of that which they oppose and fashionably worn-torn garments become another range of commodities: the raggedness of worn-out jeans, far from opposing consumerism, is turned into a way of extending and enhancing it.

Such explanations of popular culture tell us only part of the story; they concentrate almost exclusively on the power of the dominant groups to maintain the system that advantages them and thus they assume, rather than question, the success of the strategy. They fail to recognize the social differentiation that still exists between the wearers of 'really' old, torn jeans and Macy's customers, and thus overlook any resistances to incorporation that ensure that its victories are never more than partial.

Consequently, they paradoxically align themselves with the forces of domination, for, by ignoring the complexity and creativity by which the subordinate cope with the commodity system and its ideology in their everyday lives, the dominant underestimate and thus devalue the conflict and struggle entailed in constructing popular culture within a capitalist society.

De Certeau (1984 . . .) uses a military metaphor to explain this struggle; he talks about the strategy of the powerful, deploying their huge, well-organized forces, which are met by the fleeting tactics of the weak. These tactics involve spotting the weak points in the forces of the powerful and raiding them as guerrilla fighters constantly harry and attack an invading army. Guerrilla tactics are the art of the weak: they never challenge the powerful in open warfare, for that would be to invite defeat, but maintain their own opposition within and against the social order dominated by the powerful. Eco (1986), too, speaks of 'semiotic guerrilla warfare' as being the key to understanding popular culture and its ability to resist the dominant ideology. This, in its turn, I would argue, helps to maintain the sense of social differences that is essential if the heterogeneity of our society is to be productive and not static, progressive and not reactionary.

Change can come only from below: the interest of those with power are best served by maintaining the status quo. The motor for social change can come only from a sense of social difference that is based on a conflict of interests, not a liberal pluralism in which differences are finally subordinated to a consensus whose function is to maintain those differences essentially as they are.

Popular culture always is part of power relations; it always bears traces of the constant struggle between domination and subordination, between power and various forms of resistance to it or evasions of it, between military strategy and guerrilla tactics. Evaluating the balance of power within this struggle is never easy: Who can say, at any one point, who is 'winning' a guerrilla war? The essence of guerrilla warfare, as of popular culture, lies in not being defeatable. Despite nearly two centuries of capitalism, subordinated subcultures exist and intransigently refuse finally to be incorporated – people in these subcultures keep devising new ways of tearing their jeans. Despite many more centuries of partriarchy, women have produced and maintained a feminist movement, and individual women, in their everyday lives, constantly make guerrilla raids upon patriarchy, win small, fleeting victories, keep the enemy constantly on the alert, and gain, and sometimes hold, pieces of territory (however small) for themselves. And gradually, reluctantly, patriarchy has to change in response. Structural changes at the level of the system itself, in whatever domain – that of law, of politics, of industry, of the family – occur only after the system has been eroded and weakened by the tactics of everyday life.

Until recently, the study of popular culture has taken two main directions. The less productive has been that which has celebrated popular culture without situating it in a model of power. It has been a consensual model, which viewed popular culture as a form of the ritual management of social differences out of which it produced a final harmony. It is a democratic version of elite humanism, which merely resituates the cultural life of a nation in the popular rather than the highbrow.

The other direction has been to situate popular culture firmly within a model of power, but to emphasize so strongly the forces of domination as to make it appear impossible for a genuine popular culture to exist at all. What replaced it was a mass culture imposed upon a powerless and passive people by a culture industry whose interests were in direct opposition to theirs. A mass culture produces a quiescent, passive mass of people, an agglomeration of atomized individuals separated from their position in the social structure, detached from and unaware of their class consciousness, of their various social and cultural allegiances, and thus totally disempowered and helpless.

Recently, however, a third direction has begun to emerge, one to which I hope this book will contribute. It, too, sees popular culture as a site of struggle, but, while accepting the power of the forces of dominance, it focuses rather upon the popular tactics by which these forces are coped with, are evaded or are resisted. Instead of tracing exclusively the processes of incorporation, it investigates rather that popular vitality and creativity that makes incorporation such a constant necessity. Instead of concentrating on the omnipresent, insidious practices of the dominant ideology, it attempts to understand the everyday resistances and evasions that make that ideology work so hard and insistently to maintain itself and its values. This approach sees popular culture as potentially, and often actually, progressive (though not radical), and it is essentially optimistic, for it finds in the vigor and vitality of the people evidence both of the possibility of social change and of the motivation to drive it.

References

De Certeau, M. (1984) *The Practice of Everyday Life*, Berkeley, CA: University of California Press.

Dyer, R. (1986) *Heavenly Bodies: Film Stars and Society*, New York: St Martin's Press.

Eco, V. (1986) *Travels in Hyperreality*, London: Picador.

Chapter 12

Gregory Woods

'WE'RE HERE, WE'RE QUEER AND WE'RE NOT GOING CATALOGUE SHOPPING'

ANYONE WHO HAS BEEN on a Gay Pride march in London will have heard the chant: 'We're here, we're queer and we're not going shopping!' Of these three assertions, everything one sees on the march will confirm the first two; but the third is likely to be open to doubt. Many of the women and men chanting, particularly those who have travelled to the city for the day, tend to be carrying shopping bags. The march does not start until the early afternoon – which leaves all morning for visiting shops.

Writing in *Marxism Today* in 1988, Frank Mort and Nicholas Green remarked that, 'Marketers and advertisers have always had designs on our images as much as our pockets.' After all, any company which can influence how we perceive ourselves and how we want ourselves to be perceived, is guaranteed influence on how we spend our money. Mort and Green continued: 'The buzz word is *lifestyles* – a concept which goes hand-in-hand with the retail revolution. Lifestyle advertising is all about designer-led retailing which reflects changing consumer demand. In essence it is marketing's bid to get to grips with today's social agenda' (Mort and Green 1988: 32). Among the items on that agenda, of course, are the needs and demands of lesbians and gay men.

Since the late 1980s it has become increasingly commonplace to speak, not only of the purchasing power of the so-called 'pink economy', but also of the pink pound's extraordinary resilience during the recession of the early 1990s. A 1992 article in the London *Times* spoke rather enviously of 'a thriving subculture in which pink pounds are spent on pink services in a private micro-economy where spend, spend, spend! is still the watchword'. Intimidated by the homophobic Section 28 of the Thatcher government's Local Government Act (banning the 'promotion of homosexuality' with public funds) and by initial media responses to the AIDS epidemic – the argument goes – the gay community turned in on itself and unwittingly discovered economic virtue in old-fashioned solidarity (David 1992: 10).

The gay media are currently burgeoning, not only with advertisements for gay goods and services, but also with articles on the phenomenon of conspicuous gay consumption; and not all such articles are entirely taken in by the impression of general affluence. Bill Short, for instance, has questioned a number of rather slapdash assumptions shared by both straight and gay commentators, among them the myth that gay men necessarily have more spending power than their straight counterparts. He makes a point which is also evident in the fiction of contemporary writers like Neil Bartless, that 'many gay men appear to be living the high life when in fact they have no disposable income at all'. However, Short agrees that, to a large extent, lifestyle is determined by economic considerations: 'Many of us who wish to maintain a gay identity, actually *buy* that identity.' The reason for this is fundamental, relating to how we meet each other and how we appear to the rest of society: 'We are forced to prove we exist by projecting a gay image or lifestyle' (Short 1992: 20). Thus, it is in quite a literal sense that one can say: I shop, therefore I am.

Speaking of the demise of the golden age of department stores, Harvie Ferguson has outlined a crucial shift in ways of showing off commodities: 'The larger propaganda aspect of display has been usurped by the more powerful, private and intimate form of television advertising. The shop window now opens directly into the home; the *flâneur* has become the somnambulist' (Ferguson 1992: 32). Indeed so. But the trouble with television advertising is that it tends to offer a limited range of goods, and it displays them for only a limited length of time between distractingly irrelevant programmes. To browse at one's leisure, one needs a catalogue; better still, a whole collection of competing catalogues.

With reference to sexuality, the cultural values and assumptions of mail order catalogues from Britain and the United States are not difficult to read. The consumer goods they advertise are arranged around implied narratives of heterosexual courtship and home-building. While it is clear that such catalogues as *Argos*, *Burlington*, *Index* and *Littlewoods* now make some slight genuflection in the direction of anti-sexism and multiculturalism, they exhibit no acceptance of any world order other than the strictly heterosexual. For a start, the nuclear family (father, mother, son, daughter) is always present as being the ideal living arrangement. Whole catalogues are predicated on the assumption that no greater happiness can be found than in the combination of such a family and well-chosen consumer goods.

Many catalogues are friendly only to the family. Take the example of the *Avon* collection (Campaign 9), the front cover of which shows a father (dark) and mother (blonde) running in a shallow sea with their son and daughter. The catalogue opens with three double-page spreads of sun tan lotions, each illustrated with a photograph of a nuclear family. Cosmetics follow, all clearly aimed at women; there is even a page of 'Little Blossom' make-up for 'young ladies aged 5 to 8' – but none for boys or men. There are, eventually, four double-page spreads of toiletries for men; but each of these is conspicuously headed 'Father's Day Sunday June 21st'. There are no gifts here for the family's favourite bachelor uncle.

The *Ace* Christmas catalogue (1992) is aimed principally at the family, even if the written copy does not overtly push this fact. The cutesy cover photograph is of a boy and girl, cheek to cheek, evidently preparing for the kind of material future the catalogue then maps out. Roles are conventionally divided; for instance, there are only girl models playing with the advertised dolls. Sexuality is acknowledged – sex sells, after all, and in any case the company needs its buyers to produce new generations of buyers – but the nature of sexual pleasure is closely policed. On the bathroom page, opposite a family in co-ordinated bathrobes (tall, dark father in royal blue; shorter, blonde mother in white; daughter in pink; son in pale blue) a teenage couple, he with his arm around her, are wearing personalised sarongs (Mike in 19 inches of royal blue, Susan in 29 inches of pink). Thus, exoticism and eroticism are reassuringly anglicised and tamed; even the lovers' towelling dictates their sexual roles.

A later page advertises musical boxer shorts for men: when you press the picture on the shorts (Santa Claus, a pink pig or a woman's lips) they play a tune. Three pairs are shown, but not on a model. Each is being pressed – by a woman's finger. God forbid that any man should press his own, or even get a male friend to press it for him. When a potentially disruptive item appears in the middle of this system of unquestioned heterosexualism, its use has to be firmly signalled and limited in the descriptive copy. So a Chippendales mug is captioned 'Ladies this is for you!' lest any of the gents should start buying them for each other.

This Christmas catalogue, finally, asserts its values in a double-page display of wedding stationery. What is being purveyed in these pages is a fresh-faced, jolly conventionality. Love is signalled here in a number of ways, since one is, after all, meant to be browsing for presents for one's 'loved ones'; but the company seems to have an oddly commodified idea of what love means. The material accompanying the catalogue is headed by the disturbing promise: 'You'll fall in love with your new *Ace* Christmas catalogue.' It is clear that we must add a new concept to our psychoanalytic lexicon: the phenomenon of catalogophilia.

The typical structure of a mainstream British catalogue (*Littlewoods, Janet Frazer, Burlington*, etc.) is as follows: women's clothes, children's clothes, men's clothes, sports clothes, soft furnishings, hard furnishings and leisure goods (an odd combination of jewellery, toys and bicycles). Because they segregate women and men for the sake of this schematic order, these catalogues end up subjecting themselves to a kind of semiotic panic about homosexuality. It must not appear that the lives the models in the photos are enjoying with such ostentatious pleasure are in any way abnormal. All items have to appeal to the average, even if when purchased they will be used as the currency for (un)neighbourly one-upmanship. You do not keep up with, still less outdo, the Joneses by adopting what are perceived to be eccentric or abnormal styles; you have to buy things that they will recognise and envy you for. You must not look lonely, of course. The best way of avoiding that is to create an impression either of sexual good fortune – in the case of single people – or of complete marital harmony. The one thing you must avoid is the slightest whiff of deviancy.

These worries manifest themselves in all kinds of ways: sometimes in the structure of the catalogue, sometimes in its written copy, most often in its illustrations. Many details, barely perceptible to the casual browser, become crystal clear when subjected to a moment's thought. For instance, the *L. L. Bean* catalogue genuflects to the anti-sexist tenor of our times by offering the 'River Driver's Shirt' – which is described as being 'Named for the rugged men who once worked the spring log drive on Maine's rivers' – to purchasers of both sexes. But although a wide range of colours is available to both women and men, women are offered one extra colour, 'Rose' – that is to say, pink. It is hard to imagine the kind of meeting at which such decisions are made; but even if the significance of the ban on pink shirts for men was not made explicit then, it cannot be attributed to anything but homophobia. Whether we attribute this fault to the L. L. Bean company itself or, more plausibly, to the prejudices they perceive in their customers, its name is homophobia none the less. Later in the same catalogue, silk underwear is offered to men in navy blue and 'natural' (the undyed fabric) but to women in 'natural' and pink.

The poses adopted by models seem to be under close scrutiny, particularly on the relatively uncommon occasions when two or more men appear together in the same photograph. Physical contact between them is clearly discouraged. They do, however, have to seem to be enjoying themselves, and it follows that they ought to look as though they enjoy each other's company. They should look like friends, even very good friends – but never lovers. Elaborate conventions, therefore, surround male bodily contact. Manly sporting activities are acceptable, of course. One man may place his fist, or less often his open palm, on the nearside shoulder, or less often the far shoulder of his friend. Ideally, they should look into the distance rather than at each other. Only very rarely do you see them looking into each other's eyes.

Given the difficulties raised by the juxtaposition of male bodies, many catalogues simply ration the number of times the difficulties arise. Take the example of two recent *Racing Green* catalogues. In the Autumn 1992 edition, as well as many photos containing single female or male models, there are seven photos of a male and a female; one of two males and two females, but arranged in the sequence male–female–male–female, so as not to suggest two queer couples; two of two women and a man, with the man in the middle, keeping the women apart; and just one of two women. In the whole catalogue there is no photograph of two men. Likewise, the Christmas 1992 edition contains many photos of single models, plus five of a man and a woman, just one of two women and, again, none of two men. Interestingly, *Racing Green*'s edition of Summer 1992 contains several pleasantly affectionate images of two women – perhaps because the models look sufficiently alike to be twin sisters.

While it is true that most kinds of commercial promotion are at pains to preserve conventions and not to violate the status quo, they must also create at least an impression of moving smartly with the times. After all, we buy new things because they are new. There is evidence, therefore, of the urge to change in most catalogues, particularly those aimed at young people. But such signs of change have a limited scope.

Despite a general tendency to subscribe to the values of its Littlewoods Group stable-mates, including the usual rigorous segregations and heavy semiotic hints (yet another bride who has donned her head-dress and picked up her bouquet while still only dressed in her underwear), the *Janet Frazer* catalogue shows unusual signs of relaxation on some of its informal menswear pages. While there are still plenty of fist-on-shoulder shots of macho camaraderie, several poses allow an arm around the shoulder, one even around the neck instead. The context is of healthy beach sports, of course, but the general atmosphere is emotionally warmer than most catalogues seem to allow. There is even one shot in which a man appears to be affectionately patting his chum on the backside. The swimwear photos, although truncated in the usual fashion so that one cannot see nearly enough of the models' bodies, are group shots posed in what must have been very close groups, pelvis to pelvis, of up to five men; these contribute to the mood of unselfconscious friendliness which makes this section of the catalogue worth both looking at and commenting on. However, *Janet Frazer* soon reverts to type. We find that neither men's dressing gowns nor their underwear can be promoted without the admiring and endorsing gaze of an otherwise supernumerary female model.

Superficially modern and young in its values, the hardback *Next Directory*, for which one has to pay, turns out to be only a slight advance on its more dowdy competitors. The structure is conventional (women, men, children, household) and as you leaf through the pages you see that the compilers are suffering from familiar anxieties.

Most models are pictured singly, lest they compromise each other by look or gesture. (In the women's section there is, however, one peculiar exception: two women appear together in bathing costumes, both evidently delighted that one has pressed her knee between the other's legs.) It is the male models, as usual, whose hetero credentials are considered more in need of endorsement. So several shirts and sweaters are shown to be huggable by women; as is the male body itself, on the swimwear pages and, later, the underwear pages. Although Next has gone to some trouble to present good-looking men in a relatively sexy range of shorts and briefs, the message is clear: these bodies are available to the female customer only. As if to prove that these signals are not merely fortuitous, the children's clothing section, which follows, shows a broad range of child models, both white and black, both female and male, in a wide variety of poses and degrees of affectionate physical contact, evidently unpoliced.

Even *International Male*, a catalogue plainly dedicated to the proposition that men can be mouth-wateringly sexy, only has a handful of photos of two men together, and in each of these cases the models are fully clad. In all photos of shorts, underwear and swimming trunks, each model is on his own. Although this catalogue does include instances of heterosexualisation by the otherwise superfluous presence of a woman, this occurs in only two out of several hundred images.

The problem, therefore, is not that such catalogues do not recognise the existence of non-heterosexual buyers. The signs are that, on the contrary, they do. Lesbians and gay men represent a significant absence from their pages, an absence which is enforced with evident nervousness. There is, for instance, a kind of desperation in the way photographic displays of goods for sale make claims on the heterosexuality of the models being photographed. Women modelling lingerie are shown wearing bridal veils. Single sex pairs of models are posed with detailed and obvious care so that the women are seen to be available only to browsing men, and the men do not conform to the myth that all male models are queer. Attractive individuals are often shown with a person of the opposite sex, in soft focus, in the background. One of the worst examples of this tendency occurs in the 1992–3 edition of the *Ciro Citterio* menswear catalogue. To start with, the written copy appropriates that most ungendered item of clothing, the pair of denim jeans, for exclusively male use: 'JEANS masculine, hard, brash, sexy, comfortable, cool, utilitarian.' This is accompanied by a photograph of a white and a black man, both shirtless, in jeans. Behind these two figures, a naked woman is lying face-down on a wall. In a subsequent photo, the men have more clothes on but the woman does not.

Given that lesbians and gay men are imagined as a small minority of the credit card-carrying population, no major company seems yet to have recognised a source of profit in representing any of its models – and, therefore, any of its customers – as likely to live in a single sex household. For obvious economic reasons, each catalogue is addressing a notional 'majority', and protecting that audience from any influence which might lead them to question their established values.

The closer a catalogue's implied narratives come to moments in which sexual events might take place, the more nervous their imagery seems to become. In a situation where sex has to be evoked, since everyone knows it helps sell consumer goods – it seduces customers into handing over money to buy the props for their fantasies – sex must also be kept under control. The wrong kind of imagery would evoke the wrong kind of sex, which would then taint the goods in question; and goods which seem queer will not be bought by people who do not want to seem queer themselves. So, if one imagines a typical narrative of seduction as proceeding logically through the various subdivisions of the domestic space – let us say from dining room to living room, then from bathroom to bedroom – each of these rooms will, in turn, cause the advertiser a bigger headache.

As far as one can tell, there is not a lot of difference between a man's and a woman's bathrobe; it would not seem to matter which gender modelled one. However, shoppers' insecurities are generally calmed with a photo of robes being worn by a woman and a man together (*Choice*, *Family Album*, *Kays*). To underline the point, such images may be accompanied by explanatory copy – 'Although made for men they are equally suitable for women' (*Sander & Kay's Mail Mart*) or, more pithily, 'Luxurious Unisex Towelling Bath Robe' (*Green Shield*). Adjacent to the latter is a display of His and Hers towels. The overall impression these pages leave is of bathtime as a shared experience, but shared only by opposite sex couples.

That there are sexual concerns behind these various idiosyncrasies is further proved when one turns to pages concerning the bedroom. Anxieties surround what the consumer is expected to see there, to wear (and take off) there and, by implication, to do there. Again, these anxieties seem to be focused on unmarried men. Among their many pages displaying bed linen, most catalogues include one double-page spread intended to appeal to the single man – the so-called bachelor. Here, suddenly, instead of pastel colours, floral patterns, flounces and frills, the browsing eye encounters bold stripes, scarlet, a lot of black, and the trademark of the Playboy bunny. Three designs are offered: 'Bucks Fizz', an image of cascading champagne and bunny heads; 'Raffles', one large, black bunny head against a dark background; and 'Cabaret', a duvet-sized image of a woman's hat, face and gloved hand above the key word 'Playboy'. All this bedding can be matched with Playboy wallpaper and friezes, thereby making of the bachelor bedroom a perfect den for heterosexual seduction – or, perhaps more plausibly, a space in which to masturbate while fantasising such narratives.

An interesting accompaniment to this display is a bedding design called 'Censored'. This consists of a duvet cover in bold black and white stripes, with bright red highlights, down the full length of which is unambiguously printed, in black, the word 'PRIVATE'. On its other side, the reversible cover bears a large 'No Entry' sign. The complementary pillow case, mainly black, is liberally scattered with the legends 'Private', 'No Entry' and 'Keep Out'. Not surprisingly, this design is available only for a three-foot bed. It seems to be aimed at curiously demonstrative celibates.

Bedtime itself is, of course, the key moment for ideological and semiotic policing. Even more than the bathroom, the bedroom is desired and feared as the prime locus for the definition of sexualities. It is here that, perhaps under 'Frilled bedding with a floral stripe design and a contrast frill and trim', a groom might slip out of his 'PRINTED COTTON JERSEY PYJAMAS with fashionable classic motif', negotiate his way into his bride's 'WARM-HANDLE NIGHTDRESS with lace and ribbon trim' and ensure the survival of the species. (Thoughtlessly, however, most catalogues do not advertise maternity clothes.) But it is here, too, that the wrong combinations of bodies may occur: uncomplementary pairs – which is to say, of course, pairs which match. Queers.

In a display of bedtime wear for men which appears in several catalogues (*Burlington*, *John Moores*), on two double-page spreads, nine pictures of individual men in pyjamas or dressing gowns are accompanied by two in which a woman is kneeling or sitting on the bed behind the man, and two more in which the man is accompanied by a woman in a smaller version of the same dressing gown ('Judo-style robes IN SIZES TO SUIT BOTH OF YOU'). Yet the women's pages in the same catalogue are often significantly different. In the *Burlington* and *John Moores* catalogues, for instance, of thirty-five photos of women in nightdresses, pyjamas or dressing gowns, seven show two women together; and of these, two have them posing demurely together at the foot of their bed. Several catalogues promote garments which they describe as Samurai Yukatas, intended for use as dressing gowns, with an image of a man with his arm around a woman (*Home Free*, *Reader Offers from the Observer*, *Self Care*), ignoring or ignorant of the proudly homoerotic history of the Samurai themselves.

Only rarely do two men ever appear together in their dressing gowns or pyjamas. In the *J. D. Williams* collection, a catalogue aimed mainly at middle aged and old customers, two male models pose unproblematically, once with one in conventional pyjamas and the other in a bathrobe, then with both in pyjamas. Several factors seem to make these two images acceptable: because of its target age group, the catalogue does not seem much concerned to evoke sexual allure; the models, their clothing and their poses somehow look too conventional to be queer; photographed against a blank studio background, the models *look like* models, rather than the occupants of a real bedroom and bed.

A more daring image which appears in several catalogues (*Choice*, *Family Album*, *Kays*) shows two much younger models – both of whom also appear in a sexy display of underwear on an earlier double-page spread – dressed in Fido Dido and Spiderman [*sic*] 'short pyjama sets' (these being a combination which looks like tee-shirt and boxer shorts). One sits at a table, the other on it, with a portable backgammon board between them; behind them is a nondescript room with bare floorboards and a framed picture on the wall. Although ready for bed, these boys are not yet ready for each other: they are still concentrating on the game. But before long they will have to move: the one on the table has obviously not settled down for a protracted game. Although the marketers presumably do not intend this, the gay browser is prompted to ask one crucial question. In the unseen portion of the room, are the sleeping arrangements single or double?

It should be added that consumers are clearly expected to conform to company guidelines on sleeping arrangements even when on holiday. In the *L. L. Bean* catalogue, sleeping bags are advertised with an image of a nuclear family, the four of them lying in a row, each in a single bag. Even here, members of the same sex are kept apart: the family has organised itself into a strict male–female–male–female sequence. A double sleeping bag is shown with a heterosexual couple in it. In the *Index* catalogue, even what is promisingly called a '2-man' tent is pictured being used by a straight couple. Needless to say, holiday brochures – apart from those few specifically aimed at gay tourists – indulge in the same appropriations of all spaces for the enjoyment of heterosexual couples and nuclear families.

Writing on the topic of recent advertising, Frank Mort has spoken of how 'male sexuality is conjured up *through the commodity*, whether jeans, hair-gel, aftershave or whatever' (Mort 1988: 201). It is worth taking into account also, that 'through the commodity' is one of relatively few ways in which male bodies are acceptably conjured up in Western societies. Consequently one often hears of gay men whose first images of sexy men – their earliest masturbatory icons – were the men and boys in the underwear and swimwear sections of mail order catalogues. This use of catalogues as pornography seems to be tacitly accepted and, indeed, encouraged by companies selling 'exotic' underwear for men.

If one thing is clear about the promotion of men's underwear, it is that heterosexual men, although they constitute the major part of the market, are not the principal focus of the marketing. Because straight men apparently do not buy their own underwear – we are told that the majority of pants, pouches and shorts are bought by women for men (Blanchard 1992) – one even finds, on occasions, men's underwear in the middle of the women's sections of the catalogues. For example, on a page of women's knickers by Sloggi, a large photo shows a man and a women with their arms around each other, his face laughingly pressed to her cheek, both clad in Sloggi underwear. The copy across the top of the picture says, 'Women know why MEN should wear Sloggi for Men' (*Choice, Family Album*). The unstated reason is, of course, that the gym-toned model looks delicious in his little white briefs.

It is difficult not to deduce from what we are told of straight men's indifference to their own underwear that the most appreciative browsers of the men's underwear pages of general catalogues, and of men's underwear catalogues, are straight women and gay men. Some companies – Body Aware and Shamian being two recent examples – may go so far as to acknowledge gay interest by advertising in the gay press; but their catalogues are still at pains to suppress all imagery of male interest in men.

The aim of such catalogues is, of course, mainly to sell knickers (or, at the very least, the next edition of the catalogue), but they need to do so by effecting or reinforcing a change in attitudes. Richard Dyer has spoken of how, in Britain, there used to be only two main ways of perceiving the very topic of male underwear, 'medical' and 'giggling' – the latter point emphasised by a proliferation of 'novelty' underwear emblazoned with jokey illustrations or slogans (Dyer 1989: 43). In common with 'high' fashion companies such as Calvin Klein and Nikos, the underwear catalogues are obviously trying to replace the therapeutic and comic images with the erotic. The more seriously sexy an item looks on the page, the sexier it promises to become when one puts it on or prepares to take it off. The seriousness of the focused eroticism is a major selling point. (I should add, however, that even in an intensely eroticised display of items for women and men, the *Bronson Collection* still includes such novelty items for men as the 'Chef's Special Pouch', the 'Old Man Pouch', the 'Indian Pouch', the 'Coco Pouch' and the 'Long John Plonker Pirate Pouch'. One item, an elephant's-head pouch called 'Williphants', is pictured being fed a cupcake by a semi-naked woman.)

The *Shamian* catalogue is relaxed enough to show two men in one photo – but only once, and both are wearing both vest and shorts. Only when on their own or with a woman do they wear any less. Similarly, *Body Aware* publish a catalogue of men's underwear with eighteen photos of male models on their own, and two of male models accompanied by a female. Since the women's clothes are not on sale, the women are clearly included only for what their presence implies about the men. The *Designs in Leather* catalogue of erotic underwear never has more than one man in any photo, though its rear cover does show that pet fantasy of straight males, two women together on a bed. Inside the catalogue, no man appears without one (seven times), two (five times) or three women (once) to endorse his heterosexual credentials. The catalogue thus promotes its wares within the narrow swingers' fantasy world whose unwaveringly straight men make it with eagerly convertible lesbians. In the *Kiniki*

Catalogue, the majority of photographs are of single male models, but thirteen heterosexualise the display by including women in various stages of undress.

It is worth lingering on the *Kiniki* collection, to attend to the names with which all these briefs and pouches for straight men have been characterised. Some names are pithily descriptive of structure (Boxer, Ultrabox, Super-G, Contour, Zipper, Wispy); others bear the names of the men who might wear them, whether classy anglo (Marcus, Adam, Max, Barclay, James, Monty, Jasper), routinely suggestive (Roddy, Randy), continental or Latin (Pierre, Rico, Diego, Dino). The upper class theme is continued with underwear suggesting well-heeled leisure (Cabaret, Party, Stringfellow, Raffles, Ritzy), high status (Squire, Sloane, Top Notch, Elite) and dubious moral fibre (Charmer, Swinger, Dandy, Cad). Some briefs are named after the exotic locations they are intended to conjure up (Riviera, San Tropez, Brazil, Havana, Amazon, Hawaii, Mexico), others after the leisure activity one might enjoy in them (Sandtrecker, Windsurf, Beach Boy, Cruiser). Some are routinely macho (Beefcake, Tiger, Magnum) or evocative of macho narratives (Commander, Hero, High Flyer). Of these latter, the Hero briefs are shown in the silliest of photographs: he looks valiant in flying jacket, briefs, sun glasses and white silk scarf; she – the endorser of his sexuality – gazes into the sky beside him, dressed in nothing but the end of his scarf. One pair of padded briefs for men who do not measure up to requirements – 'Boost your credentials when you're eager to make an impression in this spectacular bulging brief' – is called Bandingo, presumably as intentional echo of the name of the West African tribe the Mandingo (Malinka), popularised in the developed world by the novels of Kyle Onstott. The racist message may be subliminal, but is perfectly clear: wear these pants and you will look as well hung as if you were black.

Eventually, anyone who browses the catalogues from a gay point of view must consider the topic – perhaps the myth – of gay 'style'. How willing are gay consumers to be seen in/with items bought from certain catalogues which have 'naff' reputations? Do they *want* to be, or to look, 'homely'? (How many self-respecting scene queens could survive the discovery that they buy their shoes from Argos or their maquillage from Avon?) On the other hand, it is not insignificant that shopping by catalogue may be the safest way for cross-dressers of either sex to stock up their closets. The drag queen does not have to be up to date. Indeed, she is more or less obliged not to be. Her nostalgia for pre-feminist styles, whether heartfelt or bogus, is adequately fed by the unassuming range of the catalogues – though she may well have to add sequins to taste.

Whether expressed as personality or sensibility, Camp is in need of both costumes and props. In general, its theatricality is not simply performed; it has to be staged. Male-as-female drag, in particular, has always been commodity-based in so far as it obviously relies on clothing, make-up and other accessories of constructed femininity. Men who cannot bring themselves either to outstare impertinent shop assistants and fellow customers, or to pretend they are shopping on behalf of non-existent wives with suspiciously large shoe sizes, may have recourse to mail order. The fact remains, though, that such customers know they are not included in the dreams promoted by the straight catalogues. It is only the lack of an alternative that forces people to go on supporting commercial organisations which do not acknowledge their existence. Imagine what a fabulous text a glossy catalogue for drag queens might be!

PART FOUR

The spectator and the audience
Shifts in screen theory

Introduction

FROM MULVEY THROUGH TO Schlesinger *et al.*, the essays in this Part indicate a journey in Film Studies, from the primacy of 'the spectator' as a hypothetical subject position constructed by the filmic text, to an increasingly expansive recognition of 'the audience', as actual, empirical viewers belonging to distinct sociohistorical contexts. This gradual shift in focus owes much to the more traditionally ethnographic approach of Cultural Studies, which was steadily accruing a seminal body of work on 'real' audiences and their relationships with media texts over the same period. In contrast, the concept of the spectator has remained one of Film Studies' most focal and contentious issues since the 1970s, when the impact of psychoanalysis and semiotics first put spectatorship at the forefront of film theory. It is hardly surprising then, that perhaps the most controversial and debated single essay in the history of Film Studies, Laura Mulvey's 'Visual Pleasure and Narrative Cinema', took spectatorship as its subject. Originally published in *Screen* journal in 1975, Mulvey's essay in Chapter 13 set the agenda for discussion of spectatorship and feminist film criticism for years to come and it is for this reason, despite its being widely reproduced elsewhere, that we open with it here. This Part, then, charts some of the key shifts Film Studies has travelled since Mulvey in pursuit of the female spectator and later, more tentatively, the female audience.

Before we look at Mulvey's intervention, some contextualisation. Judith Mayne (1993) identifies two broad strands of work from the 1970s that sought to analyse cinema as an institution, each conceptualising cinema's positioning of the spectator and its presumed alignment of the spectator with dominant ideology. First, 'apparatus theory' (as developed most prominently by Christian Metz and Jean-Louis Baudry in France and Mulvey in Britain) examined how the physical conditions of the cinematic space and its machinery encouraged the spectator to (falsely) imagine themselves as the author of meaning. A second, more text-based strand of theory (led by Raymond Bellour, Stephen Heath and Thierry Kuntzel) examined how the specifics of Hollywood's visual and narrative systems interpellated the spectator (see also Rosen, 1986).

Mulvey's key intervention was to argue that any conceptualisation of spectatorship in mainstream cinema had to engage with its representation of the female form. Her polemical essay brought together the era's prevailing interests in structuralism, feminism, psychoanalysis and Marxism to argue that the classical Hollywood cinema was dominated by a monolithic, patriarchal male gaze that offered pleasure only to the male spectator. Women's role within mainstream cinema was essentially passive, primarily pivoting on their 'to-be-looked-at-ness'. Drawing on Freud and Lacan, she argued that the conventions of Hollywood narrative and its voyeuristic and fetishistic approach to the female form conspired to control woman as image and to privilege the male spectator. Though many of the essay's findings have proved both enduringly provocative and all too prevalent, its shortcomings soon became apparent. While the male spectator in Mulvey's analysis was revelling in the male gaze or narcissistic identification, the female spectator seemed strangely and conspicuously absent. And couldn't the male body too be the object of an erotic gaze?

Mulvey herself would shortly address some of these omissions in her 1981 essay 'Afterthoughts on "Visual Pleasure and Narrative Cinema" inspired by *Duel in the Sun*'. Here she formulated a more mobile concept of female spectatorship, suggesting that the female spectator could move between an active 'masculine' and a passive 'feminine' identity. This conceptualisation was widely received as ultimately pessimistic, however, since it still fundamentally suggested that action was 'masculine'. In Chapter 14, however, we look at how Miriam Hansen's work on spectatorship in American silent film further problematised Mulvey's original essay. Hansen argues that early film had to cater to the needs of a variety of audience groups; needs which included female fantasy, as her case study of Rudolph Valentino – one of the biggest male stars and 'sex symbols' of the era – demonstrates. Hansen notes that 'whenever a woman initiates the look, she is invariably marked as a vamp' (1991: 269). But as she goes on to argue, it is nevertheless the case that the exchange of looks that Valentino participates in, as both object and subject of the look, is marked by ambivalence and instability rather than the rigid gendered dichotomy identified by Mulvey. Valentino, then, is very much the object of a 'desiring female gaze' within the filmic world, and by extension beyond it, challenging 'the notion of a unified position of scopic mastery' (1991: 281) formulated in Mulvey's original analysis. Elsewhere theorists have formulated a 'queer gaze' as another way in to reading Classical Hollywood, again enabling a conceptualisation of mainstream cinema's ideological operations as flexible and fissured in ways that early accounts of spectatorship didn't imagine (see Doty, 1993; Weiss, 1991).

By the time we reach Jackie Stacey's analysis of British female cinema audiences of the 1940s and 1950s and their relationships with the female stars of the era (Chapter 15), Film Studies has gone a step further; not just investigating how the *text* constructs or allows a space for female desire, as Hansen does, but actually going out and speaking with 'real' *audiences* about their experiences of that desire. In a letter published in two of Britain's leading women's magazines, Stacey appealed to 'keen cinema-goers in the 1940s and 1950s' to contact her with their memories. In the resulting work Stacey combines theories of escapism, identification and consumption with ethnographic research to give a fascinating account of some of the ways in which British women actively emulated and engaged with the stars of the classical period. As such, it pursues a more empirical analysis of film reception, garnering insights which theories of spectatorship, in their relative abstraction, could not yield. The reluctance of feminist film theorists to venture into the perplexity of audience research may well be understandable given the comparative ease, accessibility and order of conducting textual analysis. Moreover, textual analysis has also enabled feminist film theorists to largely evade the difficult *ethical* issues which come with actually meeting audiences and subsequently having to make 'critical judgements' about how 'real' women engage with the cinema machine (Stacey, 1994: 12). But feminist film analysis shuns audience research at its peril according to Stacey. As she notes:

> I would argue that it is only by combining theories of the psychic dimensions of cinematic spectatorship with analyses that are socially located that the full complexity of the pleasures of the cinema can be understood. The analysis of female spectators' accounts of the cinema may open up multiple or contradictory readings, depending on variables such as context, company, mood or differences amongst female spectators.
>
> (ibid.: 33)

However, as always and as Stacey notes, the methodological and ideological pitfalls of ethnography make themselves felt. In the extract here, for example, she reflects that her work has to negotiate the respondents' selection and construction – and the researcher's processing and inevitable interpretation – of audience memories. Potential problems also emerge in the way that some respondents evidently form an affectionate affiliation with her as a kind of researcher-cum-confidante. The allure of nostalgia is all too clear as one woman wistfully recollects, 'Oh Jackie, what lovely memories are being recalled . . .' (1994: 64). In fact, Stacey subsequently argues that nostalgia is a pleasure that is particularly potent for the female audience given their cultural investment in idealised images of the feminine.

On a very different tack, Schlesinger *et al.*'s work with female audiences (Chapter 16), undertaken in much the same period as Stacey's, explores women's relationships with screen violence. Their respondents watched a variety of film and TV texts; the extract here examines the nuances of their responses to *The Accused* (Jonathan Kaplan, US, 1989), a major Hollywood production which notoriously featured a lengthy and controversial gang-rape scene. Interestingly (and in contrast with Stacey), Schlesinger *et al.* organise their respondents systematically according to prescribed and foregrounded categories, classifying them according to class, nationality, race and whether or not they had 'experienced violence'. This latter subdivision in particular – how precisely can one classify and identify a shared concept of 'experience of violence'? – seems to demonstrate how audience research's efforts to maintain discrete classificatory divisions inevitably sometimes risk a degree of indeterminacy or subjectivity. Nevertheless, the researchers' attention to differences in the respondents' personal experience and cultural and social distinctions between them highlights significant differences in the way the women responded to the film. For example, they found that far fewer Asian women than white or Afro-Caribbean women 'related' to the characters or situations depicted in *The Accused*, a pattern which the researchers posit results from the Asian women's relative detachment 'from the cultural context of the film' (Schlesinger *et al.*, 1992: 141). This demonstrates again how any invoking of 'the audience' or 'the female audience' as a homogeneous group is destined to prove reductive in the face of differences in the interpretation and reception of the film text, wrought by the individual's membership of specific socio-cultural groups and indeed the historical context of its viewing.

Finally, it is also worth acknowledging here that the terrain may be shifting again according to Pam Cook's reflective reassessment of spectatorship debates in Film

Studies; or more specifically, of these debates as they refer to feminist analysis of the women's picture'. In a recent essay, 'No Fixed Address: The Women's Picture From *Outrage* to *Blue Steel*' (1998), Cook has suggested that we once again reconsider our assumptions about the nature of audience engagement with popular films. Cook acknowledges that feminist analysis of the women's picture has been 'enormously productive' (ibid.: 230), partly facilitating the shift away from a position which maintained that Hollywood cinema marginalised or even omitted female spectatorial pleasure, to a position which recognises that mainstream cinema has always enabled female audiences to derive identification and empowerment. But what if the fundamental premises underlying this body of work were misguided? What if generic boundaries and gendered address in Hollywood were in fact more permeable and fluid than Film Studies has hitherto recognised?

Cook suggests that the Western, that most 'masculine' of genres, may have more in common with the melodramatic structures of the women's picture than has yet been explored. Looking again at the work of Mary Ann Doane, Judith Mayne and the women's films of the 1940s, Cook finds that these women's pictures' multiple masochistic scenarios 'impl[y] a dual address to male and female spectators' which demands we reconsider 'the widely accepted notion that the woman's film is primarily addressed to female spectators' (ibid.: 235). The implications of Cook's analysis are striking, both for our understanding of the operation of classical and post-classical Hollywood and for our evaluation of the history of spectatorship and audience theory. Recent 'cracks appearing in the surface of film theory' suggest that 'popular cinema is more ideologically open, and processes of identification more fluid than has previously been imagined', while feminist film theory's enduring critique of Hollywood's marginalisation of women both on and off the screen 'is radically questioned by the idea that all spectators may redefine themselves in relation to the dominant social categories, not only in the darkened space of the cinema, but outside it too' (ibid.: 234).

Further reading

Clover, Carol J. (1992) *Men, Women and Chainsaws: Gender in the Modern Horror Film*, London: BFI Publishing.

Cook, P. (1998) 'No Fixed Address: The Women's Picture from *Outrage* to *Blue Steel*', in S. Neale and M. Smith (eds) *Contemporary Hollywood Cinema*, London and New York: Routledge.

Doane, M. A. (1982) 'Film and the Masquerade: Theorising the Female Spectator', *Screen*, vol. 23, nos. 3–4.

Doty, A. (1993) *Making Things Perfectly Queer: Interpreting Mass Culture*, Minneapolis: University of Minnesota Press.

Hansen, M. (1991) *Babel and Babylon: Spectatorship in American Silent Film*, Cambridge, MA: Harvard University Press.

Mayne, J. (1993) *Cinema and Spectatorship*, New York and London: Routledge.

Mulvey, L. (1981) 'Afterthoughts on "Visual Pleasure and Narrative Cinema" inspired by *Duel in the Sun*', *Framework* 6, 15/16/17, pp. 12–15.

Mulvey, L. (1989) *Visual and Other Pleasures*, London: Macmillan.

Rosen, P. (1986) *Narrative, Apparatus, Ideology*, New York: Columbia University Press.

Schlesinger, P., Dobash, R. E., Dobash R. P. and Weaver, C. K. (1992), *Women Viewing Violence*, London: BFI Publishing.

Stacey, J. (1994) *Star Gazing: Hollywood Cinema and Female Spectatorship*, London and New York: Routledge.

Weiss, A. (1991) '"A queer feeling when I look at you": Hollywood stars and lesbian spectators in the 1930s', in C. Gledhill (ed.) *Stardom: Industry of Desire*, London and New York: Routledge.

Chapter 13

Laura Mulvey

VISUAL PLEASURE AND NARRATIVE CINEMA

I. Introduction

A. A political use of psychoanalysis

THIS PAPER INTENDS TO use psychoanalysis to discover where and how the fascination of film is reinforced by pre-existing patterns of fascination already at work within the individual subject and the social formations that have moulded him. It takes as its starting point the way film reflects, reveals and even plays on the straight, socially established interpretation of sexual difference which controls images, erotic ways of looking and spectacle. It is helpful to understand what the cinema has been, how its magic has worked in the past, while attempting a theory and a practice which will challenge this cinema of the past. Psychoanalytic theory is thus appropriated here as a political weapon, demonstrating the way the unconscious of patriarchal society has structured film form.

The paradox of phallocentrism in all its manifestations is that it depends on the image of the castrated woman to give order and meaning to its world. An idea of woman stands as lynch pin to the system: it is her lack that produces the phallus as a symbolic presence, it is her desire to make good the lack that the phallus signifies. Recent writing in *Screen* about psychoanalysis and the cinema has not sufficiently brought out the importance of the representation of the female form in a symbolic order in which, in the last resort, it speaks castration and nothing else. To summarise briefly: the function of woman in forming the patriarchal unconscious is twofold, she first symbolises the castration threat by her real absence of a penis and second thereby raises her child into the symbolic. Once this has been achieved, her meaning in the process is at an end, it does not last into the world of law and language except as a memory, which oscillates between memory of maternal plenitude and memory of lack. Both are posited on nature (or on anatomy in Freud's famous phrase). Woman's desire is subjected to her image as bearer of the bleeding wound, she can exist only in relation to castration and cannot transcend it. She turns her child into the signifier of her own desire to possess a penis (the condition, she imagines, of entry into the symbolic). Either she must gracefully give way to the word, the Name of the Father and the Law, or else struggle to keep her child down with her in the half-light of the imaginary. Woman then stands in patriarchal culture as signifier for the male other, bound by a symbolic order in which man can live out his phantasies and obsessions through linguistic command by imposing them on the silent image of woman still tied to her place as bearer of meaning, not maker of meaning.

There is an obvious interest in this analysis for feminists, a beauty in its exact rendering of the frustration experienced under the phallocentric order. It gets us nearer to the roots of our oppression, it brings an articulation of the problem closer, it faces us with the ultimate challenge: how to fight the unconscious structured like a language (formed critically at the moment of arrival of language) while still caught within the language of the patriarchy. There is no way in which we can produce an alternative out of the blue, but we can begin to make a break by examining patriarchy with the tools it provides, of which psychoanalysis is not the only but an important one. We are still separated by a great gap from important issues for the female unconscious which are scarcely relevant to phallocentric theory: the sexing of the female infant and her relationship to the symbolic, the sexually mature woman as non-mother, maternity outside the signification of the phallus, the vagina. But, at this point, psychoanalytic theory as it now stands can at least advance our understanding of the status quo, of the patriarchal order in which we are caught.

B. Destruction of pleasure as a radical weapon

As an advanced representation system, the cinema poses questions of the ways the unconscious (formed by the dominant order) structures ways of seeing and pleasure in looking. Cinema has changed over the last few decades. It is no longer the monolithic system based on large capital investment exemplified at its best by Hollywood in the 1930's, 1940's and 1950's. Technological advances (16mm, etc.) have changed the economic conditions of cinematic production, which can now be artisanal as well as capitalist. Thus it has been possible for an alternative cinema to develop. However self-conscious and ironic Hollywood managed to be, it always restricted itself to a formal mise-en-scène reflecting the dominant ideological concept of the cinema. The alternative cinema provides a space for a cinema to be born which is radical in both a political and an aesthetic sense and challenges the basic assumptions of the mainstream film. This is not to reject the latter moralistically, but to highlight the ways in which its formal preoccupations reflect the psychical obsessions of the society which produced it, and, further, to stress that the alternative cinema must start specifically by reacting against these obsessions and assumptions. A politically and aesthetically avant-garde cinema is now possible, but it can still only exist as a counterpoint.

The magic of the Hollywood style at its best (and of all the cinema which fell within its sphere of influence) arose, not exclusively, but in one important aspect, from its skilled and satisfying manipulation of visual pleasure. Unchallenged, mainstream film coded the erotic into the language of the dominant patriarchal order. In the highly developed Hollywood cinema it was only through these codes that the alienated subject, torn in his imaginary memory by a sense of loss, by the terror of potential lack in phantasy, came near to finding a glimpse of satisfaction: through its formal beauty and its play on his own formative obsessions. This article will discuss the interweaving of that erotic pleasure in film, its meaning, and in particular the central place of the image of woman. It is said that analysing pleasure, or beauty, destroys it. That is the intention of this article. The satisfaction and reinforcement of the ego that represent the high point of film history hitherto must be attacked. Not in favour of a reconstructed new pleasure, which cannot exist in the abstract, nor of intellectualised unpleasure, but to make way for a total negation of the ease and plenitude of the narrative fiction film. The alternative is the thrill that comes from leaving the past behind without rejecting it, transcending outworn or oppressive forms, or daring to break with normal pleasurable expectations in order to conceive a new language of desire.

II. Pleasure in looking/fascination with the human form

A. The cinema offers a number of possible pleasures. One is scopophilia. There are circumstances in which looking itself is a source of pleasure, just as, in the reverse formation, there is pleasure in being looked at. Originally, in his *Three Essays on Sexuality*, Freud isolated scopophilia as one of the component instincts of sexuality which exist as drives quite independently of the erotogenic zones. At this point he associated scopophilia with taking other people as objects, subjecting them to a controlling and curious gaze. His particular examples centre around the voyeuristic activities of children, their desire to see and make sure of the private and the forbidden (curiosity about other people's genital and bodily functions, about the presence or absence of the penis and, retrospectively, about the primal scene). In this analysis scopophilia is essentially active. (Later, in *Instincts and Their Vicissitudes*, Freud developed his theory of scopophilia further, attaching it initially to pre-genital autoeroticism, after which the pleasure of the look is transferred to others by analogy. There is a close working here of the relationship between the active instinct and its further development in a narcissistic form.) Although the instinct is modified by other factors, in particular the constitution of the ego, it continues to exist as the erotic basis for pleasure in looking at another person as object. At the extreme, it can become fixated into a perversion, producing obsessive voyeurs and Peeping Toms whose only sexual satisfaction can come from watching, in an active controlling sense, an objectified other.

At first glance, the cinema would seem to be remote from the undercover world of the surreptitious observation of an unknowing and unwilling victim. What is seen on the screen is so manifestly shown. But the mass of mainstream film, and the conventions within which it has consciously evolved, portray a hermetically sealed world which unwinds magically, indifferent to the presence of the audience, producing for them a sense of separation and playing on their voyeuristic phantasy. Moreover, the extreme contrast between the darkness in the auditorium (which also isolates the spectators from one another) and the brilliance of the shifting patterns of lights and shade on the screen helps to promote the illusion of voyeuristic separation. Although the film is really being shown, is there to be seen, conditions of screening and narrative conventions give the spectator an illusion of looking in on a private world. Among other things, the position of the spectators in the cinema is blatantly one of repression of their exhibitionism and projection of the repressed desire onto the performer.

B. The cinema satisfies a primordial wish for pleasurable looking, but it also goes further, developing scopophilia in its narcissistic aspect. The conventions of mainstream film focus attention on the human form. Scale, space, stories are all anthropomorphic. Here, curiosity and the wish to look intermingle with a fascination with likeness and recognition: the human face, the human body, the relationship between the human form and its surroundings, the visible presence of the person in the world. Jacques Lacan has described how the moment when a child recognises its own image in the mirror is crucial for the constitution of the ego. Several aspects of this analysis are relevant here. The mirror phase occurs at a time when the child's physical ambitions outstrip his motor capacity, with the result that his recognition of himself is joyous in that he imagines his mirror image to be more complete, more perfect than he experiences his own body. Recognition is thus overlaid with misrecognition: the image recognised is conceived as the reflected body of the self, but its misrecognition as superior projects this body outside itself as an ideal ego, the alienated subject, which, re-introjected as an ego ideal, gives rise to the future generation of identification with others. This mirror moment predates language for the child.

Important for this article is the fact that it is an image that constitutes the matrix of the imaginary, of recognition/misrecognition and identification, and hence of the first articulation of the I, of subjectivity. This is a moment when an older fascination with looking (at the mother's face, for an obvious example) collides with the initial inklings of self-awareness. Hence it is the birth of the long love affair/despair between image and self-image which has found such intensity of expression in film and such joyous recognition in the cinema audience. Quite apart from the extraneous similarities between screen and mirror (the framing of the human form in its surroundings, for instance), the cinema has structures of fascination strong enough to allow temporary loss of ego while simultaneously reinforcing the ego. The sense of forgetting the world as the ego has subsequently come to perceive it (I forgot who I am and where I was) is nostalgically reminiscent of that pre-subjective moment of image recognition. At the same time the cinema has distinguished itself in the production of ego ideals as expressed in particular in the star system, the stars centring both screen presence and screen story as they act out a complex process of likeness and difference (the glamorous impersonates the ordinary).

C. Sections II. A and B have set out two contradictory aspects of the pleasurable structures of looking in the conventional cinematic situation. The first, scopophilic, arises from pleasure in using another person as an object of sexual stimulation through sight. The second, developed through narcissism and the constitution of the ego, comes from identification with the image seen. Thus, in film terms, one implies a separation of the erotic identity of the subject from the object on the screen (active scopophilia), the other demands identification of the ego with the object on the screen through the spectator's fascination with and recognition of his like. The first is the function of the sexual instincts, the second of ego libido. This dichotomy was crucial for Freud. Although he saw the two as interacting and overlaying each other, the tension between instinctual drives and self-preservation continues to be a dramatic polarisation in terms of pleasure. Both are formative structures, mechanisms not meaning. In themselves they have no signification, they have to be attached to an idealisation. Both pursue aims in indifference to perceptual reality, creating the imagised, eroticised concept of the world that forms the perception of the subject and makes a mockery of empirical objectivity.

During its history, the cinema seems to have evolved a particular illusion of reality in which this contradiction between libido and ego has found a beautifully complementary phantasy world. In *reality* the phantasy world of the screen is subject to the law which produces it. Sexual instincts and identification processes have a meaning within the symbolic order which articulates desire. Desire, born with language, allows the possibility of transcending the instinctual and the imaginary, but its point of reference continually returns to the traumatic moment of its birth: the castration complex. Hence the look, pleasurable in form, can be threatening in content, and it is woman as representation/image that crystallises this paradox.

III. Woman as image, man as bearer of the look

A. In a world ordered by sexual imbalance, pleasure in looking has been split between active/male and passive/female. The determining male gaze projects its phantasy onto the female figure, which is styled accordingly. In their traditional exhibitionist role women are simultaneously looked at and displayed, with their appearance coded for strong visual and erotic impact so that they can be said to connote *to-be-looked-at-ness*. Woman displayed as sexual object is the leitmotif of erotic spectacle: from pin-ups to stripe-tease, from Ziegfeld to Busby Berkeley, she holds the look, plays to and signifies male desire. Mainstream film neatly combines spectacle with narrative. (Note, however, how in the musical song-and-dance numbers break the flow of the diegesis.) The presence of woman is an indispensable element of spectacle in normal narrative film, yet her visual presence tends to work against the development of a story line, to freeze the flow of action in moments of erotic contemplation. This alien presence then has to be integrated into cohesion with the narrative. As Budd Boetticher has put it:

> What counts is what the heroine provokes, or rather what she represents. She is the one, or rather the love or fear she inspires in the hero, or else the concern he feels for her, who makes him act the way he does. In herself the woman has not the slightest importance.

(A recent tendency in narrative film has been to dispense with this problem altogether; hence the development of what Molly Haskell has called the 'buddy movie', in which the active homosexual eroticism of the central male figures can carry the story without distraction.) Traditionally, the woman displayed has functioned on two levels: as erotic object for the characters within the screen story, and as erotic object for the spectator within the auditorium, with a shifting tension between the looks on either side of the screen. For instance, the device of the show-girl allows the two looks to be unified technically without any apparent break in the diegesis. A woman performs within the narrative, the gaze of the spectator and that of the male characters in the film are neatly combined without breaking narrative verisimilitude. For a moment the sexual impact of the performing woman takes the film into a no-man's-land outside its own time and space. Thus Marilyn Monroe's first appearance in *The River of No Return* and Lauren Bacall's songs in *To Have and Have Not*. Similarly, conventional close-ups of legs (Dietrich, for instance) or a face (Garbo) integrate into the narrative a different mode of eroticism. One part of a fragmented body destroys the

Renaissance space, the illusion of depth demanded by the narrative, it gives flatness, the quality of a cut-out or icon rather than verisimilitude to the screen.

B. An active/passive heterosexual division of labour has similarly controlled narrative structure. According to the principles of the ruling ideology and the psychical structures that back it up, the male figure cannot bear the burden of sexual objectification. Man is reluctant to gaze at his exhibitionist like. Hence the split between spectacle and narrative supports the man's role as the active one of forwarding the story, making things happen. The man controls the film phantasy and also emerges as the representative of power in a further sense: as the bearer of the look of the spectator, transferring it behind the screen to neutralise the extra-diegetic tendencies represented by woman as spectacle. This is made possible through the processes set in motion by structuring the film around a main controlling figure with whom the spectator can identify. As the spectator identifies with the main male[1] protagonist, he projects his look onto that of his like, his screen surrogate, so that the power of the male protagonist as he controls events coincides with the active power of the erotic look, both giving a satisfying sense of omnipotence. A male movie star's glamorous characteristics are thus not those of the erotic object of the gaze, but those of the more perfect, more complete, more powerful ideal ego conceived in the original moment of recognition in front of the mirror. The character in the story can make things happen and control events better than the subject/spectator, just as the image in the mirror was more in control of motor coordination. In contrast to woman as icon, the active male figure (the ego ideal of the identification process) demands a three-dimensional space corresponding to that of the mirror recognition, in which the alienated subject internalised his own representation of this imaginary existence. He is a figure in a landscape. Here the function of film is to reproduce as accurately as possible the so-called natural conditions of human perception. Camera technology (as exemplified by deep focus in particular) and camera movements (determined by the action of the protagonist), combined with invisible editing (demanded by realism), all tend to blur the limits of screen space. The male protagonist is free to command the stage, a stage of spatial illusion in which he articulates the look and creates the action.

C.1 Section III. A and B have set out a tension between a mode of representation of woman in film and conventions surrounding the diegesis. Each is associated with a look: that of the spectator in direct scopophilic contact with the female form displayed for his enjoyment (connoting male phantasy) and that of the spectator fascinated with the image of his like set in an illusion of natural space, and through him gaining control and possession of the woman within the diegesis. (This tension and the shift from one pole to the other can structure a single text. Thus both in *Only Angels Have Wings* and in *To Have and Have Not*, the film opens with the woman as object of the combined gaze of spectator and all the male protagonists in the film. She is isolated, glamorous, on display, sexualised. But as the narrative progresses she falls in love with the main male protagonist and becomes his property, losing her outward glamorous characteristics, her generalised sexuality, her show-girl connotations; her eroticism is subjected to the male star alone. By means of identification with him, through participation in his power, the spectator can indirectly possess her too.)

But in psychoanalytic terms, the female figure poses a deeper problem. She also connotes something that the look continually circles around but disavows: her lack of a penis, implying a threat of castration and hence unpleasure. Ultimately, the meaning of woman is sexual difference, the absence of the penis as visually ascertainable, the material evidence on which is based the castration complex essential for the organisation of entrance to the symbolic order and the law of the father. Thus the woman as icon, displayed for the gaze and enjoyment of men, the active controllers of the look, always threatens to evoke the anxiety it originally signified. The male unconscious has two avenues of escape from this castration anxiety: preoccupation with the re-enactment of the original trauma (investigating the woman, demystifying her mystery), counterbalanced by the devaluation, punishment or saving of the guilty object (an avenue typified by the concerns of the *film noir*); or else complete disavowal of castration by the substitution of a fetish object or turning the represented figure itself into a fetish so that it becomes reassuring rather than dangerous (hence over-valuation, the cult of the female star). This second avenue, fetishistic scopophilia, builds up the physical beauty of the object, transferring it into something satisfying in itself. The first avenue, voyeurism, on the contrary, has associations with sadism: pleasure lies in ascertaining guilt (immediately associated with castration), asserting control and subjecting the guilty person through punishment or forgiveness. This sadistic side fits in well with narrative. Sadism demands a story, depends on making something happen, forcing a change in another person, a battle of will and strength, victory/defeat, all occurring in a linear time with a beginning and an end. Fetishistic scopophilia, on the other hand, can exist outside linear time as the erotic instinct is focussed on the look alone. These contradictions and ambiguities can be illustrated more simply by using works by Hitchcock and Sternberg, both of whom take the look almost as the content or subject matter of many of their films. Hitchcock is the more complex, as he uses both mechanisms. Sternberg's work, on the other hand, provides many pure examples of fetishistic scopophilia.

C.2 It is well known that Sternberg once said he would welcome his films being projected upside down so that story and character involvement would not interfere with the spectator's undiluted appreciation of the screen image. This statement is revealing but ingenuous. Ingenuous in that his films do demand that the figure of the woman (Dietrich, in the cycle of films with her, as the ultimate example) should be identifiable. But revealing in that it emphasises the fact that for him the pictorial space enclosed by the frame is paramount rather than narrative or identification processes. While Hitchcock goes into the investigative side of voyeurism, Sternberg produces the ultimate fetish, taking it to the point where the powerful look of the male protagonist (characteristic of traditional narrative film) is broken in favour of the image in direct erotic rapport with the spectator. The beauty of the woman as object and the screen space coalesce; she is no longer the bearer of guilt but a perfect product, whose body, stylised and fragmented by close-ups, is the content of the film and the direct recipient of the spectator's look. Sternberg plays down the illusion of screen depth; his screen tends to be one-dimensional, as light and shade, lace, steam, foliage, net, streamers, etc, reduce the visual field. There is little or no mediation of the look through the eyes of the main male protagonist. On the contrary, shadowy presences like La Bessière in *Morocco* act as surrogates for the director, detached as they are from audience identification. Despite Sternberg's insistence that his stories are irrelevant, it is significant that they are concerned with situation, not suspense, and cyclical rather than linear time, while plot complications revolve around misunderstanding rather than conflict. The most important absence is that of the controlling male gaze within the screen scene. The high point of emotional drama in the most typical Dietrich films, her supreme moments of erotic meaning, take place in the absence of the man she loves in the fiction. There are other witnesses, other spectators watching her on the screen, their gaze is one with, not standing in for, that of the audience. At the end of *Morocco*, Tom Brown has already disappeared into the desert when Amy Jolly kicks off her gold sandals and walks after him. At the end of *Dishonoured*, Kranau is indifferent to the fate of Magda. In both cases, the erotic impact, sanctified by death, is displayed as a spectacle for the audience. The male hero misunderstands and, above all, does not see.

In Hitchcock, by contrast, the male hero does see precisely what the audience sees. However, in the films I shall discuss here, he takes fascination with an image through scopophilic eroticism as the subject of the film. Moreover, in these cases the hero portrays the contradictions and tensions experienced by the spectator. In *Vertigo* in particular, but also in *Marnie* and *Rear Window*, the look is central to the plot, oscillating between voyeurism and fetishistic fascination. As a twist, a further manipulation of the normal viewing process, which in some sense reveals it, Hitchcock uses the process of identification normally associated with ideological correctness and the recognition of established morality and shows up its perverted side. Hitchcock has never concealed his interest in voyeurism, cinematic and non-cinematic. His heroes are exemplary of the symbolic order and the law – a policeman (*Vertigo*), a dominant male possessing money and power (*Marnie*) – but their erotic drives lead them into compromised situations. The power to subject another person to the will sadistically or to the gaze voyeuristically is turned onto the woman as the object of both. Power is backed by a certainty of legal right and the established guilt of the woman (evoking castration, psychoanalytically speaking). True perversion is barely concealed under a shallow mask of ideological correctness – the man is on the right side of the law, the woman on the wrong. Hitchcock's skilful use of identification processes and liberal use of subjective camera from the point of view of the male protagonist draw the spectators deeply into his position, making them share his uneasy gaze. The audience is absorbed into a voyeuristic situation within the screen scene and diegesis which parodies his own in the cinema. In his analysis of *Rear Window*, Douchet takes the film as a metaphor for the cinema. Jeffries is the audience, the events in the apartment block opposite correspond to the screen. As he watches, an erotic dimension is added to his look, a central image to the drama. His girlfriend Lisa had been of little sexual interest to him, more or less a drag, so long as she remained on the spectator side. When she crosses the barrier between his room and the block opposite, their relationship is re-born erotically. He does not merely watch her through his lens, as a distant meaningful image, he also sees her as a guilty intruder exposed by a dangerous man threatening her with punishment, and thus finally saves her. Lisa's exhibitionism has already been established by her obsessive interest in dress and style, in being a passive image of visual perfection; Jeffries's voyeurism and activity have also been established through his work as a photo-journalist, a maker of stories and captor of images. However, his enforced inactivity, binding him to his seat as a spectator, puts him squarely in the phantasy position of the cinema audience.

In *Vertigo*, subjective camera predominates. Apart from one flash-back from Judy's point of view, the narrative is woven around what Scottie sees or fails to see. The audience follows the growth of his erotic obsession and subsequent despair precisely from his point of view. Scottie's voyeurism is blatant: he falls in love with a woman he follows and spies on without speaking to. Its sadistic side is equally blatant: he has chosen (and freely chosen, for he had been a successful lawyer) to be a policeman, with all the attendant possibilities of pursuit and investigation. As a result, he follows, watches and falls in love with a perfect image of female beauty and mystery. Once he actually confronts her, his erotic drive is to break her down and force her to tell by persistent cross-questioning. Then, in the second part of the film, he re-enacts his obsessive involvement with the image he loved to watch secretly. He reconstructs Judy as Madeleine, forces her to conform in every detail to the actual physical appearance of his fetish. Her exhibitionism, her masochism, make her an ideal passive counter-part to Scottie's active sadistic voyeurism. She knows her part is to perform, and only by playing it through and then replaying can she keep Scottie's erotic interest. But in the repetition he does break her down and succeeds in exposing her guilt. His curios-ity wins through and she is punished. In *Vertigo*, erotic involvement with the look is disorientating: the spectator's fascination is turned against him as the narrative carries him through and entwines him with the processes that he is himself exercising. The Hitchcock hero here is firmly placed within the symbolic order, in narrative terms. He has all the attributes of the partriachal superego. Hence the spectator, lulled into a false sense of security by the apparent legality of his surrogate, sees through his look and finds himself exposed as complicit, caught in the moral ambiguity of looking. Far from being simply an aside on the perversion of the police, *Vertigo* focuses on the implications of the active/looking, passive/looked-at split in terms of sexual difference and the power of the male symbolic encapsulated in the hero. Marnie, too, performs for Mark Rutland's gaze and masquerades as the perfect to-be-looked-at image. He, too, is on the side of the law until, drawn in by obsession with her guilt, her secret, he longs to see her in the act of committing a crime, make her confess and thus save her. So he, too, becomes complicit as he acts out the implications of his power. He controls money and words, he can have his cake and eat it.

IV. Summary

The psychoanalytic background that has been discussed in this article is relevant to the pleasure and unpleasure offered by traditional narrative film. The scopophilic instinct (pleasure in looking at another person as an erotic object), and, in contradistinction, ego libido (forming identification processes) act as formations, mechanisms, which the cinema has played on. The image of woman as (passive) raw material for the (active) gaze of man takes the argument a step further into the structure of representation, adding a further layer demanded by the ideology of the patriarchal order as it is worked out in its favourite cinematic form – illusionistic narrative film. The argument returns again to the psychoanalytic background in that woman as representation sig-nifies castration, including voyeuristic or fetishistic mechanisms to circumvent her threat. None of these interacting layers is intrinsic to film, but it is only in the film form that they can reach a perfect and beautiful contradiction, thanks to the possibility in the cinema of shifting the emphasis of the look. It is the place of the look that defines cinema, the possibility of varying it and exposing it. This is what makes cinema quite different in its voyeuristic potential from, say, strip-tease, theatre, shows, etc. Going far beyond highlighting a woman's to-be-looked-at-ness, cinema builds the way she is to be looked at into the spectacle itself. Playing on the tension between film as controlling the dimension of time (editing, narrative) and film as controlling the dimension of space (changes in distance, editing), cinematic codes create a gaze, a world, and an object, thereby producing an illusion cut to the measure of desire. It is these cinematic codes and their relationship to formative external structures that must be broken down before mainstream film and the pleasure it provides can be challenged.

To begin with (as an ending), the voyeuristic-scopophilic look that is a crucial part of traditional filmic pleasure can itself be broken down. There are three different looks associated with cinema: that of the camera as it records the pro-filmic event, that of the audience as it watches the final product, and that of the characters at each other within the screen illusion. The conventions of narrative film deny the first two and subordinate them to the third, the conscious aim being always to eliminate intrusive camera presence and prevent a distancing awareness in the audience. Without these two absences (the material existence of the recording process, the critical reading of the spectator), fictional drama cannot achieve reality, obviousness and truth. Nevertheless, as this article has argued, the structure of looking in narrative fiction film contains a contradiction in its own premises: the female image as a castration threat constantly endangers the unity of the diegesis and bursts through the world of illusion as an intrusive, static, one-dimensional fetish. Thus the two looks materially present in time and space are obsessively subordinated to the neurotic needs of the male ego. The camera becomes the mechanism for producing an illusion of Renaissance space, flowing movements compatible with the human eye, an ideology of representation that revolves around the perception of the subject; the camera's look is disavowed in order to create a convincing world in which the spectator's surrogate can perform with verisimilitude. Simultaneously, the look of the audience is denied an intrinsic force: as soon as fetishistic representation of the female image appears directly (without mediation) to the spectator, the fact of fetishisation, concealing as it does castration fear, freezes the look, fixates the spectator and prevents him from achieving any distance from the image in front of him.

This complex interaction of looks is specific to film. The first blow against the monolithic accumulation of traditional film conventions (already undertaken by radical film-makers) is to free the look of the camera into its materiality in time and space and the look of the audience into dialectics, passionate detachment. There is no doubt that this destroys the satisfaction, pleasure and privilege of the 'invisible guest', and highlights how film has depended on voyeuristic active/passive mechanisms. Women, whose image has continually been stolen and used for this end, cannot view the decline of the traditional film form with anything much more than sentimental regret.

Note

1 There are films with a woman as main protagonist, of course. To analyse this phenomenon seriously here would take me too far afield. Pam Cook and Claire Johnston's study of *The Revolt of Mamie Stover* in Phil Hardy, ed., *Raoul Walsh*, Edinburgh, 1974, shows in a striking case how the strength of this female protagonist is more apparent than real.

Chapter 14

Miriam Hansen

BABEL AND BABYLON
Spectatorship in American silent film

Patterns of vision, scenarios of identification

AT FIRST GLANCE VALENTINO'S films seem to rehearse the classical choreography of the look almost to the point of parody, offering point-of-view constructions that affirm the cultural hierarchy of gender in the visual field. From *The Four Horsemen* to his death, Valentino starred in fourteen films, produced by different studios and under different directors. Illustrating the significance of the star as *auteur* as much as the economic viability of vehicles, each of these films reiterates a familiar pattern in staging the exchange of looks between Valentino and the female characters. Whenever Valentino lays eyes on a woman first, we can be sure that she will turn out to be the woman of his dreams, the legitimate partner in the romantic relationship. Whenever a woman initiates the look, she is invariably marked as a vamp, to be condemned and defeated in the course of the narrative.

In the opening sequence of *The Eagle* (United Artists, 1925; based on Pushkin's novella *Dubrovsky*), the Czarina (Louise Dresser) is about to inspect her favorite regiment, 'the handsomest in all Russia,' when a runaway carriage nearby prompts the hero into a Fairbanks-like rescue. The first shot of Valentino shows him from the rear, looking through a pocket-sized telescope. The first time we see his face, it is framed, medium close-up, by the window of the coach, directing a curious gaze inside. The reverse shot completing the point of view, however, is illegible, hiding the object under a bundle of fur; only his repeated look makes the image readable, distinguishes the female figure from the setting, literally produces her for the spectator. As the young woman (Vilma Banky) returns the glance, she enters the romantic pact, acknowledging the power of his look(s). Her negative counterpart is the Czarina, a stout, elderly woman who is shown catching sight of Valentino independent of his look, which momentarily transfigures her face in desire. While she is masculinized by a military outfit and at the same time ridiculed for her lack of masculine physical skills, desire on her part is most crucially discredited through its association with political power. As she continues her inspection of Valentino's body in the privacy of the imperial suite, encircling and immobilizing him (no point-of-view shot), the expression of horror in his eyes pinpoints the scandal of the situation, the reversal of gender positions in the visual field, unilaterally enforced by the monarch. As soon as Valentino understands the sexual implications of his position, he determines to restore the traditional (im)balance, risking death as a deserter, yet regaining the mastery of the look.

A similar pattern can be observed in *Blood and Sand* (Famous Players-Lasky, 1922): Doña Sol (Nita Naldi), the President's niece, is shown admiring the victorious torero through opera glasses, prior to his looking at her, syntactically, this marks her as a vamp. His future wife, Carmen (Lila Lee), on the other hand, is singled out by the camera within his point of view, similar to the coach sequence in *The Eagle*. A close-up of his face signals the awakening desire, alternating with an undecipherable long shot of a crowd. The repetition of the desiring look, provoking a dissolve that extricates her from the crowd, resolves the picture puzzle for the spectator and, by the same logic of vision, establishes her as the legitimate companion (further sanctioned by the inclusion of his mother in the point-of-view construction that follows). Thus, the legitimate female figure is deprived of the initiative of the erotic look, relegated to the position of scopic object within the diegesis. In relation to the spectator, however, she shares this position of scopic object with Valentino.

Valentino's appeal depends to a large degree on the manner in which he combines masculine control of the look with the feminine quality of 'to-be-looked-at-ness,' to use Laura Mulvey's rather awkward term. When he falls in love – usually at first sight – the close-up of his face surpasses that of the female character in its value as spectacle. In a narcissistic doubling, the subject of the look constitutes itself as object, graphically illustrating Freud's formulation of the autoerotic dilemma: 'Too bad that I cannot kiss myself.'[1] Moreover, in their radiant pictorial quality, such shots temporarily arrest the metonymic drive of the narrative, similar in effect to the visual presence of the woman, which, as Mulvey observes, tends 'to freeze the flow of action in moments of erotic contemplation.'[2] In Valentino's case, however, erotic contemplation governs an active as well as a passive mode, making spectator and character the subject of a double game of vision.

To the extent that Valentino occupies the position of primary object of spectacle, he incurs a systematic feminization of his persona. But as with the publicity discourse, his feminization on the level of filmic enunciation involves more complex processes than mere sexual objectification. Complementing the specular evocation of feminine narcissism, the mise-en-scène of many of his films makes him enact an exhibitionism, which, with the 'Great Masculine Renunciation' of fashion in the eighteenth century, became culturally assigned to women.[3] Although the narration tries to motivate this exhibitionism by casting Valentino as a performer (torero, dancer) or by situating him in a historically or exotically removed setting, the connotation of femininity persists in the choice of costumes, such as flared coats and headdress reminiscent of a bridal wardrobe, as well as a general emphasis on dressing and disguises. *Monsieur Beaucaire*, a 1924 Paramount costume drama based on the Booth Tarkington novel, combines the effect and its disavowal in a delightfully self-reflective manner. Valentino, playing the Duke of Chartres alias Monsieur Beaucaire, is introduced on stage playing the lute in an attempt to entertain the jaded King, Louis XV. The courtly mise-en-scène ostensibly legitimizes the desiring female gaze, contained in the alternation of relatively close shots of Valentino and the female members of the audience within the film. Unfailingly, however, this sequence enacts the paradox of female spectatorship. As one woman is shown *not* focusing her eyes upon him in rapture, he stops midway in indignation and a title redundantly explains: 'the shock of his life: a woman not looking at him.' Sure enough, this refers to the leading romantic lady.[4] The partial reversal of the gender economy of vision is prepared by the film's opening shot, a close-up of hands doing needlepoint. As the camera pulls back, the hands are revealed to be the King's. In the effeminate universe of the French court, Valentino asserts his masculinity only by comparison, staging it as a difference that ultimately fails to make a difference.

Before considering the possibilities of identification implied in this peculiar chore-ography of vision, I wish to recapitulate some thoughts on female visual pleasure and its fate under the patriarchal taboo. Particularly interesting are certain aspects of scopophilia that Freud analyzes through its development in infantile sexuality, a period in which the child is still far from having a stable sense of gender identity. Stimulated in the process of mutual gazing between mother and child, the female scopic drive is constituted with a bisexual as well as an autoerotic component. Although these components subsequently succumb to cultural hierarchies of looking that tend to fixate the woman in a passive, narcissistic-exhibitionist role, a basic ambivalence in the structure of vision as a component drive remains. As Freud argues in 'Instincts and Their Vicissitudes' (1915), the passive component of a drive repre-sents a reversal of the active drive into its opposite, redirecting itself to the subject. Such contradictory constitution of libidinal components may account for the coex-istence, in their later fixations as perversions of diametrically opposed drives within one and the same person, even if one tendency usually predominates. Thus a voyeur is always to some degree an exhibitionist and vice versa, just as the sadist shares the pleasure of masochism.[5]

The notion of ambivalence is crucial to a theory of female spectatorship, precisely because the cinema, while enforcing patriarchal hierarchies in its organization of the look, also offers women an institutional opportunity to violate the taboo on female scopophilia. The success of a figure like Valentino, himself overdetermined as both object and subject of the look, urges us to insist upon the ambivalent constitution of scopic pleasure, the potential reversibility and reciprocity of roles. Moreover, as one among a number of the more archaic partial drives whose integration is always and at best precarious, scopophilia needs to be distinguished, conceptually, from its return in the adult perversion of voyeurism, culturally assigned to men and predicated on the one-sided regime of the keyhole and the threat of castration. Although scopophilia as a component drive does not exist outside the norms of genitality, collapsing it a priori into an Oedipal teleology restricts the possibility of conceptualizing the female spec-tator (or, for that matter, the male spectator as well) in other than binary, ahistorical terms; it thus tends to reproduce a phallic economy on the level of critique.[6]

The potential dissociation of sexual and survival instincts, which is implicit in Freud's notion of 'anaclisis' and which he discusses with reference to the scopic drive in his analysis of cases of psychogenic disturbance of vision, is equally pertinent to an alternative conception of visual pleasure. The eye serves both a practical function for the individual's orientation in the external world and the function of an erotogenic zone. If the latter refuses to accept its subservient role in the forepleasure and takes over, the balance between sexual and survival instincts is threatened. To this the ego may react by repressing the dangerous component drive. The psychogenic disturbance of vision in turn represents the revenge of the repressed instinct, retrospectively interpreted by the individual as the voice of punishment which seems to be saying: 'Because you sought to misuse your organ of sight for evil sensual pleasure, it is fitting that you should not see anything at all any more.'[7]

While the psychogenic disturbance of vision, in the framework of psychoanalytic theory, clearly functions as a metaphor of castration,[8] the potentially antithetical relation of sexual and survival instincts could also be taken to describe the cultural and historical differentiation of male and female forms of vision. Although the neurotic dissociation may occur in patients of both sexes, the balance effected in so-called normal vision seems more typical of the pyschic disposition by means of which the male subject controls the practical world as well as the sexual field. Suffice it here to allude to the historical construction of monocular vision in Western art since the Renaissance, the instrumental standards imposed upon looking in technical and scientific observation and other disciplines, areas of cultural activity from which for centuries women were barred. On the flipside of this coin we find a variety of social codes enforcing the taboo on female scopophilia, ranging from make-up fashions like belladonna through the once popular injunction, parodied by Dorothy Parker, not to 'make passes at girls who wear glasses.'

The construction of femininity within patriarchal society, however, contains the promise of being incomplete. Women's exclusion from mastery of the visual field may have diminished the pressure of the ego instincts toward the component drives, which are probably insufficiently subordinated to begin with. Thus the potential dissociation of the scopic drive from its function for survival may not be that threatening to the female subject, may not necessarily provoke the force of repression that Freud holds responsible for certain cases of psychogenic blindness. If such generalization is permissible, women might be more likely to indulge, without immediately repressing, in a sensuality of vision that contrasts with the goal-oriented discipline of the one-eyed masculine look. Christa Karpenstein speaks in this context of 'an unrestrained scopic drive, a swerving and sliding gaze which disregards the meanings and messages of signs and images that socially determine the subject, a gaze that defies the limitations and fixations of the merely visible.'[9]

If I seem to belabor this notion of an undomesticated gaze as a historical aspect of female subjectivity, I certainly do not intend to propose yet another variant of essentialism. To the extent that sexual difference is culturally constructed to begin with, the subversive qualities of a female gaze may just as well be shared by a male character. This is precisely what I want to suggest for the case of Valentino, contrary to the official legend, which never ceased to assert the power of his look in terms of aggressive mastery. The studios and fan magazines persistently advertised his hypnotic gaze, and the state of bliss in store for the woman who would be discovered by it, in the measure that he himself was becoming an erotic commodity at the mercy of the gaze of millions.[10]

On the level of filmic enunciation, the feminine connotation of Valentino's 'to-be-looked-at-ness' destabilizes his own glance in its very origin, makes him vulnerable to temptations that jeopardize the sovereignty of the male subject. When Valentino's eyes get riveted on the woman of his choice, he seems to become paralyzed rather than aggressive or menacing, behaving like the rabbit rather than the snake. Struck by the beauty of Carmen, in *Blood and Sand*, his activity seems blocked, suspended; it devolves upon Carmen, who throws him a flower, to get the narrative back into gear. Later in the film, at the height of his career as a torero, Valentino raises his eyes to the

President's box, an individual centered under the benevolent eye of the State, when his gaze is sidetracked, literally decentered by the sight of Doña Sol in the box to the right. The power of Valentino's gaze depends upon its weakness – enhanced by the fact that he was actually nearsighted and cross-eyed – upon its oscillating between active and passive, between object and ego libido. The erotic appeal of the Valentinian gaze, staged as a look within the look, is one of reciprocity and ambivalence rather than mastery and objectification.

The peculiar organization of the Valentinian gaze corresponds, on the level of narrative, to conflicts between the pleasure and the reality principle. Whenever the hero's amorous interests collide with the standards of male social identity – career, family, paternal authority, or a vow of revenge – the spectator can hope that passion will triumph over pragmatism to the point of self-destruction.[11] As the generating vortex of such narratives, the Valentinian gaze far exceeds its formal functions of providing diegetic coherence and continuity, it assumes an almost figural independence. Thus the films advance an identification with the gaze itself, not with source or object but with the gaze as erotic medium, which promises to transport the spectator out of the world of means and ends into the realm of passion.

The discussion of gendered patterns of vision opens into the larger question of identification, as the matrix structuring the viewer's access to the film, the process that organizes subjectivity in visual and narrative terms. Most productively, feminist film theorists have insisted on the centrality of sexual difference, questioning the assumption of a single or neutral spectator position constructed in hierarchically ordered, linear processes of identification. Initially, Mulvey reduced cinematic identification to a basically active relationship with a protagonist of the same sex, that is, male; but she subsequently modified this notion with regard to the female viewer, who may not only cross but also be divided by gender lines (which in turn deflects identification from the fictive telos of a stable identity). The difficulty of conceptualizing a female spectator has led feminists to recast the problem of identification in terms of instability, mobility, multiplicity, and, I would add, temporality. Likewise, a number of critics are trying to complicate the role of sexual difference in identification with the differences of class and race, with cultural and historical specificity. This might make it possible to rethink the concept of subjectivity implied, beyond the commonplace that subjects are constructed by and within ideology. The question of the subject of identification is also, and not least, a question as to which part of the spectator is engaged and how, which layers of conscious or unconscious memory and phantasy are activated, and how we, as viewers and critics, choose to interpret this experience.[12]

It seems useful at this point to invoke Mary Ann Doane's distinction of at least three instances of identification that operate in the viewing process: identification *with* the representation of a person (character, star); identification (recognition) *of* particular objects, persons or actions *as* such (stars, narrative images); identification with the 'look,' with oneself as the condition of perception, which Metz, in analogy with Lacan's concept of the mirror phase, has termed 'primacy.'[13] These psychical mechanisms and their effects can be traced through the various levels of enunciation that structure cinematic identification, interlacing textual units such as shot, sequence, strategies of narrative and mise-en-scène.[14] The first form of identification discussed by Doane, identification with the integral person filmed (Metz's 'secondary' mode of identification), engages the female viewer transsexually insofar as it extends to the Valentino character as subject. Thus is raises the problem of spectatorial cross-dressing – unless we consider other possibilities of transsexual identification beside the transvestite one. The alternative option for the woman spectator, passive-narcissistic identification with the female star as erotic object, seems to have been advertised primarily by the publicity discourse; it appears rather more problematic in view of the specular organization of the films.[15]

If we can isolate an instance of 'primary' identification at all – which is dubious on theoretical grounds – Valentino's films challenge the assumption of perceptual mastery implied in such a concept both on account of the star system and because of the peculiar organization of the gaze. The star not only promotes a dissociation of scopic and narrative registers but also complicates the imaginary self-identity of the viewing subject with an exhibitionist and collective dimension. The fascination with the star, 'the observed of all observers' (Pratt), entails both a projection of the fan into the figure of the star as the object of admiration and an awareness that this projection is shared by others who contemplate that same figure.[16] The Valentino films undermine the notion of a unified position of scopic mastery by foregrounding the reciprocity and ambivalence of the gaze as an erotic medium, a gaze that fascinates precisely because it transcends the socially imposed subject–object hierarchy of sexual difference.

Moreover, the contradictions of the female address are located in the very space where the registers of the look and those of narrative and mise-en-scène intersect. In offering the woman spectator a position structurally analogous to that of the vamp within the diegesis (looking at Valentino independent of his scopic initiative) identification with the desiring gaze is both granted and incriminated, or, one might say, granted on condition of its illegitimacy. This may be why the vamp figures in Valentino films (with the exception of *Blood and Sand*) are never totally condemned, inasmuch as they acknowledge a subliminal complicity between Valentino and the actively desiring female gaze. In *The Eagle*, for instance, the Czarina is redeemed by her general's ruse of letting Valentino escape execution under an assumed identity. The closing shot shows Valentino and the Czarina waving each other a never-ending farewell, much to the concern of their respective legitimate partners.

Notes

1 Sigmund Freud, 'Three Essays on the Theory of Sexuality' (1905), *Standard Edition*, 7: 182.
2 Laura Mulvey, 'Visual Pleasure and Narrative Cinema,' *Screen* 16.3 (1975): 11.
3 See Kaja Silverman, 'Fragments of a Fashionable Discourse,' in Tania Modleski (ed.), *Studies in Entertainment: Critical Approaches to Mass Culture* (Bloomington: Indiana University Press, 1986), pp. 139–52.
4 A more misogynist version of the same pattern occurs in *Cobra* (1925), when a friend advises the unhappily courting but much pursued Valentino, 'look at the woman with the torch: she is safe!' – cut to the Statue of Liberty. For an excellent reading of these 'duels' and 'ballets' of the gaze, see Karsten Witte, 'Rudolph Valentino: Erotoman des Augenblicks,' in Adolf Heinzlmeier *et al.* (eds), *Die Unsterblichen des Kinos* (Frankfurt am Main: Fischer, 1982), I, 29–35.
5 Sigmund Freud, 'Instincts and their Vicissitudes,' trans. James Strachey, *Standard Edition*, 14: 128ff.; 'Three Essays,' *SE*, 7: 156ff, 199–200, and passim.
6 I am much indebted here to Gertrud Koch, 'Why Women Go to the Movies,' *Jump Cut* 27 (July 1982), and 'Von der weiblichen Sinnlichkeit und ihrer Lust und Unlust am Kino: Mutmaßungen über vergangene Freuden und neue Hoffnungen,' in Gabriele Dietz (ed.) *Die Überwindung der Sprachlosigkeit* (Darmstadt: Luchterhand, 1979), pp. 116–38.

7   Sigmund Freud, 'The Psycho-Analytic View of Psychogenic Disturbance of Vision' (1910), *Standard Edition*, 11: 216–17.

8   For an elaboration of this aspect of Freud's essay, see Stephen Heath, 'Difference,' *Screen* 19: 3 (Autumn 1978): 86–87.

9   Christa Karpenstein, 'Bald führt der Blick das Wort ein, bald leitet das Wort den Blick,' *Kursbuch* 49 (1977): 62. Also see Jutta Brückner's important essay on pornography, 'Der Blutefleck im Auge der Kamera,' *Frauen und Film* 30 (December 1981): 13–23; Brückner links the historical 'underdevelopment' of women's vision with the modality of dreams, as a more archaic form of consciousness: 'This female gaze, which is so precise precisely because it is not too precise, because it also has this inward turn, opening itself to phantasy images which it melts with the more literal images on the screen, this gaze is the basis for a kind of identification which women in particular tend to seek in the cinema' (p. 19).

10 The discrepancy between the advertising pitch and Valentino's actual lack of orientation and focus is obvious in the promotional short *Rudolph Valentino and His Eighty-Eight American Beauties* (1923), which shows him as a somewhat halfhearted arbiter in a beauty contest. Even Roland Barthes's compelling reading of the Valentino face emphasizes the aggressive aspect of his gaze. 'The face is mysterious, full of exotic splendor, of an inaccessible, Baudelairean beauty, undoubtedly made of exquisite dough, but one knows all too well that this cold glistening of make-up, this delicate, dark line under the animal eye, the black mouth – all this betrays a mineral substance, a cruel statue which comes to life only to thrust forth.' ('Le visage est arcane, splendeur exotique, beauté bauderlairienne, inaccessible, d'une pâte exquise sans doute, mais on sait bien que cette froid luisance du fard, ce mince trait sombre sous l'oeil d'animal, cette bouche noire, tout cela est d'un être minéral, d'une statue cruelle qui ne s'anime que pour percer' ['Visages et figures,' *Esprit* 204 (July 1953): 7]). The metaphor of piercing or thrusting, however, only conforms the suspicion that the Valentinian gaze is a substitute for phallic potency, hence the fetishistic cult that surrounds it.

11 Two of Valentino's most popular films, *The Four Horsemen* and *Blood and Sand*, actually culminate in the protagonist's death, bringing into play the deep affinity of eros and death drive that Freud observes in his fascinating paper on 'The Theme of the Three Caskets' (1913), *SE* 12: 289–301. According to Enno Patalas, Valentino identified much more strongly with these two roles than with the superficial heroism of the Sheik, *Sozialgeschichte der Stars* (Hamburg: Marion von Schröder Verlag, 1963) pp. 96–97.

12 See, for example, Janet Walker, 'Psychoanalysis and Feminist Film Theory,' *Wide Angle* 6.3 (1984): 20ff.; Teresa de Lauretis, 'Aesthetic and Feminist Theory,' *New German Critique* 34 (Winter 1985): 154–75; 164ff.

13 Mary Ann Doane, 'Misrecognition and Identity,' *Ciné-Tracts* 3.3 (Fall 1980): 25; Metz, *The Imaginary Signifier*, pp. 46ff, 56–57, and passim.

14 Suffice it here to invoke the work of Stephen Heath, Raymond Bellour, and Thierry Kuntzel, also compare the section on Point of View in *Film Reader* 4 (1979).

15 This option actually prevails in contemporary statements of female spectators; see Herbert Blumer, *Movies and Conduct* (New York: Macmillan, 1933), pp. 69–70. In retrospect, however, as I frequently found in conversation with women who were in their teens at the time, the female star has faded into oblivion as much as the narrative, whereas Valentino himself is remembered with great enthusiasm and vividness of detail.

16 John Pratt, 'Notes on Commercial Movie Technique,' *International Journal of Psycho-Analysis* 34, 3–4 (1943): 186, quoted and elaborated in Harriet E. Margolis, *The Cinema Ideal: An Introduction to Psychoanalytic Studies of the Film Spectator* (New York and London: Garland, 1988), pp. 148–49. On the theoretical blind spot of Metz's concept of primary identification, see Doane, 'Misrecognition and Identity,' pp. 28ff.; Doane's major objection is that since this concept is based on the analogy with the Lacanian mirror stage and hence the hypothetical constitution of the male subject, on a theoretical level the notion of primary identification perpetuates the patriarchal exclusion of female spectatorship.

Chapter 15

Jackie Stacey

STAR GAZING
Hollywood cinema and female spectatorship

Formations of popular memory and cinema history

> '[H]istory' is a record of subjective readings of the past; it exists
> only in the perspective of the lens through which it is viewed . . .
> History is not simply a study of the *past* by official historians. We
> are all historians of the *present*; 'popular memory' is produced
> socially and collectively as a précis of the past and everyone is a
> kind of historian.
>
> (Taylor, 1989: 203)

> Memory alone cannot resurrect past time, because it is memory
> itself that shapes it, long after historical time has passed.
>
> (Steedman, 1986: 29)

THE QUESTION OF THE relationship between memory and history is a
slippery one. Yet it is a crucial one for those interested in the historical reception
of film, if we are seriously concerned with the history of cinema audiences and not
just the history of films (Allen, 1990). The history of audiences necessitates some consideration of memory if it is not to remain at the purely quantitative level; in other
words if film history is to engage with ethnographic methods of audience analysis, as
well as detailing cinema attendance statistically, then memory has to be a central consideration. A critical analysis of the forms and mechanisms of memory is pertinent to
all ethnographic studies of media audiences, since the process of retelling is necessarily at stake in some form or another: audiences always represent their readings to
researchers retrospectively. However, in this research, the length of the gap between
the events and their recollection (forty or fifty years) highlights the question of the
processes of memory especially sharply.

Spectators' memories of Hollywood stars, then, drawn on here to construct an historical account of spectatorship, need to be considered within a critical framework highlighting these processes of memory itself. Memory is not a straightforward representation of past events to which we have direct access and which we can in turn retell to others. Instead, I would argue that it involves a set of complex cultural processes: these operate at a psychic and a social level, producing identities through the negotiation of 'public' discourses and 'private' narratives. These histories of spectatorship are retrospective reconstructions of a past in the light of the present and will have been shaped by the popular versions of the 1940s and 1950s which have become cultural currency during the intervening years.

Cultural studies work on popular memory has highlighted well some of the methodological issues of using memory for cultural and historical analysis.[1] Amongst these is the question of how personal investments shape the kinds of memories we produce and how we prioritise some of them above others: in other words the processes of selection and construction of memory. The concept of the 'treasured memory', for example, has been used to refer to memories people have in which they have a particular personal investment. Many respondents in my research wrote of such 'treasured memories' and of their continued pleasure in recollections of past times: 'I have memories I shall always treasure. Other things in life take over, visiting the cinema is nil these days, but I shall always remember my favourite films and those wonderful stars of yesteryear' (Mrs B. Morgan). Using a personal mode of address which introduces a feeling of intimacy and familiarity, another respondent writes: 'Oh Jackie, what lovely memories are being recalled – I do hope you are going to ask for lots more information as a trip down Memory Lane of this nature is most enjoyable' (Barbara Forshaw). Such memories have been likened to a personal possession never to be lost. Indeed, it has been argued that 'treasured' memories are particularly significant in conserving a past self and thereby guarding against the experience of loss (Popular Memory Group, n.d.: 26). 'Treasured memories' may thus signify past selves or imagined selves of importance retrospectively.

The notion of the treasured memory suggests a place which can be regularly revisited. One woman writes of the unexpected pleasures such a place has provided:

> My grandfather's boss was kind enough, every Christmas of my childhood, to give me a present of a film annual. I enjoyed them then, but never dreamt what a treasure trove they'd prove to be. Now in my 50s, I pore over them from time to time and it's like opening Pandora's Box (*sic*). Stars of yesteryear, long forgotten. Films I saw, but had forgotten all about. Hollywood at its height, the glitz and glamour. I can remember setting out a good hour before the film started to secure a front position in the queue.
>
> (Barbara McWhirter)

There are numerous reasons for our investments in treasured memories. It has been suggested that one such investment might be in memories as particular 'transformative moments' (Popular Memory Group, n.d.: 165). Such moments are especially pertinent to the spectator/star relationship because Hollywood stars embody cultural ideals of femininity and represent the possibility of transformation of the self to spectators. Indeed, as we shall see, many memories of Hollywood stars concern their role in the transformation of spectators' own identities . . . In addition, many respondents' memories are of a transitional period: their 'teenage' years, in which change and self-transformation were central to their desires and aspirations . . .

It has been argued that one of the pleasures of such memories might derive from the ways in which memories work as 'personal utopias' which offer a kind of escape from the constraints of daily life. This conceptualisation is particularly pertinent in the context of spectators' memories of Hollywood stars who could be seen as offering utopian fantasies to cinema audiences at that time . . . Thus the process and the subject of the memory both involve utopias of some form.

The kinds of personal utopias produced will partly depend upon present feelings about past events. Memories depend upon past expectations and the extent to which these were met or not, since unmet needs and desires may influence the continuing significance of particular memories; in other words, some memories continue to be of central importance because of past frustrations, disappointments and unfulfilled fantasies. Thus it has been suggested that memories might usefully be considered as 'stories of unfinished business' (Popular Memory Group, n.d.: 30). Women's expectations and subsequent experiences of romance, motherhood or paid work, for example, may shape their reconstructions of their relationship to Hollywood ideals of femininity in the 1940s and 1950s.

Many women looking back at the cinema of the 1940s and 1950s may have developed a critical awareness of their love of Hollywood and its stars at that time. One woman writes:

> In retrospect it's easy to see Hollywood stars for what they really were . . . pretty packaged commodities . . . the property of a particular studio. At the time I did most of my film going, while I was always aware that stars were really too good to be true, I fell as completely under the spell of the Hollywood 'Dream Factory' as any other girl of my age.
>
> (Kathleen Lucas)

Reflecting upon the role of the industry in constructing the glamour of the female stars and upon her changing feelings about this in retrospect, she continues: 'I came in contact with the glamour and expertise of film making at a particularly impressionable age. Looking back, I can see much of what I took as authenticity was really technical skill . . . Later on I realised just how much money and expertise went into creating the "natural" beauties the female stars appeared to be' (Kathleen Lucas). Thus, memory works here to define present self in contrast to past self, and whilst there may be a suggestion of retrospective wisdom, there may also be a sense of loss for the effects of the powerful magic of Hollywood.

Such feelings may be especially pertinent to an understanding of women's memories of the 1940s and 1950s, given the 'impossibility of femininity' . . . Feminine ideals are, by definition, never realisable, since they fundamentally contradict each other (such as the constructions of motherhood and of sexual desirability). Memories of Hollywood stars, then, may have a particular significance for female spectators in terms of their representation of a fantasy self never realised. In addition, given the centrality of commodities to the 'successful' construction of feminine identities, the material constraints of certain periods in women's lives, such as the austerity of the 1940s and early 1950s, and the continuing economic constraints on women outside the growing 'affluence' of the middle classes, may have shaped the kinds of investments made in particular memories.

For women in the 1980s, nostalgia is clearly one of the pleasures of remembering 1940s and 1950s Hollywood cinema and its stars. Remembrance is simultaneously an acknowledgement of the loss of those times, and a means of guarding against their complete loss. The nostalgia evoked may be for former feminine identities, for the period itself and for the cinema and stars of that time. Thus the loss of youth and of innocence articulates with a loss of a particular kind of cinematic pleasure and star status. The perception that the cinema and the stars 'are not what they used to be', 'not like the old days' is an important motivator for respondents to express their opinion about historical change in the cinema.

It has been argued that nostalgia may have particular appeal for women. Psychoanalytic theory offers an explanation of why nostalgic desire should have such a gendered appeal. According to this model our adult feelings about loss, about the past and about nostalgia are based on our early childhood understandings of our place in the world and its sexual/symbolic hierarchies. The psychoanalytic account returns us to the different meanings of sexual difference for boy and girl children represented in the Oedipal and castration scenarios: whereas the boy fears losing what he has, as he believes his mother to have done, the girl regrets what she believes she has lost. Thus femininity and nostalgia are linked through an early desire to retrieve what is believed to have been lost (see Radstone, 1993 and forthcoming).

Such an account importantly foregrounds the links between femininity and nostalgia. I do not want to take issue with some of the basic tenets of psychoanalytic theory here, since that would constitute too extended a digression . . . Rather, I would like to add to these psychoanalytic investigations my own arguments about the appeal of nostalgia for women with particular reference to the relationship between female spectators and Hollywood stars as feminine ideals during this period.

My argument hinges on the extent to which femininity is defined in patriarchal culture as an unattainable visual image of desirability . . . To present oneself to the world for approval in terms of physical attractiveness is the ultimate demand made of femininity. Few women ever overcome the sense of mismatch between their self-image and feminine ideals in terms of physical appearance, and those that do live uneasily with the inevitability of its disappearance with ageing. The attainment of feminine ideals is thus typically ephemeral. Feminine ideals are youthful ones, and thus successful femininity contains loss even in the rare sense of its attainment.

Thus the sense of loss for women evoked by nostalgic desire, I would suggest, is bound up in precisely this unattainability of the ideal feminine image. Indeed, the centrality of the visual image to feminine ideals produces lasting and powerful memories of such ideals which endure the passing of time. The feelings of loss, often experienced in the gap between the self and the ideal at the time, is deepened and extended as feminine ideals become ever-increasingly a lost possibility. Agreeing with the psychoanalytic account, then, I would argue that women's nostalgic desire is indeed bound up with their particular sense of loss, but a sense of loss which is firmly rooted in the unattainability of feminine ideal images. Thus it is the particular designation of femininity as image which gives nostalgia such potency for women.

This is not to suggest that masculinity is not also an identity which is culturally constructed through a series of ideals. Men may also feel a nostalgia for a time when attainment of desired identities still seemed a future possibility. However, masculine ideals are more diverse, less based upon image and physical appearance than on status, power and activity, and offer the possibility of improving with age in some cases. Thus, I would argue that typically nostalgia for lost ideals is very different for men and for women.

As I have discussed elsewhere . . ., Lacanian psychoanalysis would suggest that all our subjectivities are constituted in relation to the misrecognition of the self in an ideal which is ultimately illusory. However, this pre-symbolic process of 'the mirror stage' needs to be considered in the symbolic context of the centrality of the visual image in representations of femininity in this culture. The pull of such mis/recognitions may be based in very early childhood development, but its specific meaning to femininity can only be fully understood when situated within a critical analysis of representation of 'woman as image' within patriarchal culture.

The centrality of being an image to the definition of successful femininity in this culture may account for one of the forms of memory frequently used by women in this research: what I shall call iconic memory. Icon, originally used to refer to religious imagery, is apt here to describe the female stars, remembered as screen goddesses and as the objects of desire and even worship. Women's memories of 1940s and 1950s Hollywood often take the form of a particular 'frozen moment', taken out of its temporal context and captured as 'pure image': be it Bette Davis's flashing and rebellious eyes, Doris Day's fun outfits or Rita Hayworth's flowing hair. This is not only true of memories of the stars, but also of the spectators' memories of themselves. One meaning of icon is 'likeness' and this is pertinent to the use of iconic memory in the context in which female spectators remember themselves in such 'frozen moments'. One woman remembers sitting in front of the mirror brushing her hair trying to look like Bette Davis in *Dark Victory* (1939, Edmund Goulding) . . .; thus her own reflection in the mirror has replaced the image of the star on the screen and becomes the subject of this iconic memory.

The second form of memory which occurred most frequently in this research is narrative memory. Women's memories of the cinema in this period offer the opportunity for the presentation of past and present subjectivities through processes of self-narrativisation. In contrast to iconic memories, narrative memories present temporally located sequential stories of cinema-going in the 1940s and 1950s. Women's memories of Hollywood stars are specific forms of self-narrativisation in relation to cultural ideals. Female spectators thus construct themselves as heroines of their own stories which in turn deal with their own heroines at that time. Memories of Hollywood stars are thus represented through the codes and conventions of narrative form structurally connecting self and ideal.

It is not simply the case that these female spectators remembered the narratives in which their favourite screen idols starred, but also that their relationships to the stars are often recreated through narrative form of memory. One example of the use of the narrative form most conventionally associated with femininity is that of romance. This is used by some respondents in their retelling of the connections between self and ideal within the conventions of romantic narrative . . .

The ways in which I requested information may have encouraged women to use narratives to construct their memories. For example, question 13, 'describe your favourite cinema experience of the 1940s/1950s', asked respondents to tell stories. In addition, letter-writing employs certain narrative forms in the retelling of past events. Respondents wrote me letters in which they narrativised themselves in relation to their past ideals. This history of spectatorship is thus constructed through forms of private story-telling given public recognition in the research process.

Some memories combine iconic and narrative forms. Particular iconic memories may be of a narrative image, a scene from a film such as Jennifer Jones's 'last crawl towards Gregory Peck over the rocks' (Yvonne Oliver) in *Duel in the Sun* (1946, King Vidor) . . . Alternatively, women's iconic memories of themselves in the cinema of this period may be narrativised, such as descending the cinema staircase like a Hollywood heroine . . . The narrative memories of female spectators, however, are typically also iconic memories. Thus the 'hero narratives' of these female spectators involved forms of display as well as action. The gendered significance of the forms of narrative memory found in this research is discussed . . .

Each of the processes of memory formation and selection discussed so far replicates, or is replicated by, distinguishing features of Hollywood cinema. Popular memories of Hollywood cinema in these accounts thus interestingly take cinematic forms. Memories are typically constructed through key icons, significant and transformative moments, narrative structures, heroic subject positions and utopian fantasies. Thus in analysing female spectators' accounts of popular cinema it is especially important to take account of these conventions of memory formation.

Producing the past

As is true of all the sources discussed in this chapter, the rules of the enquiry frame the kind of information elicited. The form of the request for spectators' recollections of Hollywood stars will have shaped the memories sent to me. The kind of advertisement for responses clearly had a determining effect on the material I received. Answers to an advertisement asking for recollections of favourite stars inevitably produced a particular set of representations resulting from a specific cultural context. Advertising for 'keen cinema-goers of the 1940s and 1950s', for example, addressed potential respondents as a distinct group; in recognising themselves in this category, respondents were constructed as a particular kind of authority: the 'amateur expert'. The private pleasures of collecting cinema memorabilia and of having film-star expertise is thus given a kind of public importance in such research. In turn, my recognition of their 'expertise' could have been perceived to be flattering, and indeed to have set up an expectation that their 'keenness' as cinema-goers in this period had to be demonstrated either through the detail of their account, or through an expression of the significance of cinema in their lives.

The request for information about a period at such historical distance also shaped the material I received: respondents may have felt recognised as a valuable source of historical information, and thus endeavoured to give as much detail as they could remember. Indeed, the recollection of detail may have been one of the pleasures for respondents in participating in the research: 'I have enjoyed doing this questionnaire. It was so detailed, I really had to think back. Thank you for that experience' (Kathleen Sines). The detail of many of the memories is commented upon in the chapters which follow: the ability to recollect such detail might be considered evidence of devotion to favourite stars.

Furthermore, my advertisement suggested an academic recognition, or indeed, validation, of women's pleasure in Hollywood cinema during this period, thus combining two things rarely taken seriously or given much status: popular culture and its female spectators. In other research, women had expressed shame in their pleasure because they were aware of its low status (Taylor, 1989: 204). Thus my request for information served as a validation of the importance of their memories, and indeed of the significance of Hollywood cinema in their lives in the 1940s and 1950s.

The kinds of selections respondents made when remembering what Hollywood stars meant in their lives would also have been framed by the subsequent histories of the stars in question: which stars were remembered and how they were remembered must have been influenced by the cultural constructions of those stars since that time. For example, audiences may have remembered stars differently depending on whether the stars were still alive, and if not, how they had died (such as Marilyn Monroe) and indeed when they had died (Bette Davis died during the time the questionnaire was with respondents); whether they still had a fan club (such as Deanna Durbin); whether the star had continued to have a successful career (such as Katharine Hepburn and Bette Davis); whether their films had been shown frequently on television and indeed whether the stars had gone on to have a television career (such as Barbara Stanwyck).

In addition to these factors, memories are recollections of the past through the changing historical discourses. Assessments of stars will inevitably have been affected by changing notions of acceptable femininity and female sexuality. The different constructions of femininity within Hollywood, such as the power and rebelliousness of Bette Davis or the sexual attractiveness of Marilyn Monroe, or the clean-livingness of Deanna Durbin, may have had particular appeal in retrospect, and they may have come to mean something over the years which they did not in the 1940s and 1950s. For example, what effect did the 'permissive' 1960s have on discourses of stardom and glamour?[2] To what extent might stars have been re-evaluated through a post-1960s understanding of female sexuality? How might women's increased participation in the public sphere have transformed the discourses through which Hollywood's 'independent women' stars have been read? To what extent might the increased visibility of lesbians and gay men in society have encouraged a re-evaluation of early 'attachments' to stars of the same sex? . . .

What gets remembered and what gets forgotten may depend not only on the star's career and changing discourses since the time period specified, but also upon the identity of the cinema spectator. The kinds of representations offered will have been informed by issues such as the respondents' own personal histories. The ways in which their lives had changed, and the feelings they had about their past, present and future selves, will have been amongst the factors determining the memories produced for the purposes of this research.

What I have been foregrounding in these last two sections of this chapter is the specificity of the production of memories of Hollywood stars which form the basis of this research and the conventions through which knowledge about the past is formed. Rather than seeing these conditions and conventions as *barriers* to 'the real past', as if it existed separately from our retelling of it, I have instead suggested highlighting them as an integral part of the research. What is important here is to recognise the factors shaping these women's memories of Hollywood stars and to analyse the conventions through which such material is represented. Popular memories of the cinema, I have argued, replicate particular narrative and visual conventions of popular culture generally.

From the textual spectator to the spectator as text

The question of the textual conventions of popular forms is one that bridges debates about popular memory and those about ethnography, since both involve the problem of the interpretation of personal accounts. This is, however, a general issue in the analysis of media reception, be it of interviews, letters, or questionnaires. Within cultural studies audience research, attention has been paid to such conventions, in contrast to accounts which simply let the audience 'speak for itself'.

As Ien Ang has argued, when analysing the responses she received to the question 'why do you like watching *Dallas*?':

> [I]t would be wrong . . . to regard the letters as a direct unproblematic reflection of the reasons why the writers love or hate *Dallas*. What people say or write about their experiences, preferences, habits, etc., cannot be taken entirely at face value . . . we cannot let the letters speak for themselves, but they should be read 'symptomatically': we must search for what is behind the explicitly written, for the presuppositions and accepted attitudes concealed within them. In other words the letters must be read as texts, as discourses.
>
> (Ang, 1985: 11)

Ang's approach here is methodologically exemplary of the shift from the textually produced spectator of film studies to the spectator as text within cultural studies.

For feminists, this presents particular issues about the politics of interpretation and research. In particular, the power of the feminist researcher to interpret other women's feelings and thoughts from a position of expertise in the academy is highlighted. There are certainly fewer moral dilemmas for feminists who continue to analyse film texts to which they are never held accountable in terms of the politics of research methods. As I suggested . . . , this dilemma may be a reason for the reluctance of feminist film critics to engage with audiences, as well as their anxieties about committing the cardinal sin of 'empiricism'. Those who have criticised the method that treats audiences' accounts as texts may argue that it is patronising to the women concerned. It may seem more 'democratic' simply to let women speak for themselves, since, many have argued, women are rarely listened to in this culture. Indeed, much early feminist oral history and documentary film aimed to 'give women a voice' and to make visible their experiences.

However, I would argue that some kind of interpretive framework is inevitable in academic research, and that avoiding analysis of women audiences because of embarrassment or anxiety about imposing such a framework merely perpetuates their absence from feminist film theory. The role of the researcher, I would argue, is to interpret the material that audiences produce within a critical framework which is appropriate to the material, and which is made explicit and can be contested. I shall argue for the importance of textual analysis of the stories that audiences tell researchers about what the media means to them, but in a framework which is demonstrably derived from the material itself. Thus a dialectical relationship emerges between the material studied and the theory which is used to analyse it. Female spectators' accounts of the cinema are used to criticise or confirm existing film theory, and indeed produce new or refined categories which could usefully add to our understanding of how audiences watch films.

Notes

1 See, for example, Popular Memory Group, 'Popular memory: theory, politics and method', in Centre for Contemporary Cultural Studies (1982) and Frigga Haugg (1986).
2 See Sheila Jeffreys (1990) for a feminist critique of the so-called sexual revolution of the 1960s.

Chapter 16

Philip Schlesinger, Rebecca Dobash, Russell Dobash and C. Kay Weaver

WOMEN VIEWING VIOLENCE

How the respondents reacted

IN CERTAIN RESPECTS, *THE ACCUSED* was quite distinctive when compared to the other programmes screened. First, of course, it is a major feature film which has been on general release, as well as shown on satellite and terrestrial television. In a number of cases, members of our sample had actually seen the film and, where they had not, its aura of publicity had frequently ensured that at least many had some broad image or prior knowledge of it. Second, of all the material shown, it was the only programme that had originated in the USA, which meant that it offered potentially distinctive points of either identification or distancing – particularly in respect of judgments made about its 'realism' – for women living in Britain today.

Our intention in screening *The Accused* was to establish reactions to explicit scenes of sexual violence committed against women. We sought to remain within the bounds of what women could be expected to view in a formal situation. However, on those very grounds, it was considered necessary to inform members of the viewing groups they would be seeing the film, that it contained an explicit rape scene, and that, should they feel unable to view that part of the film, they would be free to leave the room. Three women actually acted upon this warning and withdrew during the scene.

The Accused offered scope for assessing the emotional impact of a graphic display of sexual violence upon women viewers. For instance, one obvious concern was whether the portrayal of the rape was considered 'justifiable'. The characterisation of the rape victim was of particular interest to us: she is portrayed as 'provocative', unsympathetic, and involved in the consumption of alcohol and drugs, opening up a wide range of possible interpretations of her character and behaviour. It was important to assess the extent to which this victim might be held responsible or blamed for her fate, and whether this had any bearing on how the film was understood. Equally, we were interested in assessing varying reactions to the rapists portrayed in the film.

The viewing groups' perceptions bear directly upon debates about whether *The Accused* may be regarded as an 'anti–rape' film, as originally publicised. A further concern is whether *The Accused* might be thought to transgress the bounds of what should be screened on television.

Placing 'The Accused'

The fact that the film was American posed no difficulties for the women viewers and, in common with the other screenings, there were some strong and persistent reactions (see Figure 16.1, Reactions to *The Accused*). In contrast to *EastEnders* and *Closing Ranks*, there was considerable commonality in the responses of the two groups of women. Around 30% of both groups had seen *The Accused* previously. The vast majority of women in both groups rated it as 'realistic' or 'very realistic', and 'believable' or 'very believable'. It is of interest in this connection to cite the professional view of a rape counsellor who took part in the study:

> Very realistic right through, everything, her emotions, the rape in itself, the courtroom, the police, everything was very true to life. It was an excellent film. Very good portrayal of what actually happens in rape cases. I mean, it was horrific, the actual rape scene. I think every woman here was taken aback, but that's the way it happens, not necessarily gang rape all the time, but that's the shock they'll feel when they're going through it. It got it across and it didn't dwell on that action scene for too long because it was giving you all her emotions and the courtroom drama, how no one believes you and guys think it's a laugh.
>
> (Scottish white woman, rape counsellor,
> member of group with experience of violence)

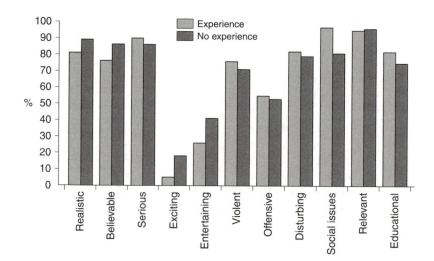

Figure 16.1 Reactions to *The Accused* – experience of violence/no experience.

Another professional judgment was expressed by a social worker, also participating in the research as a group member, who had the following (on the whole, minor) reservation about the film's realism:

> Well, for me the damage would still be done, even though they won the case. I still felt prison wasn't enough, because the damage has already been done to her and it's like saying 'it's a film'. Somebody else said earlier that . . . the effect on the victim wasn't enough, because she picks herself up out of a terrible rape and she goes out to fight a case. And the only bit is when she actually clips her hair off. Now a lot of victims do mutilate themselves because they tend to hate their own bodies, because . . . they've sort of blamed themselves and they're still trying to commit suicide. All sorts of other traumatic things happen to rape victims. That didn't come through in that film. That wasn't shown. So to me that was the only bit that wasn't realistic about it.
> (English Asian woman, social worker, with no experience of violence)

Only one woman out of all the participants said she did not take the film seriously. Most thought it was 'violent' and 'disturbing', and just over one half of the women in both groups thought it was 'offensive'. Women who had experience of violence were very unlikely to describe it as 'exciting' (6%) or 'entertaining' (26%). Nearly three-quarters of this group rated it as 'not at all exciting', and 58% rated it as 'not entertaining'. Only a small percentage (20%) of the women in groups who had not experienced violence rated it as exciting, although just over 40% found it entertaining. (see Figure 16.1).

Entertainment?

An indication of the kinds of broad expectations held by those who had gone to see *The Accused* at the cinema emerges from the following quotation:

> I must admit when I went to go and see it – it was the big thing – 'oh, there's this rape scene in it . . . everyone's got to go and see it.' So I was going to see it anyway, because I go to see all the films that come out. But I especially wanted to see it just to see what it was like and I thought it was going to be about a couple of seconds, just guys cheering it on – I didn't expect it to be anything like that.
> (Scottish white middle-class woman, with no experience of violence)

Such a comment conveys the interest aroused by the film for the cinemagoer. Obviously, enough knowledge of the central dilemmas had percolated into general circulation via media hype to arouse a motivating curiosity to see for oneself. But the impact upon the research groups was considerable. It was precisely the shock effect alluded to here that came across strongly in all of the discussions, albeit with variations described later. In fact, for the vast majority of group members, reactions encompassed shock, horror, disgust, distress and anger.

For the majority, the film's American setting was largely irrelevant, although this exchange indicates that its foreignness could very occasionally also be used as a way of distancing oneself from its message:

I didn't really watch it as American or English. I was watching that film, and, see, the inside of me was feeling everything that that woman was feeling. I don't know why. That's how close I felt to that woman.

I felt like that too. But I still felt that it was an American film and that the gang rape, it's not something you see in the news or even in the newspapers about women being gang raped.

(Scottish Asian women, with experience of violence)

As a major release, it might be expected that standard commercial assumptions about the pleasures of spectatorship would be applied, although in fact these were rarely used. The following quotation indicates how such criteria might quite exceptionally be invoked:

I thoroughly enjoyed it. I thought it was entertaining and I really thought it was an excellent film, it was good acting and, you know, you have the good guys and the bad guys and I thought it was very, very, realistic.

(English white working-class woman, with no experience of violence)

Much more common, though, in fact almost universal, were sentiments of repulsion, distress and shock. One can see from the following exchange how group members would typically try to devise the right kind of terminology for evaluating their viewing experience, and indeed for establishing a common baseline for holding the discussion at all:

Speaker 1: Even though I said – what I meant by 'not entertaining', I just think it's the wrong word . . . I enjoyed it in a way, but entertaining's not the right word for it.
Speaker 2: Gripping?
Speaker 1: No.
Speaker 3: Enthralling?
Speaker 4: Riveting – something like that?
Speaker 1: No, I just don't know. But it's not entertaining anyway.
Speaker 3: Because entertaining sometimes is something that's humorous, amusing, jovial.
Speaker 1: Yes . . . that just grabbed you.

(English white working-class women, with no experience of violence)

In general, it was simply not acceptable to define the experience of seeing *The Accused* as pleasurable, although at the same time its compelling qualities – a testament to the film-maker's skills – had also to be acknowledged. Interestingly, and this relates to how gender *differences* between masculine and feminine responses might be conceived, some made the point that certain kinds of men might find pleasure in viewing such a film because of the points of identification offered by the rapists:

To women it can't be entertaining, I wouldn't think. I don't know about the women here, I certainly don't find it that way. To men, if it is entertaining it's because they maybe think along those lines, and think, 'Oh yes, that would be good' or whatever, or give them the incentive to go out and try it and see how it really is. Because they all look as though they're having a brilliant time, these guys, don't they?

(Scottish white woman, with experience of violence)

As we shall see, this offers a pointer to the more general conceptions of masculinity and femininity that underlie such observations.

Aspects of identification

As with *EastEnders* and *Closing Ranks*, women with experience of violence were more likely than women with no experience to identify with the characters and situations depicted in *The Accused*, although this was not as strong as with the other two programmes. As shown in Table 16.1, 36% of women with experience identified with the characters in the film, overwhelmingly with the victim of rape, in contrast to 21% of women with no experience. The Yule's Q of .34 indicates that there is some association between experience of violence and identification with characters in *The Accused*, but much less than those revealed with respect to *EastEnders* and *Closing Ranks*.

However, there was a reasonably strong association between experience of violence and the ability to relate to the *situations* depicted. Over half of the women who had experienced violence (see Table 16.2) identified with situations depicting the rape, the victim's circumstances and her anger. Only 18% of the group without experience of violence related to the situations depicted, and none of them related to the portrayal of the rape. The Yule's Q of .64 indicates a reasonably strong association between past experience of violence and identification with situations in *The Accused*.

Table 16.1 Relating to characters in *The Accused*

	Violence			
	Experience		No experience	
Relate to characters	N	%	N	%
yes	14	36	6	21
no	25	64	22	79
Total	39	100%	28	100%

Note: Yule's Q= .34

Table 16.2 Relating to situations in *The Accused*

	Violence			
	Experience		No experience	
Relate to situations	N	%	N	%
yes	18	51	5	18
no	17	49	23	82
Total	35	100%	28	100%

Note: Yule's Q= .64

Thus it could be said that the uncompromising depiction of the victim of rape in *The Accused* made it difficult to identify with her personally but not with the experiences and situations she faced. This may also have been reflected in the participants' overwhelming agreement that the film is relevant to everyday life, with only three of the viewers thinking it was irrelevant.

One aspect of the process of identification that needs to be stressed is the extraordinary depth of feeling that *The Accused* aroused among the groups. Just to emphasise the point further, it is worth noting that there was a widespread need for the film to end well, which offers a powerful index of how far the identification could extend in many cases. T*he Accused* brought to the fore very strong sentiments about the need for justice to be seen to be done:

> It has a predictable ending, because I think if they had been found not guilty I would've been furious. It gets to me in the sense that they got their just desserts if you like.
> (Scottish white middle-class woman, with no experience of violence)

> I would think if they showed a different ending it would have made it a different picture. It would have been like sort of glorifying it really. It wouldn't have been like saying, 'It was all wrong', it would have been a case of 'It's all right'.
> (English Afro-Caribbean woman, with no experience of violence)

Ethnic diversity

Asian women had rather different reactions to *The Accused* than did Afro-Caribbean and white group members. Possibly they were more detached from the cultural context of the film because they did not find it as 'believable' and 'violent' as the other two groups (see Figure 16.2). Very few women in the three ethnic groups described the film as 'entertaining', with none of the Afro-Caribbean women making this assessment although more Asian women found it 'entertaining'. Only 14% of Asian women said they could relate to the characters, whereas nearly half of the white and Afro-Caribbean group members identified with characters. Additionally, over three-quarters of the Asian women (77%) could not relate to the situations depicted, in contrast to just over half for the other two groups (52% whites and 57% Afro-Caribbeans). Perhaps surprisingly, 99% of the Asian women thought the film had educational value, whereas only three-quarters of the members of the other two groups felt the same. An indication of what Asian women meant by the educational dimension of the film may be judged from points such as these:

> If she's drinking too much, you know, that's why that happened . . . Drinking is bad and [we] learn [this] from that film.

> Yes, because then it's trying to show the girls, you know, that are upset and going to the bars like that, you know. It sort of gives them a lesson that things like this happen, you know, if you behave like . . . that.
> (Scottish Asian women, with no experience of violence)

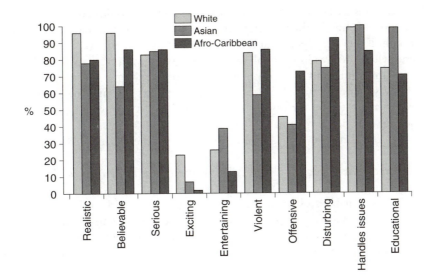

Figure 16.2 Reactions to *The Accused* – Ethnicity.

These remarks variously suggest that the film offers a warning about the dangers of drinking and of flirtation, viewed from within a cultural perspective which is relatively detached from the mainstream. There were also a few strong differences in the reactions of the Afro-Caribbean groups: a possible key to this distinctiveness is offered by observations made in the course of group discussions. One of these, which emerged with particular force amongst the group of English Afro-Caribbean women with experience of violence, concerned the ethnic dimension. The central challenge from them was: 'What if the rape victim had been black?'

> I found myself saying that in the film . . . if I change that woman into a black woman, it would be even more painful for me. Because I know that the whole line of the story would've changed . . . and I know that the verdict could have been different. And I know that the support . . . the sympathy would've been very different . . . It is a very painful film. I sat here all the time . . . sort of holding myself. I sort of felt the pain throughout the body. But I know if it was a black woman I would've felt – I probably would've been in tears, because I know that the verdict would've been different and I know that you wouldn't get the same level of sympathy.
>
> (English Afro-Caribbean woman, with experience of violence)

This observation crystallised feelings widely acknowledged in the group concerned, and brings out the identification felt with the rape victim. However, significantly, it also tempers this with reservations about equality of treatment between black and white that are based in the experience of racism.

The Accused was much more 'offensive' and 'disturbing' for Afro-Caribbean than for Asian and white viewers. Ninety-three per cent of them felt it was 'disturbing' or 'very disturbing', and 73% found it 'offensive' or 'very offensive'. An indication of the strength of feeling may be gained from considering the following views:

> I think I was all right up to before the rape scene. I could handle that and that showed, up till then it showed me actually what women have to go through, if they are raped. But the titillation bit that the media's into was the scene when she was in hospital, and her legs were up, and they were doing the examination, and then the gang rape. And for me, that was unnecessary, there was no need for that. So for me, that bit wasn't catering for women, it was actually catering for titillation, for men to say, it's okay to rape. I mean it sort of glorified it for me.
>
> (English Afro-Caribbean woman, with experience of violence)

Just over three-quarters of white and Asian women found *The Accused* 'disturbing' or 'very disturbing', and around 40% in both groups thought it was 'offensive' or 'very offensive'. Afro-Caribbean women were also twice as likely as the other two groups to say the rape scene should not be shown, and 66% of those Afro-Caribbean women offering an opinion felt the film should not be shown on television. This view was given particular strong voice by one Afro-Caribbean woman with experience of rape:

> I was gonna accept that 'OK' this is just like a film about rape and they're showing you how this woman has to stand up for her rights and everything. But once they showed the actual event, then they were endorsing it to me, because, like for a man, it's a cheap thrill. And if at the end of the day there's gonna be a big case and they're going to be dubious about whether he gets nine months or five years, then what's the big deal, you know? At least he'll remember it forever as something he did in his college days, risky but quite fun, you know, 'this was quite fun'. And that isn't good enough. Really, I don't want it on telly.
>
> (English Afro-Caribbean woman, with experience of violence)

A third of Asian viewers and a quarter of white viewers thought the film should not be shown on television. Again, ethnic background appears to make an important difference in the interpretations offered of programmes with depictions of violence.

PART FIVE

The fan audience

Cult texts and community

Introduction

H OW IS THE 'FAN' subgroup distinguished from the larger category 'audience'? According to the authors of 'Beatlemania: Girls Just Want To Have Fun',
the distinction lies in a particularly enthusiastic, even obsessive involvement with the
object of fandom – 'the appropriate reaction . . . was to sob uncontrollably while
screaming "I'm gonna die, I'm gonna die"' (p. 182) – coupled with a sense of community based around this shared fixation, which is often consolidated with visual
signs of belonging such as clothing, haircuts or related merchandise. Implied in fandom
is a sense of participation which goes beyond the 'active reading' discussed in Part
Two; rather than simply create their own meanings in the home or cinema, fans characteristically make cultural artefacts of their own, travel across the country to meet
their idols or fellow fans and often reshape their own image as a badge of their loyalty.

The Beatles fans of Barbara Ehrenreich, Elizabeth Hess and Gloria Jacobs' study
in Chapter 18 remain within the boundaries of contemporary teenage fashions, and
their 'ripping' – to return to Fiske's metaphor for cultural appropriation – is apparently
limited to cutting up any item which has come into contact with the band, whether a
friend's dress or a hotel pillowcase, and selling it for profit. However, the authors stress
the sense of community which emerged from these young female fans' shared love for
the Beatles, and suggest that for a teenage girl trapped within sexual double-standards
which demanded she both tease boys and hold back until marriage, the very act of
declaring a passionate love for these 'sexy' adult men was a form of proto-feminist
rebellion.

While sounding a note of caution about the extent to which Beatles fandom was
shaped by media influence – 'fans knew what to do. Television had spread the word . . .'
(p. 181) – the authors identify this small-scale 'social movement' as a genuine resistance against sexual repression and conformity, even if, in some ways, the fans were
simply conforming to fit a new sub-group. This ambiguity between the sense of fandom
as 'rebellion' against the world at large and as shaping oneself to fit in with a community, often with its own uniform and set of codes, is explored further in David
Muggleton's writing.

The spirit of solidarity which Camille Bacon-Smith finds among a community of female *Star Trek* fans in Chapter 20 in some ways echoes that of the Beatles followers – in place of the thirteen-year-olds' 'long discussions' about what Paul McCartney had for breakfast (p. 000), these women 'talk story' (p. 197) to work through ideas for fan fiction, and provide emotional support for each other in times of crisis. Unlike the Beatles fandom of the early 1960s, however, this community is based on a long-term commitment to a show that, in its original guise, ended in 1969. The level of commitment to the group is similarly deep-rooted, as demonstrated by Bacon-Smith's account of a conference gathering to mourn and honour a fellow fan-writer.

Significantly, these women celebrate their favoured text through a contemporary form of 'folk' culture – short stories, novels, illustrations and songs based on the *Star Trek* characters. This focus on active production, often based on an elaborate network of fanzines and conventions, is typical of media fandom, although more recently the exchange of ideas and artefacts has shifted onto the Internet.

Bacon-Smith presents her study as an ethnographic exploration into an unknown subculture, with herself as the mediator between us as readers and the arcane customs of the *Star Trek* community, and 'mentors' in turn guiding her own initiation as a 'neophyte'. Henry Jenkins in Chapter 17 espouses a different approach, and one that has become more common in writing about fandom; he introduces himself as a fan-academic, a member of the community who represents it from the inside while retaining a critical awareness. This 'intervention analysis' (p. 172) means that Jenkins has to admit to a 'partisan position', but it affords him a degree of insight and level of trust between himself and his subjects which Bacon-Smith had to establish very gradually and, arguably, never fully gained as an 'outsider'.

The 'queer' *Star Trek* fans of Jenkins' chapter, like the women in Bacon-Smith's study, find in the series' science-fiction setting a 'space' for them to explore issues from their own lives, and, again, another form of safe space in the community itself. As a futuristic utopia, *Star Trek* allows these fans to imagine a more egalitarian society, so the producers' refusal to represent gay characters in the new series was seen as a rejection and insult. While Gregory Woods' approach in Part Two shows that resistant reading can discover queerness where it appears to be repressed or absent, the Gaylaxian group of Jenkins' account demanded that the 'official' text should incorporate gay identity, and not merely in a disguised form.

As such, these fans have an intriguing relationship with the producers of the canonical *Star Trek* text: 'protective and possessive, celebratory and critical' they are used to producing their own meanings, but acknowledge that the Paramount company carries far more cultural power than their fanzine culture. However, just as *Star Trek* fans successfully lobbied for the show's third season in the 1960s, so the Gaylaxians have some genuine political leverage through their protests. Resistant readings are not always limited to the small tactical victory of personal interpretation; they can, when backed with the force of an organised group, effectively change the 'official' text.

David Muggleton's study in Chapter 21 here explores the concept of belonging and group identity which unites 'subculturalists' – in this case, fans based around a shared love of mod or punk music – and reveals deep-seated ambiguities in the relationship between 'home-made' fan culture and 'mass' media product. Muggleton explicitly questions the work of the Birmingham School, which suggested that music subcultures begin as an authentic, small-scale movement and are dissipated when dominant cultural institutions discover and mass-market them; as such, his work also has obvious relevance to John Fiske's theories of 'incorporation'.

While the subjects of this study all claim an authenticity in their own style which they distinguish from 'fake' versions on the high street and define against imitators who are 'trying to belong to a certain group' (p. 205), Muggleton points out the central ambiguities which his subculturalists apparently fail to recognise. Although punk styles became commodified, the next wave of punks continued to 'make use of incorporated styles . . . in acts of stylistic bricolage' (p. 208). A preppie girl who rips up her sorority t-shirt is regarded by 'hardcore' punks as the height of inauthenticity, but Muggleton notes that her appropriation is no less radical than the original punk mutilation of British school ties. While ostensibly based on an attitude of rebellion, then, these subculturalists are also bound by their own uniforms, grouping themselves as an 'authentic' crowd and deriding others as fakes even as they resist the idea of being labelled.

Sara Gwenllian-Jones' article on *Xena: Warrior Princess* fandom in Chapter 19 echoes the earlier work of Jenkins and Bacon-Smith while suggesting a broader view of fan activity and its potential to engage with the world beyond the chosen text. Like the female fan-writers and Gaylaxians who used *Star Trek*'s future utopia as an arena for exploring gender and sexual relationships, the fans of this study – many of whom are lesbian or bisexual – identify with *Xena*'s implicitly feminist, often knowingly-queer narratives of 'lost tribes' who were written out of official history. Significantly, Gwenllian-Jones suggests that in this case, the 'lesbian subtext' is so blatantly encoded by the producers that it becomes a preferred reading, the 'maintext' (p. 191); to interpret Xena as heterosexual would, therefore, constitute a reading 'against the grain'.

While *Xena* fans, like the longer-established *Star Trek* communities, also produce their own artefacts such as scratch video and fiction, Gwenllian-Jones notes that the development of the World Wide Web around the year of the show's debut enabled them to make the most of the Internet's facility for creating links and drawing connections. Many fans took inspiration from the show's intertextuality to investigate historical sources and research Amazon cultures. While *Xena* actively encourages what de Certeau called 'tactics' – the negotiation and resistance of imposed frameworks – these fans channel their energy outwards, using the show as a springboard for an interrogation of very real issues about the telling of history. Rather than a creative but small-scale struggle over meaning, fandom can also provide a way of engaging with the world outside.

Further reading

Brooker, W. (2002) *Using the Force*, London: Continuum.
Hall, S. and Jefferson, T. (eds) (1986) *Resistance through Rituals*, London: Hutchinson.
Hebdige, D. (1979) *Subculture: The Meaning of Style*, London: Methuen.
Jenkins, H. (1992) *Textual Poachers*, London: Routledge.
Muggleton, D. (2000) *Inside Subculture: The Postmodern Meaning of Style*, London: Berg.
Penley, C. (1997) *NASA/TREK*, London: Verso.

Chapter 17

Henry Jenkins

'OUT OF THE CLOSET AND INTO THE UNIVERSE'
Queers and *Star Trek*

> *Star Trek* celebrates its 25th anniversary in 1991. In that quarter century, one of the most important aspects of the series . . . has been the vision that humanity will one day put aside its differences to work and live in peace together. *Star Trek*, in its various television and motion picture forms, has presented us with Africans, Asians, Americans and Andorians, Russians and Romulans, French and Ferengi, Hispanics and Hortas, human and non-human men and women. In 25 years, it has also never shown an openly gay character.
>
> (Franklin Hummel, *Gaylactic Gazette*)[1]

> Perhaps someday our ability to love won't be so limited.
> (Dr Beverley Crusher, 'The Host',
> *Star Trek: The Next Generation*)

'2, 4, 6, 8, how do you know Kirk is straight?' the Gaylaxians chanted as they marched down the streets of Boston on Gay Pride day. '3, 5, 7, 9, he and Spock have a real fine time!' The chant encapsulates central issues of concern to the group: How do texts determine the sexual orientation of their characters and how might queer spectators gain a foothold for self-representation within dominant media narratives? How has *Star Trek* written gays and lesbians out of its future, and why do the characters and their fans so steadfastly refuse to stay in the closet? The chant captures the play between visibility and invisibility which is the central theme of this chapter and has, indeed, been a central theme in the struggle against homophobia in contemporary society.

The Boston Area Gaylaxians is a local chapter of the international Gaylactic Network Inc., an organization for gay, lesbian and bisexual science fiction fans and their friends.[2] Founded in 1987, the group has chapters in many cities in the United

States and Canada. Adopting the slogan, 'Out of the closet and into the universe', the group has sought to increase gay visibility within the science fiction fan community and 'to help gay fans contact and develop friendships with each other.'[3] The group hosts a national convention, Gaylaxicon, which brings together fans and writers interested in sexuality and science fiction. Although only recently given official recognition from the Network, group members have organized a national letter-writing campaign to urge Paramount to acknowledge a queer presence in the twenty-fourth-century future represented on *Star Trek: The Next Generation*. Their efforts have so far attracted national attention from both the gay and mainstream press and have provoked responses from production spokespeople and several cast members. Gene Roddenberry publicly committed himself to incorporate gay characters into the series in the final months before his death, but the producers never delivered on that promise. The series *has* featured two episodes which can loosely be read as presenting images of alternative sexuality, 'The Host', and 'The Outcast'. Although the producers have promoted these stories as responsive to the gay and lesbian community's concerns, both treat queer lifestyles as alien rather than familiar aspects of the Federation culture and have sparked further controversy and dissatisfaction among the Gaylaxians.

The fans' requests are relatively straightforward – perhaps showing two male crew members holding hands in the ship's bar, perhaps a passing reference to a lesbian lover, some evidence that gays, bisexuals and lesbians exist in the twenty-fourth century represented on the programme. Others want more – an explicitly gay or lesbian character, a regular presence on the series, even if in a relatively minor capacity. As far as the producers are concerned, homosexuality and homophobia are so tightly interwoven that there is no way to represent the first without simultaneously reintroducing the second, while for the fans, what is desired is precisely a future which offers homosexuality without homophobia.

What is at stake for these viewers is the credibility of Gene Roddenberry's oft-repeated claims about the utopian social vision of *Star Trek*. Roddenberry's reluctance to include queer characters in *Star Trek*, they argue, points to the failure of liberal pluralism to respond to the identity politics of sexual preference. As one fan wrote, 'What kind of a future are we offered when there is no evidence that we exist?'[4]

Intervention analysis and fan culture

This chapter, thus, documents the Gaylaxians' struggles with Paramount over the issue of queer visibility on *Star Trek*, their efforts to gain a public acknowledgement that gay, lesbian and bisexual people belong within the programme's utopian community. I write from a partisan position within this debate – as a *Star Trek* fan and a member of the Gaylaxians. John Hartley has called upon media scholars to engage in what he calls intervention analysis: 'Intervention analysis seeks not only to describe and explain existing dispositions of knowledge, but also to change them.'[5] Hartley advocates that media scholars write from the position(s) of media audiences, recognizing and articulating the interpretative work which viewers perform, documenting their creative engagement with the media content. Hartley continues:

> Intervention analysis certainly needs to take popular television more or less
> as it finds it, without high-culture fastidiousness or right-on political

squeamishness, but it needs to intervene *in* the media and in the production of popular knowledges *about* them.[6]

Intervention analysis, Hartley argues, speaks from, about and for the margins of popular culture.

My goal is thus to intervene in the debates about queer visibility on *Star Trek*, to trace the discursive logic by which producers have sought to exclude and fans have sought to include queer characters, to situate this issue within a larger social and cultural context of queer reception of science fiction and network representation of alternative sexuality. My goal is not to instruct or politicize audience response, since I believe that fans already exercise a form of grassroots cultural politics which powerfully reflects their interest in the media and their own ideological stakes. We need to create a context where fan politics may be acknowledged and accepted as a valid contribution to the debates about mass culture.

Such an approach may provide one way of reconciling critical work on texts, institutional analysis of the production process, and audience research on reception contexts within television studies. Rather than reading the audience from the text, an approach characteristic of ideological criticism, we would rather move to read the text from the specific perspective of particular audiences, creating our analysis in dialogue with those reception communities and in furtherance of our common interests. Such an approach need not displace but rather should supplement other modes of ethnographic research, such as those employed in earlier chapters, which continue to be appropriate for addressing other questions and issues surrounding the circulation and reception of popular texts. Such an approach will make clearer the need to contextualize work on audience resistance in relation to the conditions blocking media access and determining television content and may help us to better understand both the strengths and limitations of subcultural appropriations and resistant reading as means of reworking the dominant ideological assumptions of television science fiction.

Children of Uranus[7]

> During the course of our production, there have been many special interest groups who have lobbied for their particular cause. It is Gene Roddenberry's policy to present *Star Trek* as he sees it and not to be governed by outside influences.
> (Susan Sackett, executive assistant to Gene Roddenberry)[8]

> We have been the target of a concerted, organized movement by gay activists to put a gay character on the show.
> (Michael Piller, *Star Trek* writing staff supervisor)[9]

> In the late 1960's, a 'special interest group' lobbied a national television network to renew a series for a third season. If those networks had not listened to those with a special interest, *Star Trek* would not have returned and today *Star Trek* might very likely not be all of what it has become. You, Mr. Roddenberry, and *Star Trek* owe much to a special interest group: *Star Trek* fans. Perhaps you

> should consider listening to some of those same fans who are
> speaking to you now.
>
> (Franklin Hummel)[10]

The people who organized the national letter-writing campaign to get a queer character included on *Star Trek: The Next Generation* were not 'outside influences', 'special
interest groups' or 'gay activists'. They saw themselves as vitally involved with the life
of the series and firmly committed to its survival. As Hummel asserts, 'we are *part of
Star Trek*'. They saw their goals not as antagonistic to Roddenberry's artistic vision but
rather as logically consistent with the utopian politics he had articulated in *The
Making of Star Trek* and elsewhere. . . . fans had long drawn upon Roddenberry's own
comments about the programme and its ideology as criteria by which to evaluate the
series texts ideological consistency. If fan writers often sought to deflect anxieties
about ideological inconsistencies from producer (Roddenberry) to character (Kirk),
the Gaylaxians had no such option. What was at stake was Roddenberry's refusal to
act *as a producer* to reinforce the values he had asserted through extra-textual discourse.
The fans reminded Roddenberry that he had said:

> To be different is not necessarily to be ugly: to have a different idea is not
> necessarily wrong. The worst possible thing that can happen to humanity is
> for all of us to begin to look and act and think alike.[11]

When, they asked, was *Star Trek* going to acknowledge and accept sexual 'difference'
as part of the pluralistic vision it had so consistently evoked? They cited his successful fight to get a black woman on the *Enterprise* bridge and his unsuccessful one to
have a female second-in-command, and wondered aloud 'why can't *Star Trek* be as
controversial in educating people about our movement as they were for the black civil
rights movement?' (James).[12]

The people who organized the letter-writing campaign were *Star Trek* fans and, as
such, they claimed a special relationship to the series, at once protective and possessive, celebratory and critical. Frank Hummel, one of the key organizers of the
campaign, described his decision to take on Roddenberry:

> We expected more of *Star Trek*. A lot of the letters came from a simple, basic
> confusion. We didn't understand why *Star Trek* hadn't dealt with it. Here was
> *The Next Generation*. Here was a new series. Here was the late 1980s–1990s.
> Why didn't *Star Trek* deal with this? Why didn't they approach it the same
> way they approached casting an inter-racial crew? It was a puzzle.

Frank, like many of the others I interviewed, had started watching *Star Trek* as a child,
had grown up with its characters and its concepts. *Star Trek* provided him with a way
of linking his contemporary struggle for gay rights with successful campaigns in the
1960s on behalf of women's rights and black civil rights. The producers' refusal to
represent gay and lesbian characters cut deeply.

> They betrayed everything *Star Trek* was – the vision of humanity I have held
> for over 25 years. They betrayed Gene Roddenberry and his vision and all
> the fans. They didn't have the guts to live up to what *Star Trek* was for.

Even here, we see evidence of a desire to deflect criticism from Roddenberry onto those (the unidentified 'they') who 'betrayed' his 'vision'.

Others might point to a series of compromises Roddenberry had made in the programme ideology as evidence of a certain duplicity, or, more globally, as a failure of liberal pluralism to adequately confront issues of sexual identity:

> Todd: I think Gene Roddenberry was this prototypical liberal – and I am not saying that in the most flattering terms. Just like the characters on *Star Trek*, he wanted to convince himself he was open minded and thoughtful and growing so he would do things to present that image and make superficial changes but when it came to something that really counted, really mattered, that wasn't going to go at all.

In both versions, Roddenberry as *Star Trek*'s 'author' embodies certain myths about 1960s' activism and its relationship to contemporary social struggle.

To understand the intensity of the Gaylaxians' responses, we need to consider more closely what science fiction as a genre has offered these gay, lesbian and bisexual fans. David, a member of the Boston group, described his early experiences with the genre:

> I wasn't very happy with my world as it was and found that by reading science fiction or fantasy, it took me to places where things were possible, things that couldn't happen in my normal, everyday life. It would make it possible to go out and change things that I hated about my life, the world in general, into something that was more comfortable for me, something that would allow me to become what I really wanted to be . . . Being able to work out prejudices in different ways. Dealing with man's inhumanity to man. To have a vision for a future or to escape and revel in glory and deeds that have no real mundane purpose. To be what you are and greater than the world around you lets you be.

Lynne, another Gaylaxian, tells a similar story:

> I wasn't very happy with my life as a kid and I liked the idea that there might be someplace else where things were different. I didn't look for it on this planet. I figured it was elsewhere. I used to sit there in the Bronx, looking up at the stars, hoping that a UFO would come and get me. Of course, it would never land in the Bronx but I still had my hopes.

What these fans describe is something more than an abstract notion of escapism – the persistent queer fantasy of a space beyond the closet doorway. Such utopian fantasies can provide an important first step towards political awareness, since utopianism allows us to envision an alternative social order which we must work to realize ('something positive to look forward to') and to recognize the limitations of our current situation (the dystopian present against which the utopian alternative can be read). Richard Dyer has stressed the significant role which utopian entertainment plays within queer culture, be it the eroticism and romanticism of disco, the passion of Judy Garland, the sensuousness of ballet and opera or the plenitude of gay pornography.[13]

Utopianism, Dyer writes, offers 'passion and intensity' that 'negates the dreariness of the mundane . . . and gives us a glimpse of what it means to live at the height of our emotional and experiential capacities'.[14] The Gaylaxians describe their pleasure in science fiction both in terms of what utopia feels like (an abstract conception of community, acceptance, difference, fun) and what utopia looks like (a realist representation of alternative possibilities for sexual expression within futuristic or alien societies).

Science fiction represents a potential resource for groups which have had very limited stakes in the status quo, for whom the possibility of profound social change would be a desirable fantasy. Many of the Gaylaxians argue that science fiction is a particularly important genre for gay and lesbian readers:

> James: To me the purpose of fantasy and science fiction is to go where no one has gone before, to open our minds and to expand our intellect. The future is wider, bigger, larger and therefore that is a fertile ground for opening up possibilities that are now closed. I think it's the perfect genre to find a place where you can have your freedom because anything can happen here and anything is visible here.

Science fiction offered these readers not one but many versions of utopia, sometimes contradictory or exclusive of each other, but that was part of the pleasure. Confronted with a world which seemed all too narrow in its acceptance of a range of sexualities, they retreated into a genre which offered many different worlds, many different realties, many different futures.

> *Dana*: Science fiction allows us the flexibility to be ourselves.

The historic relations between science fiction and gay culture are complex and varied. Eric Garber and Lyn Paleo's *Uranian Worlds* lists more than 935 science fiction stories or novels which deal with gay and lesbian themes and characters, starting with Lucian's *True History* (AD 200) and ending in the late 1980s.[15] Some of the stories they cite adopt homophobic stereotypes, yet they also see science fiction as a genre which was historically open to gay, bisexual and lesbian writers who could express their sexuality in a disguised but potent form. As Garber and Paleo note, science fiction fandom in the 1950s was closely linked to the emergence of homophile organizations, with fanzines, such as Lisa Ben's *Vice Versa* and Jim Kepner's *Toward Tomorrow*, among the first gay community publications in the United States. Writers like Marion Zimmer Bradley, Joanna Russ and Samuel R. Delany were writing science fiction novels in the 1960s which dealt in complex ways with issues of sexual orientation and envisioned futures which held almost unlimited possibilities for gays and lesbians.[16] These writers' efforts opened possibilities for a new generation of queer authors, working in all subgenres, to introduce gay, bisexual and lesbian characters within otherwise mainstream science fiction stories. A key shift has been the movement from early science fiction stories that treated homosexuality as a profoundly alien sexuality towards stories that deal with queer characters as a normal part of the narrative universe and that treat sexuality as simply one aspect of their characterization.[17]

Many of these new writers, such as J. F. Rifkin, Melissa Scott, Susanna L. Sturgis and Ellen Kushner, have been actively involved with the Gaylaxians and have been featured guests at their national convention. The Boston group holds regular meetings where professional science fiction writers do readings or where struggling amateurs share their writings and receive feedback. Reviews of new books by queer writers appear regularly in the groups' newsletters, helping to alert members to new developments in this field.

For many of the Gaylaxians, fandom represented an immediate taste of what science fiction's utopian future might feel like. Fandom was a place of acceptance and tolerance. Asked to describe what science fiction offered queers, their answers focused as much on fandom as on any features of science fiction as a literary genre. The gay men contrasted belonging to fandom to the alienation of the gay bar scene and particularly to their inability to express their intellectual and cultural interests there. The female members contrasted fandom with the 'political correctness' of the lesbian community, which they felt regarded their cultural interests as trivial since science fiction was not directly linked to social and political change. Belonging to the Gaylaxians, thus, allowed them a means of expressing their cultural identity (as fans), their sexual identity (as queers) and, for some at least, their political identity (as activists).

The conception of science fiction which emerges in such a context is highly fluid as a result of the group's efforts to provide community acceptance for all those who shared a common interest in science fiction, fantasy or horror. If the MIT students offered a fairly precise and exclusive conception of the genre, one which preserved their professional status and expertise, the Gaylaxians struggle to find inclusive definitions:

Betty: Science fiction is almost impossible to define . . . Everyone you ask has a different definition.
Lynne: It can be anything from hard science to fantasy.
Dana: The author can do all kinds of things as long as the work is stable within its own universe. It can be close to present Earth reality or it can be as far-fetched as an intergalactic war from Doc Smith.
David: It's all out there! No matter what your vision of the future is, it's out there in science fiction and fantasy. It's all available to us.

Push harder and one finds that science fiction, for these fans, is defined less through its relationship to traditional science than through its openness to alternative perspectives and its ability to offer a fresh vantage point from which to understand contemporary social experience:

John: Science fiction doesn't limit its possibilities. You can constantly throw in something new, something exciting . . . Science fiction can be as outlandish as someone's imagination.
James: My definition of science fiction would be something alien, either the future, the past, different cultures, different worlds, different realities. It would have to be different from our perspective.

Many of these fans had been drawn to science fiction through *Star Trek* and saw its universe as fully embodying these principles. Nobody had expected the original *Star Trek* series, released in a pre-Stonewall society, to address directly the concerns of gay, lesbian and bisexual fans. They had taken it on faith that its vision of a United

Federation of Planets, of intergalactic cooperation and acceptance, included them as vital partners. Yet, when *Star Trek: The Next Generation* appeared, at a time when queer characters had appeared on many American series, they hoped for something more, to be there on the screen, an explicit presence in its twenty-fourth century. 'Everybody had a place in his [Roddenberry's] future,' explained one fan. 'It didn't matter if you were a man or a woman, white, black, yellow or green. If they can't take it one step further and include sexual orientation! God, if they don't have it under control in the twenty-fourth century, then it will never happen!' (James). Underlying this discussion lies a more basic concern: if *Star Trek* isn't willing to represent gay and lesbian characters in the 1990s, when would it be able to do so? As they watched a series of dramatic shifts in American attitudes towards gay and lesbian politics in the late 1980s and early 1990s, discussion of *Star Trek* provided them with one focal point for the group's discussion and comprehension of those changes, for talking about issues such as scientific research into the biological basis of sexual desire or efforts to abolish the ban on gays and lesbians serving in the United States military or the successes and setbacks of the Religious Right's campaign against Gay Rights legislation. Discussing *Star Trek* could provide a common ground for thinking through their conflicting feelings about this process of social transformation.

Notes

1   Franklin Hummel, 'Where None Have Gone Before', *Gaylactic Gayzette*, May 1991, p. 2. I am indebted to John Campbell for his extensive assistance in recruiting members of the Gaylaxians to participate in the interviews for this chapter. Interviews were conducted both in informal settings (members' homes) as well as more formal ones (my office), depending on the size and the needs of the groups. As it evolved, the groups were segregated by gender.

2   For more information on the Gaylaxian Network, see Franklin Hummel, 'SF Comes to Boston: Gaylaxians at the World Science Fiction Convention', *New York Native*, 23 October 1989, p. 26.

3   Gaylaxians International, recruitment flier.

4   Theresa M., '*Star Trek: The Next Generation* Throws Us a Bone . . .', *The Lavender Dragon*, April 1992, 2: 2, p. 1.

5   John Hartley, *Studies in Television* (New York: Routledge, Chapman and Hall, 1992), p. 5.

6   Hartley 1992, p. 7.

7   The nineteenth-century word, Uranian, was coined by early German homosexual emancipationist Karl Ulrichs and used popularly through the First World War to refer to homosexuals. As Eric Garber and Lyn Paleo note, 'It refers to Aphrodite Urania, whom Plato had identified as the patron Goddess of homosexuality in his Symposium.'

8   Susan Sackett, executive assistant to Gene Roddenberry, letter to Franklin Hummel, 12 March 1991.

9   Mark A. Altman, 'Tackling Gay Rights', *Cinefantastique*, October 1992, p. 74.

10   Franklin Hummel, Director, Gaylactic Network, letter to Gene Roddenberry, 1 May 1991.

11   Ibid.

12   The analogy John and other Gaylaxians draw between the black civil rights movement of the 1960s and the queer civil rights movement of the 1990s is a controversial one. But it is hardly unique to these fans. This analogy has been part of the discursive context surrounding Bill Clinton's efforts to end the American military's ban on gay and lesbian enlistment.

13 Many of Dyer's most important essays on this topic can be found in Richard Dyer, *Only Entertainment* (New York: Routledge, Chapman and Hall, 1992). On Judy Garland and gay audiences, see Richard Dyer, *Heavenly Bodies: Film Stars and Society* (New York: St Martin's Press, 1986). For another central text in arguments about the politics of utopian entertainment, see Frederic Jameson, 'Reification and Utopia in Mass Culture', *Social Text*, Winter 1979, pp. 130–48.

14 Richard Dyer, 'In Defence of Disco', *Only Entertainment* (London: Routledge, 1992), p. 156. What Dyer describes here as 'banality' is what fans refer to as 'the mundane', while making a similar argument about the pleasures of fandom as a repudiation or movement away from 'the mundane.'

15 Eric Garber and Lyn Paleo, *Uranian Worlds: A Guide to Alternative Sexuality in Science Fiction, Fantasy and Horror* (Boston: G. K. Hall, 1990).

16 Several of the writers associated with the original *Star Trek* series made important contributions to the development of gay and lesbian science fiction: Theodore Sturgeon, who wrote 'Amok Time' and 'Shore Leave', two of the best-loved episodes, had been dealing with issues of alien sexuality and homosexuality in his fiction as early as 1957; David Gerrold, who wrote 'Trouble with Tribbles' and was closely involved in the development of *Star Trek: The Next Generation*, was the author of a 1973 science fiction novel, *The Man Who Folded Himself*, which dealt with the auto-erotic and homo-erotic possibilities of time travel; Norman Spinrad, the author of 'The Doomsday Machine', wrote stories which dealt, not always sympathetically, with alternative sexualities and had included gay characters in his fiction prior to his involvement with *Star Trek*.

17 Clearly, these newer representations of gay characters, rather than the older representations of the problem or issue of gay sexuality, set expectations about how *Star Trek* might best address the concerns of its gay, lesbian and bisexual viewers.

Chapter 18

Barbara Ehrenreich, Elizabeth Hess and Gloria Jacobs

BEATLEMANIA
Girls just want to have fun

> . . . witness the birth of eve – she is rising she was sleeping she is fading in a naked field sweating the precious blood of nodding blooms . . . in the eye of the arena she bends in half in service – the anarchy that exudes from the pores of her guitar are the cries of the people wailing in the rushes . . . a riot of ray/dios . . .
>
> (Patti Smith, 'Notice,' in *Babel*)

THE NEWS FOOTAGE SHOWS police lines straining against crowds of hundreds of young women. The police look grim; the girls' faces are twisted with desperation or, in some cases, shining with what seems to be an inner light. The air is dusty from a thousand running and scuffling feet. There are shouted orders to disperse, answered by a rising volume of chants and wild shrieks. They young women surge forth; the police line breaks . . .

Looking at the photos or watching the news clips today, anyone would guess that this was the sixties – a demonstration – or maybe the early seventies – the beginning of the women's liberation movement. Until you look closer and see that the girls are not wearing sixties-issue jeans and T-shirts but bermuda shorts, high-necked, preppie blouses, and disheveled but unmistakably bouffant hairdos. This is not 1968 but 1964, and the girls are chanting, as they surge against the police line, 'I love Ringo.'

Yet, if it was not the 'movement,' or a clear-cut protest of any kind, Beatlemania was the first mass outburst of the sixties to feature women – in this case girls, who would not reach full adulthood until the seventies and the emergence of a genuinely political movement for women's liberation. The screaming ten- to fourteen-year-old fans of 1964 did not riot for anything, except the chance to remain in the proximity of their idols and hence to remain screaming. But they did have plenty to riot against, or at least to overcome through the act of rioting. In a highly sexualized society (one sociologist found that the number of explicitly sexual references in the mass media had doubled between 1950 and 1960), teen and preteen girls were expected to be not only 'good' and 'pure' but to be the enforcers of purity within their teen society – drawing the line for overeager boys and ostracizing girls who failed in this responsibility. To abandon control – to scream, faint, dash about in mobs – was, in form if not in conscious intent, to protest the sexual repressiveness, the rigid double standard of female teen culture. It was the first and most dramatic uprising of *women's* sexual revolution.

Beatlemania, in most accounts, stands isolated in history as a mere craze – quirky and hard to explain. There had been hysteria over male stars before, but nothing on this scale. In its peak years – 1964 and 1965 – Beatlemania struck with the force, if not the conviction, of a social movement. It begun in England with a report that fans had mobbed the popular but not yet immortal group after a concert at the London Palladium on 13 October, 1963. Whether there was in fact a mob or merely a scuffle involving no more than eight girls is not clear, but the report acted as a call to mayhem. Eleven days later a huge and excited crowd of girls greeted the Beatles (returning from a Swedish tour) at Heathrow Airport. In early November, 400 Carlisle girls fought the police for four hours while trying to get tickets for a Beatles concert; nine people were hospitalized after the crowd surged forward and broke through shop windows. In London and Birmingham the police could not guarantee the Beatles safe escort through the hordes of fans. In Dublin the police chief judged that the Beatles' first visit was 'all right until the mania degenerated into barbarism.'[1] And on the eve of the group's first US tour, *Life* reported, 'A Beatle who ventures out unguarded into the streets runs the very real period of being dismembered or crushed to death by his fans.'[2]

When the Beatles arrived in the United States, which was still ostensibly sobered by the assassination of President Kennedy two months before, the fans knew what to do. Television had spread the word from England: The approach of the Beatles is a license to riot. At least 4,000 girls (some estimates run as high as 10,000) greeted them at Kennedy Airport, and hundreds more laid siege to the Plaza Hotel, keeping the stars virtual prisoners. A record 73 million Americans watched the Beatles on 'The Ed Sullivan Show' on 9 February, 1964, the night 'when there wasn't a hubcap stolen anywhere in America.' American Beatlemania soon reached the proportions of religious idolatry. During the Beatles' twenty-three-city tour that August, local promoters were required to provide a minimum of 100 security guards to hold back the crowds. Some cities tried to ban Beatle-bearing craft from their runways; otherwise it took heavy deployments of local police to protect the Beatles from their fans and the fans from the crush. In one city, someone got hold of the hotel pillowcases that had purportedly been used by the Beatles, cut them into 160,000 tiny squares, mounted them on certificates, and sold them for $1 apiece. The group packed Carnegie Hall, Washington's Coliseum and, a year later, New York's 55,600-seat Shea Stadium, and in no setting, at any time, was their music audible above the frenzied screams of the audience. In 1966, just under three years after the start of Beatlemania, the Beatles gave their last concert – the first musical celebrities to be driven from the stage by their own fans.

In its intensity, as well as its scale, Beatlemania surpassed all previous outbreaks of star-centered hysteria. Young women had swooned over Frank Sinatra in the forties and screamed for Elvis Presley in the immediate pre-Beatle years, but the Fab Four inspired an extremity of feeling usually reserved for football games or natural disasters. These baby boomers far outnumbered the generation that, thanks to the censors, had only been able to see Presley's upper torso on 'The Ed Sullivan Show.' Seeing (whole) Beatles on Sullivan was exciting, but not enough. Watching the band on television was a thrill – particularly the close-ups – but the real goal was to leave home and meet the Beatles. The appropriate reaction to contact with them – such as occupying the same auditorium or city block – was to sob uncontrollably while screaming, 'I'm gonna die, I'm gonna die,' or, more optimistically, the name of a favorite Beatle, until the onset of either unconsciousness or laryngitis. Girls peed in their pants, fainted, or simply collapsed from the emotional strain. When not in the vicinity of the Beatles – and only a small proportion of fans ever got within shrieking distance of their idols – girls exchanged Beatle magazines or cards, and gathered to speculate obsessively on the details and nuances of Beatle life. One woman, who now administers a Washington, DC-based public interest group, recalls long discussions with other thirteen-year-olds in Orlando, Maine:

> I especially liked talking about the Beatles with other girls. Someone would say, 'What do you think Paul had for breakfast?' 'Do you think he sleeps with a different girl every night?' Or, 'Is John really the leader?' 'Is George really more sensitive?' And like that for hours.

This fan reached the zenith of junior high school popularity after becoming the only girl in town to travel to a Beatles' concert in Boston: 'My mother had made a new dress for me to wear [to the concert] and when I got back, the other girls wanted to cut it up and auction off the pieces.'

To adults, Beatlemania was an affliction, an 'epidemic,' and the Beatles themselves were only the carriers, or even 'foreign germs.' At risk were all ten- to fourteen-year-old girls, or at least all white girls; blacks were disdainful of the Beatles' initially derivative and unpolished sound. There appeared to be no cure except for age, and the media pundits were fond of reassuring adults that the girls who had screamed for Frank Sinatra had grown up to be responsible, settled housewives. If there was a short-cut to recovery, it certainly wasn't easy. A group of Los Angeles girls organised a detox effort called 'Beatlesaniacs, Ltd.,' offering 'group therapy for those living near active chapters, and withdrawal literature for those going it alone at far-flung outposts.' Among the rules for recovery were: 'Do not mention the word Beatles (or beetles),' 'Do not mention the word England,' 'Do not speak with an English accent,' and 'Do not speak English.'[3] In other words, Beatlemania was as inevitable as acne and gum-chewing, and adults would just have to weather it out.

But why was it happening? And why in particular to an America that prided itself on its post-McCarthy maturity, its prosperity, and its clear position as the number one world power? True, there were social problems that not even *Reader's Digest* could afford to be smug about – racial segregation, for example, and the newly discovered poverty of 'the other America.' But these were things that an energetic President could easily handle – or so most people believed at the time – and if 'the Negro problem,' as it was called, generated overt unrest, it was seen as having a corrective function and limited duration. Notwithstanding an attempted revival by presidential candidate Barry Goldwater, 'extremism' was out of style in any area of expression. In colleges, 'coolness' implied a detached and rational appreciation of the status quo, and it was de rigueur among all but the avant-garde who joined the Freedom Rides or signed up for the Peace Corps. No one, not even Marxist philosopher Herbert

Marcuse, could imagine a reason for widespread discontent among the middle class or for strivings that could not be satisfied with a department store charge account – much less for 'mania.'

In the media, adult experts fairly stumbled over each other to offer the most reassuring explanations. The *New York Times Magazine* offered a 'psychological, anthropological,' half tongue-in-cheek account, titled 'Why the Girls Scream, Weep, Flip.' Drawing on the work of the German sociologist Theodor Adorno, *Times* writer David Dempsey argued that the girls weren't really out of line at all; they were merely 'conforming.' Adorno had diagnosed the 1940s jitterbug fans as 'rhythmic obedients,' who were 'expressing their desire to obey.' They needed to subsume themselves into the mass, 'to become transformed into an insect.' Hence, 'jitter*bug*,' and as Dempsey triumphantly added: 'Beatles, too, are a type of bug . . . and to "beatle," as to jitter, is to lose one's identity in an automatized, insectlike activity, in other words, to obey.' If Beatlemania was more frenzied than the outbursts of obedience inspired by Sinatra or Fabian, it was simply because the music was 'more frantic,' and in some animal way, more compelling. It is generally admitted 'that jungle rhythms influence the "beat" of much contemporary dance activity,' he wrote, blithely endorsing the stock racist response to rock 'n' roll. Atavistic, 'aboriginal' instincts impelled the girls to scream, weep, and flip, whether they liked it or not: 'It is probably no coincidence that the Beatles, who provoke the most violent response among teenagers, resemble in manner the witch doctors who put their spells on hundreds of shuffling and stamping natives.'[4]

Not everyone saw the resemblance between Beatlemania girls and 'natives' in a reassuring light however. *Variety* speculated that Beatlemania might be 'a phenomenon closely liked to the current wave of racial rioting.'[5] It was hard to miss the element of defiance in Beatlemania. If Beatlemania was conformity, it was conformity to an imperative that overruled adult mores and even adult laws. In the mass experience of Beatlemania, as for example at a concert or an airport, a girl who might never have contemplated shoplifting could assault a policeman with her fists, squirm under police barricades, and otherwise invite a disorderly conduct charge. Shy, subdued girls could go berserk. 'Perky,' ponytailed girls of the type favored by early sixties sitcoms could dissolve into histrionics. In quieter contemplation of their idols, girls could see defiance in the Beatles or project it onto them. *Newsweek* quoted Pat Hagan, 'a pretty, 14-year-old Girl Scout, nurse's aide, and daughter of a Chicago lawyer . . . who previously dug "West Side Story," Emily Dickinson, Robert Frost, and Elizabeth Barrett Browning: "They're tough," she said of the Beatles. "Tough is like when you don't conform . . . You're tumultuous when you're young, and each generation has to have its idols."'[6] America's favorite sociologist, David Riesman, concurred, describing Beatlemania as 'a form of protest against the adult world.'[7]

There was another element of Beatlemania that was hard to miss but not always easy for adults to acknowledge. As any casual student of Freud would have noted, at least part of the fans' energy was sexual. Freud's initial breakthrough had been the insight that the epidemic female 'hysteria' of the late nineteenth century – which took the form of fits, convulsions, tics, and what we would now call neuroses – was the product of sexual repression. In 1964, though, confronted with massed thousands of 'hysterics,' psychologists approached this diagnosis warily. After all, despite everything Freud had had to say about childhood sexuality, most Americans did not like to believe that twelve-year-old girls had any sexual feelings to repress. And no normal girl – or full-grown woman, for that matter – was supposed to have the libidinal volt-age required for three hours of screaming, sobbing, incontinent, acute-phase Beatlemania. In an article in *Science News Letter* titled 'Beatles Reaction Puzzles Even Psychologists,' one unidentified psychologist offered a carefully phrased, hygienic explanation: Adolescents are 'going through a strenuous period of emotional and physical growth,' which leads to a 'need for expressiveness, especially in girls.' Boys have sports as an outlet; girls have only the screaming and swooning afforded by Beatlemania, which could be seen as 'a release of sexual energy.'[8]

For the girls who participated in Beatlemania, sex was an obvious part of the excitement. One of the most common responses to reporters' queries on the sources of Beatlemania was, 'Because they're sexy.' And this explanation was in itself a small act of defiance. It was rebellious (especially for the very young fans) to lay claim to sexual feelings. It was even more rebellious to lay claim to the *active*, desiring side of a sexual attraction: the Beatles were the objects; the girls were their pursuers. The Beatles were sexy; the girls were the ones who perceived them as sexy and acknowl-edged the force of an ungovernable, if somewhat disembodied, lust. To assert an active, powerful sexuality by the tens of thousands and to do so in a way calculated to attract maximum attention was more than rebellious. It was, in its own unformulated, dizzy way, revolutionary.

Notes

1 Lewis (1963, p. 124).
2 Green (1964, p. 30).
3 'How to Kick . . .' (1964, p. 66).
4 Dempsey (1964, p. 15).
5 Quoted in Schaffner (1977, p. 16).
6 'George, Paul . . .' (1964, p. 54).
7   'What the Beatles Prove . . .' (1964, p. 88).
8 'Beatles Reaction . . .' (1964, p. 141).

Chapter 19

Sara Gwenllian-Jones

HISTORIES, FICTIONS AND *XENA: WARRIOR PRINCESS*

Mapping the Xenaverse

LIKE ALL FAN CULTURES, *Xena: Warrior Princess* (*XWP*) fandom is at once typical and singular. Its commonality with other television fan cultures is nuanced by a variety of specific textual and contextual factors. These include the series' diegetic constructions, themes, and subject matter and the cultural and political contexts of its reception by its fans. These factors are consequential for the demographic profile of *XWP* fandom; for its modes of discursive engagement with and interpretative usage of the series; and for its particular character, practices, and manifestations.

XWP debuted in 1995, arriving on television screens across America during roughly the same period that the development of the World Wide Web effected a massive increase in internet usage. From the outset, *XWP* fan culture has been predominantly Net-based. Online *XWP* fandom constitutes a vast conceptual territory that fans refer to as 'the Xenaverse,' a multimedia 'environment' that encompasses everything related to the series, from its production to its diegesis to fan-produced texts. Online, fans have almost instant access to fan fiction and fan-written essays, fan art, screen captures, video and sound files, 'scratch' videos, transcripts of newspaper and magazine articles, screensavers and desktop themes, and each other. The online Xenaverse's combination of accessibility and relative anonymity means that the number of avid viewers who actively participate in *XWP* fan culture greatly exceeds the number likely to participate in offline fandom. Internet fan cultures are user friendly; fans don't need to seek out and subscribe to obscure fanzines, they don't need to travel to meet other fans, and they don't have to negotiate the negative stereotype of the nerdy Trekkie who can't get a girlfriend and still lives with his mother. In general, online fan cultures are bigger, better looking, easier to access, and much cooler than their offline equivalents.

XWP's ironic reworkings of history and mythology, together with its connotative, 'subtextual'[1] queer construction of the central Xena–Gabrielle relationship, invite, even require, active interpretation practices from the series' audience. Kathleen E.

Bennett (1999) outlines the connection between *XWP*'s postmodern constructions of the past and queer readings:

> The mythical ancient world that Xena and Gabrielle inhabit, which is clearly neither in the present era nor any definable time in the human past, is a place free of today's obsessions with sexual identity politics and not obliged to provide any historical verisimilitude. This makes it possible to be a realm open to the imagination, culturally and erotically.

The pre-Christian past, as constructed within *XWP*'s diegesis, becomes a fantastical zone of possibility in which the difficulties of the present and hopes for the future both can be addressed away from the troublesome claims, confusions, and constraints of everyday reality. *XWP*'s invocation of a world where sexism and homophobia do not and cannot triumph is inherently political; fans seize on the series' proffered ways of being female and lesbian in a mythological past so that they can formulate and explore their own modes of being in the present and the future.

XWP's postmodern fracture and excess, its ubiquitous self-referentiality and intertextuality, further draw its audience into active engagement with the series' diegetic constructions and, crucially, through and beyond them toward other texts and discourses. After all, intertextuality is a two-way mechanism that pushes as well as pulls. Its better-known function is centripetal; intertextual references weave multiple exterior meanings into the fabric of a single text. As Fiske (1987) writes,

> The theory of intertextuality proposes that any one text is necessarily read in relationship to others and that a range of textual knowledges is brought to bear upon it . . . Intertextual knowledges pre-orient the reader to exploit television's polysemy by activating the text in certain ways, that is, by making some meanings rather than others. (p. 108)

This aspect of intertextuality invites readers to bring their own cultural knowledge to bear upon the text to decode its various meanings. When a text 'quotes' from or otherwise makes reference to another text, it assumes that its readers are culturally competent enough to recognize and understand the intertextual reference. They, in turn, participate in a process of active interpretation. It is this process of intertextuality that has been most commonly addressed in studies of television readership and fandom. But intertextuality also works centrifugally, in ways that recall Derrida's notion of 'drift' but are rather more precisely motivated and oriented. Intertextuality directs readers beyond the text itself, referring them to the exterior texts that it invokes and uses. For example, when *XWP* makes reference to Orpheus, it doesn't *only* ask its audience to already possess a general understanding of who this individual is but also directs the audience *toward* Greek mythology, to themselves investigate the source of the intertextual reference.

Intertextuality is *XWP*'s primary textual strategy. The series frequently raids literary, cinematic, and other cultural texts, reworking them according to its own narrative logics and requirements. The episode 'Remember Nothing' reworks Frank Capra's *It's a Wonderful Life* as the Fates reveal to Xena what the world would have been like had she never picked up a sword (it would have been miserable, and much bloodier). 'A Solstice Carol' parodies Dickens's *A Christmas Carol*, while in 'Been There, Done That,' a none-too-amused Xena finds herself reliving a version of *Romeo and Juliet* over and over again in her own pre-Mycenaean *Groundhog Day*. In almost every episode, well-known historical and/or mythological figures and events are reworked, and it is these intertextual references above all that inspire fans to extend their interest far beyond the boundaries of the diegesis. The fan-written articles published in the fan-produced e-journal *Whoosh!* (International Association of Xena Studies web site) evidence a wide range of interests inspired and drawn together by the series. The journal carries essays on a diverse range of topics: Boudicca, Alexander the Great, battle strategy, ancient weaponry, ethical and thematic issues, hero figures, food and drink, geography, fauna and flora, ancient civilizations, spiritual beliefs, comparisons between Xena and a variety of other fictional, historical, or mythological figures, and so on. *XWP* fan fiction similarly reflects a ranger of interests and concerns inspired by or associated with, but not restricted to, the series. In fan-fiction author DJWP's carefully researched story 'Seven Days in Pompeii,' Xena and Gabrielle meet up with Sappho as Vesuvius starts to spit smoke and fire; in Melissa Good's 'Dark Comes the Morning,' the couple team up with the Amazons (for both stories, see The Bard's Corner web site).

To intertextuality's outward impetus must also be added another complication: fans' interest in the television text itself may result from, as much as produce, exterior intertextual connections. Do some *XWP* fans become interested in (for example) Greek myths as a result of watching the show, or do some people with an interest in Greek myths become *XWP* fans, recruiting the series as one part of a broader engagement with mythology? The answer is surely that both occur. The television text is not so much a source as an intertextual nexus, always overreaching the limits of its own diegesis, both drawing in and extending itself to other texts and discourses.

In the online Xenaverse, the intertextual connections of the series become manifest in the form of hypertext links that transversally connect fan web sites to other web sites of interest. Hypertextuality is the technological realization of intertextuality; with a click of the mouse, one text always leads to another, and another. As a result, the Xenaverse is not a discrete cultural territory; rather, it is a boundless, ever-evolving network of associations that exists in a constant state of flux. The television series gives the Xenaverse its name and a certain conceptual cohesion, but there are no hard-and-fast rules and no clear parameters; there is only an infinite connectivity across texts and discourses. Jenkins (1992) notes that

> while some fans remain exclusively committed to a single show or star, many others use individual series as points of entry into a broader fan community, linking to an intertextual network composed of many programs, films, books, comics, and other popular materials. (p. 40)

Hypertextuality abolishes any limitations on such intertextual networks, transforming them into the very substance of online fan cultures. Intertextuality, in its hypertextual expression, is the fabric of the Xenaverse, as it is of all online cultures. Every *XWP* (or other) fan web site furnishes a list of hypertext links selected by its author that instantly transport users to other texts – not only to those produced by the 'broader fan community' described by Jenkins but also to cybercultures of all varieties, as well as to online academic journals, political and special interest groups, and diverse informational and educational sites. Each of these web sites, in turn, makes its own hypertextual contributions to the network, and so on ad infinitum.

The task of mapping the online Xenaverse is, of course, an impossible one. The Xenaverse is too expansive, too unstructured, too fluid and fast moving to be charted; it possesses neither interior nor exterior, no clear points of entry or exit, no fixed boundaries, no overall constancy. But this is precisely the point. What hypertextuality allows to be fully realized and fully represented is the extent to which the intertextuality of the television text propels fans towards other texts, knowledges, and interests. The divide between the television text's intertextual connectivity and the internet's hypertextual connectivity is more a matter of technology and form than of textual character or cognitive process.

Between them, *XWP*'s diegesis and the online Xenaverse bring together a variety of compelling factors: a powerful, charismatic, and complex female hero; a central lesbian-inflected relationship; an explicitly postmodern take on history and mythology; an excess of intertextuality; and the complementary hypertext technologies of the internet. The interplay between these various elements takes many forms and moves in many directions, all of which involve an acute awareness of the ideological import, uses, and effects of interpretation, particularly with regard to traditional historiographical interpretations of the past. Reclamations of the Amazons and reformulations of 'Amazon' identities and cultures in and around the online Xenaverse provide perhaps the clearest example of how the interpretative and inventive practices of fans intertextually connect and hybridize fictions, myths, and histories in a highly politicized process of mythopoesis.

The Lost History of the Amazons

> The warrior women known to ancient Greek authors as Amazons were long thought to be creatures of myth. Now 50 ancient burial mounds near the town of Pokrovka, Russia, near the Kazakhstan border, have yielded skeletons of women buried with weapons . . . Some scholars have argued that the weapons found in female burials served a purely ritual purpose, but the bones tell a different story. The bowed legs of one 13- or 14-year-old girl attest to a life on horseback, and a bent arrowhead found in the body cavity of another woman suggested that she had been killed in battle. The Pokrovka women cannot have been the Amazons of Greek myth – who were said to have lived far to the west – but they may have been one of many similar nomadic tribes who occupied the Eurasian steppes in the Early Iron Age.
>
> (Davis-Kimball 1997)

In some ways, the Amazons of *XWP* bear little resemblance to those of either Greek mythology or the Eurasian steppes. Fan Robin Reed (1997) notes how 'in *Xena: Warrior Princess*, the importance of drawing in certain fans to the show has caused the dress code of the Amazons to be somewhat lacking in coverage.' Unlike their mythological or Iron Age counterparts, *XWP*'s Amazons live, hunt, and fight in the forest. They are not nomadic; they inhabit a village and a territory. However, they do constitute an all-female society, they are fierce and independent warriors, and they give at least as good as they get in battle. They are ruled by a queen, whose blood-royal is passed down the female line, and they have their own rituals, traditions, and culture.

Crucially, from the point of view of lesbian fans, they don't seem to bat an eyelid at same-sex relationships; Gabrielle is an Amazon queen 'by right of caste,' with Xena as her consort and champion. There are no questions or discussions; that's just the way things are in the Amazon nation.

For obvious reasons, *XWP*'s invocation of the Amazons has a strong appeal for both heterosexual women and lesbian fans; Amazons have long been part of feminism's symbolic lexicon, representing a wild, unfettered, heroic way of being female. Recent archaeological discoveries in Russia and Ukraine have stimulated a resurgence of interest in the idea of wandering tribes of female warriors, and nowhere more so than in the online Xenaverse. *XWP* fans demonstrate an intense interest in the Amazons, both as an emerging historical actuality and as a concept for working out new female identities and alliances in the present. The fan-produced e-journal *Whoosh!* dedicated the whole of its twelfth issue to essays about real, mythological, and fictional Amazons, reflecting a deep-seated hunger among fans for powerful, iconic female figures that is not satisfied by Xena alone. In her contribution to that issue, *XWP* fan Julie Ruffell (1997) writes,

> The myths of the Amazons are a significant part of human culture. The Amazon myth was embraced by Greece, and from there spread all over the world. They were the earliest symbols of a society's fear of feminism. They questioned the order of life and rose up against it. They would not allow themselves to be treated as less than human.

In the Xenaverse, the Amazons (and the Amazon-like warrior women of the Eurasian steppes) are a source of pride and validation. Fans' interest in the subject extends far beyond the diegetic constructions of the television series. Both within and at the edges of the Xenaverse, transversally interconnected with it, exist a number of web sites that attempt, in diverse ways, to construct virtual realizations of an idealized 'Amazon' culture and society for the twenty-first century. The 'New AmazoNation' wears its politics on its (virtual) sleeve:

> After a five thousand year reign of male icons in the Western World, we have the exhilarating privilege of witnessing a global reappearance of the Divine Feminine. Woman will retake their power in the millennium. Amazons will be in the forefront of this movement.
>
> (New AmazoNation web site n.d.)

The site presents a fully elaborated and vividly imagined blueprint for a contemporary Amazon nation. It outlines a feminist religion dedicated to Artemis and includes treatises on Amazon history and spirituality, representations of Amazons in the media and art, and a section called 'The Way of the Warrior,' which sets out a code for followers to live by. At the Amazonia web site, on the other hand, the focus is more on scholarly investigations into the existence of Amazons and Amazon-like female warriors. The site offers links to a *Time* magazine article about the Scythians and to Jeannine Davis-Kimball's (1997) article in *Archaeology* magazine about the Kazakhstan burial mounds. It also includes descriptions of Amazons in the works of Herodotus, Plato, and other classical historians and an image gallery of representations of Amazons found on ancient artifacts.

All Amazon-related web sites explicitly or implicitly seek some kind of historical redress. Almost invariably, their primary objective is to somehow counter orthodox history's dismissal of the Amazons as nothing more than myth. Backed up by increasingly persuasive archaeological evidence, such sites set out counterhistories in which female warriors and leaders, whether 'Amazon' or not, are offered as evidence that women have played independently active, important, and heroic roles throughout history. A section of the Amazonia site, pointedly titled 'The Amazons Existed,' contains the following statement:

> The reasons I believe in the existence of Amazon Women warriors in ancient history is because I think women are capable of banding together and going to war, and of defending themselves. They are certainly capable of combat, and they can certainly shoot an arrow or a spear, if they want to. Women are capable of living isolated from men.
>
> (Amazonia web site n.d.)

As on most Amazon-related web sites, the need to overturn irritating conventional constructs of women as dependent, passive, and martially challenged is foregrounded. In her concluding paragraph, the author of 'The Amazons Existed' links a feminist argument about what women are capable of to a postmodern understanding of historiographical accounts as ideologically motivated interpretations and announces her intention to play history at its own game by revising its (non)assessment of the Amazons:

> There are certain proofs (twisted and tarnished by non-believing historians as proof of the myth of Amazons); historical accounts, archaeological finds, artists renderings of Amazons in Battle, proofs heretofore squandered in 'Studies of Myths' by the academia, or chipped away at by Freudian analysts, or worse, ignored by historians, every one of which I hope to put on this site. [all *sic*]
>
> (Amazonia web site n.d.)

'Amazonism'[2] is an emerging form of lesbian/feminist activism that has strong links to the Xenaverse, though it isn't confined to it. Amazonist web sites are primarily concerned with the promotion of heroic female figures from history, mythology, and popular culture that contradict historically inscribed conventions that circumscribe female identities. Some web sites, such as Amazon Ink, Spirit Amazon, and Amazon City, go beyond the activism of representation and appropriation to constitute 'virtual tribes' where women interact to exchange information, opportunities, friendship, and support. In an ambitious attempt to 'cover the entire spectrum of meaning that has been attributed to the term Amazon,' the Amazon Connection web site offers more than 150 links arranged into seventeen categories. The categories include 'History, Culture, Mythology'; 'Philosophy, Ideology, Social Issues'; 'Goddess Spirituality and Paganism'; 'Martial Arts'; 'Science, Computers, Nrrdgrrls'; and of course, 'Xena: Warrior Princess.' Amazons are everywhere, once you know what you're looking for. In and around the Xenaverse, Amazonism manifests as another nexus; it extend hypertextually across a wide territory of texts, topics, and interest groups that may be either closely or loosely associated.

I am being tempted to describe Amazonism as the online Xenaverse's 'political wing,' but the transversal relations between these fluid, interrelated cultural zones disallow such a lazy formula. Amazonism and the Xenaverse complement each other, inform each other, interconnect and interact, blur into each other, and merge. Neither intertextuality nor hypertextuality admits boundaries. Amazonism constitutes *XWP* and the Xenaverse as part of its cultural lexicon; *XWP* features both an emphatically Amazonian hero and its own diegetic construction of a powerful Amazon nation; many parts of the Xenaverse lead into, evolve into, or dissolve into Amazonism in one form or another. Amazonism shares the Xenaverse's postmodern cultural logic; like much of the Xenaverse itself, it is what happens when feminists (male or female, straight or gay) start to think mythopoetically about the constructed nature and ideological operations of history in relation to marginalized identities.

Notes

1 Although it is commonly used in relation to *Xena: Warrior Princess*, the notion of a 'lesbian subtext' is somewhat misleading. In some episodes, either Xena or Gabrielle is involved in a heterosexual relationship, in some episodes lesbianism is subtly alluded to, and in others (e.g., 'A Day in the Life,' 'Girls Just Wanna Have Fun,' 'The Quest,' and 'The Debt'), lesbianism, while not explicit, is so strongly suggested that it could be reasonably described as 'maintext.'

2 The term 'Amazonism' is used on some Amazon web sites to describe their own particular brand of feminism; it seems appropriate and useful to adopt it here.

References

Amazon City, http://www.amazoncity. com

The Amazon Connection, http://www.math.uio.no~thomas/lists/amazon-links.html

Amazon.Ink.http://www.amazonink.com

Amazonia,http://www.speakeasy.org/~music/amazon.html

The Bard's Corner,http://ausxip.com/fanfic.html

Bennett, Kathleen E. 1999. *Xena: Warrior Princess*, Desire between Women, and Interpretive Response. Available from http://www.drizzle.com/~kathleen/zena

Davis-Kimball, Jeannine, 1977. Warrior Women of the Eurasian Steppes. *Archaeology* 50 (1, January/February). Available from http://www.archaeology.org/9701/abstracts/sarmatians.html

Fiske, John, 1987. *Television Culture*, London: Routledge.

International Association of Xena Studies. *Whoosh!* online journal. Available from http://whoosh.org

Jenkins, Henry, 1992. *Textual Poachers: Television Fans and Participatory Culture*. New York: Routledge.

The New AmazonNation,http://xenite.simplenet.com/amazons/index.html

Reed, Robin. 1997. Amazon Portrayal in *Xena: Warrior Princess*. *Whoosh!* 12 (September). Available from http://whoosh.org/issue12/reed.html

Ruffell, Julie. 1997. Brave Women Warriors of Greek Myth: An Amazon Roster. *Whoosh!* 12 (September). Available from http://whoosh.org/issue12/ruffel3.html

Spirit Amazon,http://www.globalserve,net/~oversoul/spiritamazon.html

Chapter 20

Camille Bacon-Smith

SUFFERING AND SOLACE
The genre of pain

Hurt-comfort and the ethnographer

IN HURT-COMFORT FICTION, one of the heroes suffers while the other, or a character created for the purpose, comforts him. (In *Blake's 7* fan fiction the comfortee may be one of the female characters, but is more often one of the men.) The source of the suffering may in some instances be illness, but more often inflicted injury causes the pain. Unlike sadomasochistic fantasy material,[1] hurt-comfort places the source of the injury outside of the dyad of sufferer and comforter. Alternatively, the story may originate the hurt within the relationship and move toward eradicating the hurtful behavior through better mutual understanding by the ending. At no point in any of the literature I have read does the sufferer enjoy or deliberately seek out pain.

As a researcher, I found hurt-comfort the most difficult form to study. My own strong aversion to violence inhibited my early efforts at an unbiased analysis, and the community seemed to support my negative judgments about the genre. Judy Segal, who introduced me to fandom, dismissed hurt-comfort as the special interest of a small group while she guided me toward more acceptable material for a neophyte.

As I progressed in my study of the community and its products, I asked a number of writers and editors who occasionally act as mentors to new fans why people in the community chose to write or read hurt-comfort stories. Mentors know how to talk to outsiders. They could not give me core information because I was not yet sufficiently enculturated to make sense of it, but they did mediate for me in language I could understand. Barbara Storey, co-editor of *Nome*, a fanzine that publishes homoerotic fiction, explained:

> Some people have problems with sexuality, but they do like closeness, those emotional ties. I think that's the reason why a lot of people like hurt-comfort, which happens to turn me off completely . . . they cannot allow, for whatever reason, a sexual relationship between those two characters . . . but it is all right if they are just extremely close, they hug each other, if one of

them gets hurt, that allows them an outlet for that deep emotional feeling, without having to delve into sex.[2]

Co-editor Vicki Clark seconded this opinion, including her dislike of the genre, but added, 'I can see if it's part of a whole story. What I can't see is when that is the whole point of the story.'[3]

Barbara and Vicki's explanation highlights an example of conservation of risk. The writer balances the very basic needs to be touched, caressed, against the strictures placed upon physical contact in society. Sex and pain are the two situations in which masculine culture allows physical and emotional intimacy between adults of the opposite sex. If sex is prohibited by the social constraints under which the writer works, either because the participants are not of opposite sexes or because the writer feels constrained to limit sexual material of any kind in her work, she may substitute the only symbolic alternative to sexual intimacy available to her.

Lois Welling, a frequent mentor whose stories often contain strong hurt-comfort elements, said much the same thing in more simple terms: 'I think they just like the comfort, and the hurt is an excuse to get there.'[4] When pressed for a more detailed explanation, Lois backed away from the emotionally fraught question of hurt-comfort to a mundane level I have observed among many community members who move from genre to genre and from source product to source product (Lois writes in several 'universes' and in a number of genres): 'I sometimes think that as a writer progresses in her writing, the situations get more complex and daring, and really have no subconscious meaning for the writer.'[5]

Each option available in the community affords the writer or artist a challenge to her skill as an artist and as a communicator. Can she deliver her message in this genre? In this source product? In some ways, the self-conscious writer may consider taking on a socially ambiguous genre like a mountain climber takes on the Matterhorn: she pits her skill in presenting her material against the risk she takes in the subject matter.

While some authors may engage the genre at the level of challenge, or because of sexual prohibitions, others find that their particular message places them in hurt-comfort without their volition. Shirley Maiewski wrote the story 'Mindsifter,' in which Klingon interrogation has rendered Captain Kirk bereft of both his memory and his sanity. The Klingons dispose of their victim by time-transport to the 1950s, where Kirk is hospitalized in a mental institution. In the story, a nurse helps Kirk to recover both his memory and his confidence in time for his rescue by the *Enterprise*.

According to Shirley, a mental institution near where she lives motivated her to write the story:

> . . . And you go to these state hospitals, and they're beautiful out front, and then you go 'round the back [a pregnant pause follows, giving me time to imagine the terrible conditions that lurk out of sight of casual passersby, some of which are dramatized in Shirley's story]. And there's a large one right near where we live, and a lot of my neighbors work there, and they've told me stories. Well, I got to thinking what would happen if one of our [*Star Trek*] characters, you know, was trapped in one of those places. And it wrote itself.[6]

Shirley Maiewski had an immediate and pressing social need to expose an injustice in her fiction, but she did not associate 'Mindsifter' with the genre until a reader wrote her a letter and asked her about the hurt-comfort in the story. The idea that she might be writing hurt-comfort so distressed Shirley that she stopped writing fiction altogether.

The basic plot for 'Mindsifter' grew out of the televised *Star Trek* episode 'Errand of Mercy,' in which the Klingon, Kor, interrogates Spock using a device called the mindsifter. In the episode, Spock, with his Vulcan mind controls, withstands the machine but he tells the captain that a human would not survive the ordeal with his sanity intact. Shirley was surprised to find her story considered hurt-comfort because her plot originated with the series universe itself, but many writers in the genre use series episodes as starting points for their stories. Both fans of hurt-comfort and community members who do not like the genre often dismissed my questions about its origin with the assertion that the idea wasn't theirs but came from the screen.

To test this response, I did turn to text analysis and found it to be true, up to a point. In the *Star Trek* episode 'The Empath,' Kirk, and then McCoy, are methodically tortured to test the compassion of one representative of an empathic race. Other episodes made a similar point less directly. *Starsky and Hutch* fans produce the highest percentage of hurt-comfort fiction, as writer Fanny Adams pointed out to me:

> In *Starsky and Hutch*, especially at the beginning of the fandom, there was a lot of hurt-comfort, and there may be a lot of different reasons for that, you know, I won't want to go into it, but there will always be hurt, physical hurt . . . beat 'em up, let's hurt 'em, bleed 'em.[7]

In fact, a whole *Starsky and Hutch* fanzine was dedicated to 'slow poison' stories, in honor of that common theme in action-adventure television. *Starsky and Hutch* in particular. A review of the *Starsky and Hutch* corpus was still surprising, however.

I was less interested in my interpretation of the action on the screen than in the intention to communicate hurt-comfort concepts on the part of series producers, so I examined the press release for each episode in the press pack sent to *TV Guide* magazine by the Spelling-Goldman organization. In at least 33 percent of the episodes, the press releases mentioned as central to the plot injury or directed threat of death to one of the two heroes, while the other worried or saved him. In almost as many episodes, the threat was to a friend or family member outside the dyadic hero relationship.

Clearly, fans drew basic concepts from the screen, but why these products inspired an artistic response, or why hurt-comfort fans grew decidedly misty when they admitted to their fan interest, still eluded me. To my persistent questions, most fans responded that they didn't know why they liked hurt-comfort. They just did.

While participants at the core of an esoteric practice have the most knowledge about it, those participants also have a knack for knowing when the questioner isn't ready to understand any answer they can give. My informants did not lie; the thing they did not know about their interest was how to tell me what they knew. We did not share a language, and my informants politely refrained from informing me that my question made no sense.

At this point I still had trouble reading hurt-comfort fiction, and I finally realized that I would never understand it until I had read more deeply in the genre. Armed with this grudging insight and the general explanations equally uneasily given by informants over my years studying the community, I proceeded to ask hurt-comfort fans at an action-adventure convention for the title of their favorite story. They named most frequently 'Strange Days Indeed,'[8] a story 105 single-spaced, eight-and-a-half by eleven pages long. To desensitize myself to the difficult genre so that I could work with it, I read 'Strange Days Indeed' four times in one weekend. Over that weekend I learned to look past my own response to the graphic depiction of violence and to seek out the patterns of interaction embedded within them.

In 'Strange Days Indeed,' the abuse begins when the villain beats the first hero, breaking several of the hero's ribs and damaging his appendix. An extended scene of homosexual rape of the second hero follows, from the point of view of the partner held in a room adjacent to where the rape is taking place. The partner can only hear what is happening to his friend, but at the same time he cannot stop listening. The two hurt friends are abandoned in a comfortable cottage with everything one might need but a doctor. The first hero develops a drug dependency under the pressure of caring for his raped companion. They quarrel, and finally the rape victim realizes that his companion is in equal need of attention. In spite of their respective fragile conditions, they crawl into bed together for a supportive embrace. By the end of the story, they realize they love each other.

As I have since found to be most usually the case, the violence and abuse in the story arises outside of the friendship relationship. At no point is either character attracted to the perpetrator of the violence. At no point is the abuse written as sexually exciting to the hurt characters, nor does either hero take pleasure in the abuse of the other. The presence of the friend as witness to the sexual degradation of his companion increases the suffering of the witness and the pain of humiliation of the sexually abused partner. At all times the first hero's concern is for the well-being of his companion. The second hero reciprocates this attitude and returns the care and attention as soon as he becomes aware that comforting is needed. The distinction between good and evil is clearly drawn and unambiguous. Importantly, at no point does the story seem intended to appeal sexually to its audience. Criticized by scholars for not considering the erotic possibilities of the story as I described it here, however, I returned to the community and asked those who recommended the story what they found erotic in it. The question puzzled the fans, who did not understand how anyone could find the torture portions of that particular story sexually exciting, and I had to expend some effort to rehabilitate my position among community members who took my question as an expression of my own feelings about the story. They did agree that the discovery of true love at the end was pleasurable.

I then began reading the many stories in the genre that I had put aside, and I discovered that 'Strange Days Indeed' was an unauthorized rewrite of an earlier story, also anonymous, in which the first hero is not severely beaten, and a third party with no relationship to the hero dyad attends to the care of the sexually abused man. Many fans of the genre found the first version less satisfying because the third party replaces what readers construed as the proper source of the comfort: a loving friend is present and concerned, but not the active giver of care. Other fans, however, preferred the first version because the amount of suffering depicted in the story is less extreme, and the attention of the knowledgeable third party seems more appropriate than the ministrations of his less adequately prepared friend. Both versions of the story maintain the same pattern of pain coming from outside the dyad, but the more popular version adds two interesting factors along with the additional violence that seemed gratuitous to some: (1) it reestablishes the main source of comfort within the relationship; and (2) it balances the equation – both partners experience pain and both receive comfort. In fact, the story seems to say that one way of dealing with personal pain is to recognize the suffering of those we care about and return their attention and comfort.

[. . .]

Hurt-comfort and community

I saw hurt-comfort in action in the community long before I understood the genre, but the experience has stayed with me in spite of the fact that I could neither tape nor take notes. It was my first realization that something important was going on in the genre, and it is the single reason why I never gave up trying to understand the implications for community life of stories I personally found upsetting to read.

The New York Convention Committee's More Eastly Con took place on Labor Day weekend in 1985, just weeks after the death of fanwriter Toni Cardinal-Price in a hit-and-run auto accident. Toni's work was highly respected in the fan community, and her death shocked everyone who knew her and many who had only read her poetry. I had met Vicki Clark and Barbara Storey, editors of the fanzine *Nome* and close friends of Toni, earlier that year. When they saw me in the dealers room at More Eastly Con they invited me to their room for a small get-together they were holding to remember Toni.

When I arrived the room was full of women clustered on the beds, on the floor, leaning against the walls. Around the mirror friends had taped snapshots of Toni Cardinal-Price at home and with her friends, a number of whom were present in the room. Someone had brought in a VCR, and *Star Trek* songtapes were playing. Most of the videos recounted the strong friendship between Captain Kirk and his first officer, and many dealt with Spock's death, which shocked fans when they first saw *The Wrath of Khan*.

Throughout the evening the fan women watched the videos, commented softly about them, and cried. From time to time the experience would become too much for someone in the room and she would head for the bathroom for quiet talk with one friend until she was calm enough to rejoin the group. People drifted in and out of the room, some stopping only to pay their respects, others lingering to stare at the videos and share in the warmth of each other's company and the freedom to let down the bright face and mourn. Vicki and Barbara told me how they had been on vacation in California when they received the news on the same day Toni had died in New Jersey, and how they had traveled four hundred miles off their scheduled route to be with mutual friends, who took time off from work to be with them and share their grief. It became strikingly clear to me during that weekend that fans did not write hurt-comfort for fun, but that the genre fulfilled some of the deepest needs of community life.

I kept the experience of More Eastly Con in mind while I accumulated explanations of fans and a working knowledge of the literature by title and author. Finally, I figured out where my original question had gone wrong, and once again I ventured into the field. This time, I asked a number of the writers what was happening in their lives when they wrote particular stories I mentioned by title. One woman, who wrote about a man losing his young son to leukemia, explained that she was working out her feelings about an adult daughter's drug addiction. Another woman wrote a 'get-'em' story about a hero captured and tortured while his partner, believing him dead, goes mad. At the end of the story the captured hero is rescued by third parties and brought to the place where his partner awaits his return to take him into death. Both men are debilitated almost beyond recognition, but the story offers only the glimmer of hope that they are still alive, together again. Writing the story helped that author struggle with suicidal depression. She told me that she had originally planned to write the comfort part as a sequel but found that when her depression lifted she could not go back to the story again.

In all cases when I asked about specific fictional stories I received descriptions of real psychic pain. Some fans who read but did not create in the genre dealt with physical disability in their lives. In general, however, I found that women experiencing physical turmoil in their lives were more likely to write the most idealized relationships in their fiction.

I might have been tempted to stop here, with a phenomenon and a symbolic function of the text, but my knowledge of the genre and the duration of my study put me in an ambiguous position. While some fans feared that my study might reveal too much about them, others had grown used to my presence. When I showed an interest in hurt-comfort, they included me in fan activities that focused on the genre. I had not seen these interactions earlier because it would have been inappropriate, according to fan standards of behavior, to subject me to discussions about a topic I found distasteful. Over the years fans had occasionally asked if I liked the material, but when I said that I found it uncomfortable reading they quickly dropped the subject. I now realize that I had put some of my informants in a double bind, asking about a genre while admitting I didn't like it, but at the time I thought I could learn about the fan relationship to the genre without actually reading the stories. As I later discovered, I was wrong.

When a fan has an idea, she calls friends and tells them that idea – it's called talking story, and, as discussed in earlier chapters, it is the most common activity at any fan gathering in any media product or community genre. It is far more acceptable to talk story widely in the community than to express feelings of hopelessness and despair in the outside world. Through the process of talking story, the fanwriter or reader has direct and immediate contact with warm and caring friends. She can ask for advice about her story from any fan of the genre and, while they talk story, the participants move back and forth from the personal to the grammatical, hiding in sentence structure when the feelings become too intense or when a stranger passes by. With their literature for symbolic discourse, fans band together this way in a conspiracy of support for their members.

But this support does not occur in woeful sob sessions. Pain is present, recognized, shared, but art is also present, and art is joyful. Fans learn to laugh with their friends, to stave off the fearful darkness with potato chips and chocolate ice cream and preposterous exaggerations of their own genre. 'Shot in the shoulder, point-blank range with a high-power rifle and he's up and running the next day,' one writer characterized her own story; 'What I like best is the realism.'

Further along the process, the writer may see her story incorporated into the community with illustrations in a fanzine. Its worth is reified because fans outside the immediate circle buy it. Isolation continues to break down as new readers discuss her work. The writer even finds satisfaction in helping others when fans tell her that her story has affected them and offer stories of their own in turn.

Notes

1 In the sadomasochistic fantasy material I reviewed, the violence was much less extreme than in hurt–comfort fiction (I found only one threat of permanent injury, and no representations of serious physical damage such as broken bones and abusive beatings). In most cases the point of view was that of the submissive partner, and the attitude of the submissive partner was gratitude for the humiliation and ritual abuse meted out to him by his dominant partner. Examples drawn from *Drummer* magazine, 1980–81.
2 Barbara Storey and Victoria Clark, taped interview, August 1985.
3 Ibid.
4 Personal correspondence, Lois Welling to author, 1986.
5 Ibid.
6 Shirley Maiewski, taped interview, New York, September 1985.
7 Fanny Adams, taped interview, Chicago, March 1987.
8 'Strange Days Indeed,' anonymous and undated circuit story.

Chapter 21

David Muggleton

INSIDE SUBCULTURE
The postmodern meaning of style

What we did was we opened the doors, and so all these endless punk imitators suddenly flooded in and dissipated the whole point of it, because they became clone-like. Now they totally missed the whole point, that this was all about individual expression and personality. These are the things that count in life for me, but most of the punk outfits didn't appreciate that at all. They allowed the likes of the *Daily Mirror* to dictate a uniform. *The* leather jacket; *the* safety pin; *the* torn jeans; *the* bovver boots; *the* spiky hair. And it became hideous.

> (John Lydon on the Sex Pistols and Punk Rock:
> 'Mavericks', BBC Radio One, Feb. 1995)

Our politics were clear in 'Anarchy'. We weren't political in the sense of saying: be a Socialist, be a Tory, be a Communist. We were political in the sense that we didn't even entertain the idea of politics, it was below us. It was anarchy in its purest sense: self-determination. We couldn't, we felt, do much about changing the system, but we weren't going to let the system do anything to us. We wanted to live our lives how we wanted to live them – and we went out and did it.

> (Glen Matlock: *I Was a Teenage Sex Pistol*, 1996: 163)

Defusion and diffusion

I N ANY EXAMINATION OF subcultural authenticity and resistance, a consideration of the role played by the media and commerce is indispensable. That this should be so is primarily because of the way these two pairs of factors have been almost completely counterpoised in the CCCS approach. In a two-way process, authentic stylistic resistance occurs through *bricolage*, an act of transformation by which a new and original style is formed through plunder and recontextualization as a challenge to the hegemony of the dominant culture. It is this radical creativity that, so the theory goes, is then co-opted and incorporated through media and commercial exploitation, after which those who take up the style are reduced to the status of mere fad-followers.

We discussed the initial part of this process . . . The latter part, as sketched out by Clarke (1986: 185–9) and Hebdige (1979: 92–9), itself involves two interconnected movements, defusion and diffusion. Through defusion, the subversive potential of subcultural style is sanitized, commercially, through the commodification of subcultural forms: the turning of gestures and signs of refusal into mainstream fashion – ' a pure "market" or "consumer" style' (J. Clarke 1986: 187). Diffusion is the actual geographical and social dispersal of the style from the original nucleus of innovators to new and mass publics, mediated through television and tabloid reports. In both cases, the process assumes an underground, yet internally-cohesive, clearly defined, self-contained resistance movement, untainted by the world of media and commerce until its discovery and dissipation by the institutions of dominant society – 'the element of commercial reaction which attempts to universalize, at a purely stylistic and consumption level, the innovations made by distinctive youth cultures, while simultaneously defusing the oppositional potential of the exclusive lifestyles' (J. Clarke and Jefferson 1978: 157).

. . . the increasing power of media and commerce in a postmodern society hastens this process of incorporation (Connor 1991; Redhead 1991), further negating the potential for authenticity and resistance. McRobbie (1989) and Thornton (1994, 1995) more radically demonstrate how the forces of media and commerce are, from the very outset, proactive in subcultural formation. If the postmodern thesis is fully realized we might expect subculturalists to exhibit a celebratory attitude towards style, fashion and the media rather than to view their affiliation as a normative or political gesture of resistance or rebellion. This is our hypothesis, to be supported or refuted by the data. Although the two themes of media and commerce are obviously interrelated, I will deal with them separately. First, let us consider the media. Here there are three interrelated questions: (1) How do subculturalists view the role of media and commerce in the construction of their own identity?; (2) How do they view the role of the media in the construction of others?; and (3) Are different media allocated distinct roles in the above process?

(A) MATT

M: If you actually look at the photographs of the Sex Pistols gigs there is like not a punk in the audience, they have all got long hair. They have all got, like . . . if you look at the real photographs, nobody knew what a punk was, there was no uniform. There wasn't a punk uniform. Maybe I might be wrong. There might have been people who actually thought they were punks, but um, I'm not so sure, you know, I think punk became a label possibly after Johnny Lydon, Johnny Rotten said . . . er . . . told . . . er . . . Grundy to fuck off.

In the first extract we again find Matt . . . He was then engaged in the process of authenticating his punk identity by virtue of his involvement having occurred prior to the labelling process by which punk was publicly named and identified. Not only, then, does his inception predate the point at which punk became a uniform, but he was initially unaware of his identity as a punk. As corroborative evidence he points to photographs of the Sex Pistols' gigs. It will become clear that these are the gigs taking place before the end of 1976, before punk became a focus of mass media attention. The people in the audience on these photographs not only fail to look like 'punks', they are more likely to resemble hippies or, at the very least, sport the general youth fashion of the time ('they have all got long hair').[1] As Matt points out, at this period in time 'nobody knew what a punk was.'

What is significant is the way the mass media are deemed to be fully responsible for the sudden transformation of this situation. The watershed is precisely identified as the Bill Grundy interview with the Sex Pistols. Broadcast on Thames Television in the early evening of 1 December 1976, this infamous encounter brought national notoriety to the group and punk rock in general. It is only after this event that punk becomes labelled, the style becomes identifiable as a 'uniform', and people think of themselves as punks. This not only clearly defines the subculture's identity, but the perceived movement towards homogeneity sharply demarcates it from the remnants of residual cultural movements such as hippy. This further implies that those who become punks in the wake of this event are inauthenticated, not only through their uniformity of look and rapid conversion (attributable to one specific instance of media exposure), but by the very fact of media-influenced affiliation itself. As Osgerby has perceptively argued, 'any sense of a coherent punk "movement" or punk "identity" was largely the outcome of media simplification and commercial marketing strategy' (1998: 111).

In one obvious sense, (A) follows the pattern of events set out by the CCCS work: the mass communications media are evacuated from Matt's own (authentic) inception, but construct those who enter the subculture after the Grundy interview as, for all intents and purposes, inauthentic 'followers'. Yet, as the Osgerby quotation suggests, this appears to reverse the CCCS construction of subcultural cohesion. Rather than self-contained and clearly defined subcultures being diffused and dissipated by media attention and commercial exploitation, authentic inception is characterized here by a lack of cohesion and demarcation, with the media playing a homogenizing and clarifying role. It might appear that Matt's views are more consistent with those expressed by Stanley Cohen in his seminal text, *Folk Devils and Moral Panics* (1973, 1980). As Trowler and Riley say of this work, 'its principal theme [is] that youth subculture must be seen as a media creation rather than as a reaction by the working class section of youth to their economic and social environment' (1985: 157). Similarly, according to Thornton, 'scholars of "moral panic" assume that little or nothing existed prior to *mass* media labelling' (1995: 119; original emphasis).

These, it must be said, are somewhat oversimplistic readings of Cohen, who was careful to stress in the final chapter of his book that a conventional socio-structural account is required to explain the origins of such subcultures – 'the mods and rockers did not appear from nowhere' (Cohen 1973: 191). It would be more accurate to see this as an origin in which the media are not allocated any explicit or significant role. Only in the process of societal reaction do the media really come to prominence, the effect of what is to homogenize and polarize the two subcultures. In (A), then, Matt appears to be proposing a more radical version of Cohen's thesis whereby mass media coverage does not simply intensify weakly drawn differences between already existing groups, but *actually creates the very notion* of a subcultural identification itself.

Mass, niche and micro media

That media effects are imputed to others is unsurprising, given the oft-made equation between mass media influence and a lack of capacity for critical and independent thought in those so swayed. However, this does suggest the need to examine whether subculturalists have in mind different types or forms of media, and if these are regarded as having varying implications for the construction of authenticity or inauthenticity. Relevant to such an analysis is Sarah Thornton's (1995) study *Club Cultures* . . . In her discussion of the media (see also Thornton 1994), Thornton poses two questions. First, in what way are the media involved in the actual development of subcultures? Second, how do 'subcultural ideologies' (1995: 121) – the subjective perceptions of subcultural members – construct the role of the media?

In answering the first of these questions, Thornton takes issue with Cohen (1973), who defines media solely in terms of the regional and national press. She argues instead for an internally differentiated understanding of 'the media', distinguishing between micro, niche and mass media. Thornton proposes that such distinctions undercut any simple opposition between media that are indigenous and those that are exogenous to subcultural movements. Nor, therefore, can their relationship to sub-cultures be viewed in terms of a linear process of increasing incorporation. Such a proposal is justified by three claims. First, that negative mass media coverage does not act as a mechanism of defusion and diffusion, but on the contrary, can help to render subcultures subversive and increase their longevity. Thornton notably diverges here from the CCCS view of the media-subculture relationship. Second, that niche media – the music press and style magazines – are often staffed with people previously or currently subcultural members themselves. Such media actively help to compose and structure stable subcultural entities from real yet nonetheless nebulous movements and cultural fragments. Third, that micro-media, such as fanzines, listings, posters and flyers, are also integral to the networking process of assembling individuals *as* a crowd for a specific purpose and imbuing them with a particular identity . . . Moreover, in an ironic reversal of subcultural ideologies, the tabloid mass media can often be well ahead of certain micro-media in their coverage of new developments in the subcultural arena.

Clearly, Thornton's conclusion, 'that subcultures are best defined as social groups that have been labelled as such . . . Communications media create subcultures on the process of naming them and draw boundaries around them in the act of describing them' (1995: 162), does not allow any space for a non-mediated subcultural identity. A point which, at one level, a number of my interviewees are happy to concur with; for as Oliver put it, 'everybody's influenced by the media'. However, this is precisely to raise Thornton's second question of how subculturalists position the media (or different aspects of it) in relation to their own affiliation. In much the same way as my own interviewees, Thornton's informants proclaimed their authenticity through comparisons with two types of reference groups. First, against a feminized nightclub mainstream which bears more than a passing resemblance to the 'trendie' venue and its Shaz inhabitants . . . Secondly, against a subcultural 'Other' – inauthentic clubbers known, somewhat bizarrely, as 'Acid Teds' (ibid.: 100).[2] There are really, then, two aspects of Thornton's second question: how do her clubber informants regard their own relationship to the media? And: how do they see the role of the media in the construction of these inauthentic 'Others'?

Predictably, in line with Matt in (A), we find that 'Others' are denigrated as mass-media-influenced. Sharon and Tracey, who personify the mainstream, set their cultural standards by 'Top of the Pops', while 'Acid Teds', and their feminized equivalent 'Techno Traceys', take their cues from *The Sun* newspaper (ibid.: 109). And as we might also have expected, the clubbers invert this relationship when referring to themselves, disparaging the mass media (a sure sign of 'selling-out'), yet championing micro-media such as fanzines as an authentic, grass-roots means of communication, thus confirming an earlier finding by Lull, that flyers and fanzines were 'trusted sources of information' (1987: 244) for the punks in his study. This varying regard given to different aspects of the media can, in fact, be detected in (A). Note how Matt characterizes the visual evidence of those first gigs as 'the real photographs', thereby suggesting their authenticity, presumably in relation to the 'falsity' of the mass media. Yet this is too easy a conclusion to leap to. Such remarks may be more of a comment on the people portrayed and constructed by the media than it is on the media themselves, for such a distinction seems to derive from the dichotomy between 'genuine' and 'false' members, first outlined in Chapter 5. It would also be necessary to see how subculturalists deal with the complications that arise when, unlike Matt, they would find it difficult to claim that their own inception preceded not only media attention but the very naming process of the subculture itself. Let us look then at (B) which deals not with punk, but with mod.

(B) OLIVER

DM: I mean – you know – the difference between being genuine or whatever you want to call it and not being a fad-follower. And yet I'm wondering that someone else might see you as a fad-follower and what your defence would be. Because I can't see what it is that you have which fad-followers don't. Or at least, I don't know what it is.

O: Yeah, I see what you mean. I don't know, because I got into dressing like this through sort of hanging around with people like it. And although everyone's going . . . you know, there's been that piece in that music paper, *Select*, about the mod revival, and there's like *Blow Up*, which is a mod club, and everything like that . . . but I don't know. I was sort of dressing quite sharp before I read about those, and it's more about watching *Quadrophenia* or something like that.

This extract opens with a reference to the distinction between real members and mere followers. Here, I put it to Oliver that there is nothing that obviously seems to place him in the former group rather than the latter. What we can observe in this extract is how three potential admissions of inauthenticity are counteracted by their framing within claims for authenticity. First, Oliver states that his style has emerged through peer-group interaction. While this could be interpreted as an admission of copying (following the dictates of others), the point of this statement is to highlight how the style came about through face-to-face contact rather than the influence of the media. Secondly, he does not deny knowledge of the contemporary mod revival, nor of his interest in associated media coverage. Yet he plays down any possible accusation of influence by chronologically placing his initial involvement as having preceded such developments ('before I read about those'). Note also that he does not acknowledge 'mod' as a group label relevant to his identity, but merely says that he was 'dressing quite sharp'. His alternative source of influence ('it's more about watching *Quadrophenia* or something like that') also provides the third potential admission of inauthenticity. Not only is this an explicit acknowledgement of media influence, but a particularly significant one given that *Quadrophenia* is not merely a cult film, but was popular in major cinemas at the time of its release. It could conceivably be regarded as more akin to a mass media text than *Select*, the music paper whose influence is mitigated, and which Thornton would clearly regard as an example of niche media.

But as Oliver is attempting to situate his involvement as having occurred before the, then current, 1994 mod revival, mitigation need take place only with regard to contemporary media influences. As *Quadrophenia* was originally released in 1979, it would normally be cited as having helped precipitate the 1980 mod revival. While we would therefore have expected 1980 mods to have denied such an influence at the time, Oliver was then only eight years old, and too young to be involved. It is precisely this point that allows him to cite the film as an influence rather than, say, current music papers, for he can now safely claim he saw it well before the origins of the 1994 revival. In other words, there are significant time lags between the 1980 revival and his own viewing of the film, and from then until the emergence of the 1994 mod subculture. This minimizes the likelihood of others who were similarly influenced becoming mods through viewing the film at the same time as Oliver, and emphasizes his individuality and authentic origins. An additional inference might be that contemporary revivalists are also too young to have seen the film, and would therefore have been influenced by other, more current, media material. The point is the manner in which the age of the film, Oliver's personal biography and the dates of the two revivals intersect, providing a historical conjuncture that allows this particular person to cite this specific film at this moment in time while retaining his authenticity in relation to a media-influenced collective other.

Many subculturalists fully recognize the pervasiveness of the media and the inevitability of its influence on people's lives. But consistently with findings in the previous chapters, media effects were most usually attributed to others or retrospectively to a point in one's own past in order to authenticate a more recent situation. Subculturalists did not, however, consistently differentiate along a scale of decreasing authenticity between micro, niche and mass media in the expected manner. This is because claims for authenticity are primary; the media can then be illustrative of this. In other words, one's own heterogeneity and originality is first contrasted to the relative lack of such qualities in a subcultural or conventional 'Other' or past situation. Various media are then positioned and defined as mass or otherwise on the basis of this contrast. Their relative 'massness' is therefore derived from the homogenization of the 'Other', not in terms of any pre-defined formal qualities. This means that admissions of media influence by subculturalists can in no way be considered a postmodern celebration of the media, for such references are most likely to take the form of mitigation. The claims for authenticity that they seek to establish are necessarily conditional upon the 'mass media'-influenced inauthenticity of others.

Fashion and commercialism

Empirically, the worlds of media and commerce are clearly interrelated; they are also theoretically combined in accounts of defusion and diffusion. In this chapter they are separated for analytical purposes to highlight their similar implications for subcultural authenticity. Echoing the manner in which respondents perceive their relationship to the media, the homogeneity of a look is not a quality of the style itself, not a function of where it is purchased, but depends on how it is situated within a description of the wearer's authenticity.

(C) MARC AND PAULA

M: Yeah, there are definite categories of people around. It's just that I don't really like categorizing myself.

P: There are a lot of people who do, like, belong to (indecipherable on tape). I think there are a lot in Brighton. Like recently there's been an upsurge of quite young girls, sort of between thirteen and sixteen, who think it's cool to be crusty, basically. I don't know if you've noticed that; it's quite obvious. And if you go around these pubs, you see them. There's loads of underage drinking. And they've got sort of like a uniform of holey tights on, I dunno.

M: They're like us really.

P: Well, yeah; but in certain cases they're trying to belong to a certain group, and that's really obvious. Like, you know they're obviously copying something that . . . you know. I think it's a phase they've got caught in, really.

M: You just have to look at what most of the sort of High Street shops are doing. I was looking through some magazines the other day and Top Shop are bringing out their traveller look because now they think it's trendy to look sort of crusty in a way. So they're bringing out new clothes, basically for probably your thirteen- to sixteen-year olds. I can see people do think this all has some sort of bearing on fashion.

(D) SUZIE AND MAGS

S: I got very fed up with all the clothes that I was wearing and buying cheap and wrecking being sold for huge amounts of money to people that had probably never heard of . . . they'd heard of, like *Teen Spirit*, but hadn't heard of Mudhoney or any of the other, like, grunge bands that were fairly big then, and were just buying stuff from Top Shop and stuff and thinking they were great and it got on my nerves and I thought 'I'm not wearing this any more.'

M: Got really pretentious.

S: 'Cos I was being lumped in a group with them which wasn't on really, so.

M: When the grunge look became fashionable, well, that was a piss-off. Before that, people used to have . . . rip you apart for it, really – and then all of a sudden the catwalk said it was fashionable and it was cool, do you know what I mean?

Extract (C) begins with a familiar sentiment. Marc resists categorization, but feels that it is applicable to others. Paula then nominates such a category – 'crusty'. Those designated by this term are claimed to be identifiable by their uniformity of appearance. That the description of this style could equally be applicable to the two interviewees makes this a potentially dangerous accusation. The irony is not lost on Marc ('They're like us really'). But Paula has already mitigated such a response in two ways. The first is by describing the emergence of this group through the words 'recently' and 'upsurge'. The transformation into 'crusty' has, in other words, been both rapid (superficial) and contemporary (after the original impulse), in contrast to which the interviewees can claim that they have been dressing in this style for a long time (which makes them innovators rather than followers), and that their own transition was gradual (suggesting an evolving, developing self). Paula's second mitigation, that this group 'think it's cool to be crusty' is premised on the distinction . . . between subculturalists, like the crusties, who merely adopt an image, and people, such as Marc and Paula, who wear style as a genuine expression of internally held attitudes.

Following Marc's comments, Paula commences to reinforce these initial negative group references. 'Trying to belong to a certain group . . . obviously copying something' implies a deliberate attempt by the crusties to follow a collective look, while the remarks about a 'phase' suggest that this is to be a short-lived, superficial attachment. The final claim is that the group look has been purchased from a High Street store, Top Shop, which renders it nothing more than an immediately obtained youthful trend. Just as 'preppie punks' were denigrated as 'pretenders' with a 'costume party' sensibility (Fox 1987: 361), the crusties are perceived to be interested only in subculture as fashion. As such, they resemble what Baron termed '"poseurs" (those youth who had adopted the subcultural style but did not participate in the subculture)' (1989: 231). For other examples of this distinction between genuine and fashion-oriented members see also Andes (1998); Kotarba and Wells (1987); Lull (1987); Roman (1988); Sardiello (1998); Tomlinson (1998) and Widdicombe and Wooffitt (1990, 1995).

Although slightly older and of a related rather than identical style, Suzie and Mags in extract (D) would come close to the type of people who are disparaged by Marc and Paula in (C) for their fashion mentality. Of course, as we might expect, they also impute a fashion sensibility and related negative attributes to a comparative 'Other' through which to authenticate themselves. Suzie sets herself up (singular) as a creative innovator ('buying cheap and wrecking'). This is contrasted with those (plural) who merely buy the style, presumably 'ready wrecked', after it has become an expensive fashion. Note again the use of Top Shop as a symbol of a youthful, female fashion mentality. Also, observe the description of this 'Other' as 'pretentious', used in other interviews as a synonym for both 'plastic' and 'false'. Suzie's refusal to wear the style after this point is to differentiate her individual self from this inauthentic collective. Her complaint about 'being lumped in a group with them' could easily be a direct riposte to Marc and Paula. Mags also bemoans how the turning of grunge style into fashion by 'the catwalk' (note the impersonal, collective noun) has divested it of its shock potential and ability to provoke a critical reaction ('before that, people used to . . . rip you apart for it'). Moreover, this transformation is deemed to have occurred 'all of a sudden'. In other words, those taking up the fashion would have undergone a rapid change, denoting their superficiality. By contrast, Suzie and Mags can imply that their own inception occurred gradually, took place prior to this incorporation, and thereby signified a more individualized stylistic radicalism formed in opposition to mainstream fashion and mass consumption.

Interestingly, Suzie also invokes music to make claims about her authenticity. Those who constitute the reference group are thought to have heard of *Teen Spirit*, a reference to a hit single by Nirvana, but not any other grunge bands, despite the fact that some of these, such as Mudhoney, are described as having been 'fairly big then'. However, this is not to endow such bands with the popularity and renown that ensues from a top-selling hit single; for what, then, is the point of the contrast with *Teen Spirit*? The implication is that such bands were big enough for anyone *genuinely* into grunge to have heard of. The fact that certain people were not aware of them, yet had heard a successful chart single by a grunge band, is a comment on their taste for only the commercial element of such music. The falsity of grunge 'fashion' is clearly being equated here with the superficiality of commercially successful grunge music, both being contrasted with a depth metaphor: music (or style) as a genuine expression of and belief in inner feelings. Dancis expresses this difference with regard to punk music as, 'a band that has adopted a punk image and sound because it has become marketable, rather than because they believe in what they're doing' (1978: 63). This is one reason why, in the eyes of Lull's San Francisco punks, 'rock music that makes a lot of money is suspect, and songs that are rotated regularly on commercial radio stations do not gain approval' (Lull 1987: 243–4).

What is being privileged here is the artistic integrity of the underground compared to the mass commercialism of the mainstream. In Thornton (1995: 109, 122–9), we find, for example, the association of the denigrated mainstream with 'Top of the Pops' and various forms of 'chartpop'. For Thornton's clubbers, commercialism is a sure sign of 'selling out', a threat to one's sense of exclusivity, esotericism and cultural capital.[3] But Thornton also recognizes the irony that 'nothing proves the originality and inventiveness of subcultural music and style more than its eventual "mainstreaming"' (1995: 128). On one hand, there is the desire to protect the scarcity of subcultural capital and thereby retain one's originality; on the other, the need to have this affirmed by a larger following, losing in the process what Wai-Teng Leong has termed 'the power to be different' (1992: 32). Oliver indicated as much when he said, 'It's [the mod revival] not very big at the moment, and therefore, you know, you hope it's going to get big almost, but in a way you're glad it's not, because it would be full of people who would be jumping on the bandwagon.'

The oppositions brought into play in these extracts – between alternative and commercial, minority and majority, originals and followers – are those that in the CCCS approach distinguish 'the first wave of self-conscious innovators' (Hebdige 1979: 122) from the merely fashion-conscious. We examined the theoretical basis of this distinction at the beginning of this chapter, where we also made reference to subsequent modifications of the theory that have attempted to demystify the concept of pure stylistic innovation. Of these, we have already outlined Thornton's (1995) arguments that the media are as responsible for the definition and demarcation of subcultures as they are for their defusion and diffusion. A parallel thesis is provided by Frith and Horne (1987), and Seago (1995), who examine how the art schools provided an entrepreneurial ethos and designer dynamic, a strand of bohemianism that fed straight into the innovative world of streetstyle, counterculture and subculture, yet is absent from so much theoretical analysis. The relevance of this to punk is given in Jon Savage's (1992) cultural history *England's Dreaming*, certain passages of which suggest that the 'creation' of punk as a distinctive style owes as much to the entrepreneurial impulse of Malcolm McLaren and Vivienne Westwood, and the adoption of these designs by the Sex Pistols and others, as it does to the creative originality of disaffected youth.[4]

Now let us attempt our own theoretical re-evaluation of what occurs 'after the subculture has surfaced and become publicized' (Hebdige 1979: 122). We could assume this necessarily leads to the passive and collective acceptance of a commercially produced style. Or, alternatively, we could propose that such commodified subcultural styles, whether purchased new or obtained second-hand, continue to be customized and subverted. 'Just as the innovators can construct new meanings for clothes or other symbols from the dominant culture, so too can other members adapt and change the subcultural items for their own purpose and needs' (Andes 1998: 213). Why, then, should the option of further adaptation leading to heterogeneity be any less subversive than the actions of the original innovators? The answer, of course, is that it isn't, particularly when one further considers that some of the original adapters may also have adopted. In other words, as Wai-Teng Leong realizes, 'it is difficult to establish empirically the difference between adapters and adopters of style, between innovators and followers' (1992: 46). What is being suggested here is captured by Cagle's concept of 'out-there subculture':

> Unlike Hebdige's subcultural innovators, out-there subcultures take styles from mass-mediated sources (out-there) and appropriate them in a subcultural manner. Thus the out-there subculture is not pure in that it takes particular images given to it by commercial sources that have already incorporated innovative subcultural styles. Out-there subcultures, however, may engage in the recontextualization of an already commercialized (incorporated) style, but in so doing, they also engage in an act that symbolically resists the supremacy of dominant/mainstream culture.
>
> (Cagle 1995: 45)

Cagle is proposing not only that those who make use of incorporated styles can do so in a different cultural context to that of the original innovators and thereby maintain a sense of 'otherness', but that they may additionally engage in acts of stylistic *bricolage*, further individualizing the ensemble in question (1994: 42, 97, 218). As Andes discovered, subculturalists do indeed view themselves as authentic by virtue of their individualistic innovations and adaptations, for 'regardless of when [their] involvement took place in the history of the subculture' (1998: 219) they always construct themselves as originals relative to an 'Other' who, it is claimed, merely follows in their wake, adopting mass versions of subcultural fashions. To illustrate these points let us now look at (E).

(E) PAUL AND DOUGIE

P: Yeah, I mean I'd never had any what you might call punk gear really, any bondage stuff, anything like that.

D: We used to make it myself. Sew zips on.

P: I never had anything. Exactly. All I ever had was tatty, crappy clothes, and always wrote all over my T-shirts and drew on the jacket and that, and it's all, it is just do-it-yourself stuff. It's not deliberately modelled on anything.

DM: Did you ever buy punk stuff, like, off the peg I suppose is the best way of putting it?

P: No, never ever at all. The most punk gear I've ever done is paint jackets and draw on T-shirts, it really is. I've never, I chucked bleach all over my jeans, I suppose, that's about it. If you see someone who, it just looks like they've just gone out and spent two hundred pounds in London on the right punk gear and someone's put the safety pins through it for them and someone's put the studs on for 'em and that, that's not right, is it? What's the fun of that?

We find here a number of binary oppositions in play. First, punk style is personally constructed through customizing ordinary clothes ('paint jackets, draw on T-shirts')[5] rather than having a look that is 'ready-made' to look 'subcultural' ('I never had any what you might call punk gear'). This also constructs a second distinction between, on the one hand, heterogeneity and partiality through *bricolage*, and on the other, a look that is holistic, or wholly subcultural. Third, this is therefore the difference between adapting ('do-it-yourself') and adopting ('someone's put the safety pins through it for 'em'). Also, fourth, between the original ('all I ever had') and the latest ('just gone out and . . .') immediately obtained style. Fifth, this distinguishes the old and cheap and personal ('tatty, crappy clothes . . . my jeans . . . my T-shirt') from that which is expensive, fashionable and purchased over the counter ('spent two hundred pounds in London'). Sixth, all of this also amounts to an attempt to produce something individual and unique rather than that which is merely a copy ('it's not deliberately modelled on anything') or which is meant to fit in with the dictates of the collective ('the right punk gear').

What are outlined here are sets of correspondences that, although congruent, can be selectively applied for the purpose of inauthenticating a comparative 'Other'. Let us again take the study by Fox (1987) as an example, not because it is deserving of sustained criticism, but because it is particularly illuminating on how certain members use style as such a means of inauthentication. Here, the dress of the 'preppies' is disparaged by the 'hardcores' on three main counts. First, they are considered to be into punk only as a fashion. Second, this partly derives from their purchasing of 'punk outfits from Ms. Jordan's [an exclusive clothing store]' (ibid.: 361).[6] Third, . . . their malleable appearance is indicative of a part-time affiliation. By making adjustments to the style, they can change roles and pass muster in both punk and conventional society. We hear how, 'Mary, a typical preppie punk, put her regular clothes together in a way she thought would look punk. She ripped up her sorority t-shirt. She bought outfits that were advertised as having the "punk look". Her traditional bangs transformed into "punk" bangs, standing straight up using hair spray or setting gel' (ibid.: 361).

Yet it is precisely through the reordering and customizing of conventional items that authentic subcultural style is actively created. So one can readily admit to purchasing clothes from commercial stores, because the point is not what you wear or even where you buy it from, but what you wear it with or what you do to it. This is the whole basis of *bricolage*, and this is what Mary is actually doing when transforming the meaning of her regular clothes. What could be more subversive than the desecration of a sorority T-shirt, apart perhaps from mutilating the Stars and Stripes? And why is this any different from 'original' British punks mocking and customizing school shirts and ties? – an action that Marxist theorists, had they thought about it, would have interpreted as symbolic resistance against a dominant institution. Perhaps the bone of contention is the newness of the clothes worn. But, to continue with the above line of argument, surely it is logical to view the abuse of expensive new clothes from an 'exclusive' store as an infinitely more potent gesture of defiance towards bourgeois conventions than the spoiling of one's old tatty hand-me-downs? Moreover, the obvious alternative to both partiality and adaptation is to buy ready-made outfits, indicating homogeneity and adoption. Yet this is also exactly what Mary is accused of!

Clearly, there is something contradictory in such allegations. In fact, it doesn't take much imagination to construct the 'hardcore punks' as equally inauthentic through much the same accusations. . . . their badges of permanence – the mohawk and tat-toos – can equally indicate stasis and stereotypicality. Fox does not precisely delineate the style of the hardcores compared to that of other punks. But we hear that, for the scene in general, leather jackets were favoured wear (for a choice, considered opinion on this item, see the John Lydon quotation that opens this chapter). She also notes, as does Lull (1987), that Army and military wear, along with T-shirts and unkempt jeans, are commonly worn gear for punks. Again, depending on the combination of items, this might invite the criticism that what is worn does not differ considerably from conventional wear (T-shirt, jeans), that it is not particularly punk (army boots and jackets), that it is newly purchased from outlets specifically for the purpose, and so on. To give another example applicable to almost any subculture, a band T-shirt might for the wearer be revered as a sign of authentic affiliation to a particular group or to the music in general. Yet it is precisely because of this that these and many sim-ilar items, ostensibly indicators of permanent and genuine membership, hold the potential of being dismissed by others as expensive new purchases, the sign of a fash-ion mentality, of buying into the subculture.[7]

It is again important to stress that the wearing of 'conventional' items, or the pur-chasing of them from particular shops, is not, *in itself*, an admission of inauthenticity. What is important is the manner in which this is included in a claim for the wearer's heterogeneity and originality. Similar sartorial behaviour observed in others (and observed by others in oneself) can, however, be interpreted quite differently, as evi-dence of a fashion sensibility and of the wearer's having purchased 'ready-made' subcultural 'outfits'. Hebdige is therefore correct when he observes that 'the distinc-tion between originals and hangers-on is always a significant one in subculture' (1979: 122), but he fails to realize that this dichotomy has no objective basis or tem-poral logic.

Notes

1 See, for example, the photograph in the centre pages of York (1980) of the Sex Pistols playing the 100 Club in 1976, and at the two males in the background either side of Steve Jones. The same point was made in the Granada television programme 'Mark Radcliffe's NWA', broadcast on 22 July 1996, one item of which was to commemorate the twenti-eth anniversary of the Sex Pistols playing the Lesser Free Trade Hall, Manchester. One of the original audience reminisced, 'this wasn't like a punk gig. The audience was just like us really –hippies.'

2 Tomlinson (1998: 207) likewise remarks on 'bubblegum ravers'. See also Rietveld (1993) on 'Acid Teds'.

3 For an application of this to rave, see Tomlinson (1998). Its relevance to rap music is dis-cussed in Blair and Hatala (1991) and Blair (1993).

4 But as we saw in our discussion of the media, subculturalists do not wish to be so clearly defined and labelled. Unsurprisingly, then, we find John Lydon, the singer with the Sex Pistols, claiming to have been an original *bricoleur*, and that McLaren only later commer-cialized some of these looks as 'punk' style (Lydon 1993).

5 Lull (1987: 230) also notes how punks 'inscribe sentiments directly onto the surface of clothing with a marking pen'.

6 See Lull (1987: 227) on 'punkers': inauthentic punks who 'often buy expensive "punk-chic" clothing in fancy stores'.

7 As Gross puts it, 'they can don their metal oriented teeshirts that were bought at the mall, slip on some official metal oriented jewelry and toss on an AC/DC or Harley Davidson Cap and be ready to go. Is there a dollar to be made off thecult of heavy metal? You bet your Def Leppard T-shirt, there is' (1990); 127).

PART SIX

Female audiences

Gender and reading

Introduction

THOUGH MATERIAL ON FEMALE audiences can be found in different forms throughout this collection it would be remiss indeed not to devote an entire section to them, since feminist researchers have been responsible for some of the most influential and pioneering work in audience studies. Analysis of 'the audience' in media and cultural studies in fact has very often more specifically entailed analysis of *female* audiences. In pursuing this arena in the late 1970s and 1980s, critics like Janice Radway and Angela McRobbie, whose work features here in a section devoted to the female *reader*, provided meditative accounts of female audiences engaging with popular texts that were generally held in low critical esteem, such as the romance novel and teenage girls' magazines. Their seminal research was essential to the growth and critical respectability of a wider field of work that has sought both to understand audience relationships with popular culture and, in doing so, to take popular culture 'seriously'. Similarly, the expansion of academic interest in soap operas and their audiences since the 1980s, for example, Hobson (1982) and Geraghty (1991), is testament to the accomplishments of this project elsewhere. The extracts here, then, share common ground in their privileging of the female audience, but they diverge in their summoning of it. In the spectrum of audience work seen here the visibility of the audience is inflected in different ways – sometimes evident in engagement with real, manifest consumers of the given text(s), sometimes understood as an appellation or textual/subject position. These distinct ways of locating the female audience have given rise to some potent differences of opinion about the use and value of ethnographic work (particularly versus textual analysis) as we shall see in Ien Ang's piece.

We open here with an extract from *Reading the Romance,* Radway's (1984) study of female romance readers in the suburbs of the midwestern city of 'Smithton', USA, and constructed by Radway, in Stanley Fish's term, as an 'interpretive community' (Fish, 1980). Though this work has, inevitably perhaps, attracted criticism since publication (represented here in Ang's piece which follows Radway's and indeed amply reflected on by Radway herself in the preface to later editions of the book), it remains a fascinating study. Her account of these women – and crucially not just *what* they read but *how* and *why* they read it – and the dynamics of her own relationships with them as she pursues their study, provide a series of insights into the rewards and pit-falls of ethnographic research. With the help of Dorothy Evans, a romance reader who worked at the local bookstore and recommended and reviewed romantic fiction for local women customers as well as writers and publishers, Radway was able to gain entrance to their reading community. In this section she describes how she had to relin-quish her 'inadvertent but continuing preoccupation with the text' as she comes to realise that for the women it is 'the act of romance reading' rather than the 'meaning of the romance' which is frequently the focus. The women recurrently describe how the act of reading is a quest for 'escapism', an abstract noun that regularly figures in accounts of women's engagement with popular culture. This is very often in a pejora-tive sense of course, so that escapism itself has come to be held as a kind of feminine/feminised desire. Rather than belittling this desire, Radway instead probes the mechanism of escapism as a 'compensatory function' and seeks to contextualise how these women use romance reading and its attendant 'escapism' as an intervention in and response to the demands of their 'habitual existence' as wives, mothers and home-makers.

The publication of *Watching Dallas* in 1985 placed Ien Ang at the forefront of the quest to put popular culture and its audiences on the academic map. Ang's seminal study explored the relationships between Dutch (largely female) audiences and the prime-time soap opera. In the second extract here, though, we draw on Ang's critique of Radway's work. While acknowledging the study's innovation and calling herself one of its 'enthusiastic readers', Ang nevertheless describes how for her the act of reading *Reading the Romance* produces a 'deep sense of tension' which she pinpoints as ema-nating from a number of perplexing flaws and assumptions that underlie the work. In her view Radway approaches romance-reading as a 'problem' for feminism and in the course of the study poses herself and the Smithton women as oppositional parties with fixed identities, the researcher/feminist versus interviewees/romance fans. In 'solving' the problem she ends up embroiled in a consciousness-raising project that seems to seek to 'rescue' these women from their diversionary romance reading. The 'them and us' dichotomy implied in this might finally be said to devalue romance reading by posing feminism as a more authoritative and effective pursuit, 'the superior solution for all women's problems', as if feminism can be presumed to know what's best for all or other women. Indeed, reflecting back on the original study in the new introduction to the 1991 edition, Radway has acknowledged that the original work neglected how she her-self as the researcher was a mediating influence constructing the Smithton women's community. She observes 'I would therefore now want to emphasise more insistently Angela McRobbie's assertion that "representations are interpretations".' In the same vein she comments that she would no longer defend the supremacy of ethnography over and above textual analysis but rather suggests that they might best work in tandem together as components of a 'multifocused approach' (Radway, 1991: 5-6) an approach which is arguably what Currie's study of 'teenzine' readers below is striving for.

Before Currie though, McRobbie's account of the British teenage girls' magazine *Jackie,* originally appearing in 1977, was one of the earliest efforts to subject such texts to close critical attention and, with its focus on how the magazine 'interpellates' its readers, it is very much a product of the era's preoccupation with Althusserian Marxism. She argues that women's and girls' weeklies occupy a privileged position in publishing solely concerned with 'promoting a feminine culture' to their female market. Consisting largely of romantic fiction and photo-stories, fashion and beauty advice and advertising, pop music pin-ups and interviews and features exploring the pleasures and pain of female adolescence, for McRobbie *Jackie* is a strikingly conservative text which 'asserts the absolute and natural separation of sex roles' and promotes a world where 'girls can only be feminine'. The '*Jackie* girls' who populate its pages are on a single-minded mission to find and keep a boyfriend, a quest supported and encouraged by the discourse which permeates all aspects of the magazine. In doing so, despite its efforts to depict teenage girlhood as 'fun', it nevertheless depicts a culture that pivots on distrust between women, female fear and insecurity.

But '*Jackie* is both the magazine and the ideal girl'. Its lessons in femininity reveal its vision of its readership, what they are and what they should become as they are further co-opted into the 'dominant order'. It is here, in her account of the readers' relationship with *Jackie*'s address, that McRobbie's vision of the *Jackie* reader appears ultimately pessimistic and that she sometimes seems to endorse a mass culture critique despite the progressive impulse behind her work. Though she opens up the notion of the polysemic text, she suggests that the concept of re-appropriation 'is of limited usefulness to teenage girls and their magazines' since 'they play little, if any, role in shaping their own pop culture', leaving only a negligible space, then, for them to use the text in subversive ways. McRobbie's semiological analysis of *Jackie*'s conservative codes and discourse is thoroughly illuminating and convincing – yet one is compelled to ask, particularly given her pioneering work at this time with working-class girls at a Birmingham youth club (McRobbie, 2000), how engaging with actual readers themselves here might have thrown more light on this theme. Are there ways not imagined by McRobbie through which they undermine the prescriptive engagement she describes? Given her acknowledgement of how *Jackie*'s unified feminine address 'serves to obscure differences of, for example class or race, between women' how are these differences manifested in the girls' readings of it? Our extract from McRobbie here ends with her observation that 'This is how the reader looks at *Jackie*', as if its readership, despite its inevitable diversity, can be positioned as a homogenous, unified group. Indeed, McRobbie would go on to address many of these issues in her later work on the girls' magazine *Just 17* (1991).

Two decades later the broader scope of Dawn H. Currie's approach to girls' magazines declares its intent to examine them through both sociologically-based content analysis and more literary, semiological analysis. At the same time, however, she very much places the readers themselves at the core of her study, insisting that

> in order to explore how social texts such as teenzines work as discourse rather than simply as cultural objects, we need to move beyond the text itself to its reading. Such an analytical move connects the cultural world of texts to the social world of embodied readers.
>
> (Currie, 1999: 118)

She distinguishes then between 'researcher readings' and 'everyday readings' and combines, for example, content analysis of beauty advertisements in teenzines with interviews and group discussions with readers (and non-readers) about them. Seventy-six issues of magazines were coded while ninety-one girls between the ages of 8–18 from Vancouver and the surrounding areas participated. Through this approach Currie is able to identify what she sees as 'disjunctures' between the magazines' proscriptions and the experiences of readers. In the extract that follows, like Radway, she contextualises reading as a social act. In contrast to Radway's older romance readers though, she finds that these young girls and women often cite the perceived *realism* of a favoured magazine as their motive for buying it, since they seek out texts which 'resonate with their everyday lives'. They also describe how many of them tend, at least consciously, to pay little regard to advertising and frequently reject the fashion pages. There may be a 'disjuncture' here, then, between what researchers find or expect to find important in these magazines and what the readers themselves do. These girls appear not to have been as easily interpellated as McRobbie's 'ideology of adolescent femininity' imagined.

In Ang's piece above, we saw how her reservations about Radway's project lamented its absence of *pleasurableness* and reductive concept of fantasy. The thorny issue of female readers' pleasure runs throughout these extracts and is taken up again in another generic context in the final piece in this section, in Esther Sonnet's work on women's erotic fiction. As fiction 'written by women for women' Black Lace publishing clearly forms parallels with the romance genre and Sonnet usefully contextualises her work in relation to Radway's ethnographic model. In other ways too her work seems to pick up where Radway left off; Radway noted a shift in some 1980s' American romance fiction towards a 'more active, more insistent female sexuality' (albeit still within the context of heterosexual monogamy) (Radway, 1991: 15–16), while Sonnet suggests that the reclaiming of 'the "illicit" pleasures of pornography for women' has only become possible in a 'post-feminist' age. Her work looks at how Black Lace's positioning of its readers is evident in a range of factors such as genre definition, editorial instructions and audience address. She argues that ultimately

> the production of fiction which promises to 'give women what they really want' does so by explicitly rejecting the pleasure (and with it therefore the ideology) held to govern women's consumption of the romance, in favour of 'real' female desire and sexual fantasy.

Yet the transgressive readership that female-authored erotic fiction addresses is, nonetheless, caught up in other, equally discursive formations of female sexuality, reading pleasure and empowerment. Against the backdrop of the other pieces in this Part, through the methods used to locate its audience and in opening up an emergent and still relatively unexplored arena of female readership, Sonnet's work underlines how we must continually revisit and reconfigure our grasp of who and what 'the female audience' is.

Further reading

Ang, I. (1985) *Watching Dallas: Soap Opera and the Melodramatic Imagination*, London: Methuen.

Ang, I. (1996) *Living Room Wars: Rethinking Media Audiences for a Postmodern World*, London: Routledge.

Currie, D. H. (1999) *Girl Talk: Adolescent Magazines and their Readers*, Toronto: University of Toronto Press.

Fish, S. (1980) *Is There a Text in This Class?: The Authority of Interpretive Communities*, Cambridge, MA: Harvard University Press.

Hermes, J. (1995), *Reading Women's Magazines: An Analysis of Everyday Media Use*, Cambridge: Polity Press.

McRobbie, A. (1991, 2nd edition 2000) *Feminism and Youth Culture*, London: Macmillan Press Ltd.

Radway, J. A. (1991) *Reading the Romance: Women, Patriarchy and Popular Literature*, Chapel Hill, NC, and London: University of North Carolina Press.

Chapter 22

Janice Radway

READING THE ROMANCE
Women, patriarchy and popular literature

By THE END OF MY first full day with Dorothy Evans and her customers, I had come to realize that although the Smithton women are not accustomed to thinking about what it is in the romance that gives them so much pleasure, they know perfectly well why they like to read. I understood this only when their remarkably consistent comments forced me to relinquish my inadvertent but continuing preoccupation with the text. Because the women always responded to my query about their reasons for reading with comments about the pleasures of the act itself rather than about their liking for the particulars of the romantic plot, I soon realized I would have to give up my obsession with textual features and narrative details if I wanted to understand their view of romance reading. Once I recognized this it became clear that romance reading was important to the Smithton women first because the simple event of picking up a book enabled them to deal with the particular pressures and tensions encountered in their daily round of activities. Although I learned later that certain aspects of the romance's story do help to make this event especially meaningful, the early interviews were interesting because they focused so resolutely on the significance of the *act of romance reading* rather than on the meaning of the romance.

The extent of the connection between romance reading and my informants' understanding of their roles as wives and mothers was impressed upon me first by Dot herself during our first two-hour interview which took place before I had seen her customers' responses to the pilot questionnaire. In posing the question, 'What do romances do better than other novels today?,' I expected her to concern herself in her answer with the characteristics of the plot and the manner in which the story evolved. To my surprise, Dot took my query about 'doing' as a transitive question about the *effects* of romances on the people who read them. She responded to my question with a long and puzzling answer that I found difficult to interpret at this early stage of our discussions. It seems wise to let Dot speak for herself here because her response introduced a number of themes that appeared again and again in my subsequent talks with other readers. My question prompted the following careful meditation:

It's an innocuous thing. If it had to be . . . pills or drinks, this is harmful. They're very aware of this. Most of the women are mothers. And they're aware of that kind of thing. And reading is something they would like to generate in their children also. Seeing the parents reading is . . . just something that I feel they think the children should see them doing . . . I've got a woman with teenage boys here who says 'you've got books like . . . you've just got oodles of da . . . da . . . da . . . [counting an imaginary stack of books].' She says, 'Now when you ask Mother to buy you something, you don't stop and think how many things you have. So this is Mother's and it is my money.' Very, almost defensive. But I think they get that from their fathers. I think they heard their fathers sometime or other saying, 'Hey, you're spending an awful lot of money on books aren't you?' You know for a long time, my ladies hid 'em. They would hide their books; literally hide their books. And they'd say, 'Oh, if my husband [we have distinctive blue sacks], if my husband sees this blue sack coming in the house . . .' And you know, I'd say, 'Well really, you're a big girl. Do you really feel like you have to be very defensive?' A while ago, I would not have thought that way. I would have thought, 'Oh, Dan is going to hit the ceiling.' For a while Dan was not thrilled that I was reading a lot. Because I think men do feel threatened. They want their wife to be in the room with them. And I think my body is in the room but the rest of me is not (when I am reading).

Only when Dot arrived at her last observation about reading and its ability to transport her out of her living room did I begin to understand that the real answer to my question, which she never mentioned and which was the link between reading, pills, and drinks, was actually the single word, 'escape,' a word that would later appear on so many of the questionnaires. She subsequently explained that romance novels provided escape just as Darvon and alcohol do for other women. Whereas the latter are harmful to both woman and their families, Dot believes romance reading is 'an innocuous thing.' As she commented to me in another interview, romance reading is a habit that is not very different from 'an addiction.'

Although some of the other Smithton women expressed uneasiness about the suitability of the addiction analogy, as did Dot in another interview, nearly all of the original sixteen who participated in lengthy conversations agreed that one of their principal goals in reading was their desire to do something *different* from their daily routine. That claim was borne out by their answers to the open-ended question about the functions of romance reading. At this point, it seems worth quoting a few of those fourteen replies that expressly volunteered the ideas of escape and release. The Smithton readers explained the power of the romance in the following way:

They are light reading – escape literature – I can put down and pick up effortlessly.

Everyone is always under so much pressure. They like books that let them escape.

Escapism.

I guess I feel there is enough 'reality' in the world and reading is a means of escape for me.

Because it is an Escape [*sic*], and we can dream and pretend that it is our life.

I'm able to escape the harsh world for a few hours a day.

They always seem an escape and they usually turn out the way you wish life really was.

The response of the Smithton women is apparently not an unusual one. Indeed, the advertising campaigns of three of the houses that have conducted extensive market-research studies all emphasize the themes of relaxation and escape. Potential readers of Coventry Romances, for example, have been told in coupon ads that 'month after month Coventry Romances offer you a beautiful new escape route into historical times when love and honor ruled the heart and mind.'[1] Similarly, the Silhouette television advertisements featuring Ricardo Montalban asserted that 'the beautiful ending makes you feel so good' and that romances 'soothe away the tensions of the day.' Montalban also touted the value of 'escaping' into faraway places and exotic locations. Harlequin once mounted a travel sweepstakes campaign offering as prizes 'escape vacations' to romantic places. In addition, they included within the books themselves an advertising page that described Harlequins as 'the books that let you escape into the wonderful world of romance! Trips to exotic places . . . interesting places . . . meeting memorable people . . . the excitement of love . . . These are integral parts of Harlequin Romances – the heartwarming novels read by women everywhere.'[2] Fawcett, too, seems to have discovered the escape function of romantic fiction, for Daisy Maryles has reported that the company found in in-depth interviewing that 'romances were read for relaxation and to enable [women] to better cope with the routine aspects of life.'[3]

Reading to escape the present is neither a new behavior nor one peculiar to women who read romances. In fact, as Richard Hoggart demonstrated in 1957, English working-class people have long 'regarded art as escape, as something enjoyed but not assumed to have much connection with the matter of daily life.'[4] Within this sort of aesthetic, he continues, art is conceivable as 'marginal, as "fun,"' as something 'for you to *use*.' In further elaborating on this notion of fictional escape, D. W. Harding has made the related observation that the word is most often used in criticism as a term of disparagement to refer to an activity that the evaluator believes has no merit in and of itself. 'If its intrinsic appeal is high,' he remarks, 'in relation to its compensatory appeal or the mere relief it promises, then the term escape is not generally used.'[5] Harding argues, moreover, on the basis of studies conducted in the 1930s, that 'the compensatory appeal predominates mainly in states of depression or irritation, whether they arise from work or other causes.'[6] It is interesting to note that the explanations employed by Dot and her women to interpret their romance reading for themselves are thus representative in a general way of a form of behavior common in an industrialized society where work is clearly distinguished from and more highly valued than leisure despite the fact that individual labor is often routinized, regimented, and minimally challenging.[7] It is equally essential to add, however, that although the women will use the word 'escape' to explain their reading behavior, if given another comparable choice that does not carry the connotations of disparagement, they will choose the more favorable sounding explanation. To understand why, it will be helpful to follow Dot's comments more closely.

In returning to her definition of the appeal of romance fiction – a definition that is a highly condensed version of a commonly experienced process of explanation, doubt, and defensive justification – it becomes clear that romance novels perform this compensatory function for women because they use them to diversify the pace and character of their habitual existence. Dot makes it clear, however, that the women are also troubled about the propriety of indulging in such an obviously pleasurable activity. Their doubts are often cultivated into a full-grown feeling of guilt by husbands and children who object to this activity because it draws the women's attention away from the immediate family circle. As Dot later noted, although some women can explain to their families that a desire for a new toy or a gadget is no different from a desire to read a new romantic novel, a far greater number of them have found it necessary to hide the evidence of their self-indulgence. In an effort to combat both the resentment of others and their own feelings of shame about their 'hedonist' behavior, the women have worked out a complex rationalization for romance reading that not only asserts their equal right to pleasure but also legitimizes the books by linking them with values more widely approved within American culture. Before turning to the pattern, however, I want to elaborate on the concept of escape itself and the reasons for its ability to produce such resentment and guilt in the first place.

Both the escape response and the relaxation response on the second questionnaire immediately raise other questions. Relaxation implies a reduction in the state of tension produced by prior conditions, whereas escape obviously suggests flight from one state of being to another more desirable one.[8] To understand the sense of the romance experience, then, as it is enjoyed by those who consider it a welcome change in their day-to-day existence, it becomes necessary to situate it within a larger temporal context and to specify precisely how the act of reading manages to create that feeling of change and differentiation so highly valued by these readers.

In attending to the women's comments about the worth of romance reading, I was particularly struck by the fact that they tended to use the word escape in two distinct ways. On the one hand, they used the term literally to describe the act of denying the present, which they believe they accomplish each time they begin to read a book and are drawn into its story. On the other hand, they used the word in a more figurative fashion to give substance to the somewhat vague but nonetheless intense sense of relief they experience by identifying with a heroine whose life does not resemble their own in certain crucial aspects. I think it important to reproduce this subtle distinction as accurately as possible because it indicates that romance reading releases women from their present pressing concerns in two different but related ways.

Dot, for example, went on to elaborate more fully in the conversation quoted above about why so many husbands seem to feel threatened by their wives' reading activities. After declaring with delight that when she reads her body is in the room but she herself is not, she said, 'I think this is the case with the other women.' She continued, 'I think men cannot do that unless they themselves are readers. I don't think men are *ever* a part of anything even if it's television.' 'They are never really out of their body either,' she added. 'I don't care if it's a football game; I think they are always consciously aware of where they are.' Her triumphant conclusion, 'but I think a woman in a book isn't,' indicates that Dot is aware that reading not only demands a high level of attention but also draws the individual *into* the book because it requires her participation. Although she is not sure what it is about the book that prompts this absorption, she is quite sure that television viewing and film watching are different. In adding immediately that 'for some reason, a lot of men feel threatened by this, very, very much threatened,' Dot suggested that the men's resentment has little to do with the kinds of books their wives are reading and more to do with the simple fact of the activity itself and its capacity to absorb the participants' entire attention.

These tentative observations were later corroborated in the conversations I had with other readers. Ellen, for instance, a former airline stewardess, now married and taking care of her home, indicated that she also reads for 'entertainment and escape.' However, she added, her husband sometimes objects to her reading because he wants her to watch the same television show he has selected. She 'hates' this, she said, because she does not like the kinds of programs on television today. She is delighted when he gets a business call in the evening because her husband's preoccupation with his caller permits her to go back to her book.

Penny, another housewife in her middle thirties, also indicated that her husband 'resents it' if she reads too much. 'He feels shut out,' she explained, 'but there is nothing on TV I enjoy.' Like Ellen's husband, Penny's spouse also wants her to watch television with him. Susan, a woman in her fifties also 'read[s] to escape' and related with almost no bitterness that her husband will not permit her to continue reading when he is ready to go to sleep. She seems to regret rather than resent this only because it limits the amount of time she can spend in an activity she finds enjoyable. Indeed, she went on in our conversation to explain that she occasionally gives herself 'a very special treat' when she is 'tired of housework.' 'I take the whole day off,' she said, 'to read.'

This theme of romance reading as a special gift a woman gives herself dominated most of the interviews. The Smithton women stressed the privacy of the act and the fact that it enables them to focus their attention on a single object that can provide pleasure for themselves alone. Interestingly enough, Robert Escarpit has noted in related fashion that reading is at once 'social and asocial' because 'it temporarily suppresses the individual's relations with his [*sic*] universe to construct new ones with the universe of the work.'[9] Unlike television viewing, which is a very social activity undertaken in the presence of others and which permits simultaneous conversation and personal interaction, silent reading requires the reader to block out the surrounding world and to give consideration to other people and to another time. It might be said, then, that the characters and events of romance fiction populate the woman's consciousness even as she withdraws from the familiar social scene of her daily ministrations.

I use the word ministrations deliberately here because the Smithton women explained to me that they are not trying to escape their husbands and children 'per se' when they read. Rather, what reading takes them away from, they believe, is the psychologically demanding and emotionally draining task of attending to the physical and affective needs of their families, a task that is solely and peculiarly theirs. In other words, these women, who have been educated to believe that females are especially and naturally attuned to the emotional requirements of others and who are very proud of their abilities to communicate with and to serve the members of their families, value reading precisely because it is an intensely private act. Not only is the activity private, however, but it also enables them to suspend temporarily those familial relationships and to throw up a screen between themselves and the arena where they are required to do most of their relating to others.

It was Dot who first advised me about this phenomenon. Her lengthy commentary, transcribed below, enabled me to listen carefully to the other readers' discussions of escape and to hear the distinction nearly all of them made between escape from their families, which they believed they do *not* do, and escape from the heavy responsibilities and duties of the roles of wife and mother, which they admit they do out of emotional need and necessity. Dot explained their activity, for instance, by paraphrasing the thought process she believes goes on in her customers' minds. 'Hey,' they say, 'this is what I want to do and I'm gonna do it. This is for me. I'm doin' for you all the time. Now leave me, just leave me alone. Let me have my time, my space. Let me do what I want to do. This isn't hurting you. I'm not poaching on you in any way.' She then went on to elaborate about her own duties as a mother and wife:

> As a mother, I have run 'em to the orthodontist. I have run 'em to the swimming pool. I have run 'em to baton twirling lessons. I have run up to school because they forgot their lunch. You know, I mean, really! And you do it. And it isn't that you begrudge it. That isn't it. Then my husband would walk in the door and he'd say, 'Well, what did you do today?' You know, it was like, 'Well, tell me how you spent the last eight hours, because I've been out working.' And I finally got to the point where I would say, 'Well, I read four books, and I did all the wash and got the meal on the table and the beds are all made, and the house is tidy.' And I would get defensive like, 'So what do you call all this? Why should I have to tell you because I certainly don't ask you what you did for eight hours, step by step' – But their husbands do do that. We've compared notes. They hit the house and it's like 'Well, all right, I've been out earning a living. Now what have you been doin' with your time?' And you begin to be feeling, 'Now really, why is he questioning me?'

Romance reading, it would seem, at least for Dot and many of her customers, is a strategy with a double purpose. As an activity, it so engages their attention that it enables them to deny their physical presence in an environment associated with responsibilities that are acutely felt and occasionally experienced as too onerous to bear. Reading, in this sense, connotes a free space where they feel liberated from the need to perform duties that they otherwise willingly accept as their own. At the same time, by carefully choosing stories that make them feel particularly happy, they escape figuratively into a fairy tale where a heroine's similar needs are adequately met. As a result, they vicariously attend to their own requirements as independent individuals who require emotional sustenance and solicitude.

Angie's account of her favorite reading time graphically represents the significance of romance reading as a tool to help insure a woman's sense of emotional well-being. 'I like it,' she says, 'when my husband – he's an insurance salesman – goes out in the evening on house calls. Because then I have two hours just to totally relax.' She continued, 'I love to settle in a hot bath with a good book. That's really great.' We might conclude, then, that reading a romance is a regressive experience for these women in the sense that for the duration of the time devoted to it they feel gratified and content. This feeling of pleasure seems to derive from their identification with a heroine whom they believe is deeply appreciated and tenderly cared for by another. Somewhat paradoxically, however, they also seem to value the sense of self-sufficiency they experience as a consequence of the knowledge that they are capable of making themselves feel good.

Notes

1 These coupon ads appeared sporadically in national newspapers throughout the spring and summer of 1980.
2 Neels, *Cruise to a Wedding*, p. 190.
3 Maryles, 'Fawcett Launches Romance Imprint,' p. 70.
4 Hoggart, *The Uses of Literacy*, p. 196.
5 Harding, 'The Notion of "Escape",' p. 24.
6 Ibid., p. 25.
7 For discussions of the growth of the reading public and the popular press, see Williams, *The Long Revolution*, pp. 156–213, and Altick, *The English Common Reader*, passim.
8 As Escarpit has observed in *The Sociology of Literature*, p. 91, 'there are a thousand ways to escape and it is essential to know from what and towards what we are escaping.'
9 Escarpit, ibid., p. 88. Although Dot's observations are not couched in academic language, they are really no different from Escarpit's similar observation that 'reading is the supreme solitary occupation.' He continues that 'the man [*sic*] who reads does not speak, does not act, cuts himself away from society, isolates himself from the world which surrounds him . . . reading allows the senses no margin of liberty. It absorbs the entire conscious mind, making the reader powerless to act' (p. 88). The significance of this last effect of the act of reading to the Smithton women will be discussed later . . . For a detailed discussion of the different demands made upon an individual by reading and radio listening, see Lazarsfeld, *Radio and the Printed Page*, pp. 170–79.

Chapter 23

Ien Ang

LIVING ROOM WARS
Rethinking audiences for a postmodern world

J ANICE RADWAY'S *READING THE ROMANCE* (1984), one of the most
influential studies within the so-called 'new audience research', does not exactly
read like a romance. In contrast to the typically engrossing reading experience of the
romance novel, it is difficult to go through *Reading the Romance* at one stretch. The
text contains too many fragments which compel its reader to stop, to reread, to put
the book aside in order to gauge and digest the assertions made – in short, to adopt
an *analytical* position vis-à-vis the text. Contrary to what happens, as Radway sees it,
in the case of romance novels, the value and pleasure of this reading experience does
not primarily lie in its creation of a general sense of emotional well-being and visceral
contentment (ibid.: 70). Rather, *Reading the Romance* has left me, as one of its enthusiastic readers, with a feeling of tension that forces me to problematize its project, to
ask questions about the kind of intervention Radway has tried to make in writing the
book. Such questions generally do not present themselves to romance readers when
they have just finished a particularly satisfying version of the romance genre. Radway
has argued convincingly that it is precisely a *release* of tension that makes romance
reading a particularly pleasurable activity for female readers. This release of tension is
accomplished, on the one hand, by a temporary, literal escape from the demands of
the social role of housewife and mother which is assured by the private act of picking up a book and reading a romance, and, on the other hand, by a symbolic
gratification of the psychological needs for nurturance and care that the romance
genre offers these women – needs that, given their entrapment in the arrangements
of 'patriarchal marriage', cannot be satisfied in 'real life'. This is elaborated by Radway
in her characterization of romantic fiction as compensatory literature (ibid.: 89–95).
In other words, the value of the romance reading for women is, in Radway's analysis, primarily of a *therapeutic* nature.

But this opposition – between the analytical and the therapeutic – invites a somewhat oversimplified view of the relationship between *Reading the Romance* and women
reading romances. To be sure, in Radway's book, we can distinguish an overtly therapeutic thrust. For what is at stake for Radway is not just the academic will to offer

a neat and sophisticated explanation of the whys and hows of romance reading, but also a feminist desire to come to terms, politically speaking, with this popular type of female pleasure.

The enormous popularity of romantic fiction with women has always presented a problem for feminism. It is an empirical given that pre-eminently signifies some of the limits of feminist understanding and effectivity. One of the essential aims of *Reading the Romance*, then, is to find a new feminist way to 'cope' with this 'problem'. And I would suggest that it is precisely this therapeutic momentum of *Reading the Romance* that, paradoxically enough, produces the deep sense of tension I felt after having read the book. At stake in the therapy, as I will try to show, is the restoration of feminist authority. The result, however, is not an altogether happy ending in the romance tradition. This is not to say that the book should *have* a happy ending, for *Reading the Romance* belongs to a completely different genre than the genre it is trying to understand. But because all feminist inquiry is by definition a politically motivated theoretical engagement, it always seems to present a certain articulation of the analytical with the therapeutic, both substantially and rhetorically. What I will try to do in this chapter, then, is to explore some of the ways in which this articulation materializes in *Reading the Romance*.[1]

What sets Radway's book apart in a 'technical' sense from earlier feminist attempts to grasp and evaluate the meaning of female romance reading is her methodology. In contrast, for example, to Tania Modleski's well-known *Loving with a Vengeance* (1982)[2] Radway has chosen to base her analysis upon oral interviews with a group of actual romance readers. Drawing on the insights of reader-response critics like Stanley Fish (1980) and Jane Tompkins (1980), she rejects the method of immanent textual analysis, which she criticizes as 'a process that is hermetically sealed off from the very people they [the romance critics concerned] aim to understand' (Radway 1984: 7). According to Radway, 'the analytic focus must shift from the text itself, taken in isolation, to the complex social event of reading where a woman actively attributes sense to lexical signs in a silent process carried on in the context of her ordinary life' (ibid.: 8). By leaving the ivory tower of textual analysis and mixing with actual readers, she pursues a strategy that aims at 'taking real readers seriously'. She thereby rejects the practice of treating them as mere subject positions constructed by the text, or as abstract 'ideal readers' entirely defined in terms of textual mechanisms and operations.

In her introduction to *Studies in Entertainment*, Tania Modleski has fiercely warded off Radway's criticism by arguing that conducting 'ethnographic studies' of subcultural groups may lead to a dangerous 'collusion between mass culture critic and consumer society' (1986: ii). In her view, it is virtually impossible for critical scholars to retain a 'proper critical distance' when they submit themselves to the empirical analysis of audience response. While I share Modleski's concern about the dangers and pitfalls of empiricism, I do not believe that the project of ethnography is necessarily at odds with a critical stance, both in relation to consumer society, and with respect to the process of doing research itself. On the contrary, ethnographic fieldwork among audiences – in the broad sense of engaging oneself with the unruly and heterogeneous practices and accounts of real historical viewers or readers – helps to keep our critical discourses from becoming closed texts of Truth, because it forces the researcher to come to terms with perspectives that may not be easily integrated in a smooth, finished and coherent Theory. If anything, then, *Reading the Romance* is inspired by a deep sense of the contradictions and ambivalences posed by mass culture, and by a recognition of the profoundly unresolved nature of critical theory's dealings with it.

This does not mean, however, that ethnography is an unproblematic project. In every ethnographic study the researcher has to confront very specific problems of access and interpretation, which will have a decisive impact on the shape of the eventual account that is presented by the ethnographer: the text of the written book. In this chapter, then, I would like to examine the political motifs and strategies that are laid out in *Reading the Romance*. For Radway, ethnography is more than just a method of inquiry, it is an explicitly political way of staging a new feminist 'reconciliation' with 'the problem' of romantic fiction's popularity. For one thing, *Reading the Romance* is a report on the quite difficult, but apparently very rewarding, encounter between a feminist academic and (non-feminist) romance readers. Its broader significance thus lies in its dramatization of the relationship between 'feminism' and 'women'. It is the recognition that this relationship is a problematic one, not one of simple identity, that makes Janice Radway's book so important. Yet at the same time it is Radway's proposals for the resolution of the problem that make the tension I described above so painfully felt.

In the early chapters of the book, Radway's self-chosen vulnerability as an ethnographer is made quite apparent. In these chapters, the dialogic nature of the ethnographic project, which according to Radway is one of its central tenets, is more or less actualized. Of course, the narrative voice speaking to us is Radway's, but the limits of academic writing practice seem to make a more heterologic mode of textuality as yet almost unrealizable (see Clifford and Marcus 1986). She describes her initial trepidation upon first contacting and then meeting 'Dorothy Evans', or 'Dot', her main informant and the impassioned editor of a small fanzine for romance readers, living and working in a small Pennsylvania community fictionalized by Radway into 'Smithton'. The gap between researcher and informants is apparently quickly surmounted, however:

> My concern about whether I could persuade Dot's customers to elaborate honestly about their motives for reading was unwarranted, for after an initial period of mutually felt awkwardness, we conversed frankly and with enthusiasm.
>
> (Radway 1984: 47)

From this point on, Radway ceases to reflect on the nature of her own relationship to the 'Smithton women', and offers instead an often fascinating account of what she has learned from them. She quotes them extensively and is at times genuinely 'taken by surprise' by the unexpected turns of her conversations with Dot and the Smithton women. However, precisely because she does not seem to feel any real strain about the way in which she and her informants are positioned towards each other, she represents the encounter as one that is strictly confined to the terms of a relationship between two parties with fixed identities: that of a researcher/feminist and that of interviewees/romance fans. This ontological and epistemological separation between subject and object allows her to present the Smithton readers as a pre-existent 'interpretive community', a sociological entity whose characteristics and peculiarities were already there when the researcher set out to investigate it. It may well be, however, that this group of women only constituted itself as a 'community' in the research process itself – in a very literal sense indeed: at the moment that they were brought together for the collective interviews Radway conducted with them; at the moment that they were invited to think of themselves as a group that shares something, namely their fondness for romance reading, and the fact that they are all Dot's customers. An indication of this is offered by Radway herself:

> In the beginning, timidity seemed to hamper the responses as each reader took turns answering each question. When everyone relaxed, however, the conversation flowed more naturally as the participants disagreed among themselves, contradicted one another, and *delightedly* discovered that they still agreed about many things.
>
> (Radway 1984: 48, emphasis added)

In relying on a realist epistemology, then, Radway tends to overlook the constructive aspect of her own enterprise. In a sense, doing ethnography is itself a political intervention in that it helps to *construct* the culture it seeks to describe and understand, rather than merely reflect it. The concrete political benefit, in this specific case, could be that Radway's temporary presence in Smithton, and the lengthy conversations she had with the women, had an empowering effect on them, in that they were given the rare opportunity to come to a collective understanding and validation of their own reading experiences. Such an effect might be regarded as utterly limited by feminists with grander aims, and it is certainly not without its contradictions (after all, how can we ever be sure how such temporary, cultural empowerment relates to the larger stakes of the more structural struggles over power in which these women lead their lives?), but it is worth noticing, nevertheless, if we are to consider the value and predicaments of doing feminist research in its most material aspects (see McRobbie 1982).

For Radway, however, other concerns prevail. The separation between her world and that of her informants becomes progressively more absolute towards the end of the book. In the last few chapters the mode of writing becomes almost completely monologic, and the Smithton women are definitively relegated to the position of 'them', a romance reading community towards which Radway is emphatically sympathetic, but from which she remains fundamentally distant. Radway's analysis first recognizes the 'rationality' of romance reading by interpreting it as an act of symbolic resistance, but ends up constructing a deep chasm between the ideological world inhabited by the Smithton women and the convictions of feminism:

> [W]hen the act of romance reading is viewed as it is by the readers themselves, from within the belief system that accepts as given the institutions of heterosexuality and monogamous marriage, it can be conceived as an activity of mild protest and longing for reform necessitated by those institutions' failure to satisfy the emotional needs of women. Reading therefore functions for them as an act of recognition and contestation whereby that failure is first admitted and then partially reversed. [. . .] At the same time, however, when viewed from the vantage point of a feminism that would like to see the women's oppositional impulse lead to real social change, romance reading can also be seen as an activity that could potentially disarm that impulse. It might do so because it supplies vicariously those very needs and requirements

that might otherwise be formulated as demands in the real world and lead to the potential restructuring of sexual relations.

(Radway 1984: 213)

These are the theoretical terms in which Radway conceives the troubled relationship between feminism and romance reading. A common ground – the perceived sharing of the experiential pains and costs of patriarchy – is analytically secured, but from a point of view that assumes the mutual exteriority of the two positions. The distribution of identities is clearcut: Radway, the researcher, is a feminist and *not* a romance fan; the Smithton women, the researched, are romance readers and *not* feminists. From such a perspective, the political aim of the project becomes envisaged as one of bridging this profound separation between 'us' and 'them'. Elsewhere, Radway has formulated the task as follows:

> I am troubled by the fact that it is all too easy for us, as academic feminists and Marxists who are preoccupied with the *analysis* of ideological formations that produce consciousness, to forget that our entailed and parallel project is the political one of convincing those very real people to see how their situation intersects with our own and why it will be fruitful for them to see it as we do. Unless we wish to tie this project to some new form of coercion, we must remain committed to the understanding that these individuals are capable of coming to recognize their set of beliefs as an ideology that limits their view of their situation.

(Radway 1986: 105)

Does this mean then that doing feminist research is a matter of pedagogy? The militant ending of *Reading the Romance* leaves no doubt about it:

> I think it absolutely essential that we who are committed to social change learn not to overlook [the] minimal but nonetheless legitimate form of protest [expressed in romance reading]. We should seek it out not only to understand its origins and its utopian longing but also to learn how best to encourage it and bring it to fruition. If we do not, we have already conceded the fight and, in the case of the romance at least, admitted the impossibility of creating a world where the vicarious pleasure supplied by its reading would be unnecessary.

(Radway 1984: 222)

Here, Radway's feminist desire is expressed in its most dramatic form: its aim is directed at raising the consciousness of romance reading women, its mode is that of persuasion, conversion even. 'Real' social change can only be brought about, Radway seems to believe, if romance readers would stop reading romances and become feminist activists instead. In other words, underlying Radway's project is what Angela McRobbie has terms a 'recruitist' conception of the politics of feminist research (1982: 52). What makes me feel so uncomfortable about this move is the unquestioned certainty with which feminism is posed as the superior solution for all women's problems, as if feminism automatically possessed the relevant and effective formulas for all women to change their lives and acquire happiness. In the course of the book

Radway has thus inverted the pertinent relations: whereas in the beginning the ethnographer's position entails a vulnerable stance that puts her assumptions at risk, what is achieved in the end is an all but complete restoration of the authority of feminist discourse. This, then, is the therapeutic effect of *Reading the Romance*: it reassures where certainties threaten to dissolve, it comforts where divisions among women, so distressing and irritating to feminism, seem almost despairingly insurmountable – by holding the promise that, with hard work for sure, unity *would* be reached if we could only rechannel the energy that is now put in romance reading in the direction of 'real' political action. In short, what is therapeutic (for feminism) about *Reading the Romance* is its construction of romance readers as embryonic feminists.

I do agree with Radway that the relationship between 'feminism' and 'women' is one of the most troublesome issues for the women's movement. However, it seems untenable to me to maintain a vanguardist view of feminist politics, to see feminist consciousness as the linear culmination of political radicality. With McRobbie (1982), I think that we should not underestimate the struggles for self-empowerment engaged in by 'ordinary women' outside the political and ideological frameworks of the self-professed women's movement. I am afraid therefore that Radway's radical intent is drawing dangerously near a form of political moralism, propelled by a desire to make 'them' more like 'us'. Indeed, what Radway's conception of political intervention tends to arrive at is the deromanticization of the romance in favour of a romanticized feminism!

This is not the place to elaborate on the practical implications of this political predicament. What I do want to point out, however, is how the therapeutic upshot of *Reading the Romance* is prepared for in the very analysis Radway has made of the meaning of romance reading for the Smithton women, that is, how the analytical and the therapeutic are inextricably entwined with one another.

Strangely missing in Radway's interpretive framework, I would say, is any careful account of the *pleasurableness* of the pleasure of romance reading. The absence of pleasure as pleasure in *Reading the Romance* is made apparent in Radway's frequent, downplaying qualifications of the enjoyment that the Smithton women have claimed to derive from their favourite genre: that it is a form of *vicarious* pleasure, that it is *only temporarily* satisfying because it is *compensatory* literature; that even though it does create 'a kind of female community', through it 'women join forces only symbolically and in a mediated way in the privacy of their homes and in the devalued sphere of leisure activity' (Radway 1984: 212). Revealed in such qualifications is a sense that the pleasure of romance reading is somehow not really real, as though there were other forms of pleasure that could be considered 'more real' because they are more 'authentic', more enduring, more veritable, or whatever.

Radway's explanation of repetitive romance reading is a case in point. She analyses this in terms of romance reading's ultimate inadequacy when it comes to the satisfaction of psychic needs for which the readers cannot find an outlet in their actual social lives. In her view, romance reading is inadequate precisely because it gives these women the *illusion* of pleasure while it leaves their 'real' situation unchanged. In line with the way in which members of the Birmingham Centre for contemporary Cultural Studies have interpreted youth subcultures (see Hall and Jefferson 1976; Hebdige 1979), then, Radway comes to the conclusion that romance reading is a sort of 'imaginary solution' to real, structural problems and contradictions produced by patriarchy. (The real solution, one could guess, lies in the bounds of feminism.) All this amounts to a quite functionalist explanation of romance reading, one that is pre-occupied with its effects rather than its mechanisms. Consequently, pleasure as such cannot possibly be taken seriously in this theoretical framework, because the whole explanatory movement is directed towards the *ideological function* of pleasure.

Are the Smithton women ultimately only fooling themselves then? At times Radway seems to think so. For example, when the Smithton women state that it is impossible to describe the 'typical romantic heroine' because in their view, the hero-ines 'are all different', Radway is drawn to conclude that 'they refuse to admit that the books they read have a standard plot' (ibid.: 199). In imposing such a hasty interpre-tation, however, she forgets to take the statement seriously, as if it were only the result of the women's being lured by the realistic illusion of the narrative text.[3] But perhaps the statement that all heroines are different says more about the reading experience than Radway assumes. Perhaps it could be seen as an index of the pleasure that is solicited by what may be termed 'the grain of the story': the subtle, differentiated tex-ture of each book's staging of the romantic tale that makes its reading a 'new' experience even though the plot is standard. In fact, Radway's own findings seem to testify to this when she reports that 'although the women almost never remember the names of the principal characters, they could recite in surprising detail not only what had happened to them but also how they managed to cope with particularly troublesome situations' (ibid.: 201).

Attention to this pleasure of detail could also give us a fresh perspective on another thing often asserted by many of the Smithton women that puzzled Radway, namely that they always want to ascertain in advance that a book finishes with a happy ending. Radway sees this peculiar behaviour as an indication that these women cannot bear 'the threat of the unknown as it opens out before them and demand con-tinual reassurance that the events they suspect will happen [i.e. the happy ending], in fact, will finally happen' (1984: 205). But isn't it possible to develop a more positive interpretation here? When the reader is sure *that* the heroine and the hero will finally get each other, she can concentrate all the more on *how* they will get each other. Finding out about the happy ending in advance could then be seen as a clever read-ing strategy aimed at obtaining maximum pleasure: a pleasure that is oriented towards the *scenario* of romance, rather than its outcome. If the outcome is predictable in the romance genre, the variety of the ways in which two lovers can find one another is endless. Cora Kaplan's succinct specification of what in her view is central to the plea-sures of romance reading for women is particularly illuminating here, suggesting 'that the reader identifies with both terms in the seduction scenario, but most of all with *the process of seduction*' (1986: 162, emphasis added).

This emphasis on the staging of the romantic encounter, on the details of the moments of seducing and being seduced as the characteristic elements of pleasure in romance reading, suggest another absence in the interpretive framework of *Reading the Romance*: the meaning of fantasy, or, for that matter, of romantic fantasy. In Radway's account, fantasy is too easily equated with the unreal, with the world of illusions, that is, false ideas about how life 'really' is. It is this pitting of reality against fantasy that brings her to the sad conclusion that repetitive romance reading 'would enable a reader to tell herself again and again that a love like the heroine's might indeed occur in a world such as hers. She thus teaches herself to believe that men *are able* to satisfy women's needs fully' (1984: 201). In other words, it is Radway's reductionist con-ception of phantasmatic scenarios as incorrect models of reality – in Radway's feminist

conception of social reality, there is not much room for men's potential capacity to satisfy women – that drives her to a more or less straightforward 'harmful effects' theory.

If, however, as I have already suggested in Chapter 5, we were to take fantasy seriously as a reality in itself, as a necessary dimension of our psychical reality, we could
conceptualize the world of fantasy as the place of excess, where the unimaginable can
be imagined. Fiction could then be seen as the social materialization and elaboration
of fantasies, and thus, in the words of Allison Light, 'as the explorations and productions of desires which may be in excess of the socially possible or acceptable' (1984: 7).

This insight may lead to another interpretation of the repetitiveness of romance
reading as an activity among women (some critics would speak of 'addiction'), which
does not accentuate their ultimate psychic subordination to patriarchal relations, but
rather emphasizes the rewarding quality of the fantasizing activity itself. As Radway
would have it, romance fans pick up a book again and again because romantic fiction
does *not satisfy them enough*, as it is only a poor, illusory and transitory satisfaction of
needs unmet in 'real life'. But couldn't the repeated readings be caused by the fact that
the romance novels *satisfies them too much*, because it constitutes a secure space in
which an imaginary perpetuation of an emphatically utopian state of affairs (something that is an improbability in 'real life' in the first place) is possible?

After all, it is more than striking that romance novels always abruptly *end* at the
moment that the two lovers have finally found each other, and thus never go beyond
the point of no return: romantic fiction generally is exclusively about the titillating
period b*efore* the wedding! This could well indicate that what repetitious reading of
romantic fiction offers is the opportunity to continue to enjoy the excitement of
romance and romantic scenes without being interrupted by the dark side of sexual
relationships. In the symbolic world of the romance novel, the struggle between the
sexes (while being one of the ongoing central themes of the melodramatic soap
operas; see Ang 1985: esp. chapter 4), will always be overcome in the end, precisely
because that is what the romantic imagination self-consciously tries to make repre-
sentable. Seen this way, the politics of romance reading is a politics of fantasy in which
women engage precisely because it does *not* have 'reality value'. Thus, the romance
reader can luxuriate in never having to enter the conflictual world that comes after the
'happy ending'. Instead, she leaves the newly formed happy couple behind and joins
another heroine, another hero, who are to meet each other in a new book, in a new
romantic setting.

What is achieved by this deliberate fictional bracketing of life after the wedding, it
seems to me, is the phantasmatic perpetuation of the romantic state of affairs.
Whatever the concrete reasons for women taking pleasure in this – here some further
ethnographic inquiry could provide us with new answers – it seems clear to me that
what is fundamentally involved is a certain determination to maintain the *feeling* of
romance, or a refusal to give it up, even though it may be temporarily or permanently
absent in 'real life,' against all odds. And it is this enduring emotional quest that, I
would suggest, should be taken seriously as a psychical strategy by which women
empower themselves in everyday life, leaving apart what its ideological consequences
in social reality are.

If this interpretation is at all valid, then I am not sure how feminism should
respond to it. Radway's rationalist proposal – that romance readers should be convinced to see that their reading habits are ultimately working against their own 'real'
interests – will not do, for it slights the fact that what is above all at stake in the energy

invested in romance reading is the actualization of romantic feelings, which are by definition 'unrealistic', excessive, utopian, inclined towards the sensational and the adventurous. That the daring quality of romanticism tends to be tamed by the security of the happy ending in the standard romance novel is not so important in this respect. What is important is the tenacity of the desire to feel romantically.

This is not to say that romantic fiction should be considered above all criticism. The ideological consequences of its mass production and consumption should be a continuing object of reflection and critique for feminism. Questions of sexual politics, definitions of femininity and masculinity, and the cultural meanings of the romance in general will remain important issues. However, all this should not invalidate the significance of the craving for and pleasure in romantic feelings that so many women have in common and share. In fact, I am drawn to conclude that it might be this common experience that could serve as the basis for overcoming the paralysing opposition between 'feminism' and 'romance reading'.

Notes

1 I would like to emphasize that in doing this I cannot do full justice to the accomplishments and problems of the book. Many aspects of Radway's distinctly innovative book, such as her discussion of the differences between the ideal romance and the failed romance, and her application of Nancy Chodorow's version of psychoanalysis to explain women's 'need' for romance reading, will therefore not be discussed here. I would also like to draw attention to Radway's preface to the British edition of *Reading the Romance* (1987), in which she raises some of the issues I go into in this chapter.
2 See, for a lengthy and insightful review of this book, Lynn Spigel (1985).
3 It should be noted that Radway's discussion of the narrative discourse of romantic fiction is very similar to the theory of the 'classic realist text' as developed in film theory by Colin MacCabe and others.

Chapter 24

Angela McRobbie

FEMINISM AND YOUTH CULTURE

*J*ACKIE IS ONE OF a large range of magazines, newspapers and comics published by D. C. Thomson of Dundee (five newspapers in Scotland, 32 titles in all). With a history of vigorous anti-unionism, D. C. Thomson is not unlike other mass communication groups.[1] Like Walt Disney, for example, it produces for a young market and operates a strict code of censorship on content. But its conservatism is most evident in its newspapers. The *Sunday Post* with a reputed readership of around 3 million (i.e. 79 per cent of the entire population of Scotland over the age of 15) is comforting, reassuring, and parochial in tone. Consisting, in the main, of anecdotal incidents drawn to the attention of the reader in 'couthie' language, it serves as a Sunday entertainer, reminding its readers of the pleasure of belonging to a particular national culture.

One visible result of this success has been enviably high profit margins of 20 per cent or more, at a time of inflation and crisis in the publishing world.[2] D. C. Thomson has also expanded into other associated fields with investments, for example, in the Clyde Paper Company and Southern TV3. Without adhering to a 'conspiracy plot' thesis, it would nonetheless be naive to imagine that the interests of such a company lie purely in the realisation of profit. In *Jackie*, D. C. Thomson is not merely 'giving girls what they want'. Each magazine, newspaper or comic has its own conventions and its own style. But within these conventions, and through them, a concerted effort is nevertheless made to win and shape the consent of the readers to a particular set of values.

The work of this branch of the media involves framing the world for its readers, and through a variety of techniques endowing with importance those topics chosen for inclusion. The reader is invited to share this world with *Jackie*. It is no coincidence that the title is also a girl's name. This is a sign that the magazine is concerned with the 'category of the subject',[3] in particular the individual girl and the feminine persona. *Jackie* is both the magazine and the ideal girl. The short snappy name carries a string of connotations – British, fashionable (particularly in the 1960s), modern and cute. With the 'pet-form' abbreviated ending, it sums up all those desired qualities which the reader is supposedly seeking.

This ideological work is also grounded on certain natural, even biological, categories. *Jackie* expresses the natural features of adolescence in much the same way as Disney comics capture the natural essence of childhood. As Dorfman and Mattelart writing on Disney point out, each has a 'virtually biologically captive predetermined audience'.[4] *Jackie* introduces the girl to adolescence, outlining its landmarks and characteristics in detail and stressing the problematic features as well as the fun. Of course *Jackie* is not solely responsible for nurturing this ideology of femininity. Nor would such an ideology cease to exist if *Jackie* disappeared.

Unlike other fields of mass culture, the magazines of teenage girls have not yet been subject to rigorous critical analysis, yet from the most cursory of readings it is clear that they too, like those other forms more immediately associated with the sociology of the media – the press, TV, film, radio – are powerful ideological forces. In fact, women's and girls' weeklies occupy a privileged position. Addressing themselves solely to a female market, their concern is with promoting a feminine culture for their readers. They define and shape the woman's world, spanning every stage from early childhood to old age. From *Mandy, Bunty, Judy* and *Jackie* to *House and Home,* the exact nature of the woman's role is spelt out in detail, according to her age and status. She progresses from adolescent romance where there are no explicitly sexual encounters, to the more sexual world of *19, Honey,* or *Over 21,* which in turn give way to marriage, childbirth, home-making, child-care and *Woman's Own.* There are no male equivalents to these products. Male magazines tend to be based on particular leisure pursuits or hobbies, motorcycling, fishing, cars or even pornography. There is no consistent attempt to link interests with age, nor is there a sense of natural or inevitable progression from one to another complementary to the life-cycle. Instead there are a variety of leisure options available, many of which involve participation outside the home.

It will be argued that the way *Jackie* addresses girls as a grouping – as do all the other magazines – serves to obscure differences of, for example, class or race, between women. *Jackie* asserts a class-less, race-less sameness, a kind of false unity which assumes a common experience of womanhood or girlhood. By isolating a particular phase or age as the focus of interest, one which coincides roughly with that of its readers, the magazine is ascribing to age, certain ideological meanings. Adolescence comes to be synonymous with *Jackie*'s definition of it. The consensual totality of feminine adolescence means that all girls want to know how to catch a boy, lose weight, look their best and be able to cook. This allows few opportunities for other feminine modes, other kinds of adolescence. Dissatisfaction with the present is responded to in terms of looking forward to the next stage. In this respect girls are being invited to join a closed sorority of shared feminine values which actively excludes other possible values. Within the world of *Jackie* what we find is a cloyingly claustrophobic environment where the dominant emotions are fear, insecurity, competitiveness and even panic.

There are several ways in which we can approach *Jackie* magazine as part of the media and of mass culture in general. The first of these is the traditionalist thesis. In this, magazines are seen as belonging to popular or mass culture, something which is inherently inferior to high culture, or the arts. Cheap, superficial, exploitative and debasing, mass culture reduces its audience to a mass of mindless morons:

> the open sagging mouths and glazed eyes, the hands mindlessly drumming in
> time to the music, the broken stiletto heels, the shoddy, stereotyped 'with it'

clothes: here apparently, is a collective portrait of a generation enslaved by a commercial machine.[5]

Alderson, writing explicitly on girls' weeklies takes a similar position. Claiming, correctly, that what they offer their readers is a narrow and restricted view of life, she proposed as an alternative, better literature, citing *Jane Eyre* as an example.[6]

The problems with such an approach are manifest. 'High' culture becomes a cure for all ills. It is, to quote Willis, 'a repository of quintessential human values',[6] playing a humanising role by elevating the emotions and purifying the spirit. What this argument omits to mention are the material requirements necessary to purchase such culture. And underpinning it is an image of the deprived, working-class youngster (what Alderson calls the 'Newsom girl') somehow lacking in those qualities which contact with the arts engenders. Mass culture is seen as a manipulative, vulgar, profit-seeking industry offering cheap and inferior versions of the arts to the more impressionable and vulnerable sectors of the population. This concept of culture is inadequate because it is ahistorical, and is based on unquestioned qualitative judgements. It offers no explanation as to how these forms develop and are distributed. Nor does it explain why one form has a particular resonance for one class in society rather than another.

The second interpretation has much in common with this approach, although it is generally associated with more radical critics. This is the conspiracy thesis and it, too, sees mass culture as fodder for the masses; the result of a ruling-class plot whose objective is to keep the working classes docile and subordinate and to divert them into entertainments. Writing on TV, Hall, Connell and Curti describe this approach, 'from this position the broadcaster is conceived of as nothing more than the ideological agent of his political masters'.[8]

Orwell, writing on boys' magazines in the 1930s, can be seen to take such a position, 'Naturally, the politics of the *Gem* and *Magnet* are Conservative . . . All fiction from the novels in the mushroom libraries, downwards is censored in the interests of the ruling class.'[9] By this logic, *Jackie* is merely a mouthpiece for ruling-class ideology, focused on young adolescent girls. Again, mass culture is seen as worthless and manipulative. Not only is this argument also ahistorical, but it fails to locate the operations of different apparatuses in the social formation (politics, the media, the law, education, the family) each of which is relatively autonomous, has its own level and its own specific material practices. While private sectors of the economy do ultimately work together with the State, there is a necessary separation, between them. Each apparatus has its own uneven development and one cannot be collapsed with another.

The third argument reverses both the first two arguments, to the extent that it points to pop music and pop culture as meaningful activities: 'for most young people today . . . pop music and pop culture is their only expressive outlet.'[10] Such a position does have some relevance to our study of *Jackie*. It hinges on the assumption that this culture expresses and offers, albeit in consumerist terms, those values and ideas held both by working-class youth and by sections of middle-class youth. Youth, that is, is defined in terms of values held, which are often in opposition to those held by the establishment, by their parents, the school, in work, and so on. Such a definition does not consider youth's relation to production, but to consumption, and it is this approach which has characterised that huge body of work, the sociology of culture and of youth subcultural theory, and delinquency theory.

To summarise a familiar argument which finds expression in most of these fields: working-class youth, denied access to other 'higher' forms of culture, and associating these in any case with 'authority' and the middle classes, turns to those forms available on the market. Here they can at least exert some power in their choice of commodities. These commodities often come to be a hallmark of the subcultural group in question but not exactly in their original forms. The group subverts the original meaning by bestowing additional implied connotations to the object thereby extending the range of its signifying power. These new meanings undermine and can even negate the previous or established meanings so that the object comes to represent an oppositional ideology linked to the subculture or youth grouping, in question. It then summarises for the outside observer, the group's disaffection from the wider society. This process of re-appropriation can be seen in, for example, the 'style' of the skinheads, the 'mod' suit, the 'rocker' motor-bike, or even the 'punk' safety-pin.[11]

But this approach, which hinges on explaining the choice of cultural artefacts – clothes, records or motor-bikes – is of limited usefulness when applied to teenage girls and their magazines. They play little, if any, role in shaping their own pop culture and their choice in consumption is materially extremely narrow. Indeed the forms made available to them make re-appropriation difficult. *Jackie* offers its readers no active 'presence' in which girls are invited to participate. The uses are, in short, prescribed by the 'map'. Yet this does not mean that *Jackie* cannot be used in subversive ways. Clearly girls do use it as a means of signalling their boredom and disaffection, in the school, for example. The point here is that despite these possible uses, the magazine itself has a powerful ideological presence as a form, and as such demands analysis carried out apart from these uses or 'readings'.

The fourth and final interpretation is the one most often put forward by media practitioners themselves. Writing on the coverage of political affairs on TV, Stuart Hall *et al.* label this the *laissez-faire* thesis:

> Programming is conceived, simply, as a 'window' on the campaign; it reflects, and therefore, does not shape, or mould, the political debate. In short, the objectives of television are to provide objective information . . . so that they – the public – may make up their own minds in a 'rational' manner.[12]

By this logic, *Jackie* instead of colouring the ways girls think and act merely reflects and accurately portrays their pre-existing interests, giving them 'what they want', and offering useful advice on the way.

While the argument made here will include strands from the positions outlined above, its central thrust will represent a substantial shift away from them. What I want to suggest is that *Jackie* occupies the sphere of the personal or private, what Gramsci calls 'Civil Society' ('the ensemble of organisms that are commonly called Private').[13] Hegemony is sought uncoercively on this terrain, which is relatively free of direct State interference. Consequently it is seen as an arena of 'freedom', of 'free choice' and of 'freetime'. This sphere includes, 'not only associations and organisations like political parties and the press, but also the family, which combines ideological and economic functions'.[14] And as Hall, Lumley and McLennan observe, this distinctness from the State has 'pertinent effects – for example, in the manner in which different aspects of the class struggle are ideologically inflected.'[15] *Jackie* exists within a large, powerful, privately-owned publishing apparatus which produces a vast range of newspapers, magazines and comics. It is on this level of the magazine that teenage girls are subjected to an explicit attempt to win consent to the dominant order – in terms of femininity, leisure and consumption, i.e. at the level of culture.

The 'teen' magazine is a highly privileged 'site'. Here the girls' consent is sought uncoercively and in their leisure time. As Frith observes, 'The ideology of leisure in a capitalist society . . . is that people work in order to be able to enjoy leisure. Leisure is their "free" time and so the values and choices, expressed in leisure and independent of work – they are the result of ideological conditions.'[16] While there is a strongly coercive element to those other terrains which teenage girls inhabit – the school and the family – in her leisure time the girl is officially free to do as she pleases. It is on the open market that girls are least constrained by the display of social control. The only qualification here is the ability to buy a ticket, magazine or Bay City Roller T-shirt. Here they remain relatively free from the interference by authority. Frith notes that there are three main purposes for capitalist society with regard to leisure.[17] (1) the reproduction of labour physically (food, rest, relaxation); (2) the reproduction of labour ideologically (so that the work-force will willingly return to work each day); (3) the provision of a market for the consumption of goods, thus the realisation of surplus value.

While *Jackie* readers are not yet involved in production, they are already being pushed in this direction ideologically, at school, in the home and in the youth club. *Jackie* as a commodity designed for leisure covers all three points noted above. It encourages good health and 'beauty sleep', and it is both a consumer object which encourages further consumption and a powerful ideological force.

So, using *Jackie* as an example, we can see that leisure and its exploitation in the commercial and private sector also provides capital with space to carry out ideological work. Further, it can be argued that the very way in which leisure is set up and defined is itself ideological. Work is a necessary evil, possibly dull and unrewarding. But its rationale is to allow the worker to look forward to his or her leisure as an escape. That is, leisure is equated with free choice and free time and exists in opposition to work, which is associated with necessity, coercion and authority. In this sphere of individual self-expression and relaxation, the State remains more or less hidden revealing itself only when it is deemed politically necessary (for example at football matches and rock concerts; through the laws relating to obscene publications and through licensing and loitering laws, etc.)

Commercial leisure enterprises with their illusion of freedom have, then, an attraction for youth. And this freedom is pursued, metaphorically, inside the covers of *Jackie*. With an average readership age of 10 to 14, *Jackie* prefigures girls' entry into the labour market as young workers, and its pages are crammed full of the 'goodies' which this later freedom promises. (*Jackie* girls are never at school, they are enjoying the fruits of their labour on the open market. They live in large cities, frequently in flats shared with other young wage-earners like themselves.)

This image of freedom has a particular resonance for girls when it is located within and intersects with the longer and again ideologically constructed 'phase' they inhabit in the present. Leisure has a special importance in this period of 'brief flowering',[18] that is, in those years prior to marriage and settling down, after which they become dual labourers in the home and in production. Leisure in their 'single' years is especially important because it is here that their future is secured. It is in *this* sphere that they go about finding a husband and thereby sealing their fate.

In pursuit of this image of freedom and of free choice it is in the interests of capital that leisure be to some extent removed from direct contact with the State, despite the latters' welfare and leisure provisions for youth. Thus a whole range of consumer goods, pop music, pubs, discos and in this case teen magazines occupy a space which promise greater personal freedom for the consumer. *Jackie* exists in this private sphere. The product of a privately owned industry and the prime exponent of the world of the private or personal emotions. Frith makes the point that

> The overall result for capital is that control of leisure has been exercised indirectly, leisure choices can't be determined but they do have to be limited – the problem is to ensure that workers' leisure activities don't affect their discipline, skill or willingness to work.[19]

That is, capital needs to provide this personal space for leisure, but it also needs to control it. This is clearly best done through consumption. Hence ultimately State and private spheres do function 'beneath the ruling ideology' but they also have different 'modes of insertion' on a day-to-day basis, which, as pointed out earlier, in turn produce *'pertinent effects'*. There is an *unspoken* consensus existing between those ideologies carried in State organised leisure, and those included in *Jackie*. The former is typically blunt in its concern with moral training, discipline, team spirit, patriotism, allowing the latter to dedicate itself to fun and romance!

What then are the key features which characterise *Jackie*? First there is a lightness of tone, a non-urgency, which holds true right through the magazine particularly in the use of colour, graphics and advertisements. It asks to be read at a leisurely pace indicating that its subject matter is not wholly serious, and is certainly not 'news'. Since entertainment and leisure goods are designed to arouse feelings of pleasure as well as interest, the appearance of the magazine is inviting, its front cover shows a pretty girl smiling happily. The dominance of the visual level, which is maintained throughout the magazine reinforces this notion of leisure. It is to be glanced through, looked at and only finally read. Published at weekly intervals, the reader has time to peruse each item at her own speed. She also has time to pass it round her friends or swap it for another magazine.

Rigid adherence to a certain style of lay-out and patterning of features ensures a familiarity with its structure(s). The reader can rely on *Jackie* to cheer her up, entertain her, or solve her problems each week. The style of the magazine once established, facilitates and encourages partial and uneven reading, in much the same way as newspapers also do. The girl can quickly turn to the centre page for the pin-up, glance at the fashion page and leave the problems and picture stories which are the main substance of the magazine, till she has more time.

Articles and features are carefully arranged to avoid one 'heavy' feature following another. The black-and-white-picture stories taking up between 2½ and 3 full pages are always broken up by a coloured advertisement or beauty feature, and the magazine opens and closes by inviting the reader to participate directly through the letters or the problem pages.

This sense of solidness and resistance to change (*Jackie*'s style has not been substantially altered since it began publication) is reflected and paralleled in its thematic content. Each feature consists of workings and reworkings of a relatively small repertoire of specific themes or concerns which sum up the girls' world. These topics saturate the magazine. Entering the world of *Jackie* means suspending interest in the real world of school, family or work, and participating in a sphere which is devoid of history and resistant to change.

Jackie deals primarily with the terrain of the personal and it marks a turning inwards to the sphere of the 'soul', the 'heart' or the emotions. On the one hand, of course, certain features do change – fashion is itself predicated upon change and upon being 'up to date'. But the degree of change even here is qualified – certain features remain the same, e.g. The models' looks, poses, the style of drawing and its positioning within the magazine and so on.

Above all, *Jackie*, like the girl it symbolises, is intended to be looked at. This overriding concern with visuals affects every feature. But its visual appearance and style also reflects the spending power of its readers. There is little of the extravagant or exotic in *Jackie*. The paper on which it is printed is thin and not glossy. The fashion and beauty pages show clothes priced within the girls' range and the advertisements are similarly focused on a low-budget market, featuring principally personal toiletries, tampons, shampoo and lipsticks, rather than larger consumer goods.

This is how the reader looks at *Jackie*,

Notes

1 G. Rosei, 'The Private Life of Lord Snooty', in the *Sunday Times* Magazine, 29 July 1973, pp. 8–16.

2 Ibid., see also *Willing's Press Guide*, 1977, and McCarthy Information Ltd (June 1977) where it is noted that 'Among the enviably high profit-margin firms are Shopfitters (Lancs); Birmingham satchel maker Ralph Martindale, and 'Dandy' and 'Beano' published by D. C. Thomson – all with profit margins of 20% or more.' See also Extel Card March 1977 for D. C. Thomson.

Year	Turnover	Profit after tax
1974	£18 556 000	£2 651 000
1975	£23 024 000	£2 098 000
1976	£28 172 000	£2 092 000

3 L. Althusser, 'Ideology and the State', in *Lenin and Philosophy and Other Essays*, London, New Left Books, 1971, p. 163.

4 A. Dorfman and A. Mattelart, *How to Read Donald Duck*, 1971, p. 30.

5 Paul Johnson in the *New Statesman*, 28 February 1964.

6 C. Alderson, *The Magazines Teenagers Read*, London, 1968, p. 3.

7 P. Willis, 'Symbolism and Practice: A Theory for the Social Meaning of Pop Music', in CCCS, Birmingham University, stencilled paper, p. 2.

8 S. Hall, I. Connell and L. Curti, 'The Unity of Current Affairs Television', in Working Paper in *Cultural Studies*, CCCS, University of Birmingham, no. 9. 1976, p. 51.

9 George Orwell, 'Boys' Weeklies' in his book *Inside the Whale and Other Essays*, Harmondsworth, Penguin, 1969, pp. 187–203, first published in 1939.

10 Willis, 'Symbolism and Practice', op. cit., p. 1.

11 J. Clarke, S. Hall, T. Jefferson and B. Roberts, 'Subcultures, Cultures and Classes' in S. Hall (ed.), *Resistance Through Rituals*, London, Hutchinson, 19767, p. 55.

12 S. Hall, I. Connell and L. Curti, 'The Unity of Current Affairs Television', in Working Papers in *Cultural Studies*, CCCS, University of Birmingham, no. 9, 1978, p. 53.

13 Antonio Gramsci, *Selections from the Prison Notebooks*, quoted in S. Hall, B. Lumley and G. McLennan, 'Politics and Ideology: Gramsci' in 'On Ideology', *Cultural Studies*, no. 10, 1977, p. 51.
14 Ibid., p. 51.
15 Ibid., p. 67.
16 Simon Frith, *Sound Effects*, New York, Pantheon, 1981.
17 Ibid.
18 Richard Hoggart, *The Uses of Literacy*, Harmondsworth, Penguin, 1957, p. 51.
19 Frith, *Sound Effects*, op. cit.

Chapter 25

Dawn H. Currie

GIRL TALK
Adolescent magazines and their readers

Beyond the pleasure principle

IF ASKED DIRECTLY, THE girls in this study claim, as feminist researchers do, that they read magazines 'for fun.' At first glance, this response may appear to support the characterization of magazine reading as a search for pleasure. The problem is that this interpretation places reading pleasure outside the realm of the social. However appealing, pleasure as an effect of reading is never 'innocent' or separate from its societal role. In this and the following chapters we explore the pleasures of teenzine reading. In order to do so we must identify which texts the girls in our study enjoy, why these texts sustain reader interest, and how these texts bring together the cultural and social realms of adolescence. As a number of writers note,[1] the construction and maintenance of any social order entails the construction of pleasures that secure participation in that order. In contrast to the notion gaining currency in cultural studies that pleasure can escape ideological manipulation and act as a form of disruption and resistance, Ballaster and colleagues (1991) point out that many commercial venues in a consumer culture will be both pleasurable and ideological – they ask, 'What else could pleasure be and how else could ideology work?' (p. 162).

Pursuing the types of questions which also motivate our study through discussions with readers, Ballaster and colleagues find that the pleasures of women's magazines derive from the magazines' ability to act both as a 'time-keeper' in women's lives and as fantasy. They link time-keeping to the way in which magazines address the particular circumstances of women's experiences at different points in their lives. They link fantasy to the opportunity provided readers to gain a sense of participation and belonging to an imagined community of women. Assigning fantasy status to this community does not mean that Ballaster and colleagues view the constructions of femininity in magazines as innocent pleasure, however. While readers are free to pick and choose the texts they read, the magazine text determines the range of possible meanings because it contains implicit assumptions about womanhood and therefore defines what kind of life can be taken for granted and what is open for struggle and renegotiation. Ballaster and colleagues advance the interesting suggestion that the fantasy element of magazines works by providing readers a fleeting sense of safety through the absolute dominion of women's domestic world.[2] 'The pleasure in safety is to be had from many elements of magazines, not least in forging of a homogeneous domestic community in contrast with the threats and confusions of the world outside. That world is constantly on the margins of the magazine's field of vision, understood both as threat and [as] *unreality*' (p. 165: emphasis in original). In short, although Ballaster and colleagues support the notion advanced by postmodern writers that women's magazines occupy fantasy status in readers' lives, they do not celebrate this status as evidence that women's magazines are an innocuous source of pleasure for women.

Similar to the (imputed) adult readers who dominate academic debate, girls in the current study found magazine reading a readily available pleasure. Some girls did refer directly to the 'fantasy' element when describing the pleasures of magazine reading. This fantasy typically arises from the visual pleasures provided by glossy beauty and fashion layouts:

> Actually, I kind of like the pictures; they're sort of interesting, exotic, but, uhm, most of the stuff I wouldn't wear. I don't know. I guess it's like a mental fantasy of what it would look like. [Later, looking at *Elle* with interviewer] I don't know. I guess it's like fantasy land for me [laughs]. Like I don't really have any clothes like this, so it's the only thing I can do! [laughs].
>
> (Seventeen-year-old Amy)

> Usually after school I have friends coming over and we sit there and we fantasize and read all these magazines articles and 'Oh, I wish that was me,' and stuff like that [laughs].
>
> (Fourteen-year-old Lauren)

Fantasy themes also surrounded depictions of romantic relationships or future roles as adult women:

> Uhm, I really like this one just because it's kind of different for a guy to be actually kissing the girl's – or look like he's *about* to kiss the girl's foot. Most of the time maybe the guy would be saying that to the girl 'Kiss my feet,' or something . . . I've actually heard guys say that [laughs]. I've never [laughs] heard a girl say that to a guy, so it's almost like a reversal.
>
> (Sixteen-year-old Melissa, looking at ad for Converse shoes)

> I like this ad. It's really natural and it's sort of like the future. You look at this and you think about what your future is going to be like, and stuff. It sort of makes you think about that.
>
> (Sixteen-year-old Erica looking at the
> bride in the ad for Beautiful perfume)

Despite the appeal of these utopian themes, however, the comments quoted above exhaust the references to fantasy themes in interview transcripts. Readers referred more frequently to favourite magazines in terms of their realistic qualities. Overall, 'realism' rather than fantasy emerged as the most important characteristic in descriptions of favoured reading. This means that, while girls cited different magazines as preferred reading, a favourite magazine was chosen from the available competing titles because it was deemed to refer to 'real' people or to address 'real' problems which readers face:

> *Teen*, I don't know, it's just more to my liking. It just seems more *realistic*. I think it deals more with the problems that people *actually* have.
>
> (Sixteen-year-old Crystal)

> And in *Seventeen*, the articles are better then *YM* . . . The ones in *Seventeen* are about like real life, or sometimes they're stories that people have wrote, and I like reading that. [Showing an example to interviewer] Well, we have had a family friend that had breast cancer, and sometimes I like things like this – they have say happened to my friends or something.
>
> (Fifteen-year-old Christina)

> *Sassy* is a little better than *YM*. I mean it's in the same category but it's a little better because they put real people on the cover and real people inside the magazine . . . *Sassy* seems to pride itself on being more realistic than the other magazines.
>
> (Thirteen-year-old Stephanie)

In contrast to the adult readers who are purported by researchers to enjoy the fantasy status of pictures and ads, the emphasis on reality by girls in this study underlies their rejection of both fashion and (other) advertising:

> I never look at the fashion stuff. 'Cause it's stuff that's almost like too weird to wear for me. I don't know, I would never think of dressing like they've dressed [pointing out fashion pages in *YM*, her favourite]. It's all – it's not real.
> [Interviewer:] It's not?
> No. A lot of it isn't real because like they all have these 'drop dead' bodies and they're not going – you know, not everyone's going to wear clothes that way. So I just, I don't know, I never look at the fashion. They're too weird.
>
> (Sixteen-year-old Melissa)

We shall see later that this rejection of magazine fashion is not an indication that dress is unimportant to these readers; on the contrary, this rejection is based on the grounds that magazine fashion is, simply, not real enough. When the girls were asked what might make their favourite magazine more enjoyable, a dominant theme which emerged[3] concerns the prominence of fashion models who are 'too perfect' or who are seen to perpetuate unrealistic body standards. This dissatisfaction does not lead girls to reject the beauty mandate itself; it does lead them to reject individual titles which emphasize fashion or contain too many ads:

I've read that [*Sassy*] a couple of times, and, ah, I don't like it.
[Interviewer:] Why?
There's no articles, every page is ads.
[Interviewer:] Really?
Yup, the whole thing.

(Fourteen-year-old Rachel)

I just found that I like *YM* better.
[Interviewer:] Is there anything in particular that is better about it?
Seventeen has columns in it too, like *good* ones, but I found that I like *YM* because it's got more – it doesn't have as much advertisement; it – it's got more writing in it.

(Thirteen-year-old Ashley)

Seventeen [is her favourite] 'cause I find I can relate to like the articles, and what they're saying in the stories, and this and that. I like the pictures – like they're kind of just fun, but the other ones, I just end up flipping through them and it's just ads and stuff – I'd rather go for a little bit more.

(Seventeen-year-old Mary)

Most of the time *Seventeen* is boring because it doesn't have as much stuff as the other two have [*Teen* and *YM*]. It's just got mostly pictures, like it's not interesting articles – it's got, like, no writing, it's just pictures and credits.
[Interviewer:] What things make *YM* better than *Seventeen*?
I don't know, it's got like interesting stories and people writing in to tell their problems and just stuff, like it's more interesting. It has lots of pictures, but it has writing too, whereas *Seventeen* just has pictures, just ads for stuff.

(Fifteen-year-old Elizabeth)

What these comments tell us is that, in contrast to the emphasis which postmodern critics give to the pleasures of reading as escape from reality, girls in this study want magazines that address the reality of teenage life:

I like reading other people's things and seeing what happens with their lives and then I'll try and make sure it doesn't happen with mine [laughs] . . . I like that [shows interviewer] – 'Problems at Home, How to Cope.' Like, if you're having family problems you could probably find out what the problems were and see how they solved their problems.

(Thirteen-year-old Brittany)

They [magazines] teach you a lot of things, like what you should do, what you should think. Sometimes they're really helpful – like your Mom dies, right? They might have advice on how to struggle through this. Like problems and things like that. And maybe make-over. Like you know, 'how to *do* a make-over.' I mean you can just look at those for suggestions.

(Fifteen-year-old Nicole)

Soap operas [another of her favourite pastimes] are sometimes a bit unrealistic – you can't really follow them to make decisions. But in magazines, they give you advice, realistic advice that you can follow.

(Sixteen-year-old Lindsey)

Because of this emphasis on what readers can learn from magazines, the girls indicated the following:

I mean, a magazine is fine to look through, but you don't really want to pay for something that you're not going to sit down and actually use, you know what I mean? Like *Sassy*, there'd actually be stuff I want to read, stuff I want to know about inside of it. I mean, I like looking through the fashion and stuff as well, but if I'm going to buy a magazine I want to have something that's going to *do* something [laughs] for me, you know what I mean?

(Seventeen-year-old Jamie)

I used to be into like *Teen*, that's when I was in Grade 7, 8. And then *YM* just seemed kind of older and more like my *style*, like it had more, like useful stuff that I'd *read* – like all the questions . . . they were kind of right for me so I've had a subscription for that for a while. It's not like a *Vogue* or anything, you know – *Vogue*, like I read it but it's not really interesting to me 'cause it has nothing to do with someone my age, or like someone I can relate to.

(Fifteen-year-old Kirsten)

Vogue, it's kind of a waste because what's the point if all you're going to do is flip, like for five seconds to look at a magazine [laughs]. If I see it on the stand it's fun to look at, but I wouldn't buy it because it's a waste of like four dollars, right?

(Sixteen-year-old Erica)

In summary, while the girls in this study, similar to adult readers, claim to read 'for fun,' most reject the glossy ads and photo-spreads of magazines in favour of written texts. As a consequence, their reading does not include very many of the magazines or specific texts studied by academic critics. While we saw in chapter 1 that the content of teenzines is very similar to that in adult magazines, we still know very little about girls' reading pleasures. In order to understand why girls enjoy teenzines, therefore, we need to pay attention to what girls rather than researchers find important. In the next section, we explore the specific parts of teenzines that the readers in this study enjoy. . . .

From pictures to written texts: girls' choice of texts

When examined only for content, the written texts of teenzines appears monolithic. Repetition could, in fact, be one of the reasons why some girls do not read very many teenzines. Sixteen-year-old Crystal quit teenzine reading because she found them boring:

It doesn't really do much. It's like the same magazine over and over again. Like a *different* way to put on every shadow, and a *different* hairdo [laughs]. You know. So that gets boring, I guess, so I don't usually buy it [*Seventeen*] unless, like I'm going somewhere on a long trip.

Magazines are not experienced this way by those who choose to read them, however, Despite the kinds of similarities . . ., teenzines are described by enthusiastic readers as offering a diverse choice of reading:

The first thing I read is the beginning where it tells all about what is in the whole magazine – the Table of Contents. Probably the first thing I read, *YM* has their article – 'disasters of the month' or 'nightmare of the month.' It's an article about a whole bunch of bad things that have happened to people and stuff. Just like embarrassing situations that have happened to people. Like you see a guy and you trip and fall, and make a fool of yourself. Things like that. And, I don't know, mainly the stories about relationships and stuff like that. Then the quizzes, I usually do those. They're about like relationships and matchmaking and things like boyfriends. I read them.

(Sixteen-year-old Lindsey)

I go for *YM* because they have romantic stories, they have like funny stories – embarrassing moments, it's just like a fun thing to read . . . As soon as I buy a magazine I have to read *every* part. I see what's on the cover, like the real headlines, and see what one interests me more, and then I'd read *that*. And then after I read whatever, I just go from beginning to end, I go through the whole thing. I read *everything*.

(Fourteen-year-old Lauren)

YM has like interesting stories, and people writing in to tell their problems and stuff. Like it's more interesting. They have advice columns and they have the 'Say Anythings,' which is like embarrassing moments and stuff. And horoscopes. And people writing to 'Dear Jill' or 'Dear Jack,' or whatever. I kind of just read through the whole magazine.

(Fifteen-year-old Elizabeth)

For the large part this sense of diversity, hence choice, in reading is a result of textual format rather than textual content. For this reason, when asked about their 'favourite' parts, the girls were more likely to mention the type of text rather than specific topics.
   Although thematic analysis requires that researchers give each unit of text equal emphasis during enumeration, adolescent readers freely 'pick and choose' their way through their magazines.

When I read, like I usually don't just look through the magazine. I kind of go to wherever it is – the stuff – and just look through it . . . I see what interests me and then I might flip through it – like just flip through the articles and then the ads and stuff.

(Sixteen-year-old Melissa)

If I'm reading I kind of, what I'll do is like skip through all the little letters and see if there's anything that kind of relates to me, and then if it's interesting, or if I want to know what the answer is, I'll read that, or whatever.

(Seventeen-year-old Jamie)

This manner of reading is made possibly by the format of teenzine texts. Much of the written material in adolescent magazines appears as small, self-contained blocks of text; very few articles are longer than the equivalent of two full pages. This format means that magazines are seldom read from 'front to back':

I usually do the tests, and then if there's certain articles or stories, I want to read them first. And then I go back and read the whole thing over again, but first I go to the parts I want to read first. Mostly the stories interest me – the stuff on the cover that they say is inside.

(Fifteen-year-old Tiffany)

It also allows magazine reading to fit into fragmented bits of available time:

Usually once you've flipped through the magazine [and] you've looked at every page, then you go back and look for articles you wanted to read. I usually put the magazine down and a couple of days later, when I've done my homework and no one's calling me, I'll pick up the magazine and read [them].

(Sixteen-year-old Crystal)

During lunch break I had nothing else to do so I went to the library and the only books that were short enough to read during lunch were magazines. So I got magazines.

(Fifteen-year-old Christina)

The discontinuous nature of magazine reading thus means that some parts of magazines are read more widely than others. The types of texts which girls like to read are shown on Table 25.1.

As seen in Table 25.1 and already discussed above, the glossy texts of teenzines are not the most frequently read part of adolescent magazines. About half of the girls claim that they look at the fashion sections of magazines when they read, while less than one third of these readers claim that they (consciously) look at ads. Fashion spreads captured interest near graduation, when girls scoured magazines for styles of dresses and new hair fashions. During the rest of the year, however, most girls indicated that they would never wear the stuff in magazines, in part because 'you wouldn't be able to get the advertised clothes even if you wanted them.'[4]

I would never wear those clothes, just because I don't dress up. It's more like dressy clothes, like things you would wear to expensive dinner parties . . . I can't imagine myself in any of those things. I don't know, it's all boring. It's just like 'Ehk,' whatever – 'Nothing special.'

(Seventeen-year-old Brianna)

Table 25.1 Parts of adolescent magazines read by participants, by age group

	% of entire group		
	13–14 yrs	15–16 yrs	17 yrs
Advice (includes relationships, beauty, and health)	73	89	36
Quizzes	60	56	36
'Say Anything' (or funny stories such as 'It Happened to Me!')	53	61	27
Fashion	47	56	45
Stuff about guys (or about romance)	47	11	27
Real-life stories/tragedies	33	67	27
Horoscopes	27	56	36
Feature article (only if 'interesting')	33	22	36
Stories/interviews with celebrities	20	17	9
Advertisements (usually only if 'catches my eye')	27	28	27
Letters from readers	27	11	9

Base *N*: 44 girls who currently read adolescent magazines or 'used to' read adolescent magazines regularly.

I'll look at a magazine and say, and just kind of think to myself 'Oh, I would really like to have *this*,' you know. 'It would be really cool to have that kind of image.' But when it comes to shopping, I can't usually look for anything because the magazines we get are usually – like, the stores we have don't actually carry the stuff shown in the magazines.

(Seventeen-year-old Amy)

Maybe like once or twice I'd seen something, like sometimes they have, like you know, a really nice shirt. I wouldn't go out and look for *that* shirt, but something like it. You know what I mean, 'cause usually all the fashions from magazines are from New York or whatever. I can never find it. Like I've seen stuff that I really want, and if it was around I'd go out and get it, but it's usually in New York or Seattle or whatever, so I never end up getting it [laughs].

(Seventeen-year-old Laura)

Very few girls indicated that they always read ads. More typically, girls claim that they look at ads 'if they catch their eye.' This finding is significant, given that the academic study of women's magazines (whether in criticism or support) has given disproportionate emphasis to the analysis of advertisements. While adult women may be attracted to the spectacle of consumption as 'wish-fulfilment' in the ways which Winship and others suggest, the girls in this study prefer texts that they claim resonate with their everyday lives. While fashion is widely read by the seventeen-year-olds in this study, readers between the ages of thirteen and sixteen prefer advice, quizzes, and real-life stories. As seen in Table 25.1, almost three quarters of thirteen- and fourteen-year-olds, and 90 per cent of fifteen- and sixteen-year-olds, mention advice pages as regular reading. McRobbie (1991: 165) also draws attention to the importance of this reading preference among young girls. It is in the problem page that she finds the strongest definitions of teenage femininity. What gives these pages such readerly appeal?

Despite their dismissal by the world of 'serious' journalism, McRobbie points out that the advice column provides an open forum for an audience with little or no access to conventional therapeutic venues. She thus claims that the question-and-answer pages of teenzines play an important social role; 'it is listening and responding to, a discourse which so far has found no other space' (p. 156). This listening and responding valorizes sexual knowledge, which is uneasily avoided in our culture, despite its cultural coding in the normative language of romance, love, and marriage. Moreover, advice columns are a distinctly feminine form because it is not only women's lot to suffer personal unhappiness in a particularly acute form, but also their duty to try to alleviate the unhappiness of other people (p. 158). Within this framework, the power of adolescent magazines can be linked to their role as a regulative, controlling mechanism which operates along the terrain of the provision of knowledge in a culturally specific way which addresses women:[5]

> From this viewpoint the problem page would represent a privileged site in the creation of a number of discourses designed so that they may be used by teenage girls to make sense of their complex and frequently contradictory feelings in relation to their own sexuality. It might even be described as a focal point for the construction of female sexuality which exists alongside other discourses, sometimes in harmony with them and on other occasions and in other contexts at odds with them. The problem pages, therefore, add to the clamour of already-existing organizing discourses, such as those found in the school, the home and elsewhere in the mass media.
>
> (p. 165)

Commentary by the girls in this study supports McRobbie's claim that advice columns appeal to readers as a source of knowledge about otherwise culturally repressed or devalued topics. The readers in this study continually refer to the usefulness of advice columns, a claim which links magazine reading to the everyday experiences of teenage girls. And yet I have also argued that it is not content alone which gives these texts appeal. . . . regular columns and feature articles similarly provide information about beauty, romance, and sex. What gives these topics more appeal when information is framed as 'problems' rather than as 'information'?

Winship (1987) maintains that 'agony' columns can actually be a source of reading pleasure. For her, the peculiar pleasure of advice lies in the relief provided by confirmation that other people's problems are worse than the reader's own. From this perspective, Winship claims that, however appealing, problem pages are not in women's interests because they reinforce both the privatized nature of magazine reading and notions that women's experiences of oppression are 'personal' rather than social problems. Like McRobbie, Winship argues that advice columns are anti-feminist because they demarcate boundaries between the private and the public: both McRobbie and Winship suggest that problem pages individualize and personalize women's experiences of oppression.

In contrast to both McRobbie's and Winship's claim that advice columns offer reading pleasure, however, McCracken suggests a somewhat opposite effect: 'The technique of question and answer encourages readers to think that their peers have written to the magazine with such problems. If a reader hasn't yet thought about herself in these fragmented terms, she should begin to do so if she wishes to be beautiful and share the concerns of her peers' (1993: 138). From this kind of reading McCracken characterizes advice columns as a potential source of anxiety and self-doubt. She claims that the authoritative tone which underlies answers to problems induces guilt and thus acts as a corrective to the otherwise pleasurable transgressions offered by fantasy elements in the text. In this way, McCracken maintains that although fantasy elements of women's magazines offer temporary release from the normative mechanisms of social control, advice columns guarantee ideological closure: while pleasurable inducements to consumption challenge or disrupt the boundaries of everyday life, advice to readers about their practical problems corrects any potential transgression of prescriptive femininity by encouraging readers to conform to established behavioural codes and standards.

Along with Winship and McRobbie, McCracken argues that, although appearing to address women's interests, women's magazines operate to reconstitute their oppression. What their analyses above have in common is reliance upon researcher rather than everyday readings.[6] In this chapter we begin instead with girls' readings. By starting our analysis from girls' accounts we have already begun to question many claims being advanced about the effect of teenzine reading. For example, we have seen that the community of teenage reading is real as well as discursive. Sharing favourite tidbits from magazines was a frequent pastime among readers:

> My friend *loves* doing the little surveys, like the 'Friends' survey and stuff. She always gets me to fill them out with her, or she'll ask me questions and we go through – actually, lately we've been going through them like crazy because it's grad. So we've been all going through those magazines you've listed, basically just for styles of grad dresses, and stuff like that. We've been going through them together a lot lately.
>
> (Seventeen-year-old Alexandra)

> If we're reading the magazine we'll talk about stuff in it. Like quizzes and – I don't know, if there is a question-and-answer like 'Dear Jill' and 'Dear Jack' – which is younger people's questions – we kind of read them and discuss them. Like if your boyfriend didn't talk to you or something and you don't know what to do and they [reader] asked what to do, then we'll start a conversation like 'What would you do?' and 'What would *you* do?' And everything. It gets into a conversation like that.
>
> (Fifteen-year-old Chelsea)

This sharing goes against the notion, described above, that advice columns individualize readers' experiences and difficulties of 'being women.' As we shall see, in this study advice columns are implicated in girls' construction of their social, as well as personal, world. We explore this process within the context of school culture in later chapters. Here Table 25.1 directs our attention to the advice columns, quizzes, and 'embarrassing moments' in teenzines.

> I read them with my friends and we might do the quizzes, or read through the questions. We have talked about the 'Say Anything' with my friends at basketball. It'd be like, 'Oh, you read *that* – eh?' and we'd laugh about it . . . If I find the 'Say Anything' hilarious, I'll phone up a friend and be like 'Oh

my God, listen to this!' Or I'll tell my mom because she thinks they're
funny.

(Fifteen-year-old Kirsten)

I do those little quizzes and tests with my friends. Usually after school I have
friends coming over and we sit there and we fantasize and read all these magazine articles, and 'Oh I wish that was me' and stuff like that [laughs]. We go,
'Oh, you should really like this article' or something like that – I'd go to
school and say that to my friends.

(Fourteen-year-old Lauren)

We have already seen from girls' accounts that their reading preferences are shaped by
texts which the girls deem to be 'realistic.' This notion of realism is important because
it is the basis for girls' claims that their magazines give them 'something useful' that
they can 'relate to.' . . .

Notes

1 See Ellen McCracken 1993 and Ballaster *et al.* 1991.
2 I do not find this suggestion to be supported by their data from discussions with readers,
   however. In fact, in the main, Ballaster *et al.* base their argument on their analysis of magazine texts, which they supplement with interview excerpts; in contrast, the current study
   uses interview data with girls as primary data, supplemented by analysis of magazine text.
3 We will see later that another dominant theme concerns the absence of social issues,
   especially racism and violence.
4 This comment suggests that the girls have actually looked for magazine fashion when shopping, however. While initial interviews included discussions of shopping for clothes for
   school, it soon became apparent that, although teenzine reading may be related to shopping, this topic requires a separate study.
5 This approach is one of three identified by McRobbie among feminist commentary on
   advice columns in women's magazines: realist, feminist, and Foucauldian (1991: pp.
   161–5).
6 Although McRobbie's position arises from her ethnographic research with young readers,
   her arguments outlined above are based on a discursive analysis (see McRobbie 1991: ch.
   6). Overall, *Feminism and Youth Culture: From Jackie to Just Seventeen* sheds little light on
   everyday, rather than researcher, reading of adolescent magazines, despite McRobbie's
   attention to the everyday 'doing' of gender.

Chapter 26

Esther Sonnet

'"JUST A BOOK", SHE SAID . . .'
Reconfiguring ethnography for the female readers of sexual fiction

> David looked out of his office door and saw that his secretary, Lisa Cresswell, was reading a book . . . He walked very softly across the carpet between them, intending to surprise her.
>
> Then he looked over her shoulder at what she was reading. His throat tightened and his heart thudded as he read, *She hung above him, gasping with suspense, and suddenly he seized her hips and pulled her down and she cried out as the great smooth shaft slid up inside her; filling her so magnificently that she screamed.*
>
> 'Christ', he hissed, his eyes skidding down the page, 'what on earth is this?'
>
> Lisa jumped and turned her elfin face to grin over her shoulder at him. 'Just a book,' she said, showing him the cover.
>
> (Juliet Hastings, *Deadly Affairs* 1997: 38-9)

THE CHARACTER OF SECRETARY Lisa Cresswell is a historically composite figure: a young woman who brazenly displays her pleasure in reading erotica at work. Confronting her male boss with the *female* consumption of sexually explicit narratives of female sexual pleasure, she is emblematic of the newly empowered 'post-feminist' who claims sex and its fictional representation for women as a right.[1] As the 'woman who reads', Lisa Cresswell is also a textual surrogate, or mirror image, for the reader of Juliet Hastings' erotic novel. This is a highly self-reflexive gesture that clearly signifies a 'knowing' awareness of contemporary concerns around transformations in contemporary mass-market fiction and its female audiences. More importantly, it prompts some fundamental questions in relation to previous ways of accounting for the audiences of women's popular fiction. Does erotica demand a different construction of its female readership than that invoked by popular romances? Do these sexually explicit fictions require a shift in the ways in which female readerships of mass-market fiction have previously been understood? What connections can be

made between Lisa Cresswell and her 'real' audience? Culturally, the erotically empowered secretary sits at the apex of major cultural challenges to traditional formulations of
women's sexuality, gender ideology and reading pleasure. Equally, the emergence of
mass market written erotica aimed directly at female readers is a hugely significant
development not least for academics who must now recognize that previous relations
between mass fiction, women's reading pleasure and feminism have to be reappraised.

By what means, then, can the 'actual' female audience of erotica be known? One
of the major avenues explored to account for female pleasure in reading has been the
ethnographic model associated chiefly with Janice Radway's (1984) study of romance
readers. I want to identify how this model produces – and then denies – the grounds
upon which knowledge of female reading pleasure might be built. This should demonstrate what is at stake in the quest for the 'real' audience of the new erotica for women.

The ethnographic turn

In a defensive new introduction to the 1991 reprint of her pioneering work *Reading
the Romance: Women, Patriarchy and Popular Literature* (1984), Radway responded to
numerous critics who, in the intervening years, had faulted her use of empiricist
ethnography to sustain her engagement with mass fiction audiences. Her adoption of
a mode of investigation derived not from indigenous literary studies but from anthro-
pology, she suggests, was part of a broader political shift in American universities,
aimed at securing methodological footing upon which popular (rather than elite) culture could enter academic cultural analysis. Ethnographic methodology effectively
abandoned the traditional terrain of 'high culture' literary studies and its concerns for
close textual analysis, canon construction and issues of aesthetic literary value. It
relocated literature instead within the social and historical communities of its users,
and thereby offered to 'guarantee a more accurate description of what a book meant
to a given audience'(Radway 1991: 5):

> If reading varied spatially and temporally, and one did wish to use literature
> in an effort to reconstruct culture, it would be necessary to connect partic-
> ular texts with the communities that produced and consumed them and to
> make some effort to specify how the individuals involved actually con-
> structed those texts as meaningful semiotic structures.
>
> (Radway, 1991: 4)

In the absence of awareness of the largely Marxist models of cultural studies developing simultaneously in Britain at CCCS, Radway explains that the anthropological
'turn' allowed her to map connections between popular literature and wider social
'belief systems' in ways that would incorporate (rather than exclude) the interpretations of its readers. As such, the study of the 'Smithton' romance readers has been
justly admired as a model of inquiry that gives methodological priority to 'how
actual communities read actual texts' (Radway 1991: 5). Further, ethnographic studies which ensure that 'actual subjects in history' appear as a vital dimension in the
social construction of 'meaning' are especially compelling for feminists; the meanings
attributed by the women readers of 'feminine' romance fiction to their activity are
granted high status and go far to offset the traditional cultural derogation of female

romance readers. It remains crucial for Radway that the view of romance readers as dupes (who willingly give up precious leisure time to take pleasure in 'compensatory' fictions that confirm their own subjection to the dictates of patriarchy) is counter-manded by their characterization in terms of personal agency and active resistance to those same dictates. To secure this, *Reading the Romance* insists on distinguishing 'ana-lytically between the significance of the *event* of reading and the meaning of the *text* constructed as its consequence' (Radway 1991: 7). From Radway's retrospective assessment of her work it is clear that its original impetus, to account for the way romances as *texts* were interpreted, cedes theoretical precedence to the way in which 'romance reading as a form of behaviour operated as a complex intervention in the ongoing life of actual social subjects, women who saw themselves first as wives and mothers' (Radway 1991: 7). Her 'unexpected' central finding was that individually atomised and socially isolated housewives engage in a proto-feminist struggle to appropriate time for romance reading not simply for its own pleasure but as a 'decla-ration of independence', an assertion of autonomous agency and resistance. While this assertion of self is fully integrated within the daily pattern of a domestic life absorbed in fulfilling the demands of husband, home and children, Radway's Smithton women rescue the act of romance reading from ideological complicity by using it to articu-late expressions of personal 'dissatisfaction' and 'protest' (Radway 1991: 220). Such a position thwarts functionalist assumptions that the final assessment of the ideological 'effect' of romance reading can be located in the pleasure taken in the textual clo-sure/resolution of the formation of the perfectly gendered heterosexual couple of heroine and hero. Reading as an act 'suggests that real people can use the romance to address their unmet needs experienced precisely because that ideal relationship is made highly improbable by the institutional structure and engendering practices of contemporary society' (Radway 1991: 221). Radway concludes that her ethno-graphic (rather than textual) methodology serves to highlight instead the 'complicated and contradictory ways in which the romance recognizes and thereby protests the weaknesses of patriarchy and the failure of traditional marriage even as it apparently acts to assert the perfection of each and to teach women how to *re*-view their own imperfect relationships in such a way that they seem unassailable' (Radway 1991: 221). However, for Ien Ang (1996), Radway's project of assessing how 'commodities like mass-produced texts are selected, purchased, constructed and used by real people with previously existing needs, desires, attentions, and interpretative strategies' (Radway 1991: 221) is fundamentally *compromised*. Ang is incisive in her deconstruction of some of the epistemological assumptions of Radway's 'ethnographic turn', not least of which is the 'dramatization' of uncomfortable tensions generated between the object/subject relations inherent in the ethnographic project: between feminist aca-demic and romance readers, feminist politics and 'ordinary life' or, most plainly, between feminism and women. Radway's view is that 'we' as 'feminists' must:

> develop strategies for making that dissatisfaction and its causes consciously available to romance readers and by learning how to encourage that protest in such a way that it will be delivered in the arena of actual social relations rather than acted out in the imagination, we might join hands with women who are, after all, our sisters and together imagine a world whose subsequent creation would lead to the need for a new fantasy altogether.
>
> (Radway 1991: 220).

In this, argues Ang, for all the epistemological weight granted to the readers' inter-pretation of the meaning of their act of romance reading, *Reading the Romance* cannot escape the logic of its 'recruitist' mission – to convert the Smithton women's sub-conscious and ill-defined reading pleasure into a conscious and explicit form of feminist politics. Their pleasure in reading is thus accounted for in highly instru-mentalist terms. As for many other critics who employ but rarely these days acknowledge a Marxist cultural studies conception of readerships, 'pleasure' is ulti-mately the *conduit of ideology*. Following Adorno's Frankfurt School tenet that a concept of 'leisure' is in itself ideological (in the sense that it is experienced as a 'pri-vate' domain outside of capitalist relations of work yet is wholly produced by them), Gramscian theory permits greater sensitivity to the specific mechanisms by which cap-italism produces and reproduces its hegemony through participation in popular leisure activities. Angela McRobbie's (1990) early work on the readers of *Jackie* magazine thus identifies that an ideology of 'romantic individualism' effectively organises and nor-malises female teenage cultural expectations through the construction of feelings, emotions and experience as private, as individually rather than socially determined. Some years later, Dawn H. Currie's (1999) study of 'actual' teenage readers of girl magazines elucidates that what is experienced by its readers as 'private' and simply entertaining 'fun' in reality confirms the view that the 'construction and maintenance of any social order entails the constructions of pleasures which secure participation in that order' (Currie 1999: 155) for their young female readers, teen magazines are sites in which 'fun' and 'pleasure' are thus intrinsically 'ideological'.

The problem set by the ethnographic model and its variants is that the ethnogra-pher's desire to grant full autonomy to her study's subjects is always compromised by the equal desire to make their subjective attributions more broadly culturally signifi-cant. In short, the interpretative framework – here, 'gender ideology' – ensures that 'fun' and 'pleasure' are understood instrumentally, that is, it over-determines the ascriptions of meaning made by the subjects to their reading activity. Conversely, what are the theoretical consequences of divorcing reading pleasure from wider social issues and dispensing with concepts such as 'ideology' or 'discourse'?

Evidently, avoiding this methodological trap runs the risk of evacuating the whole purpose of critical/political analysis; granting radical autonomy to audience 'pleasure' without an interpretative framework within which to locate the meaning of that pleasure is, epistemologically and politically, of limited value. However, the concept of 'fantasy' might profitably be explored as a term that seems to disconnect pleasure from direct control by ideology, or at least offers a mediating bridge between them. The idea of fiction as 'fantasy' should not be confused with the delusional sense that defines 'incorrect models of reality'. Rather, the concept of reader–text interaction as fantasy offers a degree of individual latitude and variation to reading encounters that ideologically-susceptible 'pleasure' alone cannot substantiate. Even so, it is within an epistemological context that is fraught with such problems that I want to locate popular erotica for women since it rests crucially upon envisaging women's 'real' fantasies as its founding rationale. Chiefly, I want to argue that, if efforts to 'know' the 'real' audience are destined to repeat prior epistemological values, then it is methodologically important to supply an alternative framework through which 'the audience' can be made visible. The foundation of my approach lies in envisag-ing the audience as a *construct*: rather than looking to the subjective meanings attributed to acts of reading by 'real' readers, I want to identify the commercial nexus

(Radway's 'institutional matrix') that *positions its readers* through a range of techniques from the invocation of broader cultural identities such as post-feminism, to genre categorization, commercial presentation, editorial instructions and audience address. Primarily, the focus here is on how the series works to re-locate the audience for erotica from the domain of romance reading. My argument is that the production of fiction which promises to give women 'what they really want' does so by explicitly rejecting the pleasure (and with it therefore the ideology) held to govern women's consumption of the romance, in favour of 'real' female desire and sexual fantasy.

Romance no more: pornography for women

In its commercial presentation, visual cover style and narrative resumés, the Black Lace series signalled an intentional address to the pre-existing markets for popular women's fiction. The series conformed to the established generic expectations of mass romance reading in splitting titles between 'historicals' and 'contemporaries' which mirrors the broad categorisation that classifies and markets the 'category romance' for the major publishers in the UK and America – Mills & Boon, Harlequin, HarperCollins, Random House, Pocket, Penguin Putnam, Kensington, Robinson, Avon, Bantam and Dell. Generic proximity to the formal conventions of romantic fiction placed them initially within pre-existing commercial narrative formulae for female-addressed fiction. Located in ordinary High Street shops, railway stations and bookstores – sometimes alongside New English Library's 'Interlover' and Headline/Delta's 'Liaison' series, selected titles from Nexus, X-Libris and 'Hard Candy' from Masquerade Books, Inc. (Harlequin) – the Black Lace series was launched by Virgin Publishing into the erotica market in July 1993. Selling two million copies of a hundred different titles in a global market extending to USA, Canada, New Zealand and South Africa and with foreign rights sold to sixteen countries in Europe as well as China, Virgin's erotica imprint professes to sell more copies than all other erotic fiction combined. The series, however, was not simply another imprint launched within a highly lucrative market for sexual fiction.[2] It was launched under a powerful new rubric – 'erotic fiction *for* women *by* women' – that defined a significant reconfiguration of traditional relations posed between women, writing and reading pleasure.

Signalled as 'new' and 'empowering' *for women*, the Black Lace series in particular seemed to proclaim a form of 'liberation' for its readers. My study of this genre of commercial-scale fiction suggests its claim to uniqueness lies at the convergence of two 'contracts' offered to its female readers to 'liberate' them from two major forms of ideological dominance: from traditionally male-defined pornography and from the sexual conformity of romance fiction. Against the historical dominance of misogynistic pornography, the notion of erotic fiction written *by women* suggested a revolutionary subversion of the textual, sexual and commercial economies of production that had previously denied women access to the pleasures of erotica. And to Freud's eternal question of 'what do women want?' Black Lace's banner of 'erotic fiction for women by women' boldly asserted that it is women who had begun to frame the terms of an answer. Equally, Black Lace fictions are avowedly set against the sexual constrictions and ideological traditionalism of putatively 'sexless' romance fiction:

Ladies who lust are a faithful market. And a big one. While men will always reach for the top shelf and go for the gyno, women want words . . . Where once the female reader liked to read about kindly Mills & Boon medics living in market towns, now they are absorbed by dark alleys and drag queens. Engagement rings and coy kisses have been replaced by whipping and ramming.

(Berens 2000: 20)

Set against the now even more 'guilty pleasures' of romance reading and its concomitant celebration of traditional female passivity, Black Lace titles are imbued with a transgressive, political edge that equates 'whipping' and 'ramming' with freedom. Black Lace narratives, then, are dually positioned: marketed within the established commercial structures of women's popular fiction while making a radical departure in content by enjoining the erotic fantasy of female fulfilment through sexual (rather than emotional) self-awareness and sexual pleasure to the romantic novel form.[3] But as Moody (1998), Thurston (1987) and Dixon (1998) have explored, modern romance narratives have long exhausted the traditional monogamous, virginal 'love and marriage' formula held by its critics to define it. Proving highly responsive to changing social definitions of female sexuality and to the place and meaning of sex within the emotional experiences encompassed by romance stories, it is equally important to place Black Lace within a larger field of fiction in which the primary distinction between asexual 'romance' and sexually explicit 'erotica' has undergone profound shifts in meaning. For example, the launch of a basically romantic narrative series that also incorporates varying degrees of sexually explicit scenes (such as Mills & Boon's *Temptation*) evidently attests to a female readership more comfortable with graphic representations of sex than the infamous 'romantic' ellipses had previously acknowledged.

But while this may be of some note as a development within the confines of the modern romance genre, in the context of other modes of mass popular fiction which are addressed specifically to a female readership, a preoccupation with sex and erotic encounters is not. In this broader context, the emergence of Black Lace – 'Erotic Fiction by Women for Women' – is perhaps the logical endpoint of transformations in women's popular fiction which, since the 'Permissive' era of Sexual Liberation of the 1970s, has seen its increasing sexualization. Through the pioneering feminist-inspired novels of Marilyn French, Lisa Alther and Erica Jong to the 'bonkbusters' of Danielle Steele, Jilly Cooper or Colleen McCullough, the 'sex-and-shopping' beach novels of Jackie Collins then to the 'media celebrity' novels of Julie Burchill, Edwina Currie and Kathy Lette, female addressed fiction has claimed sex, sexuality and the quest for sexual fulfilment as a, if not *the*, definitive domain of late twentieth century female experience.[4] But the Black Lace series is undeniably generically related to the mass romance market and its strident espousal of female-addressed erotica evidently produces anxieties around categorization already invoked by increasing sexual content in romance stories. (When does a 'romance with sex' become an 'erotic romance' or 'romantic erotica' become 'pornography'? How much sexual adventuring can a romance tolerate and still remain recognizably a romance? How far does sexual exploration and erotic experience countermand the romance's imperative to create the heterosexual romantic couple?) In this respect, it is worth noting Carol Thurston's view that such difficulties are as much the result of the manner in which romantic fiction became a subject of academic study as with any substantive issues of classification:

> Because of the heavy focus on the so-called Harlequin romance during the 1970s – studies in which 'Harlequin' often was used synonymously with 'romantic fiction', feeding the assumption that all romance novels are alike – most scholars either ignored or overlooked the 'bodice-ripper'.
>
> (Thurston, 1987: 9)

Thurston rightly argues that over-emphasis on the Harlequin/Mills & Boon romance has been made at the expense of the fact that historically, publishers since the 1970s *have* been publishing erotic material for women but 'stories were allowed to evolve as erotica without much notice and under the guise of a different label – romance'. Significantly, the Restoration, Eighteenth Century, Civil War, Regency or Western historical settings of the 'bodice-ripper' (which had largely defined the erotic romance) were in America, by 1983, superseded by contemporary ones. Thurston's sales figures confirm the massive circulation of the erotic romance, making its academic obscurity seem staggering. Of the 50 new series romance titles appearing on the market each month, at least 30 were erotic romances amounting to 4-5 million copies of erotic series romances per month or about 55 million a year, a 'conservative estimate based on an average print run of 150,000 copies (though print runs for some romance lines are known to be as high as 500,000, especially Harlequin and Silhouette, both of which have large foreign sales, and even higher for best selling authors)' (Thurston 1987: 11). Thurston suggests that these were not simply orthodox romances with the odd sex scene thrown in but, rather than 'functioning as a stronghold of conservatism', this 'type of novel has traced the evolution of the . . . liberated woman with a responsiveness unmatched by any other mass entertainment medium, changing as both its most articulate consumers and the marketplace changed.' (Thurston 1987: 7). This is diametrically opposed to the hackneyed view of romance advanced by Peter Mann (1979): 'romantic fiction is always changing gradually to reflect the views of its readers, but it rarely attempts to go beyond the more conservative mores of its period . . .'; 'Immoral behaviour, especially pre-marital or extra-marital liaisons, either do not happen or, if they do occur, are clearly labelled as wrong and likely to result in unhappiness' (Mann 1979, in Thurston, 1987: 9). Given Thurston's longer historical view of the way in which erotic fiction markets have been concealed by academics and by circumspect American publishers, Black Lace signals that it is the more general cultural exposure of women to reading erotica/erotic romances that has allowed Virgin to dispense with the need for the 'disguise' of reading romance fiction. Nonetheless, Black Lace fictions, regardless of the truth of their claims to novelty or uniqueness as women's erotica, clearly unsettle the generic, narrative and ideological boundaries marking 'romance' off from 'pornography'. But I want to ask what and why it matters to be able to say that *Desire Under Capricorn* (Louisa Francis), *Shadowplay* (Portia Da Costa) or *Silken Chains* (Jodie Nicol) is 'romantic', 'erotic romance' or more plainly 'pornography for women'? Leaving aside the possible political import of such judgement, my point is that attempting to isolate a single title in order to make that assessment brings into relief how crucial *categorization* is in assigning prior meaning to mass popular fictions. My use of the term 'categorization', however, is a complex one and goes beyond the mere genre labelling of books by publishers. It is intended to invoke some larger questions about method in studies of popular fiction by elucidating the heterogeneous economic and cultural work that 'categorization' performs.

Categorizing for audiences; audiences categorizing

From a methodological point of view, any consideration of the content of individual works (and their eventual classification) must be preceded by an understanding of their *extra-textual construction*. By this, I mean that the categorization process that Black Lace sets in play brings sharply into focus a network of *contexts of production and consumption*. These 'contexts' should be understood to operate simultaneously, as dynamic structures that *collectively* function to 'place' the individual text (and its reader) in categories that are ideologically 'meaningful'. In the economic circuit of production and consumption, books are commodities that belong within commercial structures of production and exchange (writers, editors, publishers, marketers, distributors, booksellers and individual buyers). Categorization by genre, by series and by individual writers, then, aids in the rationalizing process of commodity exchange by 'branding' books more effectively to align potential purchasers with desired products, to guarantee repeated sales through repetition in niche markets and in some measure to rationalize production. However, fiction belongs within much richer circuits of meaning than this crude economic model would suggest: in the semantic circuit of production and consumption, the cultural significance and 'meanings' of a text are produced in a context for consumption constructed by authors, editors, journalists, academics, interviews, fan magazines and readers. In other words, as the 'romance market grew bigger during the 1970s and then more competitive, the symbiotic relationship between readers and publishers became increasingly complex, more so, for example, than the one commonly existing between such products as toothpaste or beer and their consumers' (Thurston 1987: 7).

The dogged view underwriting much thinking on mass fiction markets is that it is *female* readers who are most susceptible to cynically marketed and standardized 'products'. But since the 70s, the notion of the reader as passive 'consumer' has, in the field of romantic fiction as in others, had to shift so far as to make it redundant. Any concept of the 'role of the reader' of contemporary popular fiction must take account of the extra-textual structures that assist in the unofficial yet potent 'categorization' process, not least the publishing industry's own conception of its readership. The self-identified contemporary romance reader (and, by extension, the erotic fiction reader) has a network of avenues through which to intervene actively in the text's circulation – specialist magazines featuring reader reviews, global information exchange on internet web sites, news group, fan correspondence, publisher's questionnaires, conventions, reading groups, book share schemes. In a circuit of exchange supervising the passage of texts, the role of the reader is vital in determining the cultural 'meaning' of the distinctions which are 'outside' of the text 'itself' yet construct its cultural context of consumption.

I have found no better example of this in practice than an American publication *Romantic Times*, a monthly magazine devoted to the romance fiction trade.[5] Alongside full colour publishers' promotions and straightforward booksellers' best seller lists sit numerous *Hello*-style author profiles, series previews and articles on individual sub-genres

such as 'Medical Suspense' or 'Romances Set in Texas'. But the magazine is dominated by the presence of the Reader: Reader Profiles, Letters to the Editor and
'Who's Reading What?' features are accompanied by Reader's Best lists, Books
Wanted features, personal testimonies to the pleasure and power of particular
romances in reader's lives as well as announcements of relevant websites, tours, conventions and events such as the Booklovers Club trips to Scandinavia or Caribbean
cruises. In acting as a mediator between readers, writers and industry, *Romantic Times*
articulates a strong sense of a shared community offered through participation in
female-addressed fiction culture.

One significant aspect of this culture is that the fundamental binary that is held to
consign the mass fiction reader to passivity – Author/Reader – is largely inoperative.
Throughout the magazines are repeated testimonies that romance authors are primarily ordinary romance readers who 'just' took their love of reading romances one
step further while, conversely, readers actively identify themselves as potential writers
and are solicited as active participants in critical assessments of issues such as narrative,
genre, realism and historical authenticity. The agents in the circuit of exchange whom
I argue perform cultural 'categorization' can be identified in the microcosm of 'The
Best Books Nominations' in April 1998: 'Each year ballots are sent to our Bookstores
That Care Network asking 1000 booksellers to vote for their favorite (sic) books,
authors and promotions based on overall popularity with their customers, staff and
personal picks'. Award categories include Best Historical, Best Contemporary, Best
Category Romance, Best Paranormal/Futuristic Romance, Best Regency, Best
Time-Travel, Best Romantic Suspense, Best Love & Laughter Romance, Best Sequel
(or Book in a Series), Best Bookstore Promotion, Best Poster, Best Cover and, my
favourite, Best Book Mark. More than a simple 'shopping guide', then, *Romantic
Times* defines a participatory culture of consumption that is predicated, in Pierre
Bourdieu's (1984) terms, on the exercise of 'distinction', of taste. The magazine
exhibits a proliferation of classification, of meaningful distinctions which, I suggest,
makes the monolithic genre concept of 'the romance' meaning*less*. Individual titles are
ordered by publishers' imprints: joining the more familiar Harlequin divisions
(Harlequin American, Delta Justice, Heart of Texas, Intrigue, Love and Laughter,
Presents, Romance, Super-romance, Temptation) and Silhouette (Desire, Intimate
Moments, Romance, Special Edition, 36 Hours, Yours Truly), Penguin Putnam has
Jove (Historical and Contemporary), Signet (Regency), Topaz (Historical) and Onyx
(Suspense) while Kensington offers Zebra (Time Travel, Historical and
Contemporary), Arabesque (Contemporary) and Regency (Regency). Nonetheless,
readers, booksellers and reviewers' classifications (through Monthly Top Picks, awards
and ratings) cut across the formal categorization (through series, imprints and sub-
genres) offered by publishing houses. Simultaneously, titles are ranked and star-rated
across publishers categories, by sub-genres –science fiction romance, series romance or
detective romance – though an individual title may be all of these at once. Yet one
article groups titles in a romance sub-genre category 'Mainstream & New Reality
Romance' then further distinguishes titles (within this increasingly unstable category)
according to Suspense, Romantic Suspense, Ghost (Historical), Ghost
(Contemporary), Fantasy, Mystery, Angel, Futuristic, Reincarnation, Time-Travel,
Contemporary, Contemporary Romance, New Age, Vampire and Multicultural. In
a conventional Gold Medal ratings schema, stars are awarded (1 – Acceptable to 5 –
Extraordinary) though interestingly it is not conformity to generic expectations that

are rewarded – 5 stars are 'Rarely given. Reserved for groundbreaking books that transcend the genre'.

The dizzying proliferation of distinctions and classifications in *Romantic Times* clearly subverts the possibility of stabilizing the monolithic category 'romance' which, as a result, increasingly appears as the academic construct that it is. Acknowledging the 'categorization' circuits involved in consuming women's fiction provides a much more finely nuanced way of demonstrating that the category 'romance' is evidently multiple and heterogeneously classified. This puts a different frame around the issue of how Black Lace (as 'erotica') is 'categorized': Black Lace is ardently marketed on the premise of its 'newness' and therefore by what it declares itself 'not' – romance. But it is clearly vital to dispense with the either/or, 'erotica'/'romance' binary to consider instead how Black Lace is contextually situated within the range of distinctions operating in the field of female-addressed popular fictions.

One way of gauging its claim to unprecedented sexual explicitness is to evaluate the way in which 'sexual explicitness' is itself used in the 'categorization' process of its generic kin. In a taxonomy that would make Jorgé Luis Borges blush, the *Romantic Times* is keen to offer readers guidelines on the 'sensuality' of individual works within, for example, the Historical Romance class:

Sensuality Key:
Sexy – Borders on erotica and sometimes includes alternative lifestyles. Very graphic sex.
Spicy – Similar to Sexy but not erotica. Very explicit sex.
Very Sensual – Not as explicit as Spicy but goes beyond conventional lovemaking.
Sensual – Most romance novels fall into this category. Conventional lovemaking. Explicit Sex.
Sweet – May or may not include lovemaking. No explicit sex.[6]

This allows for the possibility that what publishers classify as erotica, *Romantic Times* and romance readers might classify according to the schema as 'Spicy'. But could any classificatory endeavour determine substantively the difference between 'graphic sex' and 'very explicit sex', and between 'Sexy' which 'borders on erotica' and 'Spicy' which is 'similar to Sexy but not erotica'? More pointedly, what is the meaning of the distinction between 'conventional lovemaking' and 'explicit sex' that defines the majority of romances as 'Sensual' or 'Sweet'? What lies beyond 'conventional lovemaking' and 'explicit sex' but before 'erotica'? The setting of categories according to representations of sexuality, however ill-defined, can be taken as evidence of the impact of sexualisation on the romance fiction market, particularly in the production of romances which are specifically marked (and marketed) by its absence.

But what else is performed in categorizing for the consumer/reader (in an ostensibly non-judgemental way) the degrees of sexualization currently manifested in women's mass fiction? The Sensuality Rating functions to police boundaries that leave the space of 'erotica' (or at least a *concept* of erotica) outside that of 'romance' proper. This has normative and conservative functions in restating the age-old view that female sexuality is predicated on an emotional dichotomy between 'sex' and 'love'. Stabilizing the ideological force of that distinction in the notion of 'conventional lovemaking', the reference to 'alternative lifestyles' clearly reinforces the sense of the

Romantic Times community as straight, heterosexual and culturally 'centred' enough for these categories to function meaningfully. Between the 'sensuality' categories, though, there is a high degree of slippage. Such difficulties in categorization might be taken more progressively to indicate instead the *failure* of holding the cultural categories 'love'/romance – 'sex'/erotica apart, or, better, of a profound weakening of its contemporary ideological valence. This necessitates moving consideration of Black Lace away from women's genre fiction and towards larger determinants that act on the readers' 'categorization' process, and to transformations of Western women's relationship to Black Lace's self-announced domain: to erotica and sexual expression as it figures the reader in post-feminist heterosexuality.

As evidence of a shift in the public visibility of 'female-defined' sexuality, Black Lace confirms David Evans' observation that, while still 'severely proscribed by femininity', 'female sexuality has nevertheless become active, recreational, material, independent, consumerist and consumed, a key site of conflict, resistance and division' (Evans, 1993: 41). Its appearance certainly embodies contradictions around sexual pleasure and female desire that refuse to be easily positioned against older feminism's pro- or anti-pornography politics.[7]

Reading sex: the post-feminist audience

Post-feminist thinking during the 1990s developed two distinct trends of thought relevant here. The simplest definition suggests that feminism has achieved its major goals and become irrelevant to the lives of young women today. The 'post' therefore signifies a 'going beyond' or moving on from feminism, with the implicit assumption that its critiques and demands have been accommodated and absorbed far enough to permit 'return' to pre-feminist pleasures now transformed in meaning by a feminist consciousness. Accordingly, popular culture since the 1980s has produced Madonna, Tank Girl, 'cyber-babe' Lara Croft, and the Spice Girls and more latterly *Ally McBeal* and *Sex and the City* as evidence of new models for female identity, sexual/personal agency and sexual display.[8] With this reading, Black Lace fictions assert the existence of a 'New Woman' of the 1990s and beyond – distinguished from all other versions of the New Woman by a cultural climate in which women can now be traditionally 'feminine' and sexual in a manner utterly different in meaning from either pre-feminist or non-feminist versions demanded by phallocentrically defined female heterosexuality. The current post-feminist 'return' to feminine pleasures (to dress, cosmetics, visual display, to Wonderbra 'sexiness') is 'different' because, it is suggested, it takes place within a social context fundamentally altered by the achievement of feminist goals. The emergence of erotic fiction specifically for women can be located as part of this wider process through which a new female heterosexual identity is articulated around the active consumption of erotica. If it is feminism that enabled women to do the political work necessary to explore new modes of female sexuality outside of patriarchal givens, it is post-feminism which reclaims for women the 'illicit' pleasures of pornography.

A second version of post-feminism, more closely influenced by post-structuralist dissolution of feminism's reliance on 'identity politics', is underpinned by a narrative that casts post-feminist concern for 'difference' (race, ethnicity, class, sexual orientation, age and nationality) as a *liberation* from Second Wave feminism retrospectively constructed as a monolithic, homogeneous, puritanical and sometimes tyrannical discourse. Biddy Martin neatly encapsulates this in identifying post-feminism in 'polemical and ultimately reductionist accounts of the varieties of feminist approaches to just one feminism, guilty of the humanist trap of making a self-same, universal category of "women" – defined as other than men – the subject of feminism. At its worst, feminism has been seen as more punitively policing than mainstream culture' (Martin 1998: 12).

Taking both strands of post-feminism together, regardless of their legitimacy, would suggest a need to re-conceptualize the terms upon which a feminist-informed reading of the audience for commercial pornography for women might be made. Specifically, the post-feminism of the Black Lace texts can be found in their contradictory relationship to feminism's politicization of heterosexual pleasure. Viewed in this way, Black Lace fictions are revealing as popular cultural representations of historical shifts in discourses around feminism and female sexuality. Those shifts centre on the re-positioning of commodified pornography to align with current notions of post-feminist women's 'personal empowerment' and of sexual pleasure as a form of capitalist consumer 'entitlement'. While I am hugely sceptical about these claims, the terms of intervention in the mass popular women's fiction market are especially significant for a feminist reading of current notions on the relationship between women, politics and sexuality. Michel Foucault's oft-invoked notion of sexuality as *discourse* might fruitfully be applied here to explain how Black Lace situates its claims to be a new discourse of female pleasure (Foucault 1979).

Observing 'discourse' in Foucault's sense of bringing together power, knowledge *and* pleasure, I am concerned to identify the ways in which a commercial press proffers to 'reinvent' female sexuality within a historically unprecedented conjunction of consumerist commodity consumption. In particular, the ways in which a capitalist mass market press invokes discourses around female sexuality, feminism and the pleasures of reading sex in order to imbricate both 'power' and 'knowledge' in a specific formation of contemporary (hetero)sexuality rest, above all, upon a conception of the post-feminist female reader as self-empowered *consumer*.

One of the industry's techniques for 'knowing' its audience is the tick box questionnaire provided at the back of the novels. In the Editor's Response to the questionnaires returned, the female readership is defined by employment and age: 'Accounts Admin in her twenties', 'Bank Clerk in her forties', 'PR Executive in her twenties' and 'Journalist in her twenties'. As the age group is limited, the Ideal Reader emerges as a white-collar professional 20–40 year old presumably with enough disposable income regularly to pay £4.99 for each new title. Beyond individual pleasure, then, the newly empowered reader of Black Lace utilizes a commodified form of popular culture to signal alignment with a collective identity which exists only through that form. By connecting women in a shared fantasy world, the Black Lace philosophy mobilizes a rhetoric of community and collective female identity created around sexual fantasy. Consumption of erotica, then, works to reinforce the cultural identity of post-feminist women who are defined by their public place in the world of work and are therefore entitled to self-chosen gratification – 'It's about time we had books like this for women. I loved it', 'At last. No holds barred for the female reader', 'All women, like men, fantasize about sex. You have created what all women want and the price is just right' and 'A chance, at last, for females to enjoy erotic fiction'. Positioned as answering the needs set up by feminist demands, then, and couched in the language of revolution and change, the Black Lace fictions work by *legitimating* a space in which women can project their 'deepest' fantasies. But what is actually being legitimated? Why do women feel they must have their 'own' pornography when written pornography *per se* is widely enough available for those women who wish to use it? Perhaps the primary value of Black Lace lies with the simple functioning of giving women 'permission' to read and use written erotica in their sexual development. However, Foucault's observation that Western societies have produced discourses which construct sexuality as a force or instinct repressed by taboo and social strictures is again germane. This produces a unique conception of the series' readership that can be identified through the means by which Black Lace as a publishing event is framed specifically in terms of *feminist* intervention.

Is pornography feminism?

Having become intrigued by the emergence of the Black Lace series, I approached Virgin Publishing with a view to discussing the rationale for its appearance. Even at a general level, my interview with the Series Editor Kerri Sharp was conducted with full awareness of feminist thinking on the complexity of legitimating sexual fantasy spaces for women. Sharp's publishing career began after her academic interest in female sexuality led her to consider the historical forces which have denied women equal access to sexual fantasy material; her explicit understanding of the importance of Black Lace is that it has 'taken erotic publishing out of the hands of the sleazy porn merchants and made it available in every high street in Britain' (Black Lace Newsletter No. 1, Feb 1997). 'Only in this century has female sexual desire been gradually rediscovered. And now, as in many other areas of life, women expect to be treated on the same terms as men' (ibid.). Broadly defined, the publishing rationale is a response to a perceived need for equalising power relations for women in the sphere of pornography. Black Lace, then, expresses feminist aims. The Editor's Guidelines (August 1999) for prospective authors define the ethos:

> Talking of power differentials, we have no objection to publishing novels heavily slanted towards SM and/or bondage or fetishism, either with men dominant, women dominant, or both. But we will not publish a novel that encourages or condones hatred of women; or which suggests that all women should be, or enjoy being, subjugated to men in real life. So be careful.
>
> (Sharp 1999: 7)

There are three other ways in which those aims are articulated: through discourses around female authorship, on the reader's right to pleasure and of 'healthy' female sexuality.

Authorship and the everyday

Firstly, the fictions are framed as directly issuing out of feminist claims for women to be able to 'speak' sex in an authentic or non-colonized fashion. To do this, a language of 'female authenticity' is deployed with regard to notions of origination and authorship: the texts are sold on the pledge that the fictions are written for women only *by* women:

> Women like the fact that these books have been written and packaged specifically for them. Black Lace is written by women, from the female point of view, and with women's desires and tastes in mind.
>
> (Publicity review of readers' response)

These are, then, resolutely separatist women-only spaces. But while the intention to provide a wholly women-centred contract between publisher, author and reader sits well with the radical feminist technique of making alternative spaces outside of patriarchal traditions and practices, I would want to question what is at work in constructing erotica for and by 'women only'.

The series' publicity material includes a biography for each author detailing her lifestyle and writing philosophy. Fredrica Alleyn (author of seven titles including *Cassandra's Conflict*, *Dark Obsession* and *Deborah's Discovery*) believes that 'erotic fiction as a genre is an exciting and free area for women writers': 'At last women have the freedom to openly admit their sexual fantasies and read books based on female fantasies rather than male ones'. Juliet Hastings (author of five titles including *White Rose Ensnared*, *Forbidden Crusade* and *The Hand of Amun*) thinks that writing for Black Lace is 'the most erotic thing I can do on my own' while for Sarah Hope-Walker (author of *The Gift of Shame* and *Unfinished Business*) 'writing erotica is no big deal for Sarah. She considers sex to be as important as eating and sleeping and feels that until recently society has been educated to regard it as something that is dirty'. The great significance attached to the authorship of each title, then, is inseparable from the question of gender – it is *women* who are claiming the political and social position from which to produce erotica for other women and the sense of challenging cultural taboos, of transgressing known parameters, is strongly conveyed through the idea that, for women, engaging with erotica at all is a bold and independent act of self-will. However, if women openly enjoying the writing of erotica is one of the fruits of feminist demands for equality in all spheres of cultural life, it is curious to find that the author's biographies are carefully constructed so that an interest in erotic literature is balanced by 'healthy' interests such as 'walking her two dogs and swimming' (Fredrica Alleyn) or 'singing (she is a proficient soprano), and her husband, Jonathon' (Juliet Hastings). The bravery of these pioneers is, then, somewhat undercut by their location in the realm of the everyday: the effect is to *reassure* the readership that they will be taken to places in sexual fantasy that ordinary women with ordinary needs and desires would want to go.

Such a reading is further reinforced if the emphasis on the female-authoredness of the texts is taken as a form of guarantee that the content will not work against the interests of the readership. There is in this an awareness of anti-pornography feminist analysis that so fervently asserts a deep connection between consumption of pornography and subconscious sexual corruption. Robin Morgan's tenet that 'Pornography is the theory, rape is the practice' has, as several commentators have remarked, a much wider cultural currency than parochial debates within feminism largely because of the way in which it fits so easily with New Right, pro-family, pro-censorship politics. In this context, the femaleness of the author works to safeguard women readers: any suspicion that women might be unwittingly exploited or degraded by consuming erotica (if written by men) is alleviated by a female author. Black Lace poses itself as a new alternative where previously women's use of pornography would bring with it the bad conscience of being complicit in the objectification of other women: regardless of the content of the fictions, the series announces itself as a 'safe' space for a constructive revisioning of pornography for women readers. In this sense, Black Lace situates itself as part of what it claims is a historically unprecedented process of decolonization: challenging male-centred cultural practices by decolonizing the language of sex to stake out the territory of 'authentic' female desire. Kerri Sharp's editorial instructions to new writers make it explicit that 'erotic fiction for women by women' must make its way against an inherited tradition of written male pornography. That only a *female* author is able to accomplish this testifies to the tenacity of the notion that it is the author of a text who is responsible for its meanings. While most contemporary theories of reading have long dispensed with such intentionalism, it is interesting to see the use to which an essentialist 'female authenticity' is put here: the connection between female authorship, authorial intention, the kind of specifically 'feminine' sexual fantasies produced and the meanings of those fantasies for the readership assumes that there is an untroubled passage of meaning and understanding between women simply by the fact of being women.

Sexual pleasure and feminist entitlement

A second way in which the Black Lace series is embedded in the discourses of feminism is through its use of a language of *entitlement*. Given the historically myriad forms of radical critique that feminist politics have made, it is always more than a little disappointing to be confirmed in the view that it is liberal feminism which has found most fertile ground in Western countries because of its compatibility with individualist ideologies of self and society. Feminism of a high liberalist variety is predicated on the rights of the *individual* woman and is largely exhausted by critiques of public institutions in perpetuating social inequality (law, education, employment). Liberalism appeals to the 'rights' of the individual and liberal feminism seeks to challenge institutional sexism but has traditionally left the private sphere outside of politics. However, the last two decades have seen a shift of liberal feminist assumptions around 'entitlement' to the domain of relationships, sexuality and to personal fulfilment through sexual pleasure. Black Lace expresses a form of individualistic feminism of the *Cosmopolitan* variety which fits easily with a view of sexuality in which women can make 'demands' for what is their birthright: equal sexual gratification. If the linchpin of liberalism is its appeal to reason, then who could possibly refuse the logic of women wanting to take their 'rightful' place alongside those men who have debarred them from their personal fantasies and thus from sexual fulfilment in erotica? As a pro-pornography position, this is actually quite compelling but what it fails to provide is any analysis that connects the power relations enacted in male-defined pornography to the broader continuum of male-dominated culture. In other words, without some consideration of whether and in what ways pornography is currently related to sexist structures in society, the simple assertion of women's 'right' to consume erotica splits pornography from the social conditions which feminists have fought hard to establish necessarily locates it within politics.

Further, while one assumes that the politics of entitlement to read erotica is staked against *male* control of women's access to porn, it is interesting that several authors pose their work against the strictures of Political Correctness they find inhibiting. It does not need much interpretation to recognize the target here is anti-pornography feminism though this also subsumes any version of feminism that wishes to politicise sexual representation. It seems that the *frisson* of readers' pleasure is thus increased if this pleasure is bought at the cost of Political Correctness. In other words, the logic of the position declares that 'it is alright to read erotica even if the anti-pornography feminists wouldn't like it. In fact it is more fun to read erotica *because* the anti-pornography feminist wouldn't like it'.

The readership of Black Lace fictions, then, is addressed as consumers for whom written erotica is a site of pleasure and play, not of politics. This is a clear indication of a 'post-feminist' position that equates old-style feminism with prohibition of heterosexual enjoyment and repression of heterosexual pleasure. It is a position that taps into current perceptions (justified or not) that feminist politicization of heterosexual desire has marginalized questions of delight and sexual pleasure, that is a power discourse that is both puritanical and anti-pleasure. Hence the 'naughty but nice' effect where disapproval from Big Sister intensifies the secret/guilty pleasures offered to the 'post-feminist' consumer of the forbidden pleasures of the unreconstructed 'feminine'.

Pornography as liberation

The third association made between Black Lace erotica and the language of feminism that I want to address relates to the Editor's quite categorical statement that the series is framed by a feminist intent to open access to an area of human experience previously denied to women. In this sense, Black Lace is quite contrary to the usual correlation between mass-market fictions, patriarchal ideology and 'false consciousness' assumed to govern the meaning of the romance. Instead, consumption of popular fiction is given to be a liberating experience, an experience that immediately proposes access to a less repressed female identity through gratification in sexual fantasy. Thus a liberal feminist sense of entitlement is combined with a Freudian conception of sexuality as a 'natural' and 'healthy' dimension of human selfhood: this results in a persuasive argument for buying Black Lace. Black Lace presents sexuality as a site of liberation for women, a space in which individual gratification is almost a duty since consuming erotic fictions will make readers more psychically healthy by being more closely aligned with their 'innermost' and until recently literally unspeakable desires. What this most lucidly signifies is how adept capitalist commodity markets have become at appropriating the language of freedom and the political project of feminism to market products.

Foucault's theory that power, knowledge and pleasure come to form the discourse of sexuality in the course of the twentieth century, makes it clear why Black Lace espouses the Freudian model which places sexuality at the 'heart' and defines the 'truth' of one's self. Foucault suggests that it is functional for the operation of power that sexuality is seen as something *repressed* by social constriction for this implies the possibility of its revelation. Ignoring the gendered pronouns of the following, Foucault suggests:

> There may be another reason that makes it so gratifying for us to define the relationship between sex and power in terms of repression: something that one might call the speaker's benefit. If sex is repressed, that is, condemned to prohibition, non-existence and silence, then the mere fact that one is speaking about it has the appearance of deliberate transgression. A person who holds forth in such language places himself to a certain extent outside the reach of power; he upsets established law; he somehow anticipates the coming freedom.
>
> (Foucault 1979: 6)

In the economic circuit of commodities in which Black Lace is located, the claim to know the 'truth' of sex for women can be converted into hard capitalist cash from those seeking to know: it is Virgin Publishing which accrues the 'speaker's benefit' of fulfilling the need to 'know'.

This is part of a wider late-twentieth-century process by which dominant culture has begun to trade upon 'transgression' as cultural capital. The economies structured around the pink and lavender pounds are also symptomatic of social shifts in which once 'alternative' political/sexual identities have become accommodated through commercialisation. The emergence of new 'bodice ripper' imprints to cater for gay and lesbian as well as post-feminist heterosexual readerships testifies to the power of capitalist commodification to co-opt sexual lifestyles for niche marketing and product differentiation. Hence Virgin's newer gay list named 'Idol' works under the same rubric as Black Lace: 'Homoerotic Fiction by Men for Men' as does its 'Sapphire' series for lesbian women. That the net effect of such processes is the facilitation of a wider acceptance of sexually 'deviant' identities by mainstream hetero-society is not at issue here. Rather, all forms of mass marketed pornography attest to social changes in which sexual citizenship has become a profitable basis for the construction of readerships: sexuality has become inextricable from consumption – if our 'sexual identities are our imperative, inescapable and the deepest reality with which it is our duty to come to terms', then 'we must come to terms not only with sexuality as bio-political acts, drives, dysfunctions, "the Big "O"", health, pleasure and happiness, but also with sexuality as commodities' (Evans 1993: 45). The act by women of purchasing and reading mass market written erotica can be viewed as the most heightened manifestation of the more generalized and dispersed 'logic' of desire driving consumer culture since the 'pursuit of the commodified self is the pursuit of the sexual self; individual, private, innermost, accomplished through the acquisition and conspicuous manifestations of style' (Evans, 1993: 45). In this sense, the Black Lace series is significant for the ways in which boundaries between the 'personal' and 'public' sexual self are produced in the late twentieth-century commodity form:

> The material construction of sexualities within consumerism lies at the very heart of the modern era's instrumental self-interest for whilst consumption and sexual identity and expression are pursued in public, both their objectives remain resolutely fetishised as 'personal' and 'private'.
>
> (Evans, 1993: 45)

Evans' work argues that the articulation of a 'private' domain is as crucial for the formation of sexual identities as the public spaces of work and production. The discourse of sexuality offered as 'private' pleasure, as the individual's 'self-fulfilment' and as 'immediate gratification', obscures recognition that these terms are themselves produced as 'fetishized consequences of consumerist alienation' (Evans, 1993: 46).

Discursive connections which attempt to tie the 'Implied Reader' more tightly to the 'real' reader are effected through a lengthy questionnaire enclosed, until recently, with each Black Lace title. Requesting readers to return them with a view to 'mapping' the fantasy-scape of the putative 'terra incognita' of female sexual desire, the responses to these questionnaires formed the basis of a subsequent Virgin publication *The Black Lace Book of Women's Sexual Fantasies* (1999) as an updated and British companion to Nancy Friday's *My Secret Garden* (1963). In line with the Freudian conception of sexuality that frames the construction of the female reader of Black Lace fictions, the questionnaires can be understood as symptomatic of libertarian 'pro-sex' feminism in its pursuit of the audience in order to tap the 'unprecedented' reserves of female sexual fantasy. But counter to this, they might also be read as Taylorist techniques of a 'will-to-know' which attempt to align commodity production, subjective fantasy and 'real' readers – not the 'healthy' expression of female sexual freedom but the insertion of production procedures (standardization, repetition and predictability) in the domain of fantasy where books are subsequently tailored to meet the 'demands' of the female psyche. This, I would conclude, represents what Foucault might call the 'disciplining' of fantasy in which the language of sexual freedom speaks instead as a colonising discourse: to the female reader who is the gendered subject of knowledge, power and pleasure. The Black Lace reader is thus locked into a circuit of desire and consumption which veils the commodity object with the libidinal pleasure of the *self-defined* sexual citizen.

This conclusion, perhaps inevitably, recalls the public/private collapse embodied in the scenario of Lisa Cresswell reading her Black Lace fiction at work. Further, it returns us to the debate on pleasure and its place in ethnographic studies of female audiences. It restates the theoretical impasse that 'private pleasure' is always and already ideologically complicit; it secretes again the anti-'active audience' position that, despite the 'empowerment' experienced by its readers, Black Lace is inevitably haunted by the ghost of the notion that all mass culture produces masses of cultural dupes who perform sexual identity through commodity form.[9]

Whether the complexities of audience construction to which my research testifies suggests otherwise, the 'will-to-know' that underpins much audience study cannot be ignored. As I have demonstrated, the academic's epistemophilic desire for knowledge of the 'real' audience is hazardously compatible with capitalist imperatives that consumer 'desires' are rendered transparent to it. In the context of fictions that deal in what is taken to be 'real' female sexual desire and fantasy, the feminist intention to 'understand' how sexual fictions incite female pleasure similarly requires vigilance.

Notes

1 This present article is part of a forthcoming book-length study *Masquerades of Desire: Women's Popular Fiction in the Age of Postfeminism* that investigates the historical and contemporary relations between women and written pornography, and sets these against the commercial and ideological transformations of women's popular fiction. In other chapters, I make close linguistic analysis and textual readings not offered here; I am developing a new

theory of *masquerade* to explore the construction of fantasy scenarios (and the ways in which heterosexuality is produced and reproduced through these). Some parts of this present article have appeared in different forms in 'Erotic Fiction for Women By Women: The Pleasures of Post-feminist Heterosexuality' *Sexualities*, Vol. 2, No. 2, 1999, pp. 167–187 and 'What the Woman Reads: Categorising Contemporary Popular Erotica for Women', in J. Hallam and N. Moody (eds) *Consuming for Pleasure: Selected Essays on Popular Fiction* Liverpool, John Moores, 2000, pp. 246–267. My sincere thanks to Peter Stanfield for generous critical commentary and informative debates on the commercial contexts of popular fiction, audiences and genre.

2 This article is explicitly concerned with the contemporary repositioning of erotica within *heterosexual* post-feminism. It is important to signal that these transformations sit alongside lesbian, gay and 'queer' readings of pornography that have similarly challenged its containment within patriarchal, heterosexist and gendered culture.

3 How far women's fiction has abandoned the path of 'virtue and virginity' can, as Radway notes, be measured by the fact that 'even the most progressive of recent romances continue to bind female desire to a heterosexuality constructed as the only natural sexual alliance, and thus continue to prescribe patriarchal marriage as the ultimate route to the realization of mature female subjectivity' (1991: 16). My textual analysis of Black Lace 'contemporaries' largely contradicts this but the 'historicals' tend to confirm the 'rightness' of the heterosexual couple that comes to centre narratives of sexual diversity and multiple partners.

4 See Marilyn French, *The Women's Room* (1977), Lisa Alther, *Kinflicks* (1976) and Erica Jong, *Fear of Flying* (1973). Danielle Steele, *Changes* (1983) and *Wanderlust* (1986), Jilly Cooper, *Riders* (1985) and *Rivals* (1988) and Collen McCullough, *The Thorn Birds* (1977) and *Indecent Obsession* (1981). Jackie Collins, *Sinner* (1984) and *Lucky* (1985) and Shirley Conran, *Lace* (1982), *Lace II* (1984) and *Crimson* (1992). Julie Burchill, *Ambition* (1986), Kathy Lette, *Foetal Attraction* (1994) and *Mad Cows* (1996) and Edwina Currie, *A Parliamentary Affair* (1994) and *A Woman's Place* (1996). The massive expansion of 'chicklit' (paralleling the novels of 'Lad' culture) in the 1990s also warrants further consideration within the context supplied by post-feminism.

5 *Romantic Times* was founded and run by Kathryn Falk, Lady of Barrow and is published at 55, Bergen Street, Brooklyn, NY 11201. Awareness of the romantic reader's interest in the erotica market is demonstrated in the fact that, by February 2002, *Romantic Times* runs a feature – 'Erotic Spotlight: Do steamy novels push your buttons? Explore this forbidden genre and its appeal to women'. Its internet site can be found at http://www.romantic-times.com.

6 The Sensuality Key is a usual feature of the magazine's reviews of new titles each month and may or may not operate with the Gold Medal Ratings Key to classify within a sub-genre such as 'Mainstream Romance' or 'Series Romance'.

7 The literature on women, pornography, sexuality and feminism is now extensive. For a full bibliography of key texts in the pro- and anti-censorship debates and my examination of the historical context of feminism's politics of pornography, see Sonnet (1999).

8 The emergence of the New 'post-feminist' Woman in contemporary women's magazines (straight and gay) suggests a wider context for popular disengagement with feminist thinking explored here. See Angela McRobbie (1990), E. Sonnet and I. Whelehan (1995) and I. Whelehan (2000).

9 Thomas Frank (2000) *One Market Under God: Extreme Capitalism, Market Populism and the End of Economic Democracy* (New York: Anchor Books expressly connects American/global cooperate 'free market' ethics with the rush to embrace 'active audience' ethnographies in Cultural Studies via an anti-intellectual, 'anti-elitist' populism that sustains both.

References

Ang, I. (1996) *Living Room Wars: Rethinking Media Audiences for a Postmodern Age*, London: Routledge.

Assiter, A. (1988) 'Romance Fiction: Porn for Women?' in Gary Day and Clive Bloom (eds) *Perspectives on Pornography: Sexuality in Film and Literature*, 101–09, Basingstoke: Macmillan.

Berens, J. (2000) 'She's Gotta Have It', *The Observer Magazine*, 10 October, 20–25.

BLACK LACE (1997, 1999) Promotional Packs (including Newsletters, Editor's Guidelines for Authors and Editorial Response to Reader Questionnaires) Compiled and edited by Kerri Sharp, London: Virgin Publishing.

Bourdieu, P. (1984) *Distinction: A Social Critique of Taste*, trans. R. Nice, London: Routledge.

Currie, D. (1999) *Girl Talk: Adolescent Magazines and their Readers*, Toronto: University of Toronto Press.

Dixon, J. (1998) *The Romantic Fiction of Mills & Boon 1905–1995,* London: UCL Press.

Evans, D. T. (1993) *Sexual Citizenship: The Material Construction of Sexualities,* London: Routledge.

Foucault, M. (1979) *The History of Sexuality – Vol. I: An Introduction,* trans. Robert Hurley, Harmondsworth: Penguin.

Frank, T. (2000) *One Market Under God: Extreme Capitalism, Market Populism and the End of Economic Democracy,* New York: Anchor Books.

Hastings, J. (1997) *Deadly Affairs*, London: Virgin.

Mann, P. (1979) 'Romantic Fiction and its Readers' in H. D. Fischer and S. R. Melnick (eds) *Entertainment: A Cross-Cultural Examination*, New York: Hastings House.

Martin, B. (1998) 'Sexualities without Genders and Other Queer Utopias', in M. Merck, N. Segal and E. Wright (eds) *Coming Out of Feminism?*, 11–35, London: Blackwell.

McRobbie, A. (1991, 2000) *Feminism and Youth Culture*, London: Macmillan.

Modleski, T. (1982) *Loving with a Vengeance: Mass Produced Fantasies for Women*, New York/London: Methuen.

Moody, N. (1998) 'Mills & Boon's *Temptations*: Sex and the Single Couple in the 1990s', in L. Pearce and G. Wisker (eds) *Fatal Attractions: Rescripting Romance in Contemporary Literature and Film*, 141–156, London: Pluto.

Pearce, L. and Stacey, J. (eds) (1995) *Romance Revisited*, New York and London: New York UP.

Radway, J. ([1984] 1991) *Reading the Romance: Women, Patriarchy and Popular Literature*, Chapel Hill: North Carolina University Press.

Sharp, K. (ed.) (1999) *The Black Lace Book of Women's Sexual Fantasies*, London: Virgin Publishing.

Sonnet, E. (1999) '"Erotic Fiction by Women for Women": The Pleasures of Post-feminist Heterosexuality', *Sexualities* 2(2): 167–187.

Sonnet, E. (2000) 'What the Woman Reads: Categorising Contemporary Popular Erotica for Women', in J. Hallam and N. Moody (eds) *Consuming for Pleasure: Selected Essays on Popular Fiction*, 246–267, Liverpool: John Moores.

Sonnet, E. and Whelehan, I. (1995) 'Freedom From or Freedom To . . . Contemporary Identities in Women's Magazines', in M. Maynard and J. Purvis (eds) *(Hetero)Sexual Politics*, 81–94, London: Taylor & Francis.

Thurston, C. (1987) *The Romance Revolution: Erotic Novels for Women and the Quest for a New Sexual Identity*, Chicago: University of Illinois Press.

Whelehan, I. (2000) *Overloaded: Popular Culture and the Future of Feminism*, London: The Women's Press.

PART SEVEN

Interpretive communities
Nation and ethnicity

Introduction

P REVIOUS ARTICLES IN THIS Reader have questioned the extent to which audiences can draw their own meanings from a media text. We have seen how the assumption that texts carry the producers' message to consumers in a straightforward process of cause and effect was problematised by research into actual audiences (Part One), and that studies of active, resistant readings tended to employ a modified version of uses and gratifications theory whereby a text's possible interpretations were limited by the producers' intention and shaped by the recipient's social affiliations (Part Three). Subsequent chapters explored the role of cultural identity in forming interpretations, whether related to the group membership of fandom, the broader sense of belonging implied by specifically female or gay readings, and indeed a combination of the two (Parts Five and Six).

The four extracts in this final Part explore the importance of national and ethnic identity to audience readings. As such, they are based on the assumption that while texts may be open to any number of individual interpretations in principle, in practice these interpretations will depend on the viewer or reader's membership of specific cultural communities.

Elihu Katz and Tamar Liebes' research in Chapter 28, for instance, concentrates on the ways in which religious belief and cultural experience affects their reading of the American soap opera *Dallas*. Intriguingly, while these viewers are aware that they use the show as a form of fantastical escape comparable to getting drunk – 'in giving relief from the structures of religious observance, the constriction of living quarters and the terrible strain of the war in Lebanon' (p. 289) – they also draw from it a confirmation and validation of their own cultural ethics which are favourably contrasted to the unscrupulous behaviour of *Dallas*' 'American' values. As one of the respondents proudly states, 'You see, I'm a Jew wearing a skullcap, and I learned from this film to say "Happy is our lot" that we're Jewish' (p. 294).

Zehava, Yossi and their friends interpret and explain the soap opera in terms familiar from their own lives – the series is a 'film', with connotations of a special event; the Ewing mansion is an 'apartment'; a dead character is given an ironic Jewish blessing –

and adapt it to specific cultural uses. *Dallas* becomes the basis for a 'forum' where the group can discuss philosophical issues such as the corruptive power of money. While part of the show's pleasure is an immersion in unfamiliar lifestyles, these viewers also continually refer the text back to the reality they know, 'negotiating' between American culture and their own, and – like the audiences of Marie Gillespie's study below – finding different levels of enjoyment in the patterns of similarity and difference.

Sut Jhally and Justin Lewis' research in Chapter 27 takes American nationality as a given, and asks how ethnicity shapes interpretations of *The Cosby Show*. The parallels are as telling as the contrasts: both white and black audiences, according to Jhally and Lewis, are trapped by their own cultural beliefs into arguing that the success of the African American Huxtable family in *Cosby* 'proves' an absence of racial prejudice in the United States, even while their own experience, and their very responses, indicate the opposite.

An earlier chapter reveals that white respondents saw the Huxtables as 'just like white people' and used their fondness for the show to reassure themselves of their own liberal, 'color-blind' beliefs. The black viewers of this study, on the other hand, invest a great deal of pride in the Huxtable family as a representation of middle-class black professionals, and contrast the show with 'negative stereotypes' of working-class black families in other sit-coms. Yet while the black audiences attempt to hold *Cosby* up as a 'typical' example of African American success, and the contrasting white response argues that blacks could succeed like Cosby if only they would work hard, both groups are, in Jhally and Lewis' analysis, guilty of ignoring the intrinsic relationship between race and social class.

Chapter 30 by Marie Gillespie bears some similarity to Liebes and Katz's study in its tracing of the way teenage Punjabi viewers in the London borough of Southall find useful parallels, as well as fascinating differences, between their own experience and the ostensibly very different culture of the Australian soap opera *Neighbours*. As with the *Dallas* viewers, these respondents use the show as a way into discussion; in this case, the fictional characters provide a means of talking about otherwise taboo or sensitive topics at one remove. 'In school or at home we often have teenage problems which relate to our soap . . . you can think back to what the character did and see if they did things the right way' (p. 319).

While *Neighbours* seems to echo these viewers' experience in key respects – a tight-knit community which is highly-dependent on gossip and rumour – it also has some radical differences. The code of *izzat*, or family honour, prevents the Punjabi teenagers from enjoying anything like the level of freedom they observe in the *Neighbours* characters, and as such the soap is valued as a glimpse into the culturally 'other' society of white teenagers. This research also makes the point that interpretations are shaped by more than one aspect of social identity: here, ethnicity is the main factor and Gillespie's primary focus, but she also notes that the code of *izzat* affects young women far more than it does young men, and that female viewers' engagement with the soap is subtly different from that of their male friends.

Jacqueline Bobo's study in Chapter 29 employs the structures we saw in David Morley's research (Morley, 1999) to explore African American women's negotiated reading of a mainstream film. Significantly, even though Steven Spielberg intended his adaptation of *The Color Purple* to avoid black stereotypes, Bobo argues that, as a white man, he could not help but encode the text with dominant ideology. The black women readers she interviewed approach the film from a specific cultural position, accustomed – in an interesting parallel with Geoffrey Woods' account (Chapter 12, p. 117; Woods, 1995) of gay male interpretation – to picking their own resistant readings from texts which exclude or demean them.

Despite the film's political failings, these women were able to 'ferret out the beneficial and put up blinders against the rest' (p. 309), finding a progressive, empowering meaning which had a direct relation to their own lives; and which stood in marked contrast to the generally-hostile black male reaction to the film. Even within a marriage, Bobo notes, 'two people can watch the same film and have opposite reactions'. Like the other research in this section, Bobo's research reminds us that we may all belong to several interpretive communities at once – gay, female, black, American, working-class – and that our membership of these groups can sometimes draw us into complex affiliations, shaping our response according to a number of overlapping cultural factors.

Further reading

Bourdieu, P. (1987) *Distinction*, Cambridge, MA: Harvard University Press.
Fish, S. (1980) *Is There a Text in This Class?*, Cambridge, MA: Harvard University Press.

Chapter 27

Sut Jhally and Justin Lewis

ENLIGHTENED RACISM

The Cosby Show, audiences and the myth of the American dream

Positive images and the search for prosperity

AS WE READ THE comments of black focus groups about stereotyping on *The Cosby Show* and other black sitcoms, it became clear that characters portrayed as working class (let alone poor and struggling) were perceived negatively. As we have seen . . ., this notion is broadly accepted in our culture by both black and white people, by blue-collar workers and professionals alike. It is, nonetheless, a notion that takes on a greater degree of urgency for black people, who feel (with some justification) that they have been the victims of years of negative stereotyping. *The Cosby Show*, in this context, is much more than entertainment; it is a cultural breakthrough. Whatever their qualms about the show, most black viewers enthuse about it for this reason alone:

> It's not just a typical – being stereotyped as having only this kind of an interest or going out and partying or you know, loud music or drinking or whatever.

> I admire him. I like his show because it depicts black people in a positive way. I think he's good. It's good to see that blacks can be professionals.

> That it was a black, clean show and comedy. I like comedy and it wasn't so, it didn't have us acting so stereotype, you know?

> You don't see many African-American role models as them on television. Unfortunately, what we get to see is backstairs at the White House, you know, the maid, the servant; so it is really great to see two intelligent black professionals.

> The things that you see on *The Cosby Show* you probably will not see on a lot of other places, because they are caught up in old stereotypical white programming.

There is a great deal at stake here, and most black respondents felt enormous pride in the images of 'themselves' that were finally visible to society at large. One mother regarded the series as an important source of nurturing for her children:

> When it first came on, it was required watching. The kids knew that. Thursday night was required watching . . . PBS, *Cosby* and the news were always free time or anything that we felt that they needed to watch. I mean it was required watching.

Bill Cosby, with his well-known emphasis on the value of education, would find this a glowing testimony indeed.

If only it were that easy. Beneath this celebration of *The Cosby Show* lies a troublesome contradiction. As a reader will observe, Cosby's apparent move to a TV world beyond the confines of stereotyping is dependent upon the Huxtables' lofty class status as 'intelligent black professionals.' Without that status, the show would be seen as sliding back into the negative territory occupied by more traditional black sitcoms. This status requirement has deeply damaging consequences.

Requiring upper middle class status as a mark of normalcy creates a world that forces black viewers to accept a value system in which they are the inevitable losers. A value system based upon social class (upper equals good, lower equals bad: a notion with a sinister Orwellian ring) devalues most black people, for whom a high-income life-style like the Huxtables' is quite unattainable. Black viewers are thus caught in a trap because the escape route from TV stereotyping comes with a set of ideologically loaded conditions. To look good, to look 'positive,' means accepting a value system in which upper middle class status is a sign of superiority. This is more than crude materialism; for a group that has been largely excluded from these higher socioeconomic echelons, it is cultural and political suicide.

So powerful is the desire among blacks to escape the negative world of stereotyping that the representation of social reality, the reality of which most of them are a part, becomes a necessary sacrifice. The question of whether the Huxtables are typical or atypical, black or white, real or unreal, is resolved in terms of the broader concerns of the black audience, the desire to overcome TV racial stereotyping. Blacks are willing to accept the unreality because of the broader role played by *The Cosby Show*. They assume that the Huxtables' status is somehow linked to their wholesomeness. A black male middle class respondent, for example, makes the link by constructing a dichotomy between the unreal upper middle class world of the Huxtables and a grisly (and by implication, more 'real') alternative:

> You know, it's always that upper middle class, upper class mentality. . . . It's just not real for me. Again, I like the show per se because it does depict blacks in a more positive way than we usually – we're not killing each other. We're not raping people. You know, we're sane, ordinary people who like the nice things in life like everybody else.

The Cosby Show may not, in other words, be real; but it is a necessary illusion. There is no space in this dichotomy for depicting blacks 'in a more positive way' without elevating them to a world that most black people cannot attain. Other respondents revealed a similar unease with the Huxtables' class status but were willing to accept it because it presented images that the culture accepted as positive:

> Because to me it puts blacks in, you know, it's a positive thing for blacks, but it's unrealistic; and most blacks, you know . . . This is a middle class show, but it's appreciated by everybody.

> I like Clair's character per se. She's a strong black woman, very independent . . . I like her character per se because it depicts blacks in a different mold than what white America thinks. I like the character but again it's TV. It's sort of made up. It just doesn't seem real, but I do like the character.

The debate about the show's typicality is thus secondary to its power to promote positive images of black life. If the display of wealth is a necessary part of this process, so be it:

> I've watched talk shows where people made adverse comments about, I mean blacks even made adverse comments, like our children. They say it's not typical. A typical black family. Wwhere you gonna find a lawyer and people dressed like that . . . It's just a part of life . . . the way things are; but I view this as clean and wholesome . . . In fact I'd say it's not stereotype, you know, in the negative sort of way that makes it black female, or black male view of downtrod or suppressed.

Not all black viewers were able to strike this bargain with the series in which a highly selective picture of black experience is accepted because it breaks down stereotypes. Some black respondents found themselves caught in a more self-deceptive logic. Because *The Cosby Show*, as a benevolent intervention in a hitherto hostile world, matters so much to its black viewers, a great deal of emotional energy is invested in it. If this is the show that breaks away from stereotyping, it has to be regarded as real. If it is not real, it is merely another empty image. The tremendous sense of pride in being a part of the Huxtables' world (as African Americans) means that, for some black viewers, any doubts about the reality of the class position of the series have to be suppressed. For it to perform the role assigned to it (showing black people as human and ordinary), the Huxtables have to be reflections of the real world otherwise hidden from public view. As one female respondent put it:

> I like it because if nothing else, it's giving America a chance to see another side of African-American families that they may not necessarily come into contact with.

This logic is, on one level, indisputable. If the Huxtables are unrepresentative or unreal, then they are simply another fiction. For if the move beyond traditional stereotyping requires a move into the upper middle class, the pleasure and pride that are experienced in images of yourself that at last you can positively identify with require the existence of a significant and visible black professional class. The credibility of *The Cosby Show*'s move beyond stereotyping is, in this logic, dependent upon demonstrating such a professional class. If it cannot be demonstrated, then the show is only a fiction, just another deceptive image.

The battle for respect

Because black people have made heavy emotional investments in the show on the premise that it realistically depicts black life, a number of viewers, we found, were vehement in their contention that they knew families 'just like the Huxtables.' This assertion came from viewers regardless of class position. A middle-aged working class man commented:

> Well, I know there has been a lot of criticism of *Cosby* because people would say that it was not realistic, but it is realistic to have a doctor and lawyer, but the neighborhood that I lived at, may be a little difficult for them to imagine that there are families like this. It's good for me because we are not always showing poverty, despair; we are showing the progress that our race has achieved. That is what makes it real; we have achieved progress. We have black millionaires all over the place. It is not uncommon to have a black man and a black woman, both professional making a lot of money, living together. It is not uncommon these days. But, I think in terms of the media and television it is uncommon because they choose not to show blacks in this light. They like to show blacks in terms of crime and in despair, or in negative situations, and that is why, I think, a lot of people say it is unreal. It is only because we are not shown in this light.

The irony of this argument is that, in the 1990s, black prosperity really is quite common in the TV world. In the real world, it is not.

In part, the show is defended so powerfully by black viewers because to deny its reality would also be to deny that black people are just normal, just human. That is, the criticism of the show, especially from white people, is seen as an attack not just on the show but on black people in general. A black make respondent observed:

> What bothers me about that is this is television. But in real life people don't want to accept the fact that there is a black family, positive, black family, intact, in the home, yeah? If Daddy came home drunk and kicked the butt, that would be all right. If she was big, fat, and ugly, that would be all right. If the son was in jail, that would be all right . . . They disagree and squabble, but they don't knock each other down and fight, and they don't call each other motherfucker and all this kind of stuff. The world has to accept the fact that there are black families, period.

A female respondent reflected the idea that this 'insult to *Cosby* is an insult to us':

> It's time that the blacks, middle to upper middle class are celebrated on TV because it's happening now and there are other families like that . . . But there are some folks that go to our church that are white, and I'll never forget when that first came out, she started talking and she joined the group and

talking, and she said 'but that's not real. That's not realistic. There aren't black families like that.' And of course the black people sitting around completely blew up, you know, but she is not alone.

The battle over *The Cosby Show* then, is a battle for respect. Once prosperity becomes the basic symbol of human worth, it is necessary to argue that black people are just as likely to achieve prosperity as anyone else. Although some such comments came from the more prosperous focus groups (who were, at least, talking about their own reality), many did not:

> I mean for every person who doesn't know that setting, there is an African American who can say 'I know somebody who is a doctor' or 'I know some-body who's a lawyer' or those professional people. . . . And perhaps it does happen to be where you are living . . . But in segments of Springfield you'll run into it.

> It's just one little show, black people, I think; you know, living decent. It's life; they may not have jokes every few minutes. It may be a little more seri-ous, even in disciplining in one thing or another, but it's. . . . Lots of black people are living now in the upper middle class, or whatever.

> Well, let me tell you something, she [Clair] is for real. She's like a lot of sister lawyers that I know.

> The whole thing is very for real. And the whites say, 'No, that's not for real.' A lot of black people are lawyers.

> Yet we know there's a lot of black attorneys being lawyers. I know a couple of judges who are women, black, you know, professional wives.

> Now I've been in school, and I've heard some kids say that's not real life and putting it down; but there are families like that. It's not a one in a million thing, and there are families like that; and also I think you will find people like that.

One respondent took special pleasure in retelling a story of how he took a white business associate to the home of a black upper middle class friend to prove to him that the Huxtables were real:

> This white person, looking from white perspectives, and he was amazed and his eyes just couldn't believe there was a black family that lived like this. It was almost like the Cosbys, you know . . . So when we left . . . it left an impression on him.

The same respondent went to great lengths to point out that the representation of Cliff Huxtable as a black gynecologist was realistic:

> And I know a lot of people around the country, black and white, will whis-per and say, this is unrealistic. He's a baby specialist, specializing in women

and you know, how the feeling is, whites thrown in a black situation like that. But then, in real life, right here in Springfield there's Doctor Jones . . . He has so many, he's a gynaecologist . . . There are criticisms of the show, but there are some Dr Huxtables out there.

This firm insistence that there are families like the Huxtables should indicate to us that this is not simply a debate about reality but about identity and respect. Because it is so important, any evidence, no matter how fragmentary or distant, becomes relevant:

I'm sure I have, I have heard, I have heard. I mean I heard . . . where the family is a reverend and the daughter is whatever. Then his daughter . . . he is paying for her college. Where I used to work in Westfield this guy was telling me about his girlfriend he knew, and how their family is well off, how they took them to dinner.

The importance of the reality of families like the Huxtables is indicated in comments about role models:

It could serve as, to a certain degree, as role models. It could be a family that youngsters, not only necessarily youngsters but middle class families and not even middle class families can aspire to. To say that you know these kinds of people do exist. And you can have two professionally successful black people doing quite well and the children under control.

As this respondent suggests, the viability of such role models depends upon their status being attainable. It is difficult to aspire to a status that can never be reached. Another male respondent talked of the need for black heroes, dismissing with some irritation the suggestion that the Huxtables are not real:

People start talking about Bill Cosby as not, Huxtable is not for real. Black folks need heroes. Everybody needs heroes.

Clinging to the American dream

This insistence upon the legitimacy and authenticity of *The Cosby Show* has its roots in two quite different notions. The first is the widespread feeling that black people have traditionally been stereotyped on television. The second is that human value can, in some way, be measured by status and wealth. In our culture, these two discrete notions have become fused together in a way that locks black people into acceptance of a system that, on the whole, works against them. The ironic consequence of this is that the battle over stereotyping is fought entirely on the turf of the dominant culture, ultimately legitimating white, upper middle class hegemony.

The welding of a critique of stereotyping to a value system based on class, as we have seen, forces many black viewers to argue that the Huxtables are typical and to suggest that this typicality is proof of racial equality. The problem with this argument is not just that it is wrong (the Huxtables are exceptional, not typical) but that it blinds us to *why* it is wrong. The Huxtables are unusual because the combination of race and class barriers works against most black people. The system is neither fair nor equal, yet many black viewers are seduced, through an argument about stereotyping, into a logic that claims that it is. After all, if the world is like it is on *The Cosby Show*, what is the problem?

To insist upon the existence of a sizable black middle class implies belief in an open meritocracy and, by implication, disbelief in the barriers of race and class. On this dimension we found a curious contradiction among black respondents. In marked contrast to the white respondents, they did not question the need for policies such as affirmative action (their qualms were about its operation and how it has come to be viewed). On this issue, black respondents were reacting to what they knew from their own experience about the problems of equitable employment opportunities. Racially inequitable preferences existed and affected their lives.

Yet many of these same respondents also believed that the black middle class was ubiquitous, the black millionaires were 'all over the place.' For middle and upper middle class blacks this belief was, not surprisingly, even more common. In comments reported in the previous section, we see the outlines of the broad contours of the American dream. And there were more explicit assertions:

> I don't believe – I get so tired of hearing 'The white man got us down.' . . . See, I don't believe that. I think blacks are their own worst enemies. And other minorities come to this country and they make it. . . . I think blacks have just as much opportunity as the whites. I really, I really feel that. I really feel that. We have too many black millionaires. We have too many black successful people in this country to say 'Oh, we can't make it.' I know too many black people who live – I know just as many black people who live in Longmeadow as I do – as white. And see, I think it's a bunch of crap. . . . I think that my forefathers, my father, they worked hard. And that's how they made it, 'cause it was a work ethic . . . You know this is bull that we can't make it in this country. It's just bull.

The notion that it is a matter of 'getting our act together' was best expressed by a young working class black male: 'I think we just need to pull ourselves together and get ourselves organized like Michael Jackson and Eddie Murphy.' And, we would add, like the Huxtables and the other well-to-do black characters who now populate prime time. Although self-help and organization are certainly ways to address the serious problems faced by large numbers of black people in this country, they will not exist or be effective unless the broader structural factors are also addressed.

Unless they address the broader structural factors, the only way that blacks can reconcile real-life economic and social problems with images of success is through individual pathology – blame and self-blame for those who have not made it in the open meritocracy. Because the invisible structures of class, and not the visible structures of race, define the workings of the economic system, the only explanation for massive black poverty must lie in blacks themselves. When this assumption of individual pathology is attached to race, we confront a system of racist belief at the heart of black culture itself, a form of self-hatred.

This is expressed clearly in the work of some of the new black conservatives, such as Shelby Steele (1990: 15). The logic of these arguments is revealing. Steele writes about the decay of inner city Detroit: 'Twenty years of decline and demoralization, even as opportunities for blacks to better themselves have increased. By many measures, the majority of blacks – those not yet in the middle class – are further behind whites today than before the victories of the civil rights movement.' The assumption here is that new opportunities make it relatively easy to move upward socially. But why has this not taken place? 'If conditions have worsened for most of us as racism has receded, then much of the problem *must be of our own making*' (emphasis added).

For all its good intentions, *The Cosby Show* leaves us with an ideological problem. It sustains and promotes the widespread assumption that a positive image of a black person is necessarily of an upper middle class black. This generates contradictory attitudes: first, it 'proves' that black people can make it in a predominantly white world, even though most black people have, on this reckoning, failed; second, it cultivates the illusion that economic success is as achievable for black people as for white people. This forces black Americans to buy into a system that handicaps them, without being able to explain (or accept) their persistently low levels of achievement.

The Cosby Show, and others like it, divert attention from the class-based causes of racial inequality. More than this, the series throws a veil of confusion over black people who are trying to comprehend the inequities of modern racism. It derails dissatisfaction with the system and converts it, almost miraculously, into acceptance of its values. In a culture where white people now refuse to acknowledge the existence of unequal opportunities, the political consequences of this acceptance are, for black people, disastrous.

Chapter 28

Tamar Liebes and Elihu Katz

THE EXPORT OF MEANING
Cross-cultural readings of *Dallas*

B EFORE ATTEMPTING ANALYSIS AND generalization across the sixty-six focus-group discussions, we present here most of the transcript of one discussion in order to share our conviction that focus-group discussions resembled the kind of day-to-day conversation that is otherwise unavailable to the researcher.

The participants in the conversation were three Jewish couples of Moroccan origin who are well integrated into Israeli society and all good friends. With one exception, the participants can all read the subtitles: they do not understand English. Adi, the interviewer, came to the home of Zehava and Yossi; two other couples – Cecile and Itzchak, and Massudi and Machluf – joined them. Even before the episode went on the air, spontaneous conversation on *Dallas* began and, therefore, taping was started early. The discussion continued during the viewing, and characters and events on the screen were sometimes incorporated into the conversation. By the time the focus discussion was due to begin, the conversation flowed quite naturally. By that time, Adi was comfortably integrated into the group, making it difficult for her to stick to her moderator's role, and some of the points of discussion had already been covered. There is no question but that the following transcript is a record of the way these people normally talk to one another, even if it is unlikely that they talk in such a sustained way about a television program. In any case, it is a rare document of television talk.

The episode discussed was entitled 'Little Boy Lost,' in which J. R. loses custody of his son to Sue Ellen, who has left him and is living with her (impotent) lover, Dusty, the scion of a competing oil dynasty. The episode is from the second season of the American television serial, broadcast in Israel during the winter of 1983 with subtitles in Hebrew and Arabic.

To illustrate how the material was coded and analyzed – the dimensions within which we worked – we have annotated the protocol of the conversation and flagged each of the notes with one or more subheads (that may help to clarify what is going on; that illustrate the coding categories which are employed in our analysis; and that raise questions of interests, theoretical and methodological, that deserve attention): (1) *understanding*, for coherent perception of the story line; (2) *interpretation*, on making sense of the story or *interpretation (attribution)*, on making sense of the motives of characters; (3) *moral evaluation*, on the acceptance and rejection of perceived values in the story; (4) *interaction*, on the social dynamics and roles within the group; (5) *para-social interaction* (Horton and Wohl, 1956), on relating to the characters as if they were real; (6) *identification*, both positive and negative, with characters; (7) *acculturation*, on bringing communal or traditional sources to bear on interpretation; (8) *mutual aid*, group interaction with respect to understanding, interpretation, or evaluation; (9) *referential*, on spontaneous use of the text as a springboard for relating to personal, interpersonal, or communal problems, or *referential forum*, when the referential constitutes the basis for group discussion; (10) *critical*, for statements that reveal understanding of the genre or of dramatic requirements of television fiction; (11) *narrative*, for ethnic or personal patterns of retelling the story; (12) *gratifications*, for self-defined uses of the program in connection with social and personal needs; (13) *definition of the (interview) situation*; and (14) *methodology*.

In addition to the three couples and Adi, the observers Gil and Elihu were present, operating the tape recorders and making notes. Some preliminary conclusions may be suggested on the basis of this case study (which serves as part of the subsample of preliminary readings):

1. The group clearly understood the basic narrative, unimpeded by subtitles and cultural differences. Their focus on primordial passions and the patterns of interpersonal relations may conceal a lesser understanding of the intricate machinations of a particular subplot (cf. note 21, where the meaning of the secretary's phone call to the restaurant is misunderstood). The universality of these elemental relationships seems to be a key to the ease with which the program is understood.

2. Retelling of the narrative by group members was in an interpretative and evaluative mode. They edited the story as if it were more linear than it is on the screen, stringing together the segments of only one of the main themes, and they treated it as if it were leading to a final resolution rather than to a never-ending and potentially reversible serial. They were certainly closer to Tannen's (1982) Greek storytellers, who defined their task as telling an interesting story, than to her Americans, who tried to be as detailed and precise as possible, even at the expense of being boring.

3. Their reediting of the story invokes a moral frame, whereby the plot rewards and punishes characters according to the moral or immoral motives that are attributed to them. Approval of a character entails attribution of an intrinsic moral motive to explain action. Our Moroccan viewers would surely disagree with Arlen's (1980) proposal that the fascination of *Dallas* is its moral improvisation and equivocation and its consequent unpredictability. Their reading is more lawful, their characters less ambiguous. That Sue Ellen discovers true love with Dusty (note 61) may not be in the text; it is in the reading. The story may be anomic: this reading is not.

4. It is likely, therefore, that the program serves as more of a forum (Newcomb and Hirsch, 1983) for Israeli Moroccans than for Americans. The constant negotiation between their own values and those of the program leads the group to commute between discussion of the program and discussion of life. The conversation is replete with referential allusions to issues of family, sex roles, justice, standards of living, and the like. On the basis of issues raised in the discussion of the program, reference is made to social issues raised in the immediate group itself, to personal relations in the community of group members, to problems of Israeli society, to American society

(where *Dallas* is often treated as equivalent to America), and to philosophical issues more generally. Interchanges of this kind are another of the keys to the process whereby American television programs penetrate linguistic and cultural frontiers. People help one another to decode them. The same interchanges constitute the filters through which the story – as hero, metaphor, message – makes its way into the culture. This group is of particular interest because it illustrates vividly how community members negotiate meanings by confronting the text with their own tradition and their own experience. The conversation suggests that the program serves viewers as a forum for discussion of personal, interpersonal, and social issues such as justice (our notes 41, 52); whether or not fathers have equal rights in their children (note 73); child-rearing problems (note 59); gender-role differences (notes 27, 73); attitudes toward adultery and divorce (notes 13, 40, 84, 85); the problem of cramped quarters (note 86); religious demands (note 20); and the harsh reality of prolonged war in Lebanon (note 89). Consider also the references to other texts – especially religious ones (notes 12, 28, 83, 85).

5. The reciprocal of referential allusion is critical distance, that is, discussion of the program as genre, as formula, as a story governed by aesthetic and business constraints and not necessarily related to life. Not so much of this sort of distancing is displayed in the present discussion. Occasionally, however, there is a flash of critical insight, as when the Mafia is alluded to (note 80), echoing the critical analysis by Mander (1983), who argues that *Dallas* is a version of the newly prevalent Godfather myth in America. The group is strongly aware of escapist gratifications of the program – in giving relief from the structures of religious observance, the constriction of living quarters, and the terrible strain of the war in Lebanon.

6. The group, of course, had dynamics of its own, and if certain roles emerged during the course of the conversation, and even if certain members were more dominant than others, this may well be an accurate simulation of everyday television talk. If Machluf prevails in his view, the group may well refuse entry of the values of the program into their lives as traditional Jews; if Yossi prevails, the program is altogether unworthy of serving as a forum for discussion of real problems. Among the roles engendered by the discussion, one can discern that of commuter (triggering transitions between the story and real life) and resource person (providing details from past programs). Note also the way in which knowledge of the program is used as a source of status (Cecile at note 38), just as knowledge of traditional texts conferred status.

Discussion before viewing begins

1. MACHLUF: Even when I look at it and I know it's an actor, that it's only cinema, but they act so much theater, they play it so much from their gut, especially J. R.; he's great.

Methodology. Following completion of the background questionnaire and because the viewing of the episode, an informal chat began, and the tape recorder was turned on. Machluf is teetering on the borderline of what we code as *critical* in the sense of betraying a clear awareness of the story as a construction in spite of being carried away by its reality. This is not explicit enough, however, for us to apply the *critical* subcode, 'mimetic.' We wish to point out that we are not here coding the discussion systematically but illustrating the several codes and explicating their use. We urge attention to the ways in which context functions to influence our own understanding and, thus, the coding.

2. ADI: Do you understand what he says, or do you read the subtitles?

MACHLUF: I understand what he says and what he acts, and I understand him.

YOSSI: She (the interviewer) means the translation (subtitles). Do you read the translation?

MACHLUF: Of course, the translation.

ADI: Anybody here understand English?

MACHLUF: Well, unfortunately, we studied French in our town, only French.

YOSSI: Yes, we all read the translation.

CECILE: I was in France a month ago, and I saw a few episodes. In French it was simply a pleasure. Here I enjoy it less, that is, there I discovered I enjoyed it more. Because I saw it here all the while without knowing whether I enjoy it more or less. I don't read Hebrew 100 percent, and it takes me time to read, it's a pity.

ADI: (to Massudi) What do you think?

Referring to the background questionnaire, Adi discusses the extent of dependence on the subtitles.

3. MACHLUF: I don't see *Dallas* at all.

MACHLUF: I see it for her – and in the middle of the night, I tell her everything. (general laughter)

CECILE: I always see it even though I get fed up. I anticipate what's going to happen, and sometimes I think, well, what did I sit for? But anyway, I do sit and watch . . .

Understanding: Unlike the other participants, Massudi does not know Hebrew and is, therefore, reluctant to answer questions. There are indications that she does watch *Dallas* and comprehends it, such as her remark during the viewing of the program regarding J. R.'s unsuitably informal dress in court (cf. note 34) which shows that she can both understand and criticize the basic plot. This would explain why her husband fills her in at night on the more detailed *Dallas* gossip.

4. CECILE: The landscape.

ITZCHAK: The landscape.

CECILE: It's rich . . .

ITZCHAK: It's rich like all American movies.

Interaction: Cecile's repeatedly breaking into her husband's sentences should not necessarily be looked at as interruption. In certain cultural settings, this constitutes what sociolinguists call 'corporate sentence building' (Bennet, 1978). This form of conversation characterizes cultures in which there is need for reassurance and encouragement – being polite, therefore, means cooperating in presenting oneself and the other. This does not exist in cultures where the need for privacy and autonomy is considered crucial and, therefore, being polite consists of respecting the boundaries of each individual (Brown and Levinson, 1979). Conversations in which there are frequent pauses and strict turn-taking belong to the second type of politeness, as it is concerned with respect for the distance among people. The discussion of the Moroccan group under consideration here, characterized by frequent overlaps, is associated with the first type of politeness, which creates an atmosphere of intimacy. Thus, Cecile's overlapping with Itzchak is probably (1) an indication of intimacy and consensus between husband and wife and (2) her particular way of joining the conversation and adding to the discussion rather than interrupting it.

5. MACHLUF: The beach, the pool, the colors, the apartment.

ZEHAVA: The house.

ITZCHAK: But after a while the subject becomes a little tiring because there are unacceptable things.

MACHLUF: For example?

ITZCHAK: Things that don't happen in life, let's say things that happen in a family, all the stories . . .

CECILE: They exaggerate sometimes.

ITZCHAK: It's exaggerated that they all give in to somebody like that. It's simply not real. It doesn't seem as true

Interpretation: Since most Israelis live in apartments, Machluf slips into calling the Ewing mansion 'the apartment.' He is immediately corrected by Zehava who, as we later discover, was just in the process of trying to find a way to move her own family from a two-room apartment to a slightly larger one.

to life as it was at the beginning (of the serial). After a while it starts to become boring. Even annoying.

ADI: But you see it faithfully?

CECILE: Yes, yes.

ITZCHAK: I see it for two reasons. The first reason to our regret, is that we don't . . .

6. CECILE: We don't have programs here.

Israel has one television channel. About half of the programs are imported from abroad, mostly from the United States. Subtitles are in Hebrew and Arabic.

7. ITZCHAK: We don't have very good programs. The second reason is that it's done so well – the setting and all – it attracts one; simply that. But I think it's good they stopped showing it for the time because we became almost slaves to this subject (the serial), even though I'm sure everybody knew what was going to happen.

ZEHAVA: There are also books (about *Dallas*).

Gratifications: Itzchak's comment suggests that viewing *Dallas* provides a different kind of experience than, say, viewing *Kojak*. He is, in effect, saying that the pleasure of watching does not arise from being curious about what the characters are going to do but about *how* they do it. Not having to worry about the technicalities of the plot, viewers can relax and enjoy following the Ewings, whose idiosyncrasies are anticipated. For the viewers, the pleasure of seeking out and discovering all the intricate details of the TV program may be similar to the pleasure of a reader in reading a novel for the second time (Barthes, 1975a).

8. CECILE: And people see it in Jordan, and it's more advanced.

ITZCHAK: It's something that almost repeats itself. The same mistakes that J. R. made repeat themselves, and it's no longer a subject for study.

ELIHU: What mistakes?

ITZCHAK: For example, when the father capitulates to J. R.'s mistakes in business.

MACHLUF: Which cost many millions . . .

One source of information on future developments in the story is Jordanian television, which is one season ahead of Israeli television.

9. ITZCHAK: And he always makes sure that he will succeed at any cost, and the women fall into his arms like I don't know what, and this is something in the story which is not really normal ('normal' = normative) in life.

Moral evaluation: Itzchak is raising a central moral and philosophical issue concerning the viewing of *Dallas*. Describing it in terms of the celebration of the success of ruthless power over moral values, of the victory of id over superego, leads him to consider whether this is a reflection of what happens in real life. Itzchak's answer is negative because normal to him means normative. This means a better interpretation of Itzchak's meaning than the mimetic concern with the relation between the program and life. Throughout this discussion *normali* and *lo normali* mean normative and deviant.

10. MACHLUF: Don't forget that J. R. is very good-looking and very rich.

ZEHAVA: And what do people like? Money.

MACHLUF: Good-looking and rich is something which attracts many women.

Referential forum: This leads to a discussion about social norms in interpreting the story. Machluf and Zehava draw on knowledge of life – and vice versa. They generalize about life, and this provides an interpretation of the story. Either way, they talk about *Dallas* as if it were real.

These generalizations about what 'people' like contradict what the group members say they themselves like and identify with. *They* select and evaluate characters on a strictly moral basis. When they are asked to name the central character in the episode, J. R. is not included. The difference between talking about what 'they' (people, mostly women) like and what 'we' (Jews, Moroccans) like shows that normative rules are invoked when speakers feel personally responsible for their statements. In Newcomb's (1984) terms, they might be employing different or even conflicting discourse systems in the two cases. Whereas here they talk as if they were participating observers in informal chatting about *Dallas*, later, in answering the interviewer's questions, they define themselves with the voice of a particular social and cultural community.

11. CECILE: Everybody, more or less, also in the film, knows what he's worth.

ADI: What does that mean?

MACHLUF: His character, his character . . .

CECILE: That he is not honest in business, with women, in everything. But nevertheless, the women continually . . .

The group regularly refers to the serial as a film; we have retained this usage. It seems to connote a festive involvement to which one looks forward, etc.

MACHLUF: . . . go after him.

CECILE: Anybody he wants . . .

MACHLUF: . . . gets caught in his net.

CECILE: . . . fall very fast.

YOSSI: . . . are attracted to him.

12. MACHLUF: Are attracted to him. Kristen, *zichrona livracha* ('her memory be blessed'), was also attracted.

YOSSI: The truth is, he's attractive: he's a good-looking fellow.

CECILE: They don't want to believe what they hear. They love him, and they don't want to accept the complaints against him. What one hears.

Acculturation: *Zichrona livracha*, the traditional Jewish way of alluding to someone who has died, is used ironically in this case. The term still gives a sense of how the participants chat about *Dallas*'s characters as if real people who live or, as in this case, die.

13. MACHLUF: You see, I'm a Jew wearing a skullcap, and I learned from this film to say (quoting from Psalms), 'Happy is our lot' that we're Jewish. Everything about J. R. and his baby, who has maybe four or five fathers. I don't know. The mother is Sue Ellen of course, and the brother of Pam left; maybe he's the father . . . I see that they're all bastards. Isn't that true Doctor Katz?

ELIHU: Really bastards or bastards in character?

MACHLUF: According to the movie, this son is literally a bastard. She was pregnant from Pam's brother.

Moral evaluation: This is just one instance in which Machluf invokes quotations from religious sources as a way of relating to the invading world of television. Here a quotation is used to contrast and express the mores of *Dallas* with those of Jewish culture; thus, he reinforces traditional values.

14. CECILE: . . . but the tests show that J. R. is the father . . .

MACHLUF: . . . and J. R. recognizes this himself. She told him the truth. She says: 'I am pregnant from Pamela's brother.' What's his name.

ITZCHAK: Bobby.

MACHLUF: No, no. Bobby is Pam's husband.

CECILE: Cliff. Cliff.

ITZCHAK: But, in fact he (J. R.) saw that it was his son.

GIL: OK, we're beginning. The program is starting.

Mutual aid: The debate over J. R.'s paternity points to the kind of involvement through speculation that *Dallas* arouses: the 'facts' of the story turn out to be a matter of interpretation. Different, sometimes contradictory bits of information are brought forth as evidence for various ways of understanding the story. Machluf knows the baby is *not* J.R.'s and proves it with Sue Ellen's words: 'She *told* him the truth.' Cecile brings up the laboratory test as proof of the opposite.

Discussion while viewing – from observers' notes, not recorded

15. MACHLUF: There's Miss Ellie.
ITZCHAK: Miss Ellie is wonderful, but the queen is Pam.

Methodology: Taping was discontinued here on the assumption that there would be little or no conversation during the viewing. Fortunately, the observers took notes verbatim until the recording resumed.

16. YOSSI: It's only the second time I'm seeing *Dallas*. It looks like an Arabic film, begins with an accident (*te'una*) and ends with a wedding (*hatuna*).
ZEHAVA: The men see the film because of the beautiful girls.

Critical: Yossi places *Dallas* within the genre of Arab melodrama. These shows are popular on Israeli television. His use of the rhyming words *te'una* and *hatuna* accentuates his awareness of the repetitive, formulaic nature of the succession of crises that lead, à la Propp (1968), from a 'lack' to a 'coronation.' (Compare our analysis . . . of the linear style used by Arabs and Moroccans in their retellings of the episode.) Parenthetically, there is reason to doubt Yossi's declaration that he is not a *Dallas* regular on the basis of his other statements.

17. CECILE: And there's a good mother. (*on screen: Miss Ellie is reprimanding J. R. because he intends to buy off the judge.*) Bravo. Bobby is too good and J. R. too bad, both extremes.
YOSSI: J. R. looks like Tony Curtis.

Interaction, mutual aid, critical: Cecile is here making her bid for the role of moral pedagogue or authoritative interpreter on the *Dallas* goings-on. There is also a parasocial note in the 'Bravo' she awards Miss Ellie. Also note the exaggerated polarization of Bobby and J. R., which has overtones of both the moral and the critical (in the sense of identifying the nexus of the dramatic tension). Our own analysis of the episode . . . will argue that this polarization of the two men is unwarranted, as is the group's tendency to overdetermine other characters as well, such as Sue Ellen (see note 60).

18. CECILE: There's Rebecca, Cliff's mother. Suddenly she's here again.
YOSSI: What business are they talking about?
MACHLUF: Oil. These are the actors who were in Israel.
YOSSI: Who's the boss; who decides things.
MACHLUF: J. R.
CECILE: Jock.

Mutual aid: Continuing her expertise, Cecile's surprised comments on seeing Cliff's mother sound like those of someone meeting an almost-forgotten old acquaintance. Characters are typically identified in terms of their family relations, 'Cliff's mother,' especially in the more traditional groups.

19. ITZCHAK: Look at how money corrupts things, corrupts people.

CECILE: A little money doesn't hurt; a lot does. The money simply pours out in this film.

Moral evaluation, forum: An illustration of how Dallas becomes a *forum* for the articulation of social issues (Newcomb and Hirsch, 1983) can be found in this discussion which starts with Itzchak pointing to the message of *Dallas*. Itzchak chooses to apply a moral criterion for judging characters, which is psychologically gratifying for the group because although they cannot be as successful as the Ewings, they can be more honest.

Machluf introduces an academic or spiritual standard of measuring success, alluding to tradition and to a type of success where the children of the poor may outdo the others. Thus, Itzchak and Machluf suggest two ways of using *Dallas* as a morality play, useful in defining success in ways that provide 'substitute frames for self-judgment' (Merton, 1946).

20. MACHLUF: I've seen how well poor children do at school and how rich children are just spoiled and fail. (referring to the women on screen) They're like Hanukkah lights, only there to be seen.

CECILE: My child sees swimming pools on TV and says how good it is to be rich.

YOSSI: (referring to a car on screen) What a Mercedes!

Acculturation: Machluf's metaphor again refers to a traditional source (cf. note 12) by drawing an analogy between the women in the program and Hanukkah candles, which are forbidden for practical use but are there to be admired. Use of this traditional Jewish allusion for defining the pleasures of TV is intended to be funny and serves to contribute to the group's cohesion versus the screen.

21. CECILE: Afton knows what J. R. is asking her to do is not kosher. She said as much to her brother. But, nevertheless, she goes on being with him. They choose beautiful women, one after the other. We see one beautiful girl, and after her appearance another even more beautiful girl. (*on screen: J. R.'s secretary calls to give him an excuse to leave Afton alone with the judge.*) She is waiting to be next in line. (general laughter)

ITZCHAK: J. R. is a bastard.

Understanding: This is a rare example of a viewer who may be said not to understand the plot. Trapped in her theory, according to which all women are attracted to J. R., Cecile misses the point of the secretary's call, prearranged by J. R. in order to carry out his scheme.

ZEHAVA: Would you like to be in his place? I don't think there are many people in the world like him as far as trickery goes. That's why it's not real.

MACHLUF: J. R. is the perfect man. J. R. only loves himself. Couldn't care less about the others.

22. CECILE: In real life Sue Ellen is better than Pam. They say that Pam in real life is not good; she takes drugs.

MACHLUF: (shakes his head unbelievingly)

YOSSI: There is too much cinema here. You know what movies are? Business, money. (*on screen: J. R. is trying to set the judge up with Afton.*)

MACHLUF: Filth, that's what we're seeing.

In Israel, as elsewhere, much is known about the well-publicized private lives of the stars. As Machluf has already noted, some of the *Dallas* stars made a royal visit to Israel, and Prime Minister Begin received them.

23. MACHLUF: (*on screen: Afton sings in a nightclub.*) Moroccans are drinkers; what can we do? It causes us to forget about kosher rules, about our tiny flats. Thank God for that . . . Look at how she sings.

ZEHAVA: He is simply a good-looking man (J. R.). (turning to the others) We are always talking about good-looking women – talk a bit about men.

CECILE: (referring to Mitch on screen) *Voilà le plus beau.*

ZEHAVA: Who?

Forum: Watching the bar scene on screen triggers a comment on the reasons for the prevalence of drinking in Machluf's own milieu. The function of drinking as a means of escape from sordid reality is talked about in the group in the same way that they talk about the function for them of *Dallas* (cf. note 89).

24. CECILE: Mitch. *mitz*.

MASSUDI: Not *mitz tapuzim.*

CECILE: (referring to the woman who was choking on screen) Mitch will help her. He studied medicine.

Interaction, acculturation: Cecile and Massudi make a play on words in Hebrew in saying that 'Mitch' is not *mitz* – the Hebrew word for fruit juice.

25. MACHLUF: Something like that happened to us at work; do you remember?

ZEHAVA: My friend almost died because of this. She swallowed a piece of meat.

MACHLUF: One woman actually fasted two days because there was a wedding reception.

CECILE: (referring to Mitch on screen) That's it. They got it out.

Referential: Machluf and Zehava by association, are reminded of two similar choking instances they have witnessed. Both give parallel, competing dramatic scenarios resembling the one taking place on the screen, which does not in the least disturb Cecile, who is absorbed in the program and maintains her own dialogue with the screen.

MACHLUF: . . . and she came and fell over a tray of turkey meat and put it into her mouth and choked. Thank God, among the guests, there was a doctor; he gave her a stroke on the back, pah, got it all out, very very hard. And she returned to life.

CECILE: That's it. He's saved her.

ZEHAVA: This girlfriend of mine practically choked to death. They took her in the ambulance to the operating theater, and the fear, when she saw everything, made her spit it up all at once. And they took it out: the doctor couldn't believe it. He saw this meat and said: 'How could she do such a thing?' A friend of mine told her . . .

MACHLUF: It's a whole cow's tongue she swallowed in one breath.

26.   ZEHAVA: She should eat like a human being. (asked by her husband to serve tea) Sorry, I'm watching (the program). Otherwise, afterwards, when they (the interviewers) ask me, what shall I answer?

Definition of the situation: Zehava defends herself against her husband's request that she serve tea by referring to the role of focus-group members.

27.   YOSSI: With us, it's not like with J. R. With J. R. The woman looks after everything. He's got a servant girl. (Zehava and Cecile laugh)

ZEHAVA: Why, do you mean to say I am your servant?

Interaction, gratification (uses):   TV here provides shared associations, which are activated, as it were, for expressing negative feelings in a subtle way, thus preventing a direct confrontation.

This is only one of the ways in which the program is used to comment on present problems that occupy viewers in their personal or social lives. Whereas this switch to talking about life deals with gender roles in marriage (cf. note 59), the next transition to real life (note 31) deals with the norms of Israeli society in contrast to the presumed norms of *Dallas*.

28.   MACHLUF: No, this is your house. You will be given 'up to half the kingdom' – it is Purim.

ZEHAVA: (reacting to coffee offered to Mitch in the film) Coffee, Cecile?

This is a quote from the biblical book of Esther associated with the carnivalesque holiday of Purim, which was being celebrated at the time of the interview session.

CECILE: (*on screen*:   *The doctor examines Pamela.*) What a show-off.

MACHLUF: Who's the old man?

29. CECILE: A doctor.

YOSSI: I thought they have some private doctor.

CECILE: (*in French, offering her diagnosis*) *Depression*.

MACHLUF: Why?

CECILE: *Ell veut un bébé*, and they ask her to wait too long. She wants it too much.

Cecile continues her pedagogic leadership.

30. YOSSI: The same story all the time. He (J. R.) feels himself strong with his money. I'm telling you, who in Israel could get away with that?

Critical: Recognition of the formulaic character of the plot by Yossi is continued also in Yossi's next intervention.

31. MACHLUF: Akiva Nof, the member of Knesset, had a similar story with his wife. The journalists have shaken the whole country with Akiva Nof until now. In Israel he (J. R.) cold not possibly behave in such a way.

Referential: By comparing J. R. to a member of the Israeli Parliament who went through a well-publicized divorce case, Machluf is assuming (1) that *Dallas* reflects American society, (2) that America is corrupt, and (3) that Israel is not. Thus, he again uses *Dallas* to reinforce his own values.

32. ZEHAVA: 'The taste of life.'

Critical: In order to support Yossi's argument, Zehava quotes Coca-Cola's frequently broadcast commercial (in Hebrew). She chooses an example par excellence of America inundating the world with its idea of taste – the equivalent of *Dallas* in the area of material consumption – where (1) both represent American (consumer) hegemony, (2) both are relentlessly repetitive, and maybe (3) both add flavor to ordinary life.

33. CECILE: (*on screen*:   *Mitch is having breakfast with a plastic surgeon and his wife whom he saved from choking.*) But (please) without the bones.

Para-social interaction: In conducting a conversation directly with the characters, Cecile brings them into the living room, so to speak, so that she can joke with them, give them advice, and even criticize their actions. In rebuking the doctor, she introduces her own social norms, implying that his invitation to Mitch to come for a meal defines their conversation as something personal, so that offering money seems in bad taste.

34. MASSUDI: (*on screen: J. R. enters the court.*) He came without a jacket.
ZEHAVA: (asked again to bring some tea) Well, I got an order from the captain, so I have to bring it.
CECILE: (*on screen: J. R. insults Pamela at the breakfast table.*) Now there's violence.

Understanding: Massudi, who cannot read the subtitles and claims she does not understand what is occurring on the screen (cf. note 3), nevertheless criticizes J. R. for not showing more respect to the court by dressing more formally.

35. MACHLUF: Why does Pam go to work? Her husband is so rich.
CECILE: But they have no satisfaction in life. So they search . . .
YOSSI: Satisfaction in life.
CECILE: What does it mean, why does she go to work? What will she do? Wait until Bobby comes home?
YOSSI: Does she lack anything? Of course, she does not have to wait that much for her salary. She couldn't care less. I stand in the queue at the bank on the first of the month.
CECILE: Too much money.
YOSSI: (*on screen: Another glamorous woman appears in a car.*) She doesn't work. (everybody laughs)

Forum: Although the group's discussion overtly deals with what is happening on the screen, they are, in effect, making use of *Dallas* to enter into a debate on the roles of the sexes. Machluf and Yossi voice the traditional position in this debate, while Cecile brings up the concept of the right of women to self-realization. (This discussion happens to follow closely after Zehava's joking remark about getting an order from 'the captain.')

36. CECILE: (*Cliff is introduced to his new sister.*) Suddenly he discovers a half-sister. It's lucky that she said to him she's a sister, otherwise, he could have fallen in love with her.
YOSSI: They all have blue eyes.
CECILE: Now, please. (quiet) That's the trial for the child.
ZEHAVA AND YOSSI: Moroccans want only food.
YOSSI: Not *Dallas*.
CECILE: (responding to the general noise) You've no heart; this is a trial about the child.

Referential: Cecile's relief upon hearing the formal definition of family relationship is a sign of her awareness that *Dallas* scripts hover on the borderline of kinship taboos, which the characters constantly threaten to – and sometimes do – break (cf. note 13, 78). We would have coded this as *critical* had Cecile betrayed awareness that this policy of brinkmanship is caused by (1) the need to produce new entanglements within the rather closed *Dallas* circle (a new relative has to provide a new twist in the plot) and (2) the need to provide new excitement to viewers who, due to the socializing influences of television, become more and more immunized against shock.

37. ZEHAVA: (If) it was a *Beit Din* (rabbinical court), this would be a trial. Of course, the child will go back to his mother.

YOSSI: Is this Sue Ellen's lawyer?

ZEHAVA: (when Gil gestures her to stay in her seat rather than get the tea) I get up – immediately he looks at me. (to the interviewer) Don't worry. You will ask me, I will answer you.

Acculturation: It is not clear whether Zehava considers the *Dallas* custody trial real or not when she compares it to the *Beit Din*, which deals with cases of marriage and divorce in Israel.

38. CECILE: (*on screen: Sue Ellen's lawyer discloses he has a doctor's certificate about Dusty.*) Oh, what they're going to discover now. It's not nice, in public like that.

GIL: What is not nice?

CECILE: (shaking her head) What they're going to discover . . .

GIL: Do you know what they'll discover?

CECILE: I know.

GIL: How do you know?

Referential: The same norm that is behind participants' embarrassment over public discussions of sex (see discussion of Dusty 'not (being) a man,' below) may also underlie Cecile's reluctance to see Dusty's impotence made public in the show. Another, less conscious reason might be that one of the sources of enjoyment of the series is in the arid, viewers' 'privileged' position over that of other characters in the show and over less knowledgeable viewers.

39. CECILE: For some time he's not been a man.

GIL: From former episodes?

ZEHAVA: Yes.

CECILE: Since the accident.

Interaction: Cecile's tactful way of describing Dusty's impotence is indicative of the way group members tend to use euphemisms and literary or biblical expressions – or may even leave sentences unfinished – when sex is being discussed. Note how Cecile continues her expertise.

40. ZEHAVA: And he told her beforehand: 'It's a pity for you to go on with me, I don't want to go on.' And it was because of her. He was in the airplane because of her.

CECILE: (*Sue Ellen's lawyer calls her 'the girl he (Dusty) intends to marry – his future wife.'*) 'His future wife.' Here, at least, there's a nice contrast. The second family she's falling into – people . . . not just . . . people with heart, people – not just money.

ITZCHAK: Just for that, she will get the child now.

Mutual aid in interpretation: The discussion provides a running commentary on what is happening on the TV screen, beginning with definitions of the conflict (Cecile sees it from Sue Ellen's point of view – money versus heir; Itzchak sees it from the court's point of view – sex versus love), moving on to predictions about the outcome of the trial and speculation about Sue Ellen's motives. Note that the implicit question in Machluf's statement that Dusty is 'not a man' is understood by Cecile to mean, 'Why should Sue Ellen want to stay with

CECILE: Yes, sure. It's people . . . not just the money.

MACHLUF: After the accident he is not a man anymore.

CECILE: But she wants to be with him. Also he had the accident because of her.

ITZCHAK: So they shouldn't think as if she wanted.

MACHLUF: (to lawyer on screen) Because of love – that's right.

CECILE: J. R.'s lawyer is not pleased.

ZEHAVA: (repeating lawyer's words) 'True love.'

Dusty?' and is answered accordingly. For her, not having sex is proof of true love.

41. CECILE: (on screen: *Sue Ellen's lawyer says, 'How can we deprive her of the only child she'll ever have?'*) J. R. already has Kristen's son. It's enough.

ITZCHAK: (*Sue Ellen's lawyer wins.*) She beat him.

CECILE: He (J. R.) killed her (Kristen), and the child remains.

YOSSI: But the judge is corrupt. He talked to J. R. in the cafe. He is corrupt.

ITZCHAK: They didn't show a bribe.

CECILE: In the former . . . she was pregnant, and she came to get money out of him . . . to blackmail (J. R.) . . . if not, she would tell her sister the truth.

YOSSI: The judge . . . he talked to him in the cafe . . . he's corrupt.

MACHLUF: It looks like the end.

CECILE: And Cliff came in at that moment and accused him of murder.

Forum: Cecile introduces here a new concept of distributive justice, equal allocation of babies. The basic facts of the story – that J. R. has had a baby from Kristen – serve only as the basis for an argument over whether or not J. R. has a right to another baby. The total destruction of the institution of the family passes by unnoticed and uncriticized.

42. MACHLUF: I don't understand one thing. J. R. knows; he heard from his wife that the child (John Ross) is not his, and in spite of that, he wants to *take* him.

CECILE: But it's his name. His . . . how do you say, his *nom propre*, his name in the world.

ZEHAVA: That's right.

CECILE: His name. It's the principle. It's his wife. It has to be his son. If not, his whole name collapses; his whole honor

Mutual aid interpretation: Machluf calls attention to the improbability of some of the dynamics of family relations in *Dallas*. How can babies be bought, sold, and transferred? In their answers, Cecile and Zehava avoid the issue of how J. R. can accept the fact that the baby has another father.

in the world rises and falls with this.

MASSUDI: I never see it (the program).

43. MACHLUF: (*The judge's decision about the money Sue Ellen gets for maintenance is announced*.) $5,000 a month times 360.

ZEHAVA: It will increase. Until then it's linked.

CECILE: (anticipating the announcement on the screen) It was given to his mother. (*on screen*: '. . . *to Sue Ellen Ewing* . . .') Marvelous.

ZEHAVA: I knew.

YOSSI: $1,000 a month (for the baby).

CECILE: Oh, no. (*J. R.'s smile at the end of the show*.) What a marvelous look.

Acculturation: The award is immediately translated into Israeli currency and Zehava remarks that with the rate of inflation in Israel, this amount of money will increase considerably within a short amount of time.

44. ZEHAVA: Finished. Now the examination (the interview session).

GIL: So she got $1,000 for the child as well?

CECILE: It's nothing to him.

ZEHAVA: It's nothing to him.

ITZCHAK: $5,000 maintenance and $1,000 for clothes.

ADI: $5,000 goes straight into the fuel for the car.

ITZCHAK: Nonsense. What is $1,000? It's like 1,000 *lirot* here. (comparing it to Israeli money)

MACHLUF: $6,000 times 360 *lirot*.

ZEHAVA: He talks in millions, not, not in thousands.

ITZCHAK: (repeats) There a thousand dollars is 1,000 *lirot* here.

ZEHAVA: It's nothing. Nothing.

Definition of the situation: The transition to the more formal part of the session is immediately announced by Zehava, the hostess, defining the interview situation as an 'examination' . . . Other groups define the situation quite differently.

45. MACHLUF: That's what we're condemned to: 'We can but admire them.'

Acculturation: Machluf alludes to his earlier joke about Hanukkah candles (cf. note 20). Just as the *Dallas* women, the amounts of money that are paraded on the show are only to be admired from a distance.

Program ends, focus discussion begins

46. CECILE: (to the interviewer) I think you got your answers within this — while we were watching the movie, right?

GIL: Let's start so we can all get some sleep.

ZEHAVA: If not you can (all) sleep here tonight, with the snow we've got here.

ELIHU: It's actually snowing?

ZEHAVA: Yes, wet snow.

Methodology: To a large extent, it is true that many of the questions to be brought up in the focus discussion were already touched on before the formal discussion took place. These questions focus on characters' kinship relations and their personalities as well as on how realistic they are as people, the extent to which *Dallas* reflects America, the concern with babies, and the gratifications of watching *Dallas*. Such anticipations of our questions reassured us in our conviction that the guidelines of the questionnaire were not intrusive.

47. ADI: I'm going to ask you something simple. I want each of you to tell me what was in the film. As if I hadn't seen it or as if you were coming to tell me tomorrow morning . . . Can somebody please tell me what happened in the film?

YOSSI: The same as last week. (everybody laughs) Believe me, the same faces. Only the judge is new. (laughter)

Methodology: Having the participants recount the story of the *Dallas* episode was intended to reveal (1) the extent to which people in various cultures, who depended more or less on subtitles, understood the basic plot, (2) the extent to which this understanding was shared or universal and the points at which it varied, and (3) differences in styles of narration that reflected variations in what may be called critical distance from the story as well as various traditions in storytelling.

48. ZEHAVA: Suzi (Cecile) always sounds as if she can explain things.

Interaction, definition of the situation: Zehava demurs, passing the task on to someone else, thus betraying a newly awkward feeling of the group in organized discussion. They soon forgot about this, however. Note how Zehava tries to put the group's best foot forward by cutting short her cynical husband and proposing Cecile as the group spokesperson.

49. YOSSI: In *Dallas* there's the law of Texas. (laughter)

ADI: What's on here? Tell me what happened in the film we've just seen.

Interpretation: By 'the law of Texas,' Yossi means the law of the jungle, where those with power do as they please (cf. Yossi's comments at note 52).

Chapter 29

Jacqueline Bobo

THE COLOR PURPLE
Black women as cultural readers

TONY BROWN, A SYNDICATED columnist and host of the television programme *Tony Brown's Journal* has called the film *The Color Purple* 'the most racist depiction of Black men since *The Birth of a Nation* and the most anti-Black family film of the modern film era'. Ishmael Reed, a Black novelist, has labelled the film and the book 'a Nazi conspiracy'.[1] Since its première in December 1985, *The Color Purple* has provoked constant controversy, debate and appraisals of its effects on the image of Black people in the US.

The film also has incited a face-off between Black feminist critics and Black male reviewers. The women defend the work, or more precisely, defend Alice Walker's book and the right of the film to exist. Black males vehemently denounce both works and cite the film's stereotypical representations. In the main, adverse criticisms have revolved around three issues: a) that the film does not examine class, b) that Black men are portrayed unnecessarily as harsh and brutal, the consequence of which is to further the split between the Black female and the Black male; and c) that Black people as a whole are depicted as perverse, sexually wanton, and irresponsible. In these days of massive cutbacks in federal support to social agencies, according to some rebukes, the film's representation of the Black family was especially harmful.

Most left-wing publications in the United States, the *Guardian*, *Frontline* and *In These Times*, denounced the film, but mildly. *The Nation*, in fact, commended the film and its director for fitting the work's threatening content into a safe and familiar form.[2] Articles in the other publications praised particular scenes but on the whole disparaged the film for its lack of class authenticity. Black people of that era were poor, the left-wing critics stated, and Steven Spielberg failed to portray that fact. (Uh-uh, says Walker. She said she wrote here about people who owned land, property and dealt in commerce.)

Jill Nelson, a Black journalist who reviewed the film for the *Guardian*, felt that the film's Black protesters were naïve to think that 'at this late date in our history . . . Hollywood would ever consciously offer Black Americans literal tools for our emancipation.[3] Furthermore, Nelson refuted the charge that the film would for ever set the race back in white viewers' minds by observing that most viewers would only leave the theatre commenting on whether or not they liked the film. Articles counter to Nelson's were published in a following issue of the *Guardian* and they emphasized the film's distorted perspective on class and the ideological use to which the film would be put to show the Black family's instability.

The December première of *The Color Purple* was picketed in Los Angeles by an activist group named the Coalition Against Black Exploitation. The group protested against the savage and brutal depiction of Black men in the film.[4] That complaint was carried further by a Black columnist in the *Washington Post*, Courtland Milloy, who wrote that some Black women would enjoy seeing Black men shown as 'brutal bastards', and that furthermore, the book was demeaning. Milloy stated: 'I got tired, a long time ago, of white men publishing books by Black women about how screwed up Black men are.'[5] Other hostile views about the film were expressed by representatives of the NAACP, Black male columnists, and a law professor, Leroy Clark of Catholic University, who called it dangerous. (When Ntozake Shange's choreopoem *For Colored Girls Who Have Considered Suicide/When the Rainbow Is Enuf* opened on Broadway in autumn 1976, the response from Black male critics was similar.)

Black female reviewers were not as critical of the film in its treatment of gender issues. Although Barbara Smith attacked the film for its class distortions, she felt that 'sexual politics and sexual violence' in the Black community were matters that needed to be confronted and changed.[6] Jill Nelson, emphasizing that those who did not like what the messenger (the film) said about Black men should look at the facts, provided statistics on female-headed Black households, lack of child support, and so on.[7]

Michele Wallace, a professor of Afro-American literature and creative writing at the University of Oklahoma and author of *Black Macho: The Myth of the Superwoman*, stated that the film had some 'positive feminist influences and some positive import for Black audiences in this country'.[8]

However, in an earlier article in the *Village Voice*, 18 March 1986, Michele Wallace was less charitable to the film. Although she gives a very lucid explication of Walker's novel, citing its attempt to 'reconstruct Black female experience as positive ground', Wallace wrote of the film, 'Spielberg juggles film clichés and racial stereotypes fast and loose, until all signs of a Black feminist agenda are banished, or ridiculed beyond repair.' Wallace also noted that the film used mostly cinematic types reminiscent of earlier films. She writes: 'Instead of serious men and women encountering consequential dilemmas, we're almost always minstrels, more than a little ridiculous; we dance and sing without continuity, as if on the end of a string. It seems white people are never going to forget Stepin Fetchit, no matter how many times he dies.'[9]

Wallace both sees something positive in the film and points to its flaws. I agree with her in both instances, especially in her analysis of how it is predictable that the film 'has given rise to controversy and debate within the Black community, ostensibly focused on the eminently printable issues of the film's image of Black men.'

In an attempt to explain why people liked *The Color Purple* in spite of its sometimes clichéd characters, Donald Bogle, on the *Phil Donahue Show*, put it down to the novelty of seeing Black actors in roles not previously available to them:

> for Black viewers there is a schizophrenic reaction. You're torn in two. On the one hand you see the character of Mister and you're disturbed by the stereotype. Yet, on the other hand, and this is the basis of the appeal of that

film for so many people, is that the women you see in the movie, you have
never seen Black women like this put on the screen before. I'm not talking
about what happens to them in the film, I'm talking about the visual statement itself. When you see Whoopi Goldberg in close-up, a loving close-up,
you look at this woman, you know that in American films in the past, in the
1930s, 1940s, she would have played a maid. She would have been a comic
maid. Suddenly, the camera is focusing on her and we say, 'I've seen this
woman some place, I know her.'[10]

It appears to me that one of the problems most of the film's reviewers have in trying
to analyse the film, with all of its faults, is to make sense of the overwhelming positive response from Black female viewers.

The Color Purple was a small quiet book when it emerged on the literary scene in
1982. The subject of the book is a young, abused, uneducated Black girl who evolved
into womanhood with a sense of her own worth gained by bonding with the women
around her. When Alice Walker won the American Book Award and the Pulitzer
Prize for Fiction in 1983, the sales of the novel increased to over two million copies,
placing the book on the *New York Times* best-seller list for a number of weeks.[11] Still
the book did not have as wide an audience or the impact the film would have. In
December 1985 Steven Spielberg's *The Color Purple* exploded with the force of a land-
mine on the landscape of cultural production. Many commentators on the film have
pointed out that the film created discussion and controversy about the image of
Black people in media, the likes of which had not been seen since the films *The Birth
of a Nation* (1915) and *Gone With the Wind* (1939).

One of the reasons Alice Walker sold the screen rights was that she understood that
people who would not read the book would go to see the film. Walker and her advis-
ers thought that the book's critical message needed to be exposed to a wider audience.
The readership for the novel was a very specific one and drastically different from the
mass audience toward which the film is directed. However, the film is a commercial
venture produced in Hollywood by a white male according to all of the tenets and
conventions of commercial cultural production in the United States. The manner in
which an audience responds to such a film is varied, diverse and complex. I am especially concerned with analysing how Black women have responded.

My aim is to examine the way in which a specific audience creates meaning from
a mainstream text and uses the reconstructed meaning to empower themselves and
their social group. This analysis will show how Black women as audience members
and cultural consumers have connected up with what has been characterized as the
'renaissance of Black women writers'.[12] The predominant element of this movement
is the creation and maintenance of images of Black women that are based upon
Black women's constructions, history and real-life experiences.

As part of a larger study I am doing on *The Color Purple* I conducted a group interview with selected Black women viewers of the film.[13] Statements from members of
the group focused on how moved they were by the fact that Celie eventually tri-
umphs in the film. One woman talked about the variety of emotions she experienced:
'I had different feelings all the way through the film, because first I was very angry,
and then I started to feel so sad I wanted to cry because of the way Celie was being
treated. It just upset me the way she was being treated and the way she was so totally

dominated. But gradually, as time went on, she began to realize that she could do something for herself, that she could start moving and progressing, that she could start reasoning and thinking things out for herself.' Another woman stated that she was proud of Celie for her growth: 'The lady was a strong lady, like I am. And she hung in there and she overcame.'

One of the women in the group talked about the scene where Shug tells Celie that she has a beautiful smile and that she should stop covering up her face. This woman said that she could relate to that part because it made Celie's transformation in the film so much more powerful. At first, she said, everybody who loved Celie [Shug and Nettie], and everyone that Celie loved kept telling her to put her hand down. The woman then pointed out 'that last time that Celie put her hand down nobody told her to put her hand down. She had started coming into her own. So when she grabbed that knife she was ready to use it.' This comment refers to the scene in the film at the dinner table, when Celie and Shug are about to leave for Memphis. Mister begins to chastise Celie telling her that she will be back. He says, 'You ugly, you skinny, you shaped funny and you scared to open your mouth to people.' Celie sits there quietly and takes Mister's verbal abuse. Then she asks him, 'Any more letters come?' She is talking about Nettie's letters from Africa that Mister has been hiding from Celie and that Celie and Shug had recently found. Mister replies, 'Could be, could be not.' Celie jumps up at that point, grabs the knife, and sticks it to Mister's throat.

The woman who found this scene significant continued: 'But had she not got to that point, built up to that point [of feeling herself worthwhile], she could have grabbed the knife and turned it the other way for all that it mattered to her. She wouldn't have been any worse off. But she saw herself getting better. So when she grabbed that knife she was getting ready to use it and it wasn't on herself.'

Other comments from the women were expressions of outrage at criticisms made against the film. The women were especially disturbed by vicious attacks against Alice Walker and against Black women critics and scholars who were publicly defending the film. One of the women in the interview session commented that she was surprised that there was such controversy over the film: 'I had such a positive feeling about it, I couldn't imagine someone saying that they didn't like it.' Another said that she was shocked at the outcry from some Black men: 'I didn't look at it as being stereotypically Black or all Black men are this way' (referring to the portrayal of the character Mister).

Another related a story that shows how two people can watch the same film and have opposite reactions: 'I was thinking about how men felt about it [*The Color Purple*] and I was surprised. But I related it to something that happened to me sometime ago when I was married. I went to see a movie called *Three in the Attic*. I don't know if any of you ever saw it. But I remember that on the way home – I thought it was funny – but my husband was so angry he wouldn't even talk to me on the way home. He said, "You thought that was funny." I said that I sure did. He felt it was really hostile because these ladies had taken this man up in the attic and made him go to bed with all of them until he was . . . blue. Because he had been running around with all of these ladies. But he [her husband] was livid because I thought it was funny. And I think now, some men I talked to had a similar reaction to *The Color Purple*. That was it . . . all the men in there were dummies or horrible. And none of the men, they felt, were portrayed in a positive light. And then I started thinking about it and

I said, "well . . . I felt that somebody had to be the hero or the heroine, and in this case it just happened to be the woman."'

I have found that on the whole Black women have discovered something progressive and useful in the film. It is crucial to understand how this is possible when viewing a work made according to the encoding of dominant ideology. Black women's responses to *The Color Purple* loom as an extreme contrast to those of many other viewers. Not only is the difference in reception noteworthy but Black women's responses confront and challenge a prevalent method of media audience analysis which insists that viewers of mainstream works have no control or influence over a cultural product. Recent developments in media audience analysis demonstrate that there is a complex process of negotiation whereby specific members of a culture construct meaning from a mainstream text that is different from the meanings others would produce. These different readings are based, in part, on viewers' various histories and experiences.

Oppositional readings

The encoding/decoding model is useful for understanding how a cultural product can evoke such different viewer reactions. The model was developed by the University of Birmingham Centre for Contemporary Cultural Studies, under the direction of Stuart Hall, in an attempt to synthesize various perspectives on media audience analysis and to incorporate theory from sociology and cultural studies. This model is concerned with an understanding of the communication process as it operates in a specific cultural context. It analyses ideological and cultural power and the way in which meaning is produced in that context. The researchers at the Centre felt that media analysts should not look simply at the meaning of a text but should also investigate the social and cultural framework in which communication takes place.[14]

From political sociology, the encoding/decoding model was drawn from the work of Frank Parkin, who developed a theory of meaning systems.[15] This theory delineates three potential responses to a media message: dominant, negotiated or oppositional. A dominant (or preferred) reading of a text accepts the content of the cultural product without question. A negotiated reading questions parts of the content of the text but does not question the dominant ideology which underlies the production of the text. An oppositional response to a cultural product is one in which the recipient of the text understands that the system that produced the text is one with which she/he is fundamentally at odds.[16]

A viewer of a film (reader of a text) comes to the moment of engagement with the work with a knowledge of the world and a knowledge of other texts, or media products. What this means is that when a person comes to view a film, she/he does not leave her/his histories, whether social, cultural, economic, racial, or sexual at the door. An audience member from a marginalized group (people of colour, women, the poor, and so on) has an oppositional stance as they participate in mainstream media. The motivation for this counter-reception is that we understand that mainstream media has never rendered our segment of the population faithfully. We have as evidence our years of watching films and television programmes and reading plays and books. Out of habit, as readers of mainstream texts, we have learned to ferret out the beneficial and put up blinders against the rest.

From this wary viewing standpoint, a subversive reading of a text can occur. This alternative reading comes from something in the work that strikes the viewer as amiss, that appears 'strange'. Behind the idea of subversion lies a reader-oriented notion of 'making strange'.[17] When things appear strange to the viewer, she/he may then bring other viewpoints to bear on the watching of the film and may see things other than what the film-makers intended. The viewer, that is, will read 'against the grain' of the film.

Producers of mainstream media products are not aligned in a conspiracy against an audience. When they construct a work they draw on their own background, experience and social and cultural milieu. They are therefore under 'ideological pressure' to reproduce the familiar.[18] When Steven Spielberg made *The Color Purple* he did not intend to make a film that would be in the mould of previous films that were directed by a successful white director and had an all-Black or mostly Black cast.

Spielberg states that he deliberately cast the characters in *The Color Purple* in a way that they would not carry the taint of negative stereotypes:

> I didn't want to cast traditional Black movie stars, which I thought would create their own stereotypes. I won't mention any names because it wouldn't be kind, but there were people who wanted to play these parts very much. It would have made it seem as if these were the only Black people accepted in white world's mainstream. I didn't want to do that. That's why I cast so many unknowns like Whoopi Goldberg, Oprah Winfrey, Margaret Avery.[19]

But it is interesting that while the director of the film made a conscious decision to cast against type, he could not break away from his culturally acquired conceptions of how Black people are and how they should act. Barbara Christian, Professor of Afro-American Studies at University of California, Berkeley, contends that the most maligned figure in the film is the character Harpo. She points out that in the book he cannot become the patriarch that society demands he be.[20] Apparently Spielberg could not conceive of a man uncomfortable with the requirements of patriarchy, and consequently depicts Harpo as a buffoon. Christian comments that 'the movie makes a negative statement about men who show some measure of sensitivity to women'. The film uses the husband and wife characters, Harpo and Sofia, as comic relief. Some of the criticisms against the film from Black viewers concerned Harpo's ineptness in repairing the roof. If the film-makers have Harpo fall once, it seems they decided that it was even funnier if he fell three times.

In her *Village Voice* review, Michele Wallace attributed motives other than comic relief to the film's representations of the couple. Wallace considered their appearances to be the result of 'white patriarchal interventions'. She wrote:

> In the book, Sofia is the epitome of a woman with masculine powers, the martyr to sexual injustice who eventually triumphs through the realignment of the community. In the movie she is an occasion for humor. She and Harpo are the reincarnations of Amos and Sapphire; they alternately fight and fuck their way to a house full of pickaninnies. Harpo is always falling through a roof he's chronically unable to repair. Sofia is always shoving a baby into his arms, swinging her large hips, and talking a mile a minute. Harpo,

who is dying to marry Sofia in the book, seems bamboozled into marriage in the film. Sofia's only masculine power is her contentiousness. Encircled by the mayor, his wife and an angry mob, she is knocked down and her dress flies up providing us with a timely reminder that she is just a woman.[21]

The depiction of Sofia lying the in street with her dress up is almost an exact replica of a picture published in a national mass-circulation magazine of a large Black woman lying dead in her home after she had been killed by her husband in a domestic argument. Coincidence or not, this image among others in the film makes one wonder about Spielberg's unconscious store of associations.

[. . .]

Black women's response

Given the similarities of *The Color Purple* to past films that have portrayed Black people negatively, Black women's positive reaction to the film seems inconceivable. However, their stated comments and published reports prove that Black women not only like the film but have formed a strong attachment to it. The film is significant in their lives.

John Fiske provides a useful explanation of what is meant by the term 'the subject' in cultural analysis. 'The subject' is different from the individual. The individual is the biological being produced by nature; the 'subject' is a social and theoretical construction that is used to designate individuals as they become significant in a political or theoretical sense. When considering a text – a cultural product – the subject is defined as the political being who is affected by the ideological construction of the text.[22]

Black women, as subjects for the text, *The Color Purple*, have a different history and consequently a different perspective from other viewers of the film. This became evident in the controversy surrounding the film, and in the critical comments from some Black males about what they perceived as the detrimental depiction of Black men. In contrast to this view, Black women have demonstrated that they found something useful and positive in the film. Barbara Christian relates that the most frequent statement from Black women has been: 'Finally, somebody says something about us.'[23] This sense of identification with what was in the film would provide an impetus for Black women to form an engagement with the film. This engagement could have been either positive or negative. That it was favourable indicates something about the way in which Black women have constructed meaning from this text.

It would be too easy, I think, to categorize Black women's reaction to the film as an example of 'false consciousness'; to consider Black women as cultural dupes in the path of media barrage who cannot figure out when a media product portrays them and their race in a negative manner. Black women are aware, along with others, of the oppression and harm that comes from a negative media history. But Black women are also aware that their specific experience, as Black people, as women, in a rigid class/caste system, has never been adequately dealt with in mainstream media.

One of the Black women that I interviewed talked about this cultural past and how it affected her reaction to *The Color Purple*: 'When I went to the movie, I thought, here I am. I grew up looking at Elvis Presley kissing all these white girls. I grew up listening to 'Tammy, Tammy, Tammy'. [She sings the song that Debbie Reynolds sang in the movie of the same name.] And it wasn't that I had anything projected before me on the screen to really give me something that I could grow up to be like. Or even wanted to be. Because I knew I wasn't Goldilocks, you know, and I had heard those stories all my life. So when I got to the movie, the first thing I said was "God, this is good acting." And I liked that. I felt a lot of pride in my Black brothers and sisters . . . By the end of the movie I was totally emotionally drained . . . The emotional things were all in the book, but the movie just took every one of my emotions . . . Towards the end, when she looks up and sees her sister Nettie . . . I had gotten so emotionally high at that point . . . when she saw her sister, when she started to call her name and to recognize who she was, the hairs on my neck started to stick up. I had never had a movie do that to me before.'

The concept 'interpellation' sheds light on the process by which Black women were able to form a positive engagement with *The Color Purple*. Interpellation is the way in which the subject is hailed by the text; it is the method by which ideological discourses constitute subjects and draw them into the text/subject relationship. John Fiske describes 'hailing' as similar to hailing a cab. The viewer is hailed by a particular work; if she/he gives a co-operative response to the beckoning, then not only are they constructed as a subject, but the text then becomes a text, in the sense that the subject begins to construct meaning from the work and is constructed by the work.[24]

The moment of the encounter of the text and the subject is known as the 'interdiscourse'. David Morley explains this concept, developed by Michel Pêcheux, as the space, the specific moment when subjects bring their histories to bear on meaning production in a text.[25] Within this interdiscursive space, cultural competencies come into play. A cultural competency is the repertoire of discursive strategies, the range of knowledge, that a viewer brings to the act of watching a film and creating meaning from a work. As has been stated before, the meanings of a text will be constructed differently depending on the various backgrounds of the viewers. The viewers' position in the social structure determines, in part, what sets of discourses or interpretive strategies they will bring to their encounter with the text. A specific cultural competency will set some of the boundaries to meaning construction.

The cultural competency perspective has allowed media researchers to understand how elements in a viewer's background play a determining role in the way in which she/he interprets a text. Stuart Hall, David Morley and others utilize the theories of Dell Hymes, Basil Bernstein and Pierre Bourdieu for an understanding of the ways in which a social structure distributes different forms of cultural decoding strategies throughout the different sections of the media audience. These understandings are not the same for everyone in the audience because they are shaped by the individual's history, both media and cultural, and by the individual's social affiliations such as race, class, gender, and so on.[26]

As I see it, there can be two aspects to a cultural competency, or the store of understandings that a marginalized viewer brings to interpreting a cultural product. One is a positive response where the viewer constructs something useful from the work by negotiating her/his response, and/or gives a subversive reading to the work. The other is a negative response in which the viewer rejects the work. Both types of oppositional readings are prompted by the store of negative images that have come from prior mainstream media experience; in the case of *The Color Purple*, from Black people's negative history in Hollywood films.

A positive engagement with a work could come from an intertextual cultural experience. This is true, I think with the way in which Black women constructed meaning from *The Color Purple*. Creative works by Black women are proliferating now. This intense level of productivity is not accidental nor coincidental. It stems from a desire on the part of Black women to construct works more in keeping with their experiences, their history, and with the daily lives of other Black women. And Black women, as cultural consumers, are receptive to these works. This intertextual cultural knowledge is forming Black women's store of decoding strategies for films that are about them. This is the cultural competency that Black women brought to their favourable readings of *The Color Purple*.

Notes

1 Phil Donahue read a quote by Tony Brown with this statement on his show, *The Phil Donahue Show*, 25 April 1986. Brown was part of a panel along with Donald Bogle, Michele Wallace and Willis Edwards, debating the film. Ishmael Reed's statement was quoted by Tony Brown on his show *Tony Brown's Journal*, when Reed was a guest there. Reed was debating Barbara Smith on the topic of the show: 'Do Black Feminist Writers Victimize Black Men?' (repeat programme), 2 November 1986.

2 Andrew Kopkind, 'The Color Purple', *The Nation*, 1 February 1986, p. 124. The *Guardian* is a radical journal in the United States.

3 Jill Nelson, 'Spielberg's "Purple" is Still Black', *Guardian*, 29 January 1986, p. 1.

4 E. R. Shipp, 'Blacks in Heated Debate over *The Color Purple*', *New York Times*, 27 January 1986, p. A13.

5 Courtland Milloy, 'A "Purple" Rage Over a Rip-Off', *Washington Post*, 24 December 1985, p. B3.

6 Barbara Smith, '*Color Purple* Distorts Class, Lesbian Issues', *Guardian*, 19 February 1986, p. 19.

7 Jill Nelson, *Guardian*, p. 17.

8 Michele Wallace, *The Phil Donahue Show*, 25 April, 1986.

9 Michele Wallace, 'Blues for Mr Spielberg', *Village Voice*, 18 March 1986, p. 27.

10 Donald Bogle, *The Phil Donahue Show*, 25 April 1986.

11 William Goldstein, 'Alice Walker on the set of *The Color Purple*', *Publisher's Weekly*, 6 September, 1985, p. 48.

12 Mary Helen Washington, 'Book Review of Barbara Christian's *Black Women Novelists*', *Signs: Journal of Women in Culture and Society*, vol. 8, no. 1 (August 1982), p. 182.

13 I am at present writing a dissertation on Black women's response to the film *The Color Purple*. As part of the study I conducted what will be an ethnography of reading with selected Black women viewers of the film in December 1987 in California. All references to women interviewed come from this study. For a discussion of the issues of readers' response to texts in media audience analysis see Ellen Seiter *et al.* 'Don't Treat Us Like We're So Stupid and Naive: Towards an Ethnography of Soap Opera Viewers', in *Rethinking Television Audiences*, Ellen Seiter (ed.) Chapel Hill: University of North Carolina Press, forthcoming. See also Seiter's use of Umberto Eco's open/closed text distinction to examine the role of the woman reader. Seiter uses Eco's narrative theory to argue for the possibility of 'alternative' readings unintended by their producers in 'Eco's TV Guide: The Soaps', *Tabloid*, no. 6 (1981) pp. 36–43.

14 David Morley, 'Changing Paradigms in Audience Studies', in *Rethinking Television Audiences*, Ellen Seiter (ed.), Chapel Hill: University of North Carolina Press, forthcoming.

15 David Morley, 'Changing Paradigms', p. 4.

16 Lawrence Grossberg, 'Strategies of Marxist Cultural Interpretation', *Critical Studies in Mass Communications*, no. 1 (1984), p. 403.

17 Christine Gledhill explains the idea of 'making strange' in two articles: 'Developments in Feminist Film Criticism', *Re-Vision: Essays in Feminist Film Criticism*, Mary Ann Doane, Patricia Mellencamp and Linda Williams (eds), Frederick, Maryland: University Publications of America, in association with the American Film Institute, 1984; and 'Klute 1: A Contemporary Film Noir and Feminist Criticism', *Women in Film Noir*, E. Ann Kaplan (ed.), London: British Film Institute, 1984.

18 Lawrence Grossberg, p. 403.

19 Steven Spielberg, BBC documentary, *Alice Walker and The Color Purple*, 1986.

20 Barbara Christian, 'De-Visioning Spielberg and Walker: *The Color Purple* – The Novel and the Film', Center for the Study of Women in Society, University of Oregon, 20 May 1986.

21 Michele Wallace, 'Blues for Mr Spielberg', p. 25.

22 John Fiske, 'British Cultural Studies and Television', *Channels of Discourse: Television and Contemporary Criticism*, Robert C. Allen (ed.), Chapel Hill: Universityof North Carolina Press, 1987, p. 258.

23 Barbara Christian, University of Oregon, 20 May 1986.

24 John Fiske, 'British Cultural Studies and Television', p. 258.

25 David Morley, 'Texts, Readers, Subjects', *Culture, Media, Language*, Stuart Hill, Dorothy Hobson, Andrew Lowe and Paul Willis (eds), London: Hutchinson, 1980, p. 164.

26 David Morley, 'Changing Paradigms in Audience Studies', p. 4.

Chapter 30

Marie Gillespie

TELEVISION, ETHNICITY AND CULTURAL CHANGE

T HE CONVENTIONAL WESTERN SOAP opera constructs a 'symbolic community', weaving together the everyday lives of its inhabitants in a fine web of intricate relationships between kin and neighbours, friends and enemies. The proximity of people's lives, their closeness in time and place and in their relationships, generates narrative conflict and movement. In key respects, the soap opera embodies many of the characteristics of local life in Southall: the central importance of the family; a density of kin in a small, geographically bounded area; a high degree of face to face contact (a 'knowable community'), and a distinctive sense of local identity. Similarly, the proximity and contiguity of kin and neighbours generates much of the distinctiveness of social life in Southall.

The arguments presented in this chapter centre on the homology, which is perceived by many of my informants, between life in Southall and life in the Australian soap opera *Neighbours*. They frequently commented, in particular, on the multiple relationships between local gossip and soap gossip: the term 'gossip', in young people's talk, serves to structure the symbolic community of the televised fiction as well as that of real Southall, and it also provides the metaphorical linkage between the two.

Soap operas are seen by Southall viewers to be intrinsically based on gossip. Much information is passed between characters, and of course to the viewer, in the form of gossip. A stereotypical gossip character figures prominently in most soap casts: she (invariably it is a woman) both drives forward on screen narratives by spreading information within the fictive community, and in the process relays information to the viewer. In *Neighbours*, at the time of fieldwork, this function was performed by Mrs Mangel (later by Hilary). Mrs Mangel, the elderly woman who observes, reports and censures young people's behaviour, incarnates for Southall youth the network of relatives and neighbours, particularly aunts and other female elders, who act as the moral guardians of their neighbourhood and whose 'gossip' is feared as a force of constraint of young people's freedom. Her character, indeed her very name, became the symbolic linchpin of the connectedness of Southall and Ramsay Street (the fictional setting of *Neighbours*).

The reception of soaps is also characterised by the speech forms of gossip. Viewing generates gossip among young people about the characters and their actions. And this soap talk is also fuelled by soap gossip published by the tabloid press, which adds further dimensions by playing with the double existence of the characters within the soap text and the actors outside it. In the case of *Neighbours*, several stars of the show – Jason Donovan, Kylie Minogue and Craig McLachlan – are also pop stars, whose images and star personalities are circulated in diverse media texts. Thus gossip within the soap, gossip circulated by a variety of other media texts, and gossip generated locally by both the soap and other texts, are all integrated into young people's everyday and TV talk. And finally this talk itself is, in general, conducted in forms which they themselves refer to as gossip.

Young people's everyday interpersonal communication is informed in significant ways by their soap viewing, not simply in its content but also, more significantly, in its form. As I shall demonstrate, the very structure of the soap and the cognitive processes of reception it entails are closely akin to the processes whereby gossip is transformed into rumour in local communication networks. This offers an explanation for something that puzzled me for a long time during fieldwork, namely, the way that young people move so fluidly and seemingly unselfconsciously between 'soap talk' and 'real talk'. The two are inextricably linked and, to an outsider, often indistinguishable. The parallels which young people themselves draw also help to explain why the reception of *Neighbours* is so easy and pleasurable.

Some readers, no doubt, will find it surprising that young 'British Asians' should engage so avidly with an Australian soap featuring an all-white cast. The popularity in Britain of *Neighbours*, and its stable-mate *Home and Away*, has even been ascribed to the latent racism of British society by media commentators. Bruce Gyngell, an Australian TV producer, was quoted in the *Guardian* (2 November 1993) as claiming that the appeal of these shows lay in British audiences' nostalgic pining for an all-white society (which he located in the 'pre-immigration' era of the 1960s!). But Southall's *Neighbours* fans evidently have compelling reasons for identifying with the soap's young protagonists, which override 'racial' differences. They draw on the soap as a cultural resource in their everyday interactions both in the peer culture and with parents and other adults, as they endeavour to construct new modes of identity for themselves. In order to understand why and how they do so, it is necessary to look more closely at the main features of 'soap talk' and gossip in general; at gossip and rumour in Southall in particular, as young people living there perceive it; and at the homology between the form of soap narration and gossip as a social speech form.

Soap talk

TV genres bring a range of discourses into play and employ particular ways of speaking: popular entertainment programmes work with colloquial and vernacular speech while news, current affairs and documentary programmes employ more formal modes of address. These differences play a major role in cementing affinities between particular audiences and genres, such as that noted by numerous researchers between soaps and women (Hobson, 1989; Geraghty, 1991; Morley, 1986). Most of this research has focused on adult women, showing, for example, that one of the key pleasures that women find in soaps is the validation of their own kind of talk (Brown, 1987: 22). This validation works in two ways: the programmes use the same forms of talk that the women use among themselves; and they provide additional material for the 'small talk' and 'gossip' that bond female friendships. Both these forms of validation are involved in soap viewing and soap talk among Southall youth, and we shall return to them shortly.

A large part of the enjoyment which is derived from watching soap operas lies in talking about them with other people, a talk which predominantly takes narrative form (Hobson, 1989). While TV may be viewed in the home, talk about TV outside the home with friends at work or in leisure completes the process of communication. Pleasure is derived from exchanging views and opinions about programmes with friends and colleagues:

> Talking about soap operas forms part of the everyday work culture of both men and women. It is fitted around their working time or in their lunch breaks. The process takes the form of storytelling, commenting on the stories, relating the incidents and assessing them for realism, and moving from drama to discussing the incidents which are happening in the 'real' world.
>
> (Hobson, 1989: 150)

Retelling soap opera stories gives viewers the opportunity to be storytellers, enabling them to extend their repertoires as storytellers and at the same time to inflect stories gleaned from TV in ways relevant to their own lives. Hobson also highlights the ways in which women's talk among friends and colleagues brings the interests and concerns of the private sphere into the public domain: the fusion between the two domains characterises such talk. And indeed, it is often the talk about a soap which determines whether someone will begin watching it in the first place. Thus viewing in the private context and patterns of sociability in the public context mutually shape one another: 'When a storyline is so strong that it is a main topic of conversation it is reason enough to get someone watching so as not to be left out of the conversation' (Hobson, 1989: 161).

Such views are reiterated by my informants who claim that, for example, peer pleasure and pressure led them to start watching *Neighbours* in order to participate in everyday conversations. Thus *Neighbours* is part of young people's shared culture and acts as a collective resource through which they compare and contrast, judge and evaluate the events and characters in the soap and those in 'real' life. They make assessments about the validity of what happens in the soap and compare it with what a character should have done or what they or others might have done in the same situation. As Hobson argues, because the subject-matter of the soap operas is so familiar to the viewers, there can be a free flow of information in talk as people work on 'collaborative readings' of the TV text which are informed by, and inform, their own social experiences. It is the interweaving of fiction and real experiences that perhaps most of all characterises the nature of soap talk:

> It is the talk about TV programmes and the relating of those programmes to everyday life of viewers that moves TV into a further dimension from that which ends at the viewing moment. Indeed, talk about TV programmes and

what has happened in them is essential in making a programme popular and part of the cultural capital of general discourse.

(Hobson, 1989: 167)

The collective nature of reception as evidenced in soap talk is also commented upon by Seiter *et al*.:

> What we found in our interviews over and over again was that soap opera texts are the products not of individual and isolated readings but of collective constructions – collaborative readings, as it were, of small social groups such as families and friends [...]. It seems then that the soap opera, not least because of the strong need it creates for collaborative readings, has considerable potential for reaching out into the real world of viewers. It enables them to evaluate their own experiences as well as the norms and values they live by in terms of the relationship patterns and social blueprints the show presents.

(Seiter *et al*., 1989: 233)

Soap talk in Southall is largely enjoyed as a peer group activity. Though many young people discuss *Neighbours* and other soaps in the family, . . . 'watching with mother' evokes a pleasurable sense of intimacy, but there is often the risk of parental censure. In talk among the peer group, especially among intimate friends, young people can be less guarded about their opinions: 'You're just more relaxed, you can say what you want, you can swear and use your own language, you can be more yourself and say what you really feel'. In this context, soap talk – the construction of collaborative readings plays important functions in cementing friendships. And here, as we shall see shortly, it also serves as a means of discussing personal and family issues indirectly.

Existing audience research strongly supports the notion that soap talk is a gender-specific activity, more or less exclusively confined to women and girls. The characteristics of soap talk are sometimes described in ways which suggest that it exemplifies 'female' social virtues. Thus Thorne *et al*. (1983), for example, identify:

> recurring patterns which distinguish talk among women from mixed-sex and all-male groups: mutuality of interaction work (active listening, building on the utterances of others), collaboration rather than competition, flexible leadership rather than the strong dominance patterns found in all-male groups . . . .

(1983: 18)

My data problematises this established notion somewhat, indicating that both girls and boys engage in soap talk, though different results emerge from different research methods – a significant finding in itself in terms of the debate on methodology.

In interviews, boys generally denied any interest in soaps, dismissing them as 'sissy' programmes and professing not to discuss them with peers. Interviews with girls confirm that, while many boys are in fact keen viewers of *Neighbours*, they tend not to discuss the programme, at least not with girls:

SAIRA: You don't really know what boys are really like, they don't discuss *Neighbours*, they think it's a sissy drama, they discuss computers, the latest films, video piracy, sport and boring stuff like that, they don't like discussing relationships.

So interview data suggests that soap talk is much more a feature of female than male communication. Boys claim that, if at all, they tend to talk more about the amusing incidents, the gags and repeat funny lines. But fieldwork observation provided much evidence that no such gender distinction exists, or that it is at least increasingly permeable. Soaps like *Neighbours* appeal successfully to teenagers as a whole, with characters of both sexes providing strong points of identification for male and female viewers. The characters and their dilemmas were discussed with pleasure and animation both in all-female groups and in mixed-sex groups, where issues of gender relations were extensively thematised. I also found some evidence that boys indulge in soap talk both with close female friends and in all-make groups, though more secretively. Thus while gender distinctions still affect the perceived acceptability of soap talk, the exact equations set up by some researchers between female viewers, female patterns of social interaction and interest in relationships, emotions and problem-solving, and soap as a 'female genre', do not appear to obtain in Southall.

We saw earlier how, in the domestic context, viewing soaps such as *Neighbours* may lead to intimate as well as censorious talk. In the peer group, soap talk frequently involves the veiled discussion of personal and, in particular, family problems, as these are displaced on to soap narratives. Young people themselves see talking about soaps as important because it allows them to talk about their own problems, indirectly, through a particular character or situation. A sense of family loyalty would inhibit most young people from talking directly about their own family problems, except perhaps with the closest and most intimate of friends, and even this is very rare. The culturally central concept of *izzat* . . . prohibits public discussion of private family issues, and so soap talk often allows tensions to be ventilated, serving a therapeutic function, as informants see it. The key emphasis on such talk seems to be on how problems get solved.

GITA: In school or at home we often have teenage problems which relate to our soap . . . but you don't talk about your own family except to really close friends maybe . . . By talking to friends you come to an understanding . . . you can think back to what a character did and see if they did things the right way . . . we discuss the problems and how they get solved.

This is a highly culturally specific function of soap talk in Southall, the importance of which can hardly be overestimated.

Soap talk is also seen as a way of bonding friendships, since, in discussing the problem that characters face and how effectively they deal with them, one is giving expression to norms and values in terms of the concrete experience of others, where more direct or abstract expression of norms would be difficult:

GURVINDER: It's important to talk about soaps and share those experiences with friends because your friends get to know you better, they can understand what your views are, how you think, what you believe, what you're having difficulties in and what your weaknesses are, you get closer.

Soap talk facilitates discussion of a range of topics, such as the attractiveness of certain male characters, which would be taboo in parental company:

PARAMJIT: After watching *Neighbours* we always talk about it the next day at school, we talk about the sexy male characters like Henry and his muscles, and other things like how stupid Bronwyn is for not speaking properly to Henry . . . most of the things we talk about we wouldn't discuss with our parents for obvious reasons.

Young people identify with the situations in which particular characters find themselves:

REENA: Discussing *Neighbours* with friends can be important at times because sometimes you feel as if you are in the same position as a certain character and have to stick up for yourself and say what you think.

Especially for girls who have little direct access to people outside their kinship and peer networks, soaps are seen to provide an extension to their immediate social experience:

MEENA: Some girls, especially those who lead sheltered lives, are always talking about soaps and they're always talking in that kind of soap style, you know, 'Oh dear what's the matter? Do you want to talk about it? Can I help you?' . . . they want to talk problems . . . for those girls, who don't do much else, soaps are really important.

But, one should add, soaps are also 'really important' to many young people in Southall who do not lead particularly sheltered lives by local standards.

The local importance of *Neighbours*, then, lies in the various functions served by talking about it. Essential to all these functions are processes referred to by researchers in terms of 'identification'. The relationship between viewers and texts is often conceived of as one whereby the text offers certain 'positions' for the viewer to identify with, primarily in relation to characters in the soap:

> Viewers may identify with certain characters, seeing themselves as in that character's shoes; they may regard them as a role model, imitating that character's behaviour in order to gain some of the rewards which that character is shown to enjoy; or they may recognise aspects of a character as similar to a significant person in their own lives, engaging in . . . 'parasocial interaction', watching the action as if playing the opposite character, as if the character were interacting with them directly.
>
> (Livingstone, 1990: 22)

Thus identification is seen as a psychological process whereby the viewers either project themselves on to characters and their situations or dilemmas; or else, in the reverse case, the characters and situations are appropriated and used in mimetic or imitative fashion. My data on soap talk and 'real' talk suggests that these two processes are related to each other in a much more reciprocal and socially complex way, and furthermore that the psychological dimension is not primary.

The word which informants most commonly use to describe their relationship to the text is not 'identification' but 'association'. They claim that they 'associate' themselves and or their friends with characters, situations, feelings and problems. They link and connect aspects of the social world of *Neighbours* with their own and attempt to accommodate and integrate their perceptions of the soap world into their own and vice versa. In this process, it is not in fact characters *per se* that provide the essential point of identification, but, on the one hand, a perceived social world seen as a generational entity – the social world of teenagers – and on the other hand, the very process of narration involved in 'reading' the soap, in talking about it, and in talking about their own social experiences and aspirations.

The creation of meaning through the interaction of texts and readers is best conceived as a process of negotiation and struggle (Livingstone, 1990: 23). The processes of negotiation which are manifest in young people's soap talk are of central concern here. Talk about their viewing allows for the negotiation of what is and what ought to be both in their own social lives and in the soap world. It involves both realism and fantasy and is centrally focused on questions of morality. These negotiations are partly facilitated by the continuous soap text which refuses closure and allows viewers to adopt a 'wandering' point of view. As Allen suggests:

> The perspectival openness of the contemporary soap opera diegesis enables it to accommodate a far greater range of 'negotiated' readings than other, more normatively determinant forms of fictive narratives. Furthermore, this openness helps account for the broadening of the soap audience in recent years to include more men, adolescents and college students . . . . Becoming a competent reader . . . requires a unique investment of the reader's time and psychic energy . . . . Watching soap operas is a social act as well as an engagement with narrative text.
>
> (1985: 147–148)

It is precisely because viewing and discussing *Neighbours* is a socially shared act and experience that young people can draw upon it collectively to make sense of their own lives. Yet the talk arising from their viewing, whilst recognising certain similarities, more often tends to emphasise differences between the soap world and their own experience. The parallels which do exist between the soap world and the social world of Southall are less a matter of substantial similarity, than of formal characteristics of narration and narrative structure.

So as far as substance or content is concerned, three thematic areas dominate in young people's talk about their viewing: family and kinship relations; romance and courtship rituals; and neighbourly relations in the 'community'. In exploring these relationships in *Neighbours* and contrasting the forms they take with their own experience, young people are actively and creatively negotiating the most important sources of social tensions in their lives.

Chapter 31

CONCLUSION

Overflow and audience

> 'Well, we could let viewers access the news show in progress during the week on a web site. Give them bits of raw footage and wire copy and real e-mails and story lists and draft scripts, as if they're hooking directly into our intranet . . .'
>
> 'Multiplatform it,' Featherstone says, winking not quite meaninglessly. Then he chants, pumping one arm, 'Convergence, convergence, convergence.'
>
> (Andersen, 1999: pp. 62–63)

Convergence and overflow

THIS FINAL CHAPTER EXPLORES recent developments in the relationship which contemporary media texts offer their audiences. Although I offer a brief survey of the trend towards convergence and 'overflow', my main focus here is a case study: the BBC2 series *Attachments*, which first aired on British television from September to November 2000, and its dedicated website <Seethru.co.uk>.

Attachments is a drama series about a fledgling dotcom company, run by married couple Mike and Luce, and the problems the team has in setting up and maintaining a lifestyle and music site called <Seethru>. Viewers of the early episodes who typed in the <Seethru> URL they glimpsed during the show were often surprised to discover that the site actually existed, a simulacrum of the on-screen dotcom with no hint that Mike and Luce might be fictional characters. Designed to mirror the events of the TV programme, <Seethru> enabled viewers to enter the world of *Attachments*, read the articles discussed in that week's episodes, mail and get response from the show's protagonists, watch unseen material from the programme on 'webcams', and follow up MP3 or internet links recommended by the fictional team. A *Guardian* interview with BBC2 controller Jane Root gave a sense of the producers' intentions:

> The seethru site will go live when the first episode goes out, with the standards waxing and waning after that according to the fortunes of the fictional web business. So at the outset users will log on to the amateurish site that Mike has been running from his bedroom. The internet offering will get a more professional feel when funding is secured in the drama, but the quality will also deteriorate again at times of crisis during the series.
>
> Root stresses that *Attachments* is intended to work as a stand-alone TV show, with the viewing audience still the primary focus. But it has also been created to appeal to 'v-users' – people who experience the drama through their PC screens. Anything that provokes rows or controversy in the drama will disappear from the seethru site at the exact same moment as it is fictionally deleted, according to Root.[1]

What was on offer here was an immersive, participatory experience that went far beyond watching the TV programme for forty-five minutes a week. In theory, the *Attachments* fan could log onto <Seethru> several times a day to find out more about the characters and take their advice on various aspects of web culture; although the site content was only updated weekly, the topics of discussion on the message boards were constantly evolving and changing, and the site visitors who contributed – most of them *Attachments* viewers – quickly formed into a small web community.

<Seethru> is, as I shall discuss, in some ways unique, but in other ways it is symptomatic of a recent trend. In an earlier article, I used the term 'overflow' to describe this tendency for media producers to construct a lifestyle experience around a core text, using the Internet to extend audience engagement and encourage a two-way interaction.

> In watching, or experiencing, or engaging, or living with *Attachments* as I do, I am witness to more than just the sometimes bizarre melange of television flow which dazed Raymond Williams in the 1970s;[2] indeed, I am not just a bewildered observer, but am becoming part of the broader text. *Attachments* has deliberately 'overflowed' the bounds of television and let itself, through its simulacrum of a website, merge into the vast diversity of the Internet.[3]

The same is true, to a certain extent, of other websites built around recent television series. The British version of the game show *Big Brother*, which originally ran during Summer 2000, encouraged viewers to visit its site for updates between the evening television screenings. Visitors to <bigbrother.terra.com> could email the contestants, catch up on news about their activities, view their audition tapes and, crucially, watch live streaming video from the house. The site webcams had a significant advantage over the TV programme itself in that they showed uncensored footage of events as they occurred, albeit on a small monitor window with muddy sound. On the day that Nick Bateman was evicted for cheating, the site was able to carry the story hours before it reached the TV show; an unprecedented example of a dedicated Internet site shifting its status from spin-off and back-up reference to the primary text, with the TV programme relegated to second place as a catch-up service.

Big Brother asked audiences to vote participants out of the house by telephone or online; later in the year, Channel 5's *Jailbreak* took the process further by inviting its audience to email the contestants with advice on how to escape from the show's prison setting, with a share in their reward on offer. The British version of *Survivor*, broadcast in May 2001, offered a members' only Internet service with exclusive footage, and introduced 'Survivor SMS', a feature whereby viewers could request news, gossip and quizzes from the show sent straight to their Vodafone mobile, at a cost to the user of up to £1.65 per message. *Big Brother 2* took its interactive services to a new level with instant updates on SMS, PDA and email, and two new cameras in addition to the now-standard webcam streaming. The first, a 'fan cam', follows a chosen participant for a day according to a collective vote among site visitors, and the second, the 'pan cam', can be controlled in real time from the site, with the facility to zoom in or pull out of the action.

This invitation to incorporate a media text into your daily life – to become part of a TV programme's key decisions, to watch it potentially twenty-four hours a day, and receive urgent updates if you happen to be away from the computer – is in some ways peculiar to the 'reality TV' genre. However, a very similar dynamic exists around the WB network's teen dramas, as I investigated in the paper referred to above. The dedicated sites attached to *Dawson's Creek*, in particular, offer the visitor insight into the characters and ongoing narrative that goes beyond the information available to viewers of the show. The 'Summer Diaries' feature lets a *Dawson's Creek* fan read her favourite characters' personal journal, while <Capeside.net> presents a detailed simulation of the show's fictional setting, complete with fake banner ads and college magazine articles written by Dawson and his friends.

While my research indicated that many viewers still treated the sites as a secondary resource, this dynamic could change with the introduction of features that provide vital clues to characters' motivation and behaviour. A more recent addition to the site allows visitors to explore a mocked-up version of the characters' desktops, letting them root through Dawson's deleted mail file and discover secret correspondence that never came to light on the TV show; another gives the visitor access to scribbled notes, supposedly written by the characters and passed under the table during their college classes. The page's slogan reads: 'Think you know everything that's going on in Capeside High? Think again.'

Certainly, the producers' intention, as expressed through the official sites, seems to be to create a multi-media 'Dawson's Creek Experience', encouraging viewers to seek out the music and clothes favoured by the characters and to participate in their lives on a daily basis through online questionnaires and interactive simulations. A culture is being constructed where 'regular' teenage viewers, not just committed fans, use *Dawson's Creek* and its website as the basis for everyday shopping decisions. The respondents in my own research produced no fan culture of their own, but many of them bought singles by artists they had heard on the show or were inspired by the female characters to buy a particular style of hat or shirt at American Eagle or J. Crew.

Finally, this kind of active engagement, drawing on the Internet not just as an online reference source but as an extension of the primary text, extends also to recent cinema. The *Blair Witch Project* site, like <Seethru>, treated its source text as authentic rather than admitting the fiction, and offered its visitors documentary evidence such as journals and police reports about the filmmakers' disappearance. <Memento>'s online presence, in keeping with the film's themes of amnesiac detection, took some ingenuity even to find: the site was called <otnemem.com>, and contained half-hidden links to a series of news clippings which cast further light on mysteries unresolved by the film's conclusion.

Online promotion for Steven Spielberg's *AI* has been even more oblique; filmgoers intrigued by the crediting of a 'sentient machine therapist' called Jeanine Salla at the end of the second cinema trailer had to type her name into Google and trace her footprints across the web, from her fictional university to sites campaigning for AI rights.

> Digging about these pages and hitting some links, tells the surfer that an Evan Chan has been murdered with humans and AIs suspected . . .

> Then it gets clever. Going to the Sentient Property Crime Bureau's Most Wanted Page you can find hidden text in the page by viewing the source code, which looks like hacker talk.

> For example: 'Gosting the SPCB filz, it seemz th? R looking 4 a robot in conekshun w/the deth uv a therml enji neer cald Evan Chan. Whi the hot prsoot? – The robots a 1st ordr pees uv Belladerma as, a ? $ sex slav.'[4]

Rather than simply watching the film on its release, the user is invited to investigate the diegetic world and enter into a form of competition with the producers to discover information that the primary text omits or conceals. The interaction is more similar to playing a PC adventure game than visiting a promotional site.

The contemporary phenomenon of overflow, then, transforms the audience relationship with the text from a limited, largely one-way engagement based around a proscribed time slot and single medium into a far more fluid, flexible affair which crosses media platforms – Internet, mobile phone, stereo system, shopping mall – in a process of convergence. I use the latter term in the sense suggested by Henry Jenkins, as a drawing-together of media forms; Jenkins employs the terms 'cultural convergence' for a ground-up, tactical creativity across different media, and 'media convergence' for a top-down 'structured interactivity' which implies a pattern of marketing strategies.

The examples above would all conform to his second category, and as such could be seen to have regressive implications: rather than grassroots fan communities which produce their own artwork and stories, often with 'resistant' interpretations of the text, what we see here are communities who follow the trail laid out by the media producers, from website to merchandise to multiplex. These sophisticated websites encourage an active response, but unlike the kind of fan response which has been around for decades, producing secondary texts on its own terms, this relationship is entirely shaped from 'above'. The fact that the official *Dawson's Creek* homepage includes links to a list of fan sites could in turn be seen as a cynical process of incorporation whereby potentially radical, home-made material is drawn safely inside the corporate fence; Lucasfilm have attempted much the same strategy by offering fans <starwars.com> web pages where the content is regulated and slash fiction prohibited.

The remainder of this chapter will discuss the ways in which <Seethru>, while sharing many of the characteristics of this trend for media overflow, evolved to a point where – partly through necessity due to a lack of funding, partly as the site's content writers voluntarily joined the fan community – the boundaries between producer and visitor, media convergence and cultural convergence, were increasingly blurred.

<Seethru> and *Attachments*: dependence

While *Attachments* was being screened on BBC2, from 26 September 2000 to 28 November 2000, <Seethru> served as a particularly involved example of an 'over-flow' site. *Attachments*' features writer Soph was castigated for an article called 'Hell Is Other People Shagging'; the article appeared on <Seethru> when the episode ended. Zoe, the series' teenage runner, was shown having two disastrous dates and writing an opinion piece about them; three days later, a message appeared from Zoe on the discussion board asking visitors 'have you ever had sex with someone you didn't want to have sex with?' and directing them to her polemic.[5] Episode 6, 'Burn Rate', ended with Mike about to film a piece to camera protesting about the site's new sponsorship deal: *Attachments* cut his speech short, but <Seethru> showed it in its entirety as a video clip. In the following episode, site designer Jake decided to make a regular feature out of his father's embarrassing mail correspondence; it soon appeared on <Seethru> as 'Shit: My Dad's Online'.

The relationship between *Attachments* and <Seethru> was, therefore, running as planned: the 'real' site would mirror the on-screen site, allowing viewers of the series to extend their engagement with *Attachments* by reading the fictional characters' articles at their leisure and exploring background details which the show skimmed over, such as Jake's preference – expressed on the team's 'bio' page – for <Peter the Great> over <Peter's Friends>. The site also allowed a degree of interaction through email; contacting the team would usually earn a reply in character, as I found when I mailed 'Reece' with a correction to his 'Are You A Geek?' quiz.

> From: 'Reece Seethru' <reece@seethru.co.uk>
>
> To: <will_brooker@hotmail.com>
> Subject: geek
>
> It Soph who did the Geek quiz actually. We'll change it. I've be ordered to give you 2 god points. Less of the dogboy cracks
>
> Reece[6]

As such, <Seethru> was similar to <Capeside.net>: a very clever simulation which supported and in some cases enlarged on the television series, encouraging viewers to immerse themselves in the show's diegesis, participate with it to some extent and return to it repeatedly throughout the week. However, the scope of the Seethru 'experience' was already seeping beyond the site itself, meshing with the wider culture of the Internet through its links to Tourette's Syndrome Barbie, to Flash versions of Nintendo games, to *Airwolf* versus Mr T, to news sites, comedy sites, weird sites and geek sites.

Unlike the majority of online supplements to TV series or films, *Attachments*/<Seethru> was deliberately opening itself up and becoming part of the Internet as a whole, rather than presenting a closed, inclusive world on its own terms, a theme-park simulation with no link to the web beyond. The *Blair Witch Project* site did not offer generic links to the *Resident Evil* games or *Swamp Thing* comics; Dawson and his friends on <Capeside.net> do not contribute to the site's bulletin boards, intentionally sparking off discussion with no relation to the show itself. <Seethru>, however, was not a site about *Attachments* but the site within *Attachments*: it was a lifestyle fanzine largely directed at a young, net-literate audience, and it consistently asked for their input. It was arguably only because of this wider scope and the construction of a two-way relationship between producers and audience that the site could meaningfully be sustained after the series ended, with no promise of a sequel.

<Seethru> and *Attachments*: independence

By late November, when *Attachments* finished, <Seethru> already had a relationship with its audience that transcended the programme. More importantly, its visitors had established a relationship with each other. The discussion boards had flourished into a core community of familiar 'regulars' – 'Rick J', 'Annerobinson', 'Kitty' – and a surrounding cast of more infrequent posters. While the discussion during September and October had often returned to *Attachments*, criticising the show's lack of 'realism' from a programming perspective and referring events back to the viewers' own experience, the forum became progressively more independent until mentions of the series were rare.

Late September and early October on the 'Life' board, for instance, saw a thread about Luce – 'She's probably the brains of the outfit, but is definitely the beauty – don't you think?'[7] – a complaint about not being able to read Soph's rant on the Queen Mother,[8] a discussion about whether the show's resident geek, Brandon, would plausibly code in the nude,[9] requests for a synopsis of a missed episode[10] and an essay picking apart the programme's stereotypes.[11] In the first ten days of October, twelve threads out of a total of twenty-six were either about *Attachments* in terms of characters and plot, or the <Seethru> site with reference to *Attachments*. Most threads were relatively short, with no more than ten replies to the original post: many had no replies. In the first ten days of November, ten threads out of a total fifty-six referred to *Attachments*. The length of the average thread increased, with many posts getting twenty or thirty replies and one running to eighty-one. In the first ten days of December, three out of a total seventy-four posts mentioned *Attachments* or referred to <Seethru> in terms of the characters. Apart from those begun by one contributor, 'g money', every post developed into a fairly lengthy discussion.

By this stage the discussion forum had clearly undergone a shift. Its main reference point and common ground had originally been *Attachments*, but over the series run, regular contributors had become established as online personae with their own strong personalities – in a sense, becoming larger-than-life 'characters' just like Soph and Reece – and the topics of discussion had broadened immeasurably to take in favourite food, political beliefs, film quotes, career advice, sexual deviance and corny jokes. By the start of December, several members of the group had met in 'real life' at London pub gatherings. The regular forum contributors had arranged a boycott of the boards when <Seethru> closed down its 'Sex and Relationship' discussion for fear of censorship; they spent five days on another site's message boards, then returned, having made their protest.[12] Many contributors at this stage had joined either during the series run, or following its conclusion; while many of the original posters had typed in the URL as an experiment after watching the show, others came to the site through chance, from search engines or other links. By opening itself up to the wider discourse of the web, <Seethru> had enabled visitors to stumble across it and accept it as a 'zine and filter' in its own right, with no obvious connection to a BBC2 series.

The site was still active, with regular updates and new content, in the first months of 2001. Articles were credited to Soph and Luce, weblog finds to Reece and Brandon, even though the series had ended weeks before. *Attachments* had now become entirely secondary to the <Seethru> forum community – most people knew the site's origins, but they were no longer important to the activity on the discussion boards. As one regular recalled: 'When I first started posting – I had no idea why you were all going on about some dodgy BBC Virtua-soap . . . Still, if there is a new series – I suppose I'll have to start watching it.'[13] Indeed, any overt mention of the show or its relationship to <Seethru> was generally regarded by the community as gauche, and a ritual was tacitly established whereby regulars would pretend they had no idea that the site's team were fictional, as in this exchange.

> Ma'am
> newbie
> Who watched the first series of Attachments? Who liked? Anyone know when it's back?

> DangerousDaze
> Posts: 1485
> Was Attachments that dating gameshow on Channel 5?

> phill_haw
> Posts: 66
> NO! Its the drama serise about a company that creates a website called 'seethru' its what this whole site is based on

> DangerousDaze
> Posts: 1485
> Are you sure? It could have been E4 and not Channel 5.

> kovacs
> Posts: 999
> Phil, April Fools was a week ago.[14]

The forum community, then, had evolved well beyond the 'structured interactivity' originally offered by <Seethru>, in common with other dedicated sites. Visitors had begun by following the patterns established by the producers – watch the show, then read the article or watch Mike's webcam rant – but their discussions had rapidly moved beyond the show's characters and narrative to the point where the primary text became almost irrelevant. Contributors to the boards had met up and formed both real life and online friendships based not on a shared fandom for the BBC2 series, but their own broader discussions on the forum. A community had grown and clustered around the core of top-down media convergence originally offered by the series and its tie-in site; transforming it, for the regular visitors at least, into a far more organic, fluid, user-created experience. <Seethru> had transcended *Attachments*. Yet <Seethru>, as a self-sufficient site based around the *Attachment* characters, was still at the heart of the forum community. When Soph, Mike or Luce made occasional appearances on the boards they were treated with affectionate respect, with regular contributors choosing to entertain a consensual illusion that the characters were as real as themselves:

> tav
> I agree with not advertising at first, then when people discover it by accident it makes their day. But now we're talking economics, and they should advertise IMO. It IS a great site with great features. Maybe they could offer email addresses, get the hits up a bit.

> Soph
> Aww, thanks Tav. That's sweet! We're still very much going strong, and in the planning stages of an extremely skill revamp. We are also examining new marketing strategies (not my area though – I'm strictly about content). Like the email idea too – keep 'em coming. God points, etc . . .

> Rufus
> Lets hope seethru make it . . . But if I was analysing seethru as a potential investor I would wonder just where the money comes from . . . Or, Soph, are you a lot of independently wealthy trustafarians who do it for love ?

> Luce
> Hi – Glad to see you're all worried about Seethru's anonymity. We're not unconcerned ourselves and it is something we're working very hard to change – though we don't really have the budget or size of team for a massive splurge (your Sales and Marketing Manager announcing she's pregnant about three seconds after joining doesn't help with your longterm planning.) Look out for some top new content coming soon. Oh and please don't call Soph a trustafarian – she has rather a 'thing' about them.
> Luce
> xx[15]

As this thread shows – it was titled 'RIP Seethru?' – the forum contributors had a vested interest in keeping <Seethru> afloat, even if the TV show itself had been left far behind, and the prospect of a new series was not always welcomed.[16] When the site's creators posted a message on the boards that <Seethru> was in serious financial difficulty, the relationship between the visitors and the production team shifted subtly into a new phase.

<Seethru> and *Attachments*: interdependence

Although <Seethru> stubbornly maintained the pretence that it was run by Mike and Luce, the site was actually established by World Productions, the company behind *Attachments*. The site, like the series, was commissioned by the BBC, although World Productions' relationship with the Corporation was apparently rocky from the outset. According to one member of the World website team,[17] the BBC was always wary of the idea to run <Seethru> parallel to the series, and frequently clashed with the site editors over its content. <Seethru> was, after all, meant to be an irreverent, alternative online zine, which did not sit easily with the BBC's self-image; on one occasion Director-General Greg Dyke made a personal visit to the World Production offices to protest about the Seethru rant that mocked media coverage of the Queen Mother.[18] Eventually, the BBC simply withdrew its funding, leaving <Seethru> to fend for itself until the start of the next series in Autumn 2001.[19] This decision translated to <Seethru>'s parallel universe as an announcement by Soph on 19 April 2001.

> It is with great regret that we must announce that Seethru's large corporate backer has decided to withdraw all funding from this website – effective immediately. . . .
>
> Basically they never liked the site and nothing would make them happier than to see it bite dust.
>
> We have managed to drum up some personal investment to keep us running and we are scouting around for other deals, but it looks like we will be running at 'pilot light' status – at least until the autumn when, apparently, a TV program about our trials and tribulations will be broadcast. . . .
>
> But to keep us going, we would like to ask you to help us.
>
> We would like to open up various strands (ticklist, rants, etc) on the website for visitor contributions. We'll be posting submission guidelines and a contributors' section within the week. We know we should've done this earlier but we're crap.
>
> Also, it would be helpful if you could recommend good threads from the forums to link to from the homepage.
>
> If you have any ideas how we can further reinforce the site, please add below or email.
>
> In exchange, we will soon (fingers fucking crossed) be able to offer God Points for all contributions, plus we may well invite you to a special party at our office, where you can meet us in person and have tart alcoholic drinks.
>
> We're not particularily happy about this, but we do relish a good fight.
>
> Thanks
> The Seethru Team[20]

It was a bizarre instance of life imitating art. Just as the characters on *Attachments* had won corporate backing, had their content censored or compromised, then lost their funding, so World Productions found itself stranded by the Corporation which had grudgingly supported it for months. The difference was that the 'real-life' <Seethru> could appeal to its audience for help, inviting them to become writers and editors.

The boundaries between 'producer' and 'visitor' had in fact been blurred far earlier, although most forum contributors remained unaware of it. World Productions had employed freelancers and part-time writers since September. Some of these, like Charlie Brooker, were already established names. Others had been recruited because the World team, trawling the web, had discovered their sites and decided that the style and tone matched <Seethru>. One freelancer, who produced <Seethru>'s guide to Amsterdam, was already a regular viewer of *Attachments* when he realised the World team had been exploring his site:

> I was watching the show, and was quite surprised to see the URL of See Thru pop up on my web stats, I went over to the site, and that was it, I was hooked . . .

> I contacted 'Mike' to ask where he found the site, and we got talking (t'was at this point I found out who was really behind See Thru) . . . After a while I was offered some freelance work by the site editor and the rest is history . . . [all *sic*][21]

Another, known online as AMP, was given a three day a week contract from September to April based on her fanzine <ampnet.co.uk>: 'They saw site, dug it, hired me. Working on idea of 'Internet filter' . . . bringing in the funniest/skillest writers off the web and putting all in one place.'[22]

The fact that both of these content producers were recruited because of their own non-profit fan sites clearly begins to erode the distinction between media convergence and cultural convergence in this case. While the former term implies a canny, corporate strategy intended to guide consumers on a path of multi-platform purchase, <Seethru> was at least partly made up of fanzine editors, creators of Internet 'folk' culture. Moreover, not only did the two writers discussed above form part of *Attachments*' audience, they also joined the forum message boards. 'I assure you – I was not paid to hang out on the boards, though I do have an interest in communities', AMP told me. 'I just got sucked in. I was mocked by my co-workers for my addiction.'[23] Come April, then, these two 'producers' – who had also been both viewers of *Attachments* and regular contributors to the forum – were in the same position as the other 'visitors'.

While some forum members were sceptical about Soph's announcement, wondering if the 'pilot light' status was simply a ploy to retain <Seethru>'s continuity with the forthcoming second series, most responded eagerly to the request. It should be noted that a significant proportion of forum contributors were involved in new media, many of them as programmers – hence the complaints and debates about *Attachments*' 'realism' during the series run. The relationship between World Productions and the board contributors, then, was very different to that which would normally exist between film directors and cinema audiences, or even TV producers and viewers at home. In contrast to the conventional hierarchy whereby the production team has technical skills beyond most of the audience, many of these visitors were on an equal level to the people behind <Seethru> in terms of programming competence and experience.

<Seethru> is, in June 2001, still ticking over on its pilot light. The site features are rotated rather than added to; the Amsterdam guide and AMP's feature 'Jamie Oliver Is My Bitch' are still on the front page, alongside a spoof advertisement for a

breathaliser modem, credited to the forum contributor Vtini. The weblog, one of the few site features which is updated daily, offers a catalogue of weird news, Flash show-cases and political satire: approximately half of the finds are attributed to Reece, Soph and Brandon, and the remainder to board regulars such as Vikram, Pink, AMP, Timewaster and Street66. The front page highlights and links to active threads from the message boards, which have now become, by default, the site's most dynamic section.

It would be over-optimistic to celebrate <Seethru>, in its current state, as a joint production between World and its visitors-turned-producers and producers-turned-visitors. As usual, we should be careful to make a distinction between active contributors – the regular board members who, while often maintaining an ambivalent attitude towards *Attachments*, are undeniably fans of <Seethru> as a site – and the non-active visitors, who in this case, as so often, constitute a silent majority. In early May 2001, Soph posted up details of Seethru's traffic, indicating which parts of the site received the most hits.

> The drugs homepage is in fact the 4th most visited page on the site (after the homepage, random URL & zine home) and the whole section generates over 35% of page impressions. . . .

> I'm afraid Seethru talk did not factor in the leaderboard, except for the following threads:

> 54. IMPORTANT: Seethru's future – seethru <http://www.seethru.co.uk/ubb/Forum9/HTML/000019.html>

> 77. Top ten crap songs of all time – seethru <http://www.seethru.co.uk/ubb/Forum3/HTML/000022.html>

> 79. Do we really want cannabis legalised anyway – seethru <http://www.seethru.co.uk/ubb/Forum4/HTML/000015.html>

> Although we respect your opinions, forum regulars, the majority of people who visit Seethru do not use the boards.[24]

The <Seethru> forum community, then, effectively parallels the 'powerless elite'[25] of fandom: vocal, creative, but in the minority and likely to be overruled or ignored when it comes to production decisions about their favoured text. Despite the fact that forum regulars include at least two former <Seethru> writers, that they continue to offer material to both the features pages and the weblog, and that the message boards are currently the only constantly-updated part of the site, if World Productions decided to take <Seethru> down another route in order to attract a wider market, the forum would have no say in the matter.

However, <Seethru> does offer an unusual and in some ways inspiring example of the ways in which this new form, the dedicated 'overflow' website, can evolve organically in relation to its audience. This case study shows that what began as an inventive but in many ways conventional instance of media convergence – essentially a promotional spin-off like <Capeside.net> and the Big Brother site – challenged assumptions from the start through its recruiting of fanzine editors and developed independently of its original primary text until the distinctions between producers and audience were partially, although not entirely, eroded. The case of <Seethru> suggests that media and cultural convergence, 'structured interactivity' and online 'folk' artefacts, may overlap. It suggests a pattern that other dedicated sites may follow if they acquire a life beyond their primary text and continue to develop their own narratives and characters long after the TV series or film has reached closure.

More broadly, it demonstrates that the term 'television audience', even the term 'audience' as a whole, may need to be freshly examined. The individuals who watched *Attachments* on a Tuesday evening, went online to debate its flaws, emailed its characters, watched clips that were never shown on TV and wandered off onto other sites following the fictional team's links and recommendations, constitute a very different type of television audience from the ones we would have encountered in research ten, even five years ago.

Five years from now, this fluid, participatory engagement with the online intertexts around a television series may well be the norm, rather than the exception; we could easily see a simulation of the Sun Hill police intranet running parallel to *The Bill*, or be able to receive SMS messages from *EastEnders* characters keeping us up with gossip or even just fashion and music advice. The phenomenon is unlikely to be confined to television and film; readers could be invited into the online world of a novel or music fans into a virtual construction of a band's dressing room, just as Internet users were drawn into the cinematic diegesis of *AI*.

The experience of being part of an audience will change, and will perhaps, in its shift towards greater participation, become similar in some ways to what we are used to thinking of as fandom: a pattern of engagement characterised by detection, discussion, interaction and community. While some critics may regard this development warily, seeing the dedicated sites as offering a join-the-dots path towards further consumption and a paint-by-numbers limiting of genuine creativity, the example of <Seethru> suggests that the overflow of a media text onto the Internet can in fact make for a more egalitarian relationship between producers and their audiences.

Notes

1 'Welcome to Seethru', *The Guardian*, 28 August 2000.
2 Raymond Williams, *Television: Technology and Cultural Form*, London: Collins (1974).
3 Will Brooker, 'Living on Dawson's Creek: Teen Viewers, Cultural Convergence and Television Overflow', *International Journal of Cultural Studies* vol. 4, no. 4 (December 2001).
4 Craig McGill, 'Inside AI's Web of Intrigue', *The Guardian*, 17 May 2001.
5 Zoe Atkins, 'Have you ever had sex with someone you didn't want to have sex with?', Rants, <Seethru.co.uk> (2 Nov 2000).
6 Reece, personal email, 26 October 2000.
7 Zander47, 'Luce', <Seethru.co.uk> (27 Sept 2000).
8 PaleScene, 'More Ranting', PaleScene, <Seethru.co.uk> (28 Sept 2000).
9 Mash, 'Attachments', <Seethru.co.uk> (27 Sept 2000).
10 Brerrabbit, 'What happened Tuesday night?', <Seethru.co.uk> (5 Oct 2000).
11 Rick J, 'Less stereotypes, more substance!', <Seethru.co.uk> (4 October 2000).
12 Robin, 'Why we're not here', <Seethru.co.uk> (22 Nov 2000). The protestors moved temporarily to <http://www.egroups.com/group/seethru2>.

13 LowLevel, 'Anyone know when *Attachments* is back?' <Seethru.co.uk> (15 February 2001).

14 Ma'am, 'Attachments', <Seethru.co.uk> (4 April 2001).

15 Tav, 'RIP Seethru?' <Seethru.co.uk> (26 January 2001).

16 It was thought that new contributors, posting 'Soph is HOTT' messages about the characters and naïve observations about plot, would have a negative effect on the established community.

17 Personal conversation (28 May 2001). The team member requested anonymity.

18 Soph, 'Queen Mum Stumbles!' <http://www.seethru.co.uk/zine/rants/queen_mum .htm> (19 Jan 2001).

19 Intriguingly, the forum moderator Damon was a BBC employee who continued to work as board administrator after April on an unpaid basis.

20 Soph, 'IMPORTANT: Seethru's future', <Seethru.co.uk>, 19 April 2001.

21 Personal correspondence (27 April 2001). The writer requested anonymity.

22 AMP, personal correspondence (1 June 2001).

23 AMP, personal correspondence (30 April 2001).

24 Soph, 'Ecstasy and memory impairment', <Seethru.co.uk> (2 May 2001).

25 John Tulloch and Henry Jenkins, *Science Fiction Audiences*, London: Routledge (1995).

References

Abercrombie, N. and Longhurst, B. (1998) *Audiences: A Sociological Theory of Performance and Imagination*, London and Thousand Oaks, CA: Sage Publications.

Adorno, T. W. (1991) *The Culture Industry*, London: Routledge.

Adorno, T. W. and Horkheimer, M. (1997) *Dialectic of Enlightenment*, trans. J. Cummins, London: Verso.

Alasuutari, P. (ed.) (1999) *Rethinking the Media Audience*, London and Thousand Oaks, CA: Sage.

Allen, R. C. (1990) 'From exhibition to reception: reflections on the audience in film history', *Screen*, 31, 4, 347–56.

—— (1985) *Speaking of Soap Operas*, Chapel Hill and London: University of North Carolina Press.

Althusser, L. (1971) 'Ideology and the State', in *Lenin and Philosophy and Other Essays*, London: New Left Books.

Altick, R. (1957) *The English Common Reader: A Social History of the Mass Reading Public, 1800–1900*, Chicago: University of Chicago Press.

Altman, M. A. (1992) 'Tackling Gay Rights', *Cinefantastique*, October, 76.

Anderson, K. (1999) *Turn of the Century*, London: Headline.

Andes, L. (1998) 'Growing up Punk: Meaning and Commitment Careers in a Contemporary Youth Subculture', in J. S. Epstein (ed.) *Youth Culture: Identity in a Postmodern World*, Oxford: Blackwell.

Ang, I. (1985) *Watching Dallas: Soap Opera and the Melodramatic Imagination*, London: Methuen.

—— (1991) *Desperately Seeking the Audience*, London and New York: Routledge.

—— (1996) *Living Room Wars: Rethinking Media Audiences for a Postmodern World*, London: Routledge.

Arlen, M. (1980) *Camera Age: Essays on Television*, New York: Farrar, Strauss and Giroux.

Arnold, M. (1869, reprinted 1970) *Culture and Anarchy*, Harmondsworth: Penguin.

Assiter, A. (1988) 'Romance Fiction: Porn for Women?', in G. Day and C. Bloom (eds) *Perspectives on Pornography: Sexuality in Film and Literature*, Basingstoke: Macmillan, pp. 101–9.

Auld, F., Jr. (1952) 'Influence of social class on personality test responses', *Psychol. Bull.*, 49, 318–32.

Bacon-Smith, C. (1992) *Enterprising Women: Television Fandom and the Creation of Popular Myth*, Philadelphia: University of Pennsylvania Press.

Ballaster, R., Beetham, M., Fraser, E. and Hebron, S. (1991) *Women's Worlds: Ideology, Femininity, and the Woman's Magazine*, London: Macmillan.

Barker, M. (1984a) *A Haunt of Fears: The Strange History of the British Horror Comics Campaign*, London: Pluto Press.

—— (1984b) *Comics: Ideology, Power and the Critics*, Manchester: Manchester University Press.

—— (1984c) *The Video Nasties*, London: Pluto Press.

—— (1997) 'The Newson Report' in M. Barker and J. Petley (eds), *Ill Effects*, London: Routledge.

Baron, S. W. (1989) 'Resistance and its Consequences: The Street Culture of Punks', *Youth and Society*, 21, 2 (December), 207–37.

Barthes, R. (1975) *The Pleasure of the Text*, trans. R. Miller, New York: Hill and Wang.

Bennett, K. E. (1999) *Xena: Warrior Princess,* Desire between Women, and Interpretive Response, available from <http://www.drizzle.com/~kathleen/xena>.

Benveniste, E. (1974) *Problèmes de linguistique générale*, Paris: Gallimard.

Berens, J. (2000) 'She's Gotta Have It', *The Observer Magazine*, 10 October, 20–5.

Bernrsuter, R. G. (1935) *Manual for the Personality Inventory*, Stanford: Stanford University Press.

Black Lace (1997, 1999) Promotional Packs (including Newsletters, Editor's Guidelines for Authors and Editorial Response to Reader Questionnaires) Compiled and edited by Kerri Sharp. London: Virgin Publishing.

Blair, M. E. (1993) 'Commercialisation of the Rap Music Youth Subculture', *Journal of Popular Culture*, 27, 3, 21–33.

Blair, M. E. and Hatala, M. N. (1991) 'The Use of Rap Music in Children's Advertising', in J. Sherry and B. Sternthal (eds) *Advances in Consumer Research*, 19, 719–24.

Blanchard, T. (1992) 'Will there be a G-string in your Stocking?', *The Independent*, 17 December: 15.

Blumer, H. (1933) *Movies and Conduct*, New York: Macmillan.

Blumer, H., Hauser and Hauser, P. (1933) *Movies, Delinquency, and Crime*, New York: Macmillan.

Bobo, J. (1992) '*The Color Purple*: Black Women as Cultural Readers', in D. Pribham (ed.) *Female Spectators*, London: Verso.

Bourdieu, P. (1984) *Distinction: A Social Critique of the Judgement of Taste*, London: Routledge and Kegan Paul.

Brooker, W. (2000) *Batman Unmasked*, London: Continuum.

—— (2001) 'Living on Dawson's Creek: Teen Viewers, Cultural Convergence and Television Overflow', *International Journal of Cultural Studies*, 4, 4.

—— (2002) *Using the Force*, London: Continuum.

Brown, M. (1987) 'The Politics of Soaps: Pleasure and Feminine Empowerment', *Australian Journal of Cultural Studies*, 4.

Brückner, J. (1981) 'Der Blutfleck in Auge der Kamera', *Frauer und Film*, 30, 13–23.

Brunsdon, C. (1997) *Screen Tastes: Soap Opera to Satellite Dishes*, London and New York: Routledge.

Brunsdon, C. and Morley, D. (1978) *Everyday Television: Nationwide*, London: BFI.

Buckingham, D. (1987) *Public Secrets: EastEnders and its Audience*, London: BFI.

—— (1996) *Moving Image: Children's Emotional Responses to Television,* Manchester: Manchester University Press.

Cagle, V. M. (1995) *Reconstructing Pop/Subculture*, London: Virago.

CARE (Christian Action, Research and Education) (1994) *Evidence to the Home Affairs Committee*, London: HMSO.

Centre for Contemporary Cultural Studies, University of Birmingham (1982) *Making Histories*, London: Hutchinson.

Charters, W. W. (1933) *Motion Pictures and Youth*, New York: Macmillan.

Chein, I. and Rosenfeld, E. (1957) 'Juvenile narcotics use', *Law & Contemp. Problems*, 22, 52–68.

Chodorow, N. (1978) *The Reproduction of Mothering: Psychoanalysis and the Sociology of Gender*, Berkeley: University of California Press.

Clair, J. *et al.* (1975) *Les Machines célibataires*, Venice: Alfieri.

Clarke, J. (1986) 'Style', in S. Hall and T. Jefferson (eds) *Resistance Through Rituals: Youth Subcultures in Post-War Britain*, London: Hutchinson.

Clarke, J. and Jefferson, T. (1978) 'Working Class Youth Cultures' in G. Mungham and G. Pearson (eds) *Working-Class Youth Culture*, London: Routledge and Kegan Paul.

Clarke, J., Hall, S., Jefferson T. and Roberts, B. (1976) 'Subcultures, Cultures and Classes', in S. Hall (ed.), *Resistance Through Rituals*, London: Hutchinson.

Clifford, J. and Marcus, G. E. (eds) (1986) *Writing Culture: The Poetics and Politics of Ethnography*, Berkeley, CA: University of California Press.

Clover, C. J. (1992) *Men, Women and Chainsaws: Gender in the Modern Horror Film*, London: BFI.

Cohen, S. (1973) *Folk Devils and Moral Panics*, St Albans: Paladin.

——(1980) 'Symbols of Trouble: Introduction to the New Edition', in *Folk Devils and Moral Panics*, Oxford: Martin Robertson.

Connor, S. (1991) *Postmodernist Culture*, Oxford: Blackwell.

Cook, P. (1998) 'No Fixed Address: The Women's Picture from *Outrage* to *Blue Steel*', in S. Neale and M. Smith (eds) *Contemporary Hollywood Cinema*, London and New York: Routledge.

Cooper, E. and Dinerman, H. (1951) 'Analysis of the film *Don't be A Sucker*: A Study in Communication', *Public Opinion Quarterly*, 15, 2 (Summer).

Cowe, R. (1993) 'Cuts at Littlewoods Show British Mail Order is on Downward Slope', *Guardian*, 26 January: 13.

Cressey, P. G. (1938) 'The Motion Picture Experience as Modified by Social Background and Personality', *Amer. Soc. Rev.*, 3, 516–25.

Cumberbatch, G. and Howitt, D. (1989) *A Measure of Uncertainty: the Effects of Media*, London: John Libbey.

Currie, D. H. (1999) *Girl Talk: Adolescent Magazines and Their Readers*, Toronto: University of Toronto Press.

Dancis, B. (1978) 'Safety Pins and Class Struggle: Punk Rock and the Left', *Socialist Review*, 8, 3, 58–83.

David, H. (1992) 'In the Pink', *The Times Saturday Review*, 13 June: 10–11.

Davis-Kimball, J. (1997) 'Warrior Women of the Eurasian Steppes', *Archaeology*, 50 January/February. Available from <http://www.archaeology.org/9701/abstracts/sarmatians.html>.

De Certeau, M. (1984) *The Practice of Everyday Life*, Berkeley, CA: University of California Press.

de Laurentis, T. (1985) 'Aesthetic and Feminist Theory', *New German Critique*, 34, Winter, 154–75.

Deligny, F. (1970) *Les Vagabonds efficaces*, Paris: Maspero.

Dempsey, D. (1964) 'Why the Girls Scream, Weep, Flip', *New York Times Magazine*.

Dickinson, R., Harindranath R. and Linné, O. (eds) (1998) *Approaches to Audiences: A Reader*, London: Arnold.

Dixon, J. (1998) *The Romantic Fiction of Mills & Boon 1905–1995,* London: UCL Press.

Doane, M. A. (1980) 'Misrecognition and Identity', *Ciné-Tracts*, 3, 3, Fall, 25.

——M. (1982) 'Film and the Masquerade: Theorising the Female Spectator', *Screen*, 23, 3–4.

Doane, M., Mellencamp, P. and Williams, L. (eds) (1984) *Re-Vision: Essays in Feminist Film Criticism*, Frederic, MD: Maryland University Publications in association with the American Film Institute.

Doty, A. (1993) *Making Things Perfectly Queer: Interpreting Mass Culture*, Minneapolis: University of Minnesota Press.

Dyer, R. (1977) *Gays and Film*, London: BFI.

—— (1986) *Heavenly Bodies: Film Stars and Society*, New York: St Martin's Press.

—— (1989) 'Old Briefs for New', *New Statesman and Society*, 22 March: 43–4.

—— (1992) *Only Entertainment*, New York: Routledge, Chapman and Hall.

Eco, U. (1986) *Travels in Hyperreality*, London: Picador.

Ehrenreich, B., Hess, E. and Jacobs, G. (1992) 'Beatlemania: Girls Just Want To Have Fun', in L. A. Lewis (ed.), *The Adoring Audience*, London: Routledge.

Elliot, P. (1974) 'Uses and Gratifications Research: A Critique and a Sociological Alternative', in J. G. Blumler and E. Katz (eds) *The Uses of Mass Communication*, London and Beverly Hills: Sage, pp. 249–68.

Escarpit, R. (1965) *The Sociology of Literature*, trans. Ernest Pick, Painsville, OH: Lake Erie College Press.

Evans, D. T. (1993) *Sexual Citizenship: The Material Construction of Sexualities*, London: Routledge.

Ferguson, F. (1992) 'Watching the World Go Round: Atrium Culture and the Psychology of Shopping', in R. Shields (ed.) *Lifestyle Shopping: The Subject of Consumption*, London: Routledge, pp. 2–39.

Fish, S. (1980) *Is There A Text in This Class?: The Authority of Interpretive Communities*, Cambridge, MA: Harvard University Press.

Fiske, J. (1987) *Television Culture*, London: Routledge.

—— (1987) 'British Cultural Studies and Television', in R Allen (ed.) (1987) *Channels of Discourse: Television and Contemporary Criticism*, Chapel Hill: University of North Carolina Press.

—— (1989) *Understanding Popular Culture, Reading the Popular*, London: Routledge.

Florence, P. and Reynolds, D. (eds) (1995) *Feminist Subjects, Multi-media: Cultural Methodologies*, Manchester: Manchester University Press.

Foucault, M. (1979) *The History of Sexuality – Vol I: An Introduction*, trans. R. Hurley, Harmondsworth: Penguin.

Fox, K. J. (1987) 'Real Punks and Pretenders: The Social Organisation of a Counter-culture', *Journal of Contemporary Ethnography*, 16, 3, October, 344–70.

Frank, T. (2000) *One Market Under God: Extreme Capitalism, Market Populism and the End of Economic Democracy*, New York: Anchor Books.

Freud, S. (1905) 'Three Essays on the Theory of Sexuality', *Standard Edition*, 7, 182.

—— (1913) 'The Psycho-analytic View of Psychogenic Disturbance of Vision', *Standard Edition*, 11, pp. 216–17.

Frith, S. (1981), *Sound Effects*, New York: Pantheon.

Frith, S. and Horne, H. (1987) *Art into Pop*, London: Methuen.

Garber, P. and Paleo, L. (1990) *Uranian Worlds: A Guide to Alternative Sexuality in Science Fiction, Fantasy and Horror*, Boston: G. K. Hall.

Gauntlett, D. (1998) 'Ten Things Wrong with the "Effects" Model', in R. Dickinson, R. Harindranath and O. Linné (eds) *Approaches to Audiences: A Reader*, London: Arnold.

Geraghty, C. (1991) *Women and Soap Operas*. London: Polity.

Gilbert, J. (1986) *A Cycle of Outrage,* New York: Oxford University Press.

Gillespie, M. (1995) *Television, Ethnicity and Cultural Change*, London: Routledge.

Gledhill, C. (1984a) 'Developments in Feminist Film Criticism', in M. A. Doane, P. Mellencamp and L. Williams (eds) *Re-Vision: Essays in Feminist Film Criticism*, Frederick, MD: University Publications of America.

—— (1984b) 'Klute I: A Contemporary Film Noir and Feminist Criticism', in E. A. Kaplan (ed.) *Women in Film Noir*, London: BFI.

Goldstein, W. (1985) 'Alice Walker on the Set of *The Color Purple*', *Publisher's Weekly*, 6 September, 48.

Gray, A. (1987) 'Behind Closed Doors: Video Recorders in the Home', in H. Baehr and G. Dyer (eds), *Boxed In: Women and Television*, London: Pandora.

Gross, R. L. (1990) 'Heavy Metal Music: A New Subculture in American Society', *Journal of Popular Culture*, 24, 119–30.

Grossberg, L. (1984) 'Strategies of Marxist Cultural Interpretation', *Critical Studies in Mass Communication*, 1.

Gwenllian-Jones, S. (2000) 'Histories, Fictions and *Xena: Warrior Princess*', *Television and New Media*, 1, 4 (November).

Hagell, A. and Newburn, T. (1994) *Young Offenders and the Media: Viewing Habits and Preferences*, London: Policy Studies Institute.

Hall, S. (1980) 'Encoding/Decoding', in S. Hall, D. Hobson, A. Lowe and P. Willis (eds) *Culture, Media, Language*, London: Hutchinson.

Hall, S. and Jefferson, T. (eds.) (1986) *Resistance Through Rituals*, London: Hutchinson.

Hall, S., Connell, I. and Curti, L. (1976) 'The Unity of Current Affairs Television', *Working Papers in Cultural Studies*, no. 9, Birmingham: Centre for Contemporary Cultural Studies, University of Birmingham.

Handel, L. (1950) *Hollywood Looks at its Audience*, Urbana: University of Illinois Press, 106–108.

Hansen, M. (1991) *Babel and Babylon: Spectatorship in American Silent Film*, Cambridge, MA: Harvard University Press.

Harding, D. W. (1967) 'The Notion of "Escape" in Fiction and Entertainment', *Oxford Review* 4.

Hartley, J. (1992) *Studies in Television,* New York: Routledge, Chapman and Hall.

Hastings, J. (1997) *Deadly Affairs: A John Anderson Mystery*, London: Virgin Publishing, pp. 38–9.

Haugg, F. (ed.) (1986) *Female Sexualisation*, London: Verso.

Hay, J., Grossberge, L. and Wartella, E. (eds) (1997) *The Audience and its Landscape*, Boulder, CO: Westview Press.

Heath, S. (1978) 'Difference', *Screen*, 19, 3, 86–7.

Hebdige, D. (1979) *Subculture: The Meaning of Style*, London: Methuen.

Hermes, J. (1995), *Reading Women's Magazines: An Analysis of Everyday Media Use*, Cambridge: Polity Press.

Hobson, D. (1982) *Crossroads: The Drama of a Soap Opera*, London: Methuen.

Hobson, D (1989) 'Soap Operas at Work' in E. Seiter, H. Borchers, G. Kreutzner and E.-M. Warth (eds) *Remote Control*, London: Routledge.

Hoggart, R. (1957) *The Uses of Literacy*, Harmondsworth: Penguin.

Horton, D. and Wohl, R. (1956) 'Mass Communication and ParaSocial Interaction: Observation on Intimacy at a Distance', *Psychiatry*, 19, 3, 215–29.

Howland, C. I., Lumsdaine, A. and Sheffield, F. D. (1949) *Experiments on Mass Communication*, Princeton University Press, 284–89.

—— (1959) 'Reconciling conflicting results derived from experimental and survey studies of attitude change', *Amer. Psychol.*, 14, 3–17.

Huet, A. *et al.* (1977) *La Marchandise culturelle*, Paris: CNRS.

Hulett, J. E., Jr. (1949) 'Estimating the net effect of a commercial motion picture upon the trend of local public opinion', *Amer. Soc. Rev.*, 14, 263–75.

Hummel, F. (1991) 'Where None Have Gone Before', *Galactic Gayzette*, May.

Hunt, L. (1992) 'Women Object to Sanitary Towel Adverts', *The Independent*. 14 March: 6

Jameson, F. (1979) 'Reification and Utopia in Mass Culture', *Social Text*, Winter, pp. 130–48.

Jeffreys, S. (1990) *Anti-Climax*, London: The Women's Press.

Jenkins, H. (1992) *Textual Poachers: Television Fans and Participatory Culture*, New York: Routledge.

—— (1995) 'Out of the Closet and Into the Universe', in J. Tulloch and H. Jenkins (eds) *Science Fiction Audiences*, London: Routledge.

Jhally, S. and Lewis, J. (1992) *Enlightened Racism:* The Cosby Show, *Audiences and The Myth of the American Dream*, Oxford: Westview Press.

Kaplan, C. (1986) '*The Thornbirds*: Fiction, Fantasy and Femininity', in V. Burgin, J. Donald and C. Kaplan (eds) *Formations of Fantasy*, London, New York: Methuen.

Kaplan, E. (ed.) (1984) *Women in Film Noir*, London: BFI.

Katz, E. and Lazarsfeld, P. (1955) *Personal Influence*, Glencoe, IL: The Free Press.

Kermode, M. (1997) 'I Was a Teenage Horror Fan; or: How I Learned to Stop Worrying and Love Linda Blair', in M. Barker and J. Petley (eds) *Ill Effects*, London: Routledge.

Klaper, J. T. (1960) *The Effects of Mass Media*, Glencoe: Free Press.

Kopkind, A. (1986) '*The Color Purple*', *Nation*, 1 February.

Kotarba, J. A and Wells, L. (1987) 'Styles of Participation in an All-ages, Rock 'n' Roll Nightclub: An Ethnographic Analysis', *Youth and Society,* 18, 4, June, 398–417.

Kuhn, A. (1988) *Cinema, Censorship and Sexuality, 1909–1925*, London: Routledge.

Lazarsfeld, P. (1940) *Radio and the Printed Page: An Introduction to the Study of Radio and Its Role in the Communication of Ideas*, New York: Duell, Sloan and Pearce.

—— (1942) 'The Effects of Radio on Public Opinion', in D. Waples (ed.) *Print, Radio and Film in a Democracy*, Chicago: University of Chicago Press.

Lazarsfeld, P., Berelson, B. and Gaudet, H. (1944, 3rd edition 1968) *The People's Choice: How the Voter Makes up His Mind in a Presidential Campaign*, New York: Columbia University Press.

Leavis, F. R. (1933) *Culture and Environment,* London: Chatto and Windus.

Leong, W.-T. (1992) 'Cultural Resistance: The Cultural Terrorism of British Male Working-Class Youth', *Current Perspectives in Social Theory*, 12, 29–58.

Lewis, F. (1963) 'Britons Succumb to "Beatlemania"', *New York Times Magazine*, 1 December.

Lewis, L. (1992) *The Adoring Audience,* London: Routledge.

Liebes, T. and Katz, E. (1990) *The Export of Meaning: Cross-Cultural Readings of Dallas*, Oxford: Oxford University Press.

Lingstone, S. and Lunt, O. (1994) *Talk on Television: Audience Participation and Public Debate*, London and New York: Routledge.

Livingstone, S. M. (1990) *Making Sense of Television: The Psychology of Audience Interpretation*, London: Pergamon Press.

Lull, J. (1987) 'Thrashing in the Pit: An Ethnography of San Fransisco Punk Subculture', in T. R. Lindlof (ed.) *Natural Audiences: Qualitative Research of Media Uses and Effects*, Norwood, NJ: Ablex.

McCracken, E. (1993*) Decoding Women's Magazines: From Mademoiselle to Ms.*, London: Macmillan.

McGill, C. (2001) 'Inside AI's Web of Intrigue', *Guardian*, 17 May.

McRobbie, A. (1982) 'The Politics of Feminist Research: Between Talk, Text and Action', *Feminist Review,* 12 (October), 46–57.

—— (1989) 'Second-hand Dresses and the Role of the Rag Market' in A. McRobbie (ed.) *Zoot-Suits and Second-Hand Dresses: An Anthology of Fashion and Music*, London: Macmillan.

—— (1991) *Feminism and Youth Culture*, London: Macmillan Press Ltd.

—— (2000) *Feminism and Youth Culture*, London: Routledge.

Malinowski, B. (1915) 'Magic, Science and Religion', in J. Needham (ed.) *Science, Religion and Reality*, New York: The Macmillan Company.

Maltby, R. and Stokes, M. (eds) (2000) *Identifying Hollywood Audiences*, London: BFI.

Mander, M. S. (1983) '*Dallas*: The Mythology of Crime and the Moral Occult', *Journal of Popular Culture*, 17, 44–8.

Mann, P. (1979) 'Romantic Fiction and its Readers' in H. D. Fischer and S. R. Melnick (eds) *Entertainment: A Cross-Cultural Examination*, New York: Hastings House, pp. 34–42.

Margolis, H. E. (1988) *The Cinema Ideal*, London: Garland.

Martin, B. (1998) 'Sexualities without Genders and Other Queer Utopias', in M. Merck, N.

Segal and E. Wright (eds) *Coming Out of Feminism?*, London: Blackwell, pp. 11–35.

Maryles, D. (1977) 'B. Dalton, with 350 Outlets Due by 1970, Views Its Bookselling Future with Rosy Optimism', *Publishers Weekly*, 19 September, 126–9.

Mayne, J. (1993) *Cinema and Spectatorship*, New York and London: Routledge.

Matlock, G. with Silverton, P. (1996) *I Was a Teenage Sex Pistol*, London: Virgin.

Matthews, T (1994) *Censored: The Story of Film Censorship in Britain,* London: Chatto & Windus.

Merton, R. K. (1946, reprinted 1971) *Mass Persuasion: The Social Psychology of a War Bond Drive*, Westport, CT: Greenwood Press Publishers.

Merton, R. K. and Kendall, P. L. (1944) 'The Boomerang Response', *Channels*, xxi, 7, June.

Milloy, C. (1985) 'A "Purple" Rage over a Rip-Off', *Washington Post*, 24 December, B3.

Modleski, T. (1982) *Loving with a Vengeance: Mass Produced Fantasies for Women*, London: Routledge.

—— (1986) *Studies in Entertainment: Critical Approaches to Mass Culture*, Bloomington: Indiana University Press.

Monast, J.-E. (1969) *On Les Croyait Chrétiens: Les Aymaras*, Paris: Cerf.

Montague, R. (1968) 'Pragmatics', in R. Klibansky (ed.) *La Philosophie Contemporaine*, Florence: La Nuova Italia, vol. 1, pp. 102–22.

Moody, N. (1998) 'Mills & Boon's *Temptations*: Sex and the Single Couple in the 1990s', in L. Pearce and G. Wisker (eds) *Fatal Attractions: Rescripting Romance in Contemporary Literature and Film*, London: Pluto, pp. 141–56.

Moores, S. (1993) *Interpreting Audiences*, London: Sage.

Morgan, R. (ed.) (1970) *Sisterhood is Powerful: An Anthology of Writings from the Women's Liberation Movement*, New York: Random House.

Morley, D. (1980a) *The* Nationwide *Audience*, London: BFI.

—— (1980b) 'Texts, Readers, Subjects', in S. Hall, D. Hobson and E. McCracken (eds) (1993) *Decoding Women's Magazines: From Mademoiselle to Ms.*, London: Macmillan.

—— (1986) *Family Television: Cultural Power and Domestic Leisure*, London: Comedia.

—— (1992) *Television, Audiences and Cultural Studies*, London and New York: Routledge.

—— (forthcoming) 'Changing Paradigms', in E. Seiter (ed.) *Rethinking Television Audiences.*, Chapel Hill, NC, University of North Carolina Press.

Morrison, D. (1993) 'The Idea of Violence', in A. Millwood-Hargreave (ed.) *Violence in Factual Television*, London: John Libbey, pp. 124–8.

Mort, F. (1988) 'Boys Own? Masculinity, Style and Popular Culture', in R. Chapman and J. Rutherford (eds) *Male Order: Unwrapping Masculinity*, London: Lawrence and Wishart, pp. 193–224.

Mort, F. and Green, N. (1988) 'You've Never Had It So Good – Again!', *Marxism Today*, May, 30–3.

Muggleton, D. (2000) *Inside Subculture: The Postmodern Meaning of Style*, London: Berg.

Mulvey, L. (1975) 'Visual Pleasure and Narrative Cinema', *Screen*, 16, 3 (Autumn) 6–18.

—— (1981) 'Afterthoughts on "Visual Pleasure and Narrative Cinema" inspired by *Duel in the Sun*', *Framework* 6, 15/16/17, 12–15.

—— (1989) *Visual and Other Pleasures*, London: Macmillan.

Murphy, G., Murphy, L. and Newcomb T. (1937) *Experimental Social Psychology*, New York: Harper and Brothers.

Neels, B. (1980) *Cruise to a Wedding*, Toronto: Harlequin Books.

Nelson, J. (1986) 'Spielberg's "Purple" is Still Black', *Guardian*, 29 January.

Newcomb, H. M. and Hirsch, P. M. (1983) 'Television as a Cultural Forum: Implications for Research', *Quarterly Review of Film*, 8, 45–55.

Newson, E. (1994) *Video Violence and the Protection of Children*, Report of the Home Affairs Committee, London: HMSO, 29 June, 45–9.

Nightingale, V. (1996) *Studying the Audience: The Shock of the Real*, London and New York: Routledge.

Nyberg, A. K. (1998) *Seal of Approval: The History of the Comics Code*, Jackson: University Press of Mississippi.

Opinion Research Corporation (1957) *The Public Appraises Movies*, Princeton: The Corporation, 12–13.

Orwell, G. (1969) 'Boys' Weeklies', in *Inside the Whale and Other Essays*, Harmondsworth: Penguin.

Osgerby, B. (1998) *Youth in Britain Since 1945*, Oxford: Blackwell.

Pearce, L. and Stacey, J. (eds) (1995) *Romance Revisited,* New York and London: New York University Press.

Penley, C. (1992) 'Feminism, Psychoanalysis, and the Study of Popular Culture', in L. Grossberg *et al.* (eds) *Cultural Studies*, London: Routledge, pp. 479–500.

—— (1997) *NASA/TREK*, London: Verso.

Peterson, R. C. and Thurstone, L. L. (1935) *Motion Pictures and the Social Attitudes of Children*, New York: Macmillan, 107–28.

Popular Memory Group (n.d.) 'Popular Memory', unpublished papers, Birmingham: Centre for Contemporary Cultural Studies, University of Birmingham.

Pratt, J. (1943) 'Notes on Commercial Movie Technique', *International Journal of Psycho-Analysis*, 34, 3–4, 186.

Radway, J. (1984, reprinted 1991) *Reading the Romance: Women, Patriarchy and Popular Literature*, Chapel Hill, NC: University of North Carolina Press.

Radstone, S. (1993) 'Remembering Media: The Uses of Nostalgia', *Critical Quarterly*, 35, 3.

Raths, L. E. and Trager, F. N. (1948) 'Public opinion and Crossfire', *J. Educ. Soc.*, 21, 345–68.

Reed, R. (1997) 'Amazon Portrayal in *Xena: Warrior Princess*', *Whoosh!* 12 (September) available from <http://www.whoosh.org./issue12/reed.html>.

Rietveld, H. (1991) 'Living the Dream', in S. Redhead (ed.) *Rave Off: Politics and Deviance in Contemporary Youth Culture*, Aldershot: Surrey.

Roman, L. (1988) 'Intimacy, Labor, and Class: Ideologies of Feminine Sexuality in the Punk Slam Dance', in L. Roman and L. K. Christian-Smith (eds) *Becoming Feminine: The Politics of Popular Culture*, London: Falmer Press.

Rosen, P. (1986) *Narrative, Apparatus, Ideology*, New York: Columbia University Press.

Ruffell, J. (1997) 'Brave Women Warriors of Greek Myth: An Amazon Roster', *Whoosh!,* 12 (September) Available from <http://www.whoosh.org/issue12/ruffel3.html>.

Ryle, G. (1968) 'Use, Usage and Meaning', in G. H. R. Parkinson (ed.) *The Theory of Meaning*, Oxford: Oxford University Press.

Sanjek, D. (1990) 'Fans Notes: the Horror Film Magazine', *Literature/Film Quarterly*, 18, 3, 150–60.

Sardiello, R. (1998) 'Identity and Status Stratification in the Deadhead Subculture', in J. S. Epstein (ed.) *Youth Culture: Identity in a Postmodern World*, Oxford: Blackwell.

Savage, J. (1992) *England's Dreaming: Sex Pistols and Punk Rock*, London: Faber and Faber.

Schaffner, N. (1977) *The Beatles Forever*, New York: McGraw-Hill.

Schlesinger, P., Dobash, R., Dobash, R. and Weaver, K. (1992), *Women Viewing Violence*, London: BFI Publishing.

Sconce, J. (1996) 'Trashing the Academy: Taste, Excess and the Emerging Politics of Cinematic Style', *Screen*, 36, 4, 371–93.

Seago, A. (1995) *Burning the Box of Beautiful Things: The Development of a Postmodern Sensibility*, Oxford: Clarendon Press.

Seiter, E., Borchers, H., Kreutzner, G. and Warth, E. (1989) *Remote Control: Television, Audiences and Cultural Power*, London and New York: Routledge.

Sharp. K. (ed.) (1999) *The Black Lace Book of Women's Sexual Fantasies*, London: Virgin Publishing.

Sherif, M. and Cantril, H. (1947) *The Psychology of Ego Involvement*, New York: Wiley & Sons.

Shipp, E. (1986) 'Blacks in Heated Debate Over *The Color Purple*', *New York Times,* 27 January.

Short, B. (1992) 'Queers, Beers and Shopping', *Gay Times,* 170, November, 18–20.

Silverman, K. (1986) 'Fragments of a Fashionable Discourse', in T. Modleski (ed.) *Studies in Entertainment*, Bloomington: Indiana University Press, pp. 139–52.

Sisson, E. D. and Sisson, B. (1940) 'Introversion and the aesthetic attitude', *J. Gen. Psychol.*, 22, 203–8.

Smith, B. (1986) '*Color Purple* Distorts Class Lesbian Issues', *Guardian,* 19 February.

Sonnet, E. (1999) '"Erotic Fiction by Women for Women": The Pleasures of Post-feminist Heterosexuality', in *Sexualities*, 2, 2, 167–87.

—— (2000) 'What the Woman Reads: Categorising Contemporary Popular Erotica for Women', in J. Hallam and N. Moody (eds) *Consuming for Pleasure: Selected Essay on Popular Fiction,* Liverpool: John Moores University Press, pp. 246–67.

Spigel, L. (1985) 'Detours in the Search for Tomorrow', *Camera Obscura*,13/14, 215–34.

Springer, N. N. (1938) 'The Influence of General Social Status on the Emotional Stability of Children', *J. Genet. Psychol.*, 53, 321–8.

Stacey, J. (1994) *Star-Gazing: Hollywood Cinema and Female Spectatorship*, London and New York: Routledge.

Steedman, C. (1986) *Landscape for a Good Woman: A Story of Two Lives*, London: Virago.

Steele, S. (1990) *The Content of Our Character: A New Vision of Race in America*, New York: St Martin's Press.

Stouffer, S. A. (1942) 'A Sociologist Looks at Communications Research', in D. Waples (ed.) *Print, Radio, and Film in A Democracy*, Chicago: University of Chicago Press, 133–46.

Sullivan, H. S. (1953) *The Interpersonal Theory of Psychiatry*, New York: Norton, 28–9.

Super, D. (1942) 'The Bernreuter personality inventory: A review of research', *Psychol. Bull.*, 29, 94–120.

Tannen, D. (ed.) (1982) 'Spoken and Written Language: Exploring Orality and Literacy', in J. Pine and R. O. Freedle (eds), *Advances in Discourse Processes*, vol. 9, Norwood, NJ: Ablex.

Taylor, H. (1989) *Scarlett's Women: 'Gone With The Wind' and its Female Fans*, London: Virago.

Theresa, M. (1992) '*Star Trek: The Next Generation* Throws Us a Bone . . .', *The Lavender Dragon*, April.

Thorne, B. (1983) 'Language, Gender and Society: A Second Decade of Research', in B. Thorne, C. Kramarac and N. Henley (eds) *Language, Gender and Society*, Rowley, MA: Newbury.

Thornton, S. (1994) 'Moral Panic, the Media and British Rave Culture', in A. Ross and T. Rose (eds), *Microphone Fiends: Youth Music and Youth Culture,* New York: Routledge.

—— (1995) *Club Cultures: Music, Media and Subcultural Capital*, Cambridge: Polity Press.

Thurston, C. (1987) *The Romance Revolution: Erotic Novels for Women and the Quest for a New Sexual Identity,* Urbana, IL: University of Illinois Press.

Toffler, A. (1965) *The Culture Consumers*, Baltimore: Penguin.

Tomlinson, L. (1998) '"This Ain't No Disco" . . . Or Is It?: Youth Culture and the Rave Phenomenon', in J. S. Epstein (ed.) *Youth Culture: Identity in a Postmodern World*, Oxford: Blackwell.

Tompkins, J. (1980) 'The Reader in History: The Changing Shape of Literary Response', in J. P. Tompkins (ed.) *Reader Response Criticism: From Formalism to Post-Structuralism*, Baltimore: John Hopkins University Press, pp. 201–32.

Tran, M. (1993) '50,000 Jobs to Go as Sears Axes "Big Book" Catalogues', *Guardian,* 26 January, 13.

Trowler, P. and Riley, M. (1985) *Topics in Sociology*, Slough: University Tutorial Press.

Tulloch, J. (2000) *Watching the TV Audiences*, London: Arnold.

Tulloch, J. and Jenkins, H. (1995) *Science Fiction Audiences*, London: Routledge.

Walker, J. (1984) 'Psychoanalysis and Feminist Film Theory', *Wide Angle*, 6, 3, 20ff.

Wallace, M. (1986) 'Blues for Mr Spielberg', *Village Voice*, 18 March.

Washington, M. (1982) 'Book Review of Barbara Christian's *Black Women Novelists*', *Signs: Journal of Women in Culture and Society*, 8, 1, August .

Weiss, A. (1991) '"A Queer Feeling When I Look at You": Hollywood Stars and Lesbian Sspectators in the 1930s', in C. Gledhill (ed.) *Stardom: Industry of Desire*, London and New York: Routledge.

Wertham, F. (1955) *Seduction of the Innocent*, London: Museum Press.

Wheatley, L. A. and Summer, F. C. (1946) 'Measurement of neurotic tendency in Negro students of music', *J. of Psychol.*, 22, 247–52.

Whelehan, I. (2000) *Overloaded: Popular Culture and the Future of Feminism*, London: The Women's Press.

Widdicombe, S. and Wooffitt, R. (1990) '"Being" Versus "Doing" Punk: On Achieving Authenticity as a Member', *Journal of Language and Social Psychology*, 9, 4, 257–77.

—— (1995) *The Language of Youth Subcultures: Social Identity in Action*, Hemel Hempstead: Harvester Wheatsheaf.

Wiese, M. J. and Cole, S. G. (1946) 'A study of children's attitudes and the influences of a commercial motion picture', *J. of Psychol.*, 21, 151–71.

Williams, R. (1961) *The Long Revolution*, New York: Columbia University Press.

—— (1974) *Television: Technology and Cultural Form*, London: Fontana.

Willis, P. (1977) *Learning to Labour*, Farnborough: Saxon House.

Wilner, D. (1950) 'Attitudes as a determinant of perception in the mass media of communication: Reactions to the motion picture *Home of the Brave*', Ph.D. Dissertation, University of California at Los Angeles.

Winick, C. (1963) 'Tendency Systems and the Effects of a Movie Dealing With A Social Problem', *Journal of General Psychology*.

Winship, J. (1987) *Inside Women's Magazines*, London: Pandora.

Witte, K. (1982) 'Rudolph Valentino: Erotaman des Augenblicks', in A. Heinzlneier *et al.* (eds) *Die Unsterblichen des Kinos*, Frankfurt am Main: Fischer.

Woods, G. (1995) '"We're Here, We're Queer and We're Not Going Catalogue Shopping"' in P. Burston and C. Richardson (eds) *A Queer Romance: Lesbians, Gay Men and Popular Culture*, London: Routledge.

York, P. (1980) *Style Wars*, London: Sidgwick and Jackson.

Index